AGAINST THEIR WILL

The Secret History of Medical Experimentation on Children in America

Allen M. Hornblum,
Judith L. Newman,
and Gregory J. Dober

OXFORD SOUTHERN

an imprint of Sunbury Press, Inc.
Mechanicsburg, PA USA

OXFORD SOUTHERN

an imprint of Sunbury Press, Inc.
Mechanicsburg, PA USA

For information about special discounts for bulk purchases, please contact Sunbury Press Orders Dept. at (855) 338-8359 or orders@sunburypress.com.

To request one of our authors for speaking engagements or book signings, please contact Sunbury Press Publicity Dept. at publicity@sunburypress.com.

FIRST OXFORD SOUTHERN EDITION: March 2022

Set in Adobe Garamond | Interior design by Crystal Devine | Cover by Ashley Nichole Walkowiak | Edited by Abigail Henson.

Publisher's Cataloging-in-Publication Data
Names: Hornblum, Allen M., author | Newman, Judith L., author | Dober, Gregory J., author.
Title: The Secret History of Medical Experimentation on Children in America / Allen M. Hornblum, Judith L. Newman, and Gregory J. Dober.
Description: First trade paperback edition. | Mechanicsburg, PA : Oxford Southern, 2021.
Summary: *Against Their Will* illuminates the shocking story of some of the nation's most prestigious academic institutions such as Harvard, MIT, and Penn, as well as some of its most illustrious physicians, who used institutionalized children as cheap and convenient subjects for experimentation.
Identifiers: ISBN : 978-1-62006-893-9 (softcover).
Subjects: MEDICAL / History | MEDICAL / Ethics | HISTORY / United States / 20th Century.

Product of the United States of America
0 1 1 2 3 5 8 13 21 34 55

Continue the Enlightenment!

To A. Bernard Ackerman

Whose career exemplified the highest standards
of ethics and medicine.

CONTENTS

ACKNOWLEDGMENTS

We are indebted to the many people who enabled us to chronicle this piece of medical history. We would especially like to thank former "State Boys" Charles Dyer, Gordon Shattuck, Austin LaRocque, and Joe Almaida for their recollections of Fernald's "Science Club" and tour of the institution. We also owe a debt of gratitude to Ted Chabasinski and Karen Alves for meeting with us and sharing their recollections about painful events that happened to them or to close family members. Jessie Bly and Pat Clapp also deserve our thanks for taking the time to recall memories that became key aspects of the book. To doctors such as A. Bernard Ackerman, Hilary Koprowski, Constantine Maletskos, Chester Southam, Avir Kagan, Jim Ketchum, Enoch Callaway, and the many others who contributed to our understanding of medical research during the last century, we owe a debt of gratitude.

"THEY'D COME FOR YOU AT NIGHT."

"THEY TOLD ME I SHOULDN'T HAVE KIDS AND I SHOULDN'T GET MARRIED. They said I might have a defect, that I had something wrong with me. They said, 'You aren't stabilized, and you shouldn't have kids because of what you have.' I didn't know what I had. Nobody ever told me. I thought I was like everyone else. But I was only a kid, and I had no interest in getting married; I was only fourteen years old. And to tell you the truth, I just wanted out of there," recalls Charles Dyer of his unhappy days growing up in a bleak Massachusetts orphanage.[1] It was 1954, and America was in the thick of the Cold War. Communism was spreading around the world. The Korean War had just ended; the Army—McCarthy hearings dominated political discussions in Washington.

It was also a significant time for young Charlie. He had just completed his first year in a large, forbidding state institution that was once known as the Massachusetts School for Idiotic and Feeble-Minded Youth. Over one hundred years after its founding as a refuge for high-functioning disabled children, it was still home to what many people at the time considered a motley collection of societal refuse, "defective" humans who were commonly referred to as "morons," "mongoloids," and "gargoyles," not to mention your everyday "idiots" and "lunatics." However, by today's standards, some, like Charlie, would seem no different than the rest of us.

The Walter E. Fernald State School eventually became known as the biggest and undoubtedly most chilling institution Charlie was confined. It was not his first time in a cold, impersonal structure; for nearly ten years, Charlie had been shuffled about in a series of underfunded and overcrowded public facilities for troubled youngsters from dysfunctional homes. Charlie was born in 1940 in Auburn, a small town just south of Worcester, Massachusetts. His mother was a state employee, and his father was a long-haul trucker and lumberjack who spent much of his time working in Canada. Both were alcoholics whose parenting skills left much to be desired. "I was one of eight kids," says Charlie, recollecting his troubled youth. "There were five boys and three girls. My father was kind to us, but he was rarely home. We were lucky to see him once every six months. My mother, on the other hand, was a nasty drunk. She was particularly mean toward me and picked on me a lot. She often slapped me in the face, and a few times, she nearly pulled my arms out of their sockets."

Life outside the Dyer home was not much more appealing. Charlie never progressed past the first grade. Then, following some disciplinary problems and a third unsuccessful attempt to master reading, writing, and arithmetic, a state social worker dropped the eight-year-old off at the Lymon School for Boys in Westborough, the nation's oldest reform school. The experience was traumatic for the slight, blue-eyed, blond boy.

"They used to really come down on you when you got out of line," says Charlie of Lymon's hard-nosed staff. "It was not a place to help kids, that's for sure. Kids got punished for everything, most of the time, by having staff members sit on you until you couldn't breathe. They were rough with the kids. And that's not all; they used to take all the best stuff that was donated to the place and keep it for themselves. The best clothes, the best athletic gear; we were left with the worst of everything."

Charlie was eager to learn and initially wondered what school would be like at Lymon. "There was really no schooling there," he says, "but they did make us work. I was only a little kid, but they hooked a harness around me like you do a horse and made me, and other kids pull a plank with a rug wrapped around it to wax the wooden floors. Then, back and forth, we'd go for a couple of hours until the floor shined. And if you didn't do it right or got out of line, they'd whack you on the ass with a wooden paddle. Each paddle had a child's name stamped on it, and they'd grab one if they thought you deserved it."

Lymon followed a succession of other institutional schools, including the Home for Little Wanderers in Brookline, Massachusetts. Some, such as the Metropolitan State Hospital, had bars on the windows, which deeply impressed young boys like Charlie.

By the time he was in his early teens, Charlie was shifted to the Walter E. Fernald State Training School in Waltham, an institution with a long history steeped in the principles of eugenics. The school was founded by Samuel Gridley Howe, an antebellum doctor and reformer. He operated under the belief that somebody could educate disadvantaged and disabled children to lead productive, independent lives if taught the right skills and proper etiquette. From

1848, when it was founded in South Boston to move to rural Waltham, the school grew in size and stature.

However, by the last couple decades of the nineteenth century, Fernald and scores of other schools like it were buffeted by the strong winds of philosophical change. They demonized the mentally and physically challenged as a drain on society and deemed them unsuitable for reproduction. Severely mentally and physically challenged were the first targets, along with retiring or shy people or those who stuttered and many non-English speaking individuals, regardless of skill or intelligence. "Feeblemindedness," as one critic of the movement has written, "was truly in the eye of the beholder and frequently depended upon the dimness or brightness of a particular moment."[2] Those now thought "genetically unfit" would be sequestered in more austere institutions by those who had no real intention of releasing them back into society. Instead, they would be warehoused indefinitely, and some would face additional horrors.

Initially, this unforgiving and pessimistic movement had a positive, constructive bent. Given the name "eugenics" in the early 1880s by Sir Francis Galton, a cousin of Charles Darwin, the nascent campaign married the latter's theories of natural selection to Gregor Mendel's revolutionary work in genetics. A sprinkling of Herbert Spencer's "survival of the fittest" thinking was thrown in for additional "naturalist" seasoning. The upshot was a movement built on a simple and incontrovertible scientific principle that all human characteristics, from intelligence and morality to character and longevity, were grounded in one's biological makeup. Once the die was cast, it was thought, little could be done to alter it.

Galton believed that there were ways to capitalize on the absolute best society had to offer. Very simply, if one was part of the elite, those of heroic stature and a talented disposition, it was one's moral duty to have a more considerable number of children than the average family. According to Galton, men like Napoleon, Beethoven, Van Gogh, Pasteur, and Bismarck shaped history and moved humankind forward, and therefore should be encouraged to procreate. The best individuals should be the finest and most prolific breeders. The result would be the advance of civilization and simultaneous progress in the arts, science, literature, and politics.

However, those in the movement were less focused on this heroic class than on the human wreckage or flotsam and jetsam of society that were a constant drag on civilization and a persistent impediment to reaching its potential. One of the movement's more ardent proselytizers, Charles Benedict Davenport, regarded those with what he considered weak traits, deep-seated character flaws, and severe physical impairments as "the submerged tenth" and "defective germplasm." They were destined to become beggars, lunatics, thieves, and pros-titutes who would disrupt society and eventually fill the nation's prisons, poor-houses, and hospitals.[3] In time, impoverished urban dwellers and dispossessed farmers from Maine to California, Eastern European immigrants, southern blacks, Russian Jews, illiterate Italians, desperate Mexicans, prostitutes, pick-pockets, alcoholics, the mentally compromised, and anyone else who did not resemble the Northern European archetype would find themselves potential victims of eugenic fanaticism.

By World War I, the reform movement had focused on what it called "degeneracy" and the continuing decline of the human stock. As it would eventually be known, the goal of negative eugenics would be to prevent "the reproduction of inferior stock."[4]

For those at the bottom of the social ladder, such as individuals confined at Fernald and similar schools, this news was fierce. They were viewed as the most glaring examples of genetic failure; destined to live compromised lives, work in menial labor, and rely on the generosity of strangers or, increasingly, the state. It would not be long, however, before the "mentally deficient," especially those considered "morons, imbeciles, and idiots," were no longer merely a social burden but were also seen as a social menace and as a growing percentage of the nation's paupers, prostitutes, thieves, and criminals.[5]

It was also believed that society would do well to isolate such individuals, limit their exposure to temptation, and implement policies and laws that would prevent their procreation and their unhealthy, antisocial tendencies. Thousands were sterilized and thousands more institutionalized to spend their days locked away in terminal boredom or, in later years, a drugged stupor. The lucky ones learned basic skills, such as sewing, cleaning, and gardening. Institutions, many designed for children, such as those at Vineland (New Jersey), Letchworth Vil-lage (New York), and Pennhurst (Pennsylvania), would take their place in the pantheon of human horror shows containing every type of mental defect and physical deformity imaginable.

The eugenic enthusiasm in the United States would gradually wane during the 1920s and dissipate further during the Great Depression while speeding up and taking a more vicious form in Nazi Germany. At the same time, there were still orphanages and institutions for the disabled, and the treatments given to inmates still showed the influence of eugenics. Although no longer a philosoph-ical force, the eugenics movement had done its job: Thousands of Americans had been dehumanized and thoroughly devalued.

An argument can be made that those conditions and so-called therapeutic treatments grew considerably more punitive and frightening over the decades into the 1940s, the postwar years, and throughout the Cold War. Surgical sterilization for both men and women was widespread, practiced routinely in more than half the states, and endorsed by the highest court in the land. Shock treatments, including insulin, Metrazol, and electroshock, were now institutional staples, and lobotomy had become the new therapeutic rage among neurologists, psychiatrists, and frustrated, overworked ward physicians who were desperate to cure the thousands of mentally maimed wasting away in hospital and asylum wards throughout the country. Many doctors were willing to try anything that would turn off the faucet filling the nation's institutions.

World War II would have a profound effect on scientific research in America. Saturated in several decades of dehumanizing eugenics propaganda, enterprising researchers aggressively sought out facilities that provided access to their residents. Those abandoned by their families and warehoused in large state institutions would discover that they were finally of interest to someone, medical investigators searching for a wide assortment of preventives and treatments. Thus, a convenient pattern and ethos were established, an unquestioning open-door policy that would only become more accepted and ingrained in the culture of the research arena over time.

By the time young Charlie Dyer entered Fernald in the early 1950s, eugenics may have been a fading memory more strongly associated with its Third Reich excesses. However, remnants were still visible in this country.[6] It was quickly being replaced, however, by another even more ominous ideological challenge. This new threat was neither homegrown nor genetically based but foreign in origin and, most important, designed to "bury" the American capitalist system.[7] Long suspected and guardedly watched during the first half of the century, Communism in the postwar years was seen as a rapidly growing menace and severe challenge to world stability. Stalin and the Soviet army had withstood the Nazi invasion, developed an atomic bomb years before anyone predicted, and were secretly preparing to launch the world's first artificial satellite into space. The Soviet Union was also making no secret of its ideological and territorial expansion. Events in Eastern Europe and China provided further proof of that. The world's largest nation, Nationalist China, had been "lost" the same year the Soviets had developed the bomb, and "Red China" was now aggressively following its Marxist partner in fostering a Communist future for millions worldwide.

As one close observer has written of the period, two Communist giants were now allied. The Soviet Union, already a menacing threat to the West, now had an even larger nation on its side. "The contest between Communism and the free world had taken an ominous turn in favor of the former."[8]

Alarmed by a new, threatening challenge, American governmental, cultural, and scientific institutions reacted swiftly and in many ways. As a result, children like Charlie Dyer often found themselves in the crosshairs of a ramped-up medical and scientific crusade designed to conquer our Marxist-Leninist competitors as well as age-old public health concerns such as polio, tuberculosis, and cancer.

For the thousands of institutionalized children, the competing economic systems, vitriolic Cold War rhetoric, and pharmaceutical expansion were the farthest things from their minds. Instead, they had more immediate issues to contend with, including a stark, unforgiving environment, harsh overseers, and the threat of sexual and physical violence.

After some of the previous institutions he had been in, Charlie Dyer had a fleeting sense of optimism about Fernald. "When they brought me there," he says, "I thought it would be better. There were no bars on the windows, and I hoped they'd let us out to play occasionally. Maybe they'd have a real school, and I'd finally learn to read, and they'd teach me a trade so I could get a job one day." But unfortunately, Charlie's dreams were quickly dispelled.

"They never taught me anything there," Charlie explains. "We wanted to learn about things, but the teachers just sat on their ass. They gave us coloring books and never taught us anything. We'd get homework to do, but [they] wouldn't show us how to do it. They'd say, 'Figure it out for yourself.' They were no help at all. They gave us medicine to calm us down, but that just put us to sleep when we should have been learning something. I got so angry I told them, 'The hell with you. I'll learn it myself.'"[9] Most of the boys in Fernald never learned to read.

He and the others learned how to stuff and sew mattresses, knit blankets, and make brooms. In summer, they were marched out to the surrounding fields and picked fruit and vegetables all day, like subsistence sharecroppers. However, they were not sharecroppers; they were children with a painful past and an equally dismal future. Their grim living conditions were worsened by periodic attacks, some sexual, by older boys at the facility. However, those paled compared to the frequency and sheer terror of the assaults perpetrated on them by Fernald staff.

"They'd come for you at night when everyone was sleeping," said Charlie. "I was small; most of the kids were bigger. But they'd pull a kid out of bed and take him to another room and make him do things. It happened to all of us. That's the type of people they hired there."

One day, however, Charlie and several other boys were called down to a meeting with some well-dressed, professional-looking outsiders who began promising them trips to Fenway Park, occasional excursions to the seashore, and a tour of the laboratories at the Massachusetts Institute of Technology. "They told us if we joined this new club," says Charlie, "they'd give us a Mickey Mouse watch and send us on field trips and to baseball games. So, we jumped at the chance to get into the Science Club. We would have done anything to get out of Fernald, even if it was just for the day." For a kid who had been shipped around a lot and called mentally "retarded" most of his life, this was a very welcome change of pace. All the boys felt that way.

Those who volunteered for the new club were immediately separated from the others and sequestered on a ward where they were monitored daily, forced to give blood regularly, and ordered to urinate and defecate in glass jars and endure an assortment of metabolic tests and physical examinations. The panoply of tests and strange procedures quickly cooled the ardor of even the most enthusiastic club participants. "I hated the needles," recalls Charlie, "and I wasn't allowed to see my friends anymore. They said we were just testing vitamins, but it made no sense to me. Furthermore, the few trips we went on were not worth the pain and the isolation."

Charlie told the doctors he wanted out; he no longer wanted to be in the Science Club. Nevertheless, they told him he could not leave; no one could. So, all the boys were obligated to remain involved until the doctors told them it was okay to leave the program. Finally, after repeated attempts to gain his freedom, Charlie became so desperate that he did something that nearly cost him his life. His spur-of-the-moment actions sparked panic at the school and created an incident that eventually became part of Fernald lore.

Not until decades later, however, would Charlie and the other Science Club members—not to mention the rest of the nation—learn the truth: The club was a front that enabled private and public sector entities, including universities, corporations, and the government, to use the Fernald children in a series of secret radiation experiments. For nearly twenty years—from the 1940s, when the boys' oatmeal breakfasts were contaminated with radioisotope laced milk, to the 1960s, when more severe Cold War experiments were orchestrated—the children were used like caged guinea pigs in a laboratory. The Fernald story and other revelations of unethical medical research at the time would shock the collective conscience of America and spark a major government investigation into clandestine radiation studies in the aftermath of Hiroshima and Nagasaki. It would also cement a lasting distrust of doctors and the medical establishment among former Science Club members and their friends and families.

Many test subjects at the dawn of the Atomic Age and throughout the decades that followed, as the public would come to learn, were children. Some were only days old; some were cognitively and physically impaired. Neverthe-less, we believe this tragic chapter in twentieth-century medical history, the pur-poseful and systematic exploitation and commodification of society's weakest members, is worthy of exploration and comment.

The sad history of children, especially institutionalized ones, used as cheap and available test subjects, the raw material for experimentation, started long before the Atomic Age and went well beyond exposure to radioactive isotopes. Experimental vaccines for hepatitis, measles, polio, and other diseases; explor-atory therapeutic procedures such as electroshock and lobotomy; and untested pharmaceuticals such as curare and Thorazine were all tested on children in hospitals, orphanages, and mental asylums as if they were some widely accepted intermediary step between chimpanzees and humans. Occasionally children supplanted the chimps.

Bereft of legal status or protectors, institutionalized children were often the test subjects of choice for medical researchers hoping to discover a new vaccine, prove a new theory, or publish an article in a respected medical journal. Many took advantage of the opportunity. One would be hard-pressed to identify a researcher whose professional career was cut short because he incorporated week-old infants, ward-bound juveniles with epilepsy, or those that were pro-foundly mentally challenged in his experiments. Involuntary, nontherapeutic, and dangerous experiments on children were far from unusual or dishonorable endeavors during the twentieth century. The practice was widely accepted, rarely questioned, and integral to the phenomenal growth of medical research and human experimentation during World War II and the Cold War.

Like other vulnerable populations, including prisoners, soldiers, hospi-tal patients, and those with mental illness, institutionalized children were an attractive wellspring of opportunity for enterprising doctors and scientists. Few in the medical profession thought such practices unseemly or problematic; even fewer spoke up to express opposition or voice moral outrage at these widely known and frequently cited exercises. Instead, doctors aggressively pursued relationships with superintendents, headmasters, and matrons of institutions with vulnerable populations. Doctors quickly discovered that access to institu-tionalized populations could springboard them to lucrative contracts with drug companies and great wealth. The financial incentives became so enticing that some physicians gave up their private practices to conduct large-scale clinical trials full time.[10]

However, only in recent decades have we begun to shine a light into the dark closet of medical ignominy and illuminate the many stories of vulnerable subjects who were chosen for their perceived inadequacies and handicaps. Regrettably, for researchers seeking suitable test sites, powerlessness was every bit as enticing a feature as regimentation and convenience. Bluebloods, members of the *Social Register*, and those attending elite prep schools were rarely included in clinical trials. Those at the bottom of the socioeconomic ladder, however, were not nearly so fortunate. Social, racial, physical, and intellectual disabilities stamped such individuals as "throwaway people," classes of flawed or "defective" individuals without value, except, of course, as grist for the research mill, "material" in the medical journal lexicon of the day. Ironically, they had been selected by and would suffer at the hands of some of America's best and brightest scientific minds.

Few at the time seemed to have a problem with it. Not until the mid-1960s was there an inkling of doubt about the exploitative practices. As one eager investigator of the era who regularly incorporated mentally disabled children, prisoners, and needy senior citizens in his clinical trials nostalgically commented, "No one asked me what I was doing. It was a wonderful time."[11]

Through the efforts of scholars, investigative journalists, and medical ethicists, critical pieces of history have been reclaimed, which we hope will ensure that such grievous incidents of unethical medicine never again occur. For example, *Bad Blood*, James Jones's 1978 account of several hundred unschooled Alabama sharecroppers going untreated in a four-decade-long syphilis study by the US Public Health Service, was the first examination of vulnerable populations deceived, mistreated, and medically exploited.[12]

There have been other books about medical experimentation on institutionalized children. Still, few have attempted a pointed and frank conversation about the motivating factors that allowed so many physicians and researchers to subscribe to a system and professional ethic that routinely placed infants and children in harm's way. Alternatively, society seemed indifferent to the practice, especially when it occurred in the one nation that felt it necessary to punish the Nazi doctors for their many ethical transgressions and brutal medical experiments. The unbridled esteem and worship placed upon a generation of researchers and physicians, the ethically toxic alchemy of the eugenics movement, World War II, and the threat of Communism during the Cold War played a significant part in allowing some of our best and brightest to cavalierly use some of our youngest and those most deserving of protection. Accurate accounting and discussion of this sad phenomenon are long overdue.

We hope this volume is viewed as a positive step in that significant undertaking. Our goal is that the work provides a voice—albeit a belated one—for the thousands of children who were conscripted to serve in the name of science. The crucible of scientific advancement may have brought forth increased knowledge during the twentieth century, but the young, docile, mute soldiers in the campaign witnessed more burden than acclaim. As human guinea pigs, they received no notice, reward, or appreciation. Their story is not a pleasant one, but it deserves to be told.

CHAPTER ONE

THE AGE OF HEROIC MEDICINE

"At Their Best, Medical Men are the Highest
Type Yet Reached by Mankind."

THERE ARE FEW TODAY WHO WOULD NOT IMMEDIATELY RECOGNIZE THE names Babe Ruth, Jack Dempsey, and Red Grange. Their iconic status as sporting greats from what is usually referred to as the Golden Age of Sports is arguably unrivaled and a testament to their physical accomplishments and their stature as Mount Olympus caliber athletic competitors as well as the sports—obsessed era in which they competed. Even a horse, Man o' War, managed to cement his name and stirring victories into the consciousness of adoring sports fans during the 1920s.

Books, newspapers, magazine articles, and movie theater newsreels repeatedly showcased the era's much-celebrated champions' physical talents and athletic exploits, so it was no surprise that comic books would devote numerous titles and issues to their accomplishments on the gridiron, diamond, and track. Surprisingly, however, in addition to splendid athletes, courageous crime detectives, and all-powerful science fiction characters, some of the world's leading medical and scientific minds would grace the titles and covers of children's magazines. Moreover, they would add some cultural and substantive heft to the lowbrow and trendy newsstand magazines, under-score physicians' rising status, and highlight the importance of the medical profession in contemporary society. By World War II, for example, gallant generals and daring soldiers were cover-story topics. Still, brilliant medical sleuths on the forefront of new treatments and vaccines held their own and often shared newsstand space with them.

American medicine had come a long way. However, as Harvard sociologist Paul Starr wrote, the doctor's role did not confer a clear and distinct class position in American society before the twentieth century.[1] In the nineteenth century, most medical men were often no more than autodidacts, veterans of an apprenticeship system that required no formal education. The result was a profession that had minor status and modest earning potential.

In his Pulitzer Prize winning book, The Social Transformation of American Medicine, Starr recounts the story of J. Marion Sims, one of America's foremost 19th century surgeons. Upon Sims informing his father that he was considering a career in medicine, he heard his father reply, "I certainly should not have sent you to college . . . it is a profession for which I have the utmost contempt. There is no science in it. There is no honor to be achieved in it; no reputation to be made." Moreover, as Starr writes, "Many people thought of medicine as an inferior profession, or at least as a career with inferior prospects." Furthermore, as late as 1870, one medical journal noted that when a "young man of merit and ability chose to become a doctor, the feeling among the majority of his cultivated friends is that he had thrown himself away."[2]

Starr's book offers an excellent account of American medicine's modest roots, the profession's inability to command respect through most of the 19th century, and its gradual climb to positions of "honor, deference, and prestige," not to mention considerable "wealth and income." By establishing educational standards, licensing practitioners, forcing members to join county, state, and national medical associations, and adopting numerous other measures, the medical profession began to witness greater "homogeneity and cohesiveness" among its members. It would all serve them well. Tremendous organizational respect and power were just two of the results.

By the early years of the twentieth century, however, the prestige and income potential of the medical profession had witnessed enormous gains; in fact, medicine had become a highly desirable career choice. According to a survey of high school students and teachers, in 1925, physicians ranked just behind bankers and college professors and just ahead of clergymen and lawyers. By the 1930s, medicine had jumped to the top of every occupational category and would remain there. Only one position exceeded physicians: "Justice of the U.S. Supreme Court."[3]

Sobering accounts of medical sacrifice and the excitement of triumphant discoveries, as well as an appreciation of medical history, took off in the 1920s. Profiles of the men and women who played a role in that history became a vital part of the narrative. One of the first and most influential medical success story chroniclers during this period was Paul de Kruif. Though little remembered today, de Kruif was instrumental in illuminating the challenges and sacrifices made by the great men and women of science who had committed their lives to fight disease and pestilence.

After serving in World War I and participating in the hunt for Pancho Villa in Mexico, de Kruif earned a doctorate in bacteriology at the University of Michigan and became a research fellow at New York's prestigious Rockefeller Institute, a well-recognized powerhouse of scientific research and talent. However, de Kruif also nurtured a side interest; he wanted to become a writer. So, he began to chronicle what he was observing in the lab and write illuminating vignettes about the men searching for the answers to age-old mysteries.

Young de Kruif began what would turn out to be a long and successful writing career with a series of anonymous articles in Century magazine in 1922 and a more widely read profile of Jacques Loeb, one of the great researchers and teachers working at Rockefeller at the time. Both the unsigned piece and the Loeb profile underscored de Kruif's conflicted feelings about the profession. The hero worship component displayed itself in the Loeb piece. He "adored" the old man and admitted, "It was thrilling to sit at Jacque Loeb's table listening to that parent of fatherless sea urchins, a veritable eighteenth-century encyclopedic come back to life, making offhand wisecracks about Voltaire and Diderot and pouring sarcasm on contemporary scientists."[4] Though de Kruif admitted trying to impress Rockefeller's "frontman" intellectually and "ape his tart dialectic" manner, he also admitted to always being "a thousand miles behind him." He realized he would never be able to catch up. There were others at the Institute, however. Not all were as impressive as Loeb.

De Kruif would rub shoulders at Rockefeller with Peyton Rous, Simon Flexner, Hideyo Noguchi, and Jules Bordet, brilliant men representing the elite of contemporary medical research. Many were Nobel Prize winners or soon would be. However, despite the great minds and many awards associated with the Rockefeller Institute, de Kruif was overcome with growing skepticism. As he would recount decades later, "The years wore on, but the hoped-for parade of cures did not come off. Could it be," he asked, "that the slot machine had turned out to be a one-armed bandit . . . ?"[5]

"Where are the cures and remedies?" wondered de Kruif "of the many eminent doctors using many medicines." However, even with their impressive degrees, fancy research accommodations, and supposedly magic elixirs, "the doctors did not cure many people." Granted, "doctors were priests, medicine men, layers on of hands, exponents of the bedside manner," but where were the lifesaving treatments and preventatives? "Citizens," wrote de Kruif sadly, "went on dying like flies from the great majority of the maladies. . . ."[6]

Weighed down by doubts and personal issues that included a failing marriage and regrets on leaving a child behind, de Kruif took a leave of absence from his assignments at Rockefeller in 1922. Instead, he began writing about medical research as he knew it and the great men and institutions involved in the battle against the disease. Not all of it would be positive. One 1922 magazine project, initially titled "Doctors and Drugmongers," and his first book, *Our Medicine Men*, illuminated the pretentiousness and naïveté of American medicine. The works drew public interest, at least one lawsuit, and his prompt dismissal from the Rockefeller Institute. He was fired "for irreverently daring to write a la Henry Mencken spoofing Rockefeller science and for disrespect to medicine's holy of holies."[7]

De Kruif considered his firing a "self-inflicted kick in the teeth" that spurred his move from science to journalism. Before tackling another subject on his own, he would perform the duties of a scientific aide-de-camp and idea repository for one of the literary giants of the period, the novelist Sinclair Lewis. The much-admired erudite storyteller was searching for his next project when he met de Kruif. The relationship between the master novelist and the aspiring journalist would prove critical to one of Lewis's greatest literary triumphs. As Lewis listened to de Kruif's stories of the Institute, he increasingly perceived the seeds of a storyline with all the makings of a landmark work. De Kruif agreed. In the hands of a master storyteller like Lewis, de Kruif's account of scientific research at the highest levels could prove an "epic of medical debunkology."[8]

The result was the classic American *Arrowsmith*, a Pulitzer Prize winning novel whose heroic leading man was a dedicated research scientist, supposedly "the first of consequence in American literature." According to medical historian Charles Rosenberg, Martin Arrowsmith was a new kind of hero, "one appropriate to twentieth-century America." The book's unusual theme and hero not only appealed to aspiring science buffs but surprisingly resonated with the American public.

De Kruif and Lewis had created the protagonist Martin Arrowsmith, a genuine scientist with a religious-like zeal for the truth. His tightly conceived and meticulously coordinated experiments would be untainted by professional aspirations, commercial distractions, or government restrictions. However, unfortunately, contemporary American life, particularly as it was evolving in the Roaring Twenties, was pervasive in its demeaning and degrading materialism and endless status-seeking; even pure science had been infected and tarnished. Lewis and de Kruif had their character rebel against such corrupting influences and seductions; they had Arrowsmith jettison his family and material considerations for a simpler life consistent with pure scientific research.[9]

Arrowsmith was an enormous success, won its author a Pulitzer and even greater notoriety, and was made into a successful Hollywood film.[10] It would also give most Americans their first peek into the culture of American medicine.

With the Lewis project completed, de Kruif was in search of a project of his own.

"One day," as he would later write, he began thinking about "Leeuwenhoek, the first of the microbe men."[11] Soon he had completed a manuscript containing the contributions of twelve great scientists. Scientists included in his work included Antonie van Leeuwenhoek, who first peered into a fantastic new world of microscopic organisms in the seventeenth century, to Paul Erhlich, who discovered his groundbreaking "606" medicinal recipe that effectively destroyed spirochaetes bacteria, or the cause of syphilis, three centuries later. They were microbe hunters in de Kruif's book of that name, brilliant, dedicated men of science who had conquered insidious diseases and saved the lives of untold millions. In recounting their challenging quests, their self-sacrifice and intellectual challenges, and the grandeur of their discoveries, de Kruif transformed a piece of staid laboratory history into a series of true adventure sagas that appealed to readers who usually had little interest in science.

Harcourt Brace, the book's publisher, initially was not optimistic about de Kruif's "off-beat opus;" medical research tomes were not big sellers. The company thought it would be "lucky if it sold out its first printing," a modest 2,800 copies. As de Kruif happily recalled years later, "Immediately upon publication, the sales of the book exploded in our faces." Favorable reviews from prominent literary and social critics propelled it along. "One of the noblest chapters in the history of mankind," roared Henry Mencken. "A book for those who love high adventure, who love clear, brave writing," wrote William Allen White. The book shot up the nonfiction bestseller lists during the summer of 1926, quickly passed 100,000 copies in sales, and "became one of the big nonfiction books of the decade."[12] Finally, de Kruif had authored the right book at the right time for a hero-worshipping age.

Much of its success, no doubt, was de Kruif's accessible, breezy style of historical portraiture. By combining biographies of serious-minded men who had labored long and hard to break new scientific ground and a writing style that was more typical of tales of the Old West, de Kruif discovered the secret to seducing young and old readers alike. De Kruif was not just an academic who could craftily turn a phrase and tell an interesting story; he recognized nuance, grappled with moral boundaries, and valued visionary leadership, even when those attributes were sometimes in conflict. For example, he appreciated Walter

Reed's creative and daring pursuit of the fearsome mosquito that spread death and disease throughout the tropics. Still, he also recognized that the great American physician was rolling the dice with other people's lives—in some cases, the lives of friends and colleagues. As de Kruif wrote of Reed and his deadly experiments, "To make any kind of experiment to prove mosquitoes carry yellow fever, you must have experimental animals, and that meant nothing more nor less than human animals." De Kruif did not always sugarcoat unpleasant facts; he let readers know that Reed was involved in human experimentation and that such research often ended tragically. There was no getting around it, de Kruif informed his readers; that was the nature of human research. It was "an immoral business."[13]

The thousands of Americans who read *Microbe Hunters* in the 1920s and the decades that followed were told of the trade-offs involved with such historic undertakings. Solving an age-old riddle that had snuffed out millions of lives was not child's play; experimenting with tropical diseases was a severe and deadly affair. Nevertheless, according to de Kruif's account, Reed understood that challenge. He had "not one particle of doubt he had to risk human lives" to solve the mystery of deadly yellow fever.[14] "You must kill men to save them," argued the great microbe hunter. "Never was there a good man," wrote de Kruif admiringly, "who thought of more hellish and dastardly tests."[15]

However, de Kruif went out of his way to assure readers that men like Dr. Reed and his ilk were, above suspicion, guiltless. Yes, giving test subjects yellow fever would be considered "murder" by some, but Reed's zealousness and willingness to put people at risk were understandable. Medical science needed to determine, by any means necessary, if mosquitoes caused yellow fever.

The book caused many Americans to confront the unattractive calculus of medical research. It was not pleasant, but it paid dividends; thousands of innocent lives eventually would be spared. De Kruif's heroic accounts of great men doing dangerous things would also illuminate the majesty as well as the desperation of the various test subjects, the experimental guinea pigs. With a strong whiff of American chauvinism, de Kruif praised those educated Westerners who understood the risk, appreciated the historic moment, and offered themselves as test subjects. They were accorded heroic status. "'We volunteer solely for the cause of humanity and in the interest of science,'" says a brave army private, according to de Kruif, during one solemn scene. "'Gentlemen, I salute you,'" replies an appreciative Major Reed. In the author's eyes, all such military volunteers were "first-class, unquestionable guinea pigs, above suspicion and beyond reproach."[16]

However, many more would be needed to test the theory and solve the deadly riddle. The "dastardly experiment" designed by the "insanely scientific Walter Reed" required more subjects.[17] If there were not enough "Americans who were ready to throw away their lives in the interest of science," then "there were ignorant people" those just arriving in "Cuba from Spain and who could very well use two hundred dollars."[18] In describing the induction of these "mercenary fellows" as test subjects, although they would suffer the same raging fevers, unbearable discomfort, fits of vomiting, and diarrhea, they never came off as gallant as the American soldiers and doctors who volunteered for the research program.

De Kruif's triumphant account of the landmark yellow fever experiments and the driven, almost heartless, attitude of the chief medical investigator resonated with readers just as Martin Arrowsmith's fictional quest for scientific purity had captured the hearts and minds of readers a year earlier.

The message of *Microbe Hunters* was clear: Great men like Pasteur, Reed, Theobald Smith, and Paul Ehrlich were a rare breed. However, for all their skill, training, and dogged pursuit of that deadly microbe or magical elixir, their mission was infinitely complex, the challenges multifaceted, and the trail of disease and death a daily occurrence. They had to make difficult decisions, decisions that might look cavalier and insensitive to the casual observer. Yes, on occasion, they would even appear cruel and "less human" in the eyes of some. But suppose society was to benefit in the long run. In that case, these extraordinary men of medicine, arguably the best and brightest of their class, must have the freedom to operate and to proceed unencumbered by moral tastes of the moment or by bureaucratic constraints. Granted, some unfortunate souls would lose their lives in these roulette-like experiments, but then, as de Kruif argued, "the microbe hunters of the great line have always been gamblers." He insisted that we not dwell on the negative but think of the heroic mission and focus on "the good brave adventurer and the thousands he has saved."[19] Many did just that.

In addition to the double shot of medical research triumphalism offered by Lewis and de Kruif, 1926 would witness a literary trifecta as Harvey Cushing's biography of William Osler, the most admired physician in English and American medicine, would win the Pulitzer Prize. Rarely had literary and historical works about the culture of medicine and the men behind the healing arts so captivated readers. The staid professions of medicine and medical research had received a shot in the arm, if not a dramatic makeover. Those in the business of the "wholesome adventure" genre took notice and subsequently propelled popular heroic narratives to include men in white lab coats alongside athletic champions, battlefield heroes, and comic book characters.

Paul de Kruif may have been "the most famous writer of popular medical history . . . the most prolific, and perhaps the best," according to Bert Hansen. However, there would soon be many others who became equally fascinated with medicine and medical research as a topic of literary exploration.[20] Some of the others included Frederick Faust, A. J. Cronin, and Frank G. Slaughter.

Frederick Schiller Faust was the most interesting of these de Kruif wannabes. Born in the last decade of the 19th century, Faust dabbled in several different arenas from ranch cowhand to university student to the Canadian Army before finding his niche as a wordsmith. Prolific, he could knock off 12,000 cogent words over a weekend and nearly 30,000,000 during his lifetime. He specialized in pulp fiction cowboy yarns and created the Western hero Destry, which Hollywood turned into *Destry Rides Again* starring Jimmy Stewart. However, he may have been more famous for another character he created, a young, idealist physician named Dr. Kildare.

Faust wrote several Kildare stories that were eventually adapted to the big screen in the late 1930s. The MGM series of Dr. Kildare films starring Lew Ayres, Lionel Barrymore, and Loraine Day were extremely popular with more than one generation of American filmgoers and usually put forward a warm and compassionate "doctor knows best" message. Medical problems, however, were central to the narrative of each story. For example, in *The Secret of Dr. Kildare,* the elderly and dedicated Dr. Leonard Gillespie (Lionel Barrymore) collapses from exhaustion while finding a cure for a nasty strain of pneumonia. In Dr. Kildare's Strange Case, young Dr. Kildare (Lew Ayres) tries to assist a noted brain surgeon who is depressed over losing too many patients.

Frederick Faust's literary creation was equally famous on the radio, in comic books, and later on home television screens. The Dr. Kildare brand did much to foster a positive view of the medical profession during the middle decades of the 20th century. Faust, who created the popular lead character, is little remembered today, was partial to pen names. He used well over a dozen during his prolific career and was best known to readers as Max Brand. Nevertheless, his Western yarns are legends to his many followers. He would eventually become one of Hollywood's best-paid writers before losing his life during World War II.[21]

Another prolific American author of medical tales was Frank G. Slaughter. Born in the early years of the last century and raised on a North Carolina farm, Slaughter would graduate college and Johns Hopkins Medical School. Though working at a small Jacksonville, Florida hospital, Slaughter, like de Kruif before him, desired to write about the science and craft of medicine. After purchasing a typewriter during the Depression and numerous revisions to his autobiographical account of the trials and tribulations of a young doctor, *That None Should Die* was finally published by Doubleday in 1941. Over the next half-dozen years, he would write four more medically themed novels and, during his lengthy career, an additional four-dozen fiction and nonfiction books. With titles like *Spencer Brade M.D.*, *East Side General*, *The Healer*, *Epidemic*, and *Doctors at Risk*, which he wrote from the 1940s to the late 1980s, Slaughter's 35-cent pocket novels helped feed the public's appetite for popular medically related literature.

Hollywood certainly contributed its part in raising the profile and status of doctors and medical researchers. In addition to adapting *Arrowsmith* to celluloid, the film industry produced *The Prisoner of Shark Island* about Dr. Samuel A. Mudd, *The Story of Louis Pasteur*, *The White Angel* about Florence Nightingale, *Yellow Jack* based on the Broadway play, and *Dr. Ehrlich's Magic Bullet*. Furthermore, many would come; medical dramas were a popular draw for film-going audiences.

The stunningly long list of works by popularizers of science like Faust, Slaughter, and de Kruif, as well as the movies, books, and magazine articles generated over the years, illustrated the public's growing interest in medical history, its fascination with life and death experimental struggles, and its appreciation for hard-won medical triumphs. Popular accounts of medical research resonated with audiences. Readers enjoyed good, dramatic storytelling, but these were true-life tales with a message. With each additional newspaper article, book, and movie, medical research was increasingly perceived as honorable, altruistic, and noble professions. More and more young people were encouraged to think of the medical profession as a career. As one young scientific aspirant admitted as he embarked on many years of higher education and a career devoted to medical research, "It was largely, no, it was entirely to get the glory."[22]

The days of doctors serving as the town barber and doctors shilling bottled remedies as a cure-all for everything from gout and dyspepsia to cancer and tuberculosis were long gone. Instead, the trade had been professionalized, doctors were respected, and some like Walter Reed and Joseph Goldberger, the conqueror of pellagra, had been confirmed national heroes. If not for his premature death in 1902 at 51, Reed probably would have been the first American to win a Nobel Prize.

If the profession had improved in the public's eye, triumphant disease fighters like Walter Reed and crusading public health officials like Joseph Goldberger were the pinnacle of medical progress and humanitarian concern. Hero worship had found its rightful representatives. Stories of such laudable men were ideal for an era that valued dutiful service. Reed was a soldier, Goldberger a government public health officer who had creativity and personal resolve, sometimes at significant personal risk. Finally, Americans recognized it took those qualities and discovered the answers to age-old deadly maladies like yellow fever and pellagra.

The public testimonials to the careers of these men rarely, if ever, dwelled on the test subjects incorporated in these scientific advances. Reed used soldiers and native islanders, Goldberger used orphans and prisoners. Those few that did mention the test subjects trumpeted the courageous acts of the elite, men like Dr. Jesse Lazear, a deputy of Dr. Reed's who volunteered to be bitten by microbe carrying mosquitoes. His subsequent death and other military volunteers heightened the elements of danger and drama involved in such dicey scientific escapades. Lazear's selfless attitude had him regularly referred to as "a martyr to science."

Another in the line of great microbe hunters who was posthumously awarded that honor was Dr. Hideyo Noguchi. Considered by his peers as "one of the greatest bacteriologists of modern times" and one of the scientific Illuminati ensconced at the Rockefeller Institute for Medical Research, Noguchi was credited with "important discoveries" in everything from snake venoms and syphilis to infantile paralysis and smallpox. His death in 1931, "while seeking the cause of yellow fever in Africa," was considered a significant loss to the world of science" and an unfortunate end to an "acquisitive, ambitious brain" in the service of humankind. *Time* magazine called him "a martyr to science" and pointed out his extraordinary dedication to scientific discovery to the exclusion of everything else, including sleep. That "he left an estate of only $12,000" seemed to document his unselfish, non-materialistic lifestyle. More than a few who read the fawning obituary must have thought of Martin Arrowsmith.[23]

Interestingly, none of the *Time* articles concerning his death mentioned some of the more controversial aspects of his research. For example, twenty years earlier, Noguchi had performed promising experiments on animals and humans with lutein, an extract of treponema pallidum, the causative agent of syphilis. Lutein, according to Noguchi, was a potential diagnostic tool that was going to complement the Wasserman test in detecting syphilis.[24] To test his theory, "Noguchi injected lutein into the skin of the upper arm and a control medium into the other arm" of 400 test subjects from hospitals and asylums in the New York City area. Of that number, 46 were normal children between the ages of two and eighteen, and many others were sick children suffering from a host of maladies, including malaria, leprosy, and tuberculosis.

At the time, according to medical historian Susan Lederer, only the anti-vivisection community expressed any outrage at Dr. Noguchi's questionable experiments. One pamphlet framed the issue, "Are the helpless people in our hospitals and asylums to be treated as so much material for scientific experimentation irrespective of age or consent?"[25] Parents of some of the children used in experiments by Noguchi eventually sued him, but the lawsuits did little to damage his reputation. By the time of his death in 1931, Noguchi was one of the nation's iconic microbe hunters; news organizations were not about to clutter his flattering epitaph with negative commentary concerning his misuse of test subjects. Noguchi's prestige as a microbe hunter would serve him well, at least by biographical standards. Whereas Presidents Warren Harding and Calvin Coolidge had to wait seven years and five years respectively for a comprehensive biography of their lives and contributions, Hideyo Noguchi only had to wait three years.[26] The celebrated men of the Rockefeller Institute were of greater interest to writers and readers than the men who lived in the White House.

Doctors, particularly medical researchers on the forefront of grand discoveries, had attained special status; they were an anointed priesthood that warranted the public's admiration, respect, and unfettered freedom to ply their trade as they wished. Some observers were so respectful as to accord them God-like qualities. Paul de Kruif, who knew them as well as anyone, would inform his readers that such men "were the first to show how we may fuse the power of science with the faith of religion to build a new humanity."[27] In many of his famous works, he argued that doctors were "the frontline soldiers in the fight for life," he proved to be an incredibly persuasive propagandist for the profession. "The power in the hands of the plainest physician," De Kruif preached, "is the best gift of God, so far, to mankind." He predicted this great circle of highly trained and motivated actors would tame deadly microbes, heal the sick, and accomplish even more impressive feats. In addition, they were currently dealing with "proteins, liver extracts and yeasts, anti-biotics, synthetic vitamins, and hormones."[28] De Kruif's message, as well as that of the other famous chroniclers of science, was clear; the select circle of devoted and extraordinarily well-trained men of medical research "promise not only of lengthening human life but hint a transfiguration of humanity."

If not outright hero worship, the consequences of such reverence were critical to the profession's development. Not surprisingly, an increasing number in the medical arena was considering pure research as a career choice. Though their income, honor, and respect had escalated, books and magazine articles were rarely written about those serving at the bedside of sick patients. Instead, it was the thoughtful, hardworking laboratory researcher who went into the field and struggled with death firsthand, which seemed to be the recipient of most of the glory. The uncorrupted medical investigator garnered the headlines and heroic stature and was increasingly recognized as the equal of the great names in athletics, commerce, and government.

With hero worship as a backdrop and medical progress at stake, experimentation on humans was accepted as the vehicle for attaining more excellent medical knowledge, long—sought cures, and a healthier society. Antivivisectionists, though passionate in their moral outrage regarding the cavalier use of animals and humans as research material, were a small, motley collection of social gadflies, heckling cranks, and naive do-gooders with little political power. Though their pamphlets and newsletters vigorously decried the ethical transgressions and dangerous experiments conducted by medical researchers, their efforts had a relatively negligible impact. However, in the words of Susan Lederer, it did foster "bitter confrontations between the antivivisectionists and the leaders of the American medical profession."[29]

With the phalanx of media sources, including comic books, films, radio shows, and television, trumpeting the accomplishments of medical researchers, the profession's image was greatly enhanced. Moreover, it also helped solidify those middle decades of the twentieth century as the Golden Age of American Medicine and foster a greater public appreciation for doctors, their profession, and their soaring status in society. For doctors to be lionized with sports icons like Lou Gehrig and war heroes like General George S. Patton was no small achievement.

Louis Pasteur and Theobald Smith did not turn out tens of thousands of spectators in athletic coliseums the way Jim Thorpe, Jimmie Foxx, and Gene Tunney did or have the avid following of comic book superheroes; still, they held their own in the public-esteem category. More importantly, they were resolute in their commitment to doing good work, and their efforts proved beneficial for humankind. Thus, there were definite reasons to celebrate their lives and their contributions. A halo effect had gradually settled upon the research community's best and brightest stars.

Book readers and radio listeners were increasingly learning about Louis Pasteur and Edward Jenner as well as scientists they had never heard of, such as Elie Metchnikoff, Waldemar Haffkine, Horace Wells, Émile Roux, and Giovanni Battista Grassi—men who had made significant contributions in fighting a host of dreaded diseases. The contributions of women were also celebrated. Florence Nightingale, Clara Barton, Elizabeth Blackwell, and lesser-known figures such as Jeanne Mance and Mary Walker were for the first time receiving significant attention. Even a Siberian husky named Balto was feted for leading a team of sled dogs carrying medicine to Nome, Alaska, where a diphtheria epidemic had broken out.

With the rewards so much greater than the penalties and medical ethics in its infancy, researchers proceeded in a very laissez-faire manner. During the early decades of the twentieth century, experimentation on humans was widely accepted, with few speaking in opposition. Misuse and miscalculation in the handling and treatment of test subjects were considered more of an oversight or a minor error in judgment than an egregious criminal act. That was especially the case if the research resulted in a therapeutic breakthrough or a valuable piece of new information. It should be understood that doctors did not want to damage their patients. They were sworn to do no harm as a profession, but if they committed dastardly acts, they were more easily pardoned if something positive had come of the exercise. Experiments on humans were usually excused if the study results were substantial, the process had an element of science, and the physicians were correct in their expectations.[30]

The results were increasing instances of questionable experiments being performed by members of the medical profession. In addition to numerous experimental studies on men and women and more vulnerable populations such as hospital patients, asylum residents, and prisoners, children were frequently used as research material. In 1895, for example, Dr. Henry Heiman, a New York pediatrician, purposefully infected a four-year-old "idiot with chronic epilepsy," a sixteen-year-old "idiot," and a twenty-six-year-old man with advanced tuberculosis with active gonorrhea germs.[31] That same year, while exploring the effectiveness of vaccines against smallpox, Walter Reed and George M. Sternberg used children at several New York City orphanages for their studies.[32] It was not uncommon at the time for doctors to evaluate the immunity claims of a smallpox vaccine by injecting children with the active virus after vaccinating them. In 1907, three associates of the William Pepper Clinical Laboratory at the University of Pennsylvania used over a hundred children under the age of eight at the St. Vincent's Home for Orphans, a Catholic orphanage in Philadelphia, for a series of diagnostic tests in which a tuberculin formula was placed in the test subjects' eyes.[33] Even infants were used in research studies. For example, two-day-old babies were fed bismuth, a metal-like substance used in the manufacture of some pharmaceuticals, and then exposed to extensive X-rays to chart the course of different foods in their stomachs.[34]

Frustrated in his efforts to control the expansion of vivisection, Dr. Albert Leffingwell, an early twentieth-century physician and social reformer, led a long and energetic campaign to establish restrictions on experimenting with animals and humans. He pleaded with his medical colleagues to police their actions and develop humane guidelines. "At the beginning of a new century," he wrote in one of his pamphlets, "great problems confront us. One of them is human vivisection in the name of scientific research. We appeal, then, to the medical press of America to break that unfortunate silence which seems to justify, or at least condone it. Now and subsequently, will it not join us in condemning every such vivisector of little children, every such experimenter upon human beings. We make this appeal to it in the name of justice and humanity and for the sake of millions yet unborn."[35]

Unfortunately for reformers like Leffingwell, the scientific current was moving swiftly in the opposite direction. The twentieth century signified a new era of vital, transformative medicine and medical care, and researchers were going to be in the vanguard of it. Innovative treatments, revolutionary preventives, and a whole host of novel procedures were about to explode on the scene, and those preaching restraint, moderation, and prudent, ethical decision-making was about to be swept aside as nagging eccentrics and hysterical obstructionists holding back progress. Instead, civilization's advance, along with a healthy dose of journalistic encouragement, fostered an atmosphere that celebrated scientific achievement and medical breakthroughs with no regard for those at whose expense the triumphs were attained.

Each discovery, a mosquito's role in spreading plague, a particular bacterium doing the same, or a vaccine that could nullify the threat of both was heroically trumpeted as a significant advance. Newspapers, magazines, books, radio, and films repeatedly underscored the significance of the achievements. However, unfortunately, medical triumphalism had taken hold of a hero-obsessed culture, and little thought was given to those caught in the wake of the latest scientific success. Of course, those languishing in institutionalized settings such as asylums, hospitals, orphanages, and prisons would also contribute. Nevertheless, they would never see their names in books or newspapers; they would never earn commendations or receive lucrative endorsements. They were the grist used by the increasingly well-oiled medical mill to achieve the doctors' personal and corporate goals.

There would be no Paul de Kruif to chronicle the ordeal of inhabitants at the New Jersey State Colony for the Feebleminded at Vineland, the Ohio Soldiers' and Sailors' Home Orphans Home, Letchworth Village Colony for the

Feebleminded in Thiells, New York, or the dozens of other institutions around the nation that opened their doors and turned their wards over to investigators in white lab coats as so much cheap research material. Nevertheless, doctors had discovered a use for those locked away in state institutions. Children—mute, unwitting, and desperate for affection—would increasingly become the front-line troops in the medical community's quest to improve the world.

CHAPTER TWO

EUGENICS AND THE DEVALUING OF INSTITUTIONALIZED CHILDREN

". . . Society Has No Business to Permit Degenerates to Reproduce Their Kind."

DURING THE SPRING AND SUMMER OF 1929, GEORGIA O'KEEFE DECIDED to adopt the principles of abstract art and apply them to her close-up depictions of flowers, bleached bones, and the vast, forbidding beauty of the New Mexico desert landscape. William Faulkner would write Sartoris, his first novel about the fictional Yoknapatawpha County, and tennis great Bill Tilden would win his seventh U. S. Lawn Tennis Association Championship. It would be during this same period that three of the nation's most eminent scientists would plan and carry out the deliberate castration of a 13-year-old child of small stature with Down Syndrome (who was then referred to as a mongoloid dwarf) at a state asylum for the "feebleminded" just outside of New York City.

The non-therapeutic operation was led by Charles Benedict Davenport, America's leading eugenicist and better breeding advocate whose indefatigable efforts helped usher "pure prejudice into the stately corridors of respectability."[1] Davenport was assisted in the delicate surgical procedure by the renowned George Washington Carver, a Johns Hopkins Medical School graduate, and by cytologist Theophilus H. Painter, a Yale-trained scientist, who subsequently analyzed the tissue culture.[2]

The use of vulnerable institutionalized children for experimental procedures, investigative treatments, and experimental preventives occurred every day in the 1920s. America's leading eugenicists like Davenport branded those imprisoned in poorly funded and inadequately staffed county and state asylums, hospitals, and orphanages as devalued members of the tribe, reviled cast-offs from the human race. Therefore, eminently worthy of study for their peculiarities. Some in the eugenics community found them equally useful as "material" for scientific research, which was not necessarily related to their conditions.

With the passage of years, institutionalized children would be viewed as increasingly expendable and much sought after as test subjects. World War II and the Cold War that followed further fostered a need for test subjects. Research "volunteers" and institutions holding physically and mentally challenged children became particularly attractive for their convenience, isolation, and affordability. Many researchers viewed such facilities as a gift, a gift that kept on giving.

Utilitarianism, paternalism, and elitism have long been prevalent in the medical research community. However, America's infatuation with the better-breeding movement and the nation's involvement in two international conflicts would add a potent rationale for exploitative research practices. Armed with what they considered solid justification for their actions, some doctors who had sworn to do no harm repeatedly breached that oath. Few, if any, spoke up against the practice.

For many years, Charles D. Davenport had been fascinated by all matters of hereditary dysfunction, especially those of the "Mongoloid dwarf." As he told the superintendent of the Letchworth Village Colony for the Feebleminded, the syndrome was of unknown origin and had repeatedly proved impossible to remedy. Similar problems in his studies of "dwarf plants as well as insects" had led Davenport to a possible answer; he increasingly believed "Mongoloid dwarfs might be due to abnormalities in the chromosomal complex."[3]

Now in need of humans to test his hypothesis, he knew exactly where to go for test subjects: an institution that held an impaired population he had spent many years studying. In his letter of request, Davenport informed the Colony's superintendent that it was time "to examine the chromosomes connected with the dividing cells of a Mongoloid. The only suitable organ where one is sure to find cell divisions is in the testis. The only way to get the tissue in suitable condition for fixation of the chromosomes so they can be observed is by castration."[4]

Davenport believed that pursuing this scientific conundrum was clearly in order and that a Mongoloid child's castration was warranted "for the sake of throwing light upon this problem."[5] The request was quickly granted; no one in authority, including the child's lone parent, the facility's superintendent, or the researchers, seemed opposed to castrating a child for the sake of increased knowledge.[6]

The son of a strict New England Congregationalist and successful real estate man, Davenport grew up in Brooklyn, New York. He developed a keen interest in "measurable mysteries" such as science, math, and engineering at an early age. He would study civil engineering at Brooklyn Polytechnic, but his love of animals and natural history took him to Harvard, where he earned a doctorate in biology. Davenport would then teach zoology at Harvard and the University of Chicago.

Toward the end of the nineteenth century and while teaching at the Brooklyn Institute of Arts and Sciences, Davenport established a biological laboratory to study primitive marine and mammal life in a lush, marshy section of Long Island called Cold Spring Harbor. While overturning submerged rocks, digging up oysters, and inspecting other forms of flora and fauna, he began to seriously wade into the scientific works and theories of Francis Galton, the creator of eugenics. Davenport's intense attraction to Galton's ideas would have significant scientific and philosophical portent on both sides of the Atlantic.

Francis Galton was a cousin of the great scientist Charles Darwin and grandson of the famous physician, naturalist, and free-thinker Erasmus Darwin. Galton was expected to do great things academically. However, his record at places like King's College Medical School and Cambridge would be undistinguished, and his years in school were characterized by underachievement, frustration, and finally, a nervous breakdown. However, his academic hurdles were resolved with the sudden death of his demanding father and a substantial family inheritance that allowed him to become a world traveler, self-taught geographer, and winner of a gold medal for numerous contributions from the Royal Geographical Society.

Galton's extensive travels through the Middle East and the African continent allowed him to "joyously apply his arithmetic prowess and razor-like powers of observation to everyday life, seeking correlation . . . and patterns, thereby making him an almost unique connoisseur of nature sampling, tasting, and a discerning new character in seemingly random flavors of chaos."[7] Though many of Galton's observational and quantitative ruminations would prove of little value, some had lasting import, such as his weather maps that incorporated wind direction, temperature, and barometric pressure, and his analysis of fingerprints that would prove invaluable in the identification of criminals.

However, in the field of heredity, his innate curiosity about human differences and his love of mathematics would produce his most controversial scientific discovery. Galton speculated that cumulative differences in human variation resulted in mathematical forms and trends that would allow keen observers to predict, over time and in a given population, the variation of a specific variable, such as height, weight, or intelligence. Moreover, while there would be vast differences among large groups of people on many dimensions, differences among generations would be slight.

For Galton, heredity transmitted physical features, such as eye color, height, weight, and mental and emotional qualities. Whether an individual was creative or a laggard was not pure chance; it was inherited. Galton greatly admired men like Pasteur, Beethoven, Shakespeare, and Napoleon. He was a subscriber of the heroic theory of history, a belief that the significant advances in art, literature, politics, science, and other important milestones of civilized society were the products of exceptional minds. In short, great men did extraordinary things. According to Galton, such individuals were a national treasure, and he thought it imperative they reproduce offspring. Furthermore, they should do so more frequently than ordinary people who lack unique talents and abilities. In books such as *Hereditary Genius and Natural Intelligence*, he argued for increasing the pool of extraordinary talent as a direct way to benefit all of humanity.[8]

The more Galton thought about inheritance, particularly the inheritance of genius in distinguished British families in the 1860s, the more he came to believe that science and mathematics could discover the keys to breeding and that, once understood and properly managed, the human condition could be forever changed for the better. As he stated simply, "Could not the undesirables be got rid of and the desirables multiplied?"[9]

Like many others during the last quarter of the 1800s, Galton pondered a host of hereditary questions concerning race purification and human perfection. By 1883, the year he published his book *Inquiries into Human Faculty and Its Development*, and after years of considering various names for his new science of heredity, Galton finally settled on a combination of two Greek words, *eu* (good or well) and *genes* (born), to create the word "eugenics." The term would soon take on a life of its own and eventually manifest itself in ways, policies, and practices that its originator would hardly recognize.

According to Galton, germplasm, protoplasm, or whatever one called that crucial element responsible for transmitting physical and mental characteristics from one generation to another was the central ingredient of heredity. He and others at the time did not fully understand how hereditary traits were passed on, but they knew that environment and quality—of—life factors had little to no impact if one's germplasm declared one unfit.

Galton claimed that he was not unsympathetic to the plight of such families but insisted that if society was to progress, such elements had to be constrained and eliminated. He did not propose to neglect the sick and the unfortunate, but he did advocate their isolation to stop the production of families likely to include "degenerates."

During the last two decades of the nineteenth century, the demonizing and devaluing of specific population segments would grow in support and legitimacy. Galton emphasized getting the most out of society's best representatives. He favored placing restrictions on society's least admirable members, such as restricting the marriage license process to prevent genetically flawed unions. Eugenics was too important an issue to be a voluntary affair; government enforcement was necessary. During the early years of the twentieth century, the movement took root and developed a darker, more coercive aura. Galton's "positive eugenics" stressing biologically beneficial marriages to enhance society's benefactors was quickly being supplanted by "negative eugenics," stressing dramatically accelerated programs and policies to control, if not eradicate, the genetically unfit—those deemed to be medically infirm, racially tainted, and non-Nordic in origin. Those with inferior genetics were dealt with harshly.

A decade after Galton invented the term "eugenics" in 1883, Dr. F. Hoyt Pilcher, a U.S. physician and asylum superintendent, castrated nearly six dozen boys at the Institute for Imbeciles and Weak-Minded Children in Winfield, Kansas. Pilcher's predecessor at the institution had been treating young inmates "who were confirmed masturbators" for years without the benefit of a proven remedy. Upon assuming the position of superintendent and after "taking a rational view of the subject," Pilcher began his search for a "curative effect" or solution that would put an end to the annoying and persistent problem. He believed that he had discovered the answer through surgical intervention, specifically castration.

Many Kansans were horrified at Pilcher's actions, but the medical community was supportive, sometimes aggressively so. Calling the "bitter" attacks on Pilcher partisan bombast and "political campaign thunder," one state medical journal said, "there is growing sentiment in the profession in favor of castration" as a medicinal vehicle to stem both disease and crime. However, the journal article also made the case that there was an immediate need for the public to be "educated up" to this realization.

Other doctors soon asserted that castration could produce therapeutic wonders for various medical ailments and social problems. Dr. Everett Flood informed his colleagues at an American Medical Association convention in Philadelphia in 1897 of twenty-six children confined in an institution in Baldwinsville, Massachusetts, who had been recently castrated. According to Flood, "the first castrations were performed with the idea of preventing masturbation in certain cases where the habit was most constant." One boy, the doctor wrote, "had no sense of shame, besides being a confirmed epileptic and of course somewhat feebleminded." Flood said that parental permissions were attained for the surgeries, which a staff surgeon performed.

The outcome of the experimental surgeries was more than satisfactory, according to Flood, since "it has been found in every case that the masturbation has ceased." It was also noted that those castrated had become "fairer in complexion," taken on "additional flesh" were "more manageable, better groomed, and more truthful." Last but no less noteworthy, Flood pointed out that "the possibility of their transmitting defects to offspring is of course removed."

The last decade of the nineteenth century produced several scientific champions of eugenic castration and sterilization. One of them was Harry C. Sharp, a surgeon at the Indiana Reformatory, who became an outspoken leader of the sterilization movement. Sharp often wrote and spoke about the ever-increasing problem of defective germplasm coursing through American society. For example, he noted;

> "Take the criminal class alone for the past fifty years. We find that in 1850 there were 6,737 criminals in the United States, or one to each 3,442 of the population; while in 1890, the penal population is shown to be 83,329 or one to each 957 of the population. This is of the criminal alone. If all dependents were considered, such as inhabit public and private insane hospitals, almshouses, and institutes for the feebleminded, we should find the proportion to be in the neighborhood of one to each three hundred of the population. This is most alarming and calls for a most heroic method of treatment."[10]

Sharp's "heroic method" of ridding the world of defective germplasm was through sterilization. He would soon report that he had sterilized forty-two young men, some as young as seventeen. In addition, he would sterilize hundreds more to ensure that they did not become criminals and an economic drain on society. Delighted with his results, Sharp argued that "radical methods are necessary" and encouraged fellow physicians to press elected officials to have superintendents of insane asylums, prisons, and institutions for the feeble-minded sterilize every male inmate who walked through the front door.

His peers' reaction to Sharp's paper was favorable and supported by asylum superintendents from Cuban leper colonies to Ohio prisons. Sharp would be elected president of the Physicians Association of the National Prison Association, an office from which he could propagandize with even greater authority. Sharp was only one of an increasing number in the medical profession advocating for sterilization as an acceptable therapeutic practice. Articles written by physicians promoting "sterilization for social control" significantly increased between 1880 and 1900. Most followed the typical pattern of decrying the growth in crime and the rising cost of incarceration and proudly extolling patients' new sense of industriousness, ambition, and happiness after surgery.

More physicians were signing on, some of whom were nationally prominent. For example, Dr. William T. Belfield, a surgeon of some stature, endorsed both eugenics and mass sterilization policies in December 1907 at a Physician and Law Clubs of Chicago meeting. His presentation, which was soon after printed in the Journal of the American Medical Association, argued that the American homicide rate was spiraling out of control and already "33 times higher than London."[11] Belfield urged Illinois lawmakers to pass a sterilization law similar to the recent Hoosier state law; others would initiate a similar lobbying campaign.

Dr. David Weeks, the head physician at the New Jersey State Village for Epileptics; Dr. Charles Carrington, chief surgeon at the Virginia State Penitentiary; and Dr. F. W. Hatch, secretary of the State Lunacy Commission in California, were all actively writing, lobbying, or utilizing eugenic nostrums to deal with the nation's "social disease." Some eugenic proponents, such as Lewellys F. Barker and G. Frank Lydston, were not just directors of institutions but notable names in medicine. Barker was the physician-in-chief at Johns Hopkins Hospital; Lydston, a professor of genitourinary surgery at the University of Illinois, had some extreme views on the role of medicine in combating America's dysgenic hordes, Southern European immigrants, and was not bashful about sharing them. Along with advocating the castration of rapists and sterilization of the unfit (people with epilepsy, inebriates, consumptives, and other maladies using toxic gas in sealed compartments "to kill convicted murderers and driveling imbeciles." Barker's and Lydston's papers, especially those published in the *Journal of the American Medical Association* and the *New York Medical Journal*, signified for many Americans that eugenical surgery had been accorded a seal of approval by the profession's elite.[12]

In 1910, nearly two dozen medical articles advocated eugenical sterilization, and between 1899 and 1912, thirty-eight articles were published calling for the profession to be more proactive on the issue.[13] As one proponent of medical intervention would forcefully state, "We must face the fact the very life-blood of the nation is being poisoned by the rapid production of mental and moral defectives, and the only thing that will dam the flood of degeneracy and ensure the survival of the fittest, is abrogation of all power to procreate."[14] Clearly, the medical profession regarded criminality, feeblemindedness, and the burden and expense of degeneracy— "the very nightmare of the human race" as one eugenics activist called it—as a social and economic pox that had to be eradicated. Medical support enabled twelve states during that period to enact sterilization laws (four additional states—Pennsylvania, Oregon, Vermont, and Nebraska—passed similar legislation only to have it vetoed by the governors).

With this as a backdrop and nearly two decades later, during the dawn of the Great Depression, Davenport's desire to castrate a child for research purposes was met with something approaching casual indifference by the asylum superintendent.

Interestingly, the nascent eugenics movement would find its most ardent supporters in America. They would champion a panoply of harsh and restrictive policy initiatives, including segregation, deportation, castration, marriage prohibition, compulsory sterilization, and occasionally euthanasia or withholding medical treatment to those in need. Among such proponents, the issue of medical experimentation on "defectives" and other unfit "material" would not be viewed as a departure from standard policy and standard medical procedure.

Though many prominent Americans such as Alexander Graham Bell, Theodore Roosevelt, Luther Burbank, and Margaret Sanger would at one time or another gravitate to the eugenics cause, one of the earliest, most devoted, and hardest working of Galton's disciples would prove to be Charles Davenport.

Intellectuals were not the only ones concerned about the threat of the unfit. Readers of newspapers and magazines were getting increasing doses of alarmist stories. From 1905 to 1909, for example, there were 27 articles on eugenics according to *The Reader's Guide to Periodical Literature*. "During the next 5—year period, there was an explosion of 122 entries under the 'eugenics' listing, making it one of the most referenced subjects in the entire index."[15] Thus, both the general public and the medical establishment were getting a healthy dose of eugenics. Further complicating matters were the hordes of Asian and European immigrants who threatened to make America, according to Davenport, "darker in pigmentation, smaller in stature, more mercurial . . . and more given to crimes of larceny, kidnapping, assault, murder, rape, and sex—immorality."[16]

Negative eugenics and the prevention of the proliferation of tainted genetic material became Davenport's sole concern. The more quickly and aggressively America addressed the challenge, the better it would be for the nation's collective health and bloodlines. In Davenport's mind, the country was being overrun by an array of defective elements. Viewed as a potential and an actual threat were the "feebleminded"—a catchall term of the era that included a wide swath of mental symptoms and syndromes—who made up the bulk of any community's motley collection of mentally challenged beggars, thieves, lunatics, and worse. Those with severe mental or physical disabilities were obviously in this category and swept up in the negative eugenic dragnet. They spoke poor English, stuttered severely, or were just painfully shy around other people regardless of their actual intelligence and abilities. Davenport believed such undesirables made up 10 percent of the general population and often referred to them as the "submerged tenth."

As one ardent eugenicist complained of the unfit in 1935, "the vast sums in taking care of lower grades of our feeble-minded people . . . will necessitate our spending more and more."[17] Something needed to be done that would "work in the elimination of undesirable elements in society."[18] Like Alexander Johnson, a former secretary of the Indiana Board of State Charities in the 1930s, some advocated "segregation." Johnson believed "all such people should be taken in childhood . . . and placed in a training school . . . where they may be placed in useful labor and kept under positive control as long as they live."[19] Many others, however, believed that the nation's orphanages, prisons, and mental asylums were already overcrowded and that a more radical approach was needed to rectify the problem.

For eugenics activists like Leon Whitney, "elimination" was the answer. "If in one fell swoop," he argued, "we could eliminate all our useless degenerates, incapable of anything beyond a kind of gross animal happiness if we could awaken one morning and find all these gone in some mysterious but painless fashion, what class of persons would we fix on to be the ones eliminated?" Whitney already knew the answer. They should "start eliminating at the bottom. We should go to the institutions for the feeble-minded and look at their inmates. The first ones to be picked out would probably be those of such a low grade as to be hardly better than human vegetables."[20] Stamped with an array of mental and physical stigmata more visible and damning than any scarlet letter, "defectives" languishing in large state institutions were increasingly viewed in the early decades of the twentieth century as a public menace and a financial encumbrance requiring swift action.

Many prominent citizens joined the condemnatory bandwagon. For example, in 1913, former President Theodore Roosevelt wrote Davenport, "I agree with you . . . that society has no business to permit degenerates to reproduce their kind. However, someday, we will realize that the prime duty, the inescapable duty, of the good citizen of the right type, is to leave his or her blood behind him in the world; and that we have no business to permit the perpetuation of citizens of the wrong type."[21] Margaret Sanger, the great social activist, and birth control proponent, was even more strident in her denunciation of society's unfit elements, "vigorously opposing charitable efforts to uplift the downtrodden" and arguing that "it was better that the cold and hungry be left without help" so the eugenically fit would face less of a challenge from "the unfit." She often compared the poor and the great mass of dispossessed to "human waste" and "weeds" needing to be "exterminated."[22] Other presumably progressive citizens like G. Stanley Hall, Washington Gladden, and E. E. Southard—all established academics and respected citizens at the time—were similarly disposed.

Davenport believed that many immigrants from Europe and Asia who were entering the country were either damaged or dangerous, occasionally both, and were destined to prove an additional financial burden. Davenport was already furious that the government—and therefore the taxpaying public—was obligated to support the growing number of people in almshouses, asylums, and prisons. Many tens of millions of dollars were involved in their maintenance, and there seemed to be no end in sight.[23] With the European and Asian floodgates open, America had to protect itself. Careful observation and study could detect the most menacing of the unfit arriving on our shores. Even a cursory examination of an individual or a group's lineage could determine their social inadequacies or criminal tendencies, for, Davenport believed, there was such a thing as "racial identity," and it determined behavior. Poles, for example, were "clannish"; Italians tended toward "personal violence"; and Jews, though engaged in little "personal violence," were prone to "thieving" and "prostitution."[24]

Davenport was as much a social activist as a scholarly academic, and he targeted nearly a dozen "socially unfit" groups for "elimination." They included the poor, alcoholics; all classes of criminals; epileptics; the insane; the weak; those subject to specific diseases; the physically deformed; and the deaf, dumb, and blind.[25] Though frowned on and shunned by polite society, many of these classes were soon sought out as ideal research material.

No novice as an organizer, Davenport realized that such a battle plan required economic resources. His organizational and entrepreneurial skills would serve him well over the years, but never more so than in his 1909 meeting with Mary Harriman, the daughter of one of the nation's most prominent railroad magnates. Harriman was already familiar with the Cold Spring Harbor Laboratory from her days as a Barnard College undergraduate.

A liberal and social activist, Mary Harriman was drawn to Davenport's pitch's "social improvement" aspect, as were many progressives of the day. She encouraged her mother to support the young Brooklyn scientist's ambition to establish a serious eugenics research center. Armed with facts, a clear vision of what needed to be done, and the commitment of a faithful zealot, Davenport proved an impressive and convincing advocate. He received an endowment from Mrs. E. H. Harriman to purchase a seventy-five-acre tract of land just up the road from his Cold Spring Harbor Laboratory. The Eugenics Record Office (ERO) now had sufficient funds and staff to carry out its mission of racial hygiene and endless file cabinets to hold an ocean of extremely sensitive personal information. It would become the largest repository of genetic data in the nation. It would also be home to an army of field investigators who would make thousands of house calls and official visits to asylums, prisons, and hospitals across the country and ferret out information about inmates and their "defective lineage." Davenport saw the Harriman gift as a turning point in his eugenics campaign and referred to it in his diary as "A red—letter day for humanity."[26]

By 1918, Mrs. Harriman would give over half a million dollars to various eugenic causes, a considerable sum in those days. Davenport made sure that a portion of the money went to his front-line troops: young women from elite colleges such as Vassar, Radcliffe, and Wellesley and young men from universities such as Cornell, Harvard, and Johns Hopkins who had knowledge of biology and went into the field to spread the word and seek out information about the unfit in America.

With an information-gathering army approaching 300 trained field workers, Davenport not only had the means of spreading his alarmist vision of national decay and impending doom but was also able to collect data, family profiles, and statistics on everything from instances of pellagra and nomadism to an individual's athletic proclivities and emotional disposition. Most, if not all, of the information was used in various books, bulletins, pamphlets, and newsletters like *Eugenical News* supporting sterilization, a strict immigration policy, and other efforts to enhance American germplasm and thwart degeneracy.

Shortly after procuring the Harriman money, Davenport obtained an even larger Rockefeller Foundation contribution. Davenport and the ERO were now forces with which to be reckoned. Money made all the difference for the eugenics movement. Biological supremacy, raceology, and coercive public policies were just excess verbiage until those notions were backed by hard cash.[27] Money now greased the skids for simplistic hereditary theories to become law.

Moreover, the monetary windfall enabled Davenport to turn his data-collection system from a relatively small cottage industry into a statistical powerhouse that could not be easily ignored. In addition, by recruiting asylum superintendents to the cause, traveling to their institutions, measuring and examining the shuttered "defectives," and theorizing about the origins of degeneracy and the best methods to combat its insidious growth, he established a formidable template on how to tackle the nation's problem.

Moreover, America's growing number of asylums proved a gold mine of investigative opportunity that held "the ore of progress," according to E.E. Southard, a Harvard Medical School neuropathologist.[28] Scientists discovered the significant opportunities presented by large state institutions as human laboratories. The unfit had finally assumed some value as laboratory specimens. Davenport and other eugenics adherents immediately recognized the possibilities and became familiar figures on institutional campuses. Letchworth Village, a new facility for the "feebleminded" where Mary Harriman served as a board member, became one of his favorite venues. Designed to "provide training and education for backward children," Letchworth Village, located just north of New York City, trumpeted its goal of "increasing better human strains . . . and the right to be well-born."[29]

Davenport's legwork paid dividends as many institutional heads bought into the campaign and bid for his favor. He thanked Henry H. Goddard, the research director of the New Jersey Training School for Feeble-Minded Boys and Girls, for his efforts to hire field workers to research "the pedigree of feeble-minded children." He was "quite convinced" that the best method for procuring the necessary information was "to visit the families of your inmates in their own homes."[30] It would not be long before Davenport's ERO field workers were armed with a five-page questionnaire that asked dozens of personal questions. The questions ranged from one's religious habits, marital history, tobacco, and alcohol use, to a list of illnesses since infancy, surgical procedures, and those in the family who were cross-eyed, had "fingers with only 2 joints," and "abnormal genitalia." Intrusive inquiries were also made regarding those in the family who were guilty of "deceitfulness," "cunning," "revengefulness," and "masturbation."[31]

Some viewed the accumulation of such salacious personal information as potentially explosive, especially if it were to "fall into the hands of newspaper or magazine writers who would be very glad of an opportunity to exploit the matter," as Goddard wrote to Davenport. It was one thing for readers of *American Breeders Magazine,* which was devoted to doing to humans what cattle farmers did to their livestock, to glean information derived from the research of ERO field workers; it was a whole other thing if the mainstream press gained control of it. Goddard's "cautionary" note to Davenport suggested that the data were "in danger of being used by someone who will put it into a popular magazine and thus queer the whole country, so to speak, regarding this whole matter of Eugenics."[32]

Undaunted, Davenport admitted that it was possible that "yellow journals might succeed in using this material to put such an aspect upon all our whole work as to damage it seriously. There are scores of persons" in the newspaper business, he conceded, "who would not scruple to use their power to damage any good cause." But finally, he argued boldly, "There is no use in collecting facts unless they can be put before at least the scientific public to form the basis of eventual action."[33]

Goddard would make his contributions to eugenics history. One of them was the influential tract *The Kallikak Family: A Study in the Heredity of Feeblemindedness*, which traced the origin of an eight-year-old female Vineland resident back many generations to a Revolutionary War soldier who fathered a defective son after impregnating a feebleminded girl. Goddard's research on "mental defectives" would become increasingly important to Davenport and the eugenics cause despite its questionable conclusions and lack of sophistication.[34] As the relationship between the men grew, they would regularly notify each other of new developments and discoveries. Always on the lookout for interesting examples of unfit germplasm, Goddard and Davenport shared stories of degenerates and inbreeding they had come upon in their travels.[35]

Though Davenport may have had an academic interest in isolated instances of degeneracy, he was more concerned about winning converts, building a movement, and spreading the gospel of eugenics. Getting the message into high schools and colleges was a major preoccupation, as was keeping track of what biological material was being taught, what eugenics courses were being offered, the number of students in attendance, and the total class hours devoted to "laboratory" or "fieldwork." Davenport had the ERO and the Carnegie Institution of Washington blanket the nation's universities with questionnaires, and a surprising number of institutions replied. For example, at Adelphi College in Brooklyn, 51 females were enrolled in a seventeen-week eugenics and human heredity course. At Brown University in Providence, 75 students—45 males and 30 females—participated in a four-week course for upperclassmen; 88 males at Dartmouth College took a sixteen-week course in animal and plant heredity that included a vital eugenics component, and 187 students at Penn State were learning eugenic theory in a seventeen-week Botany and Genetics course.[36]

Some universities even offered "extension courses" to the public, allowing students and average citizens to be schooled in the new science. For example, the University of California offered a "fifteen lecture" program at the San Francisco Main Library. Lectures would present a smorgasbord of eugenic thought, including "The Transmission of Human Defects," "War and Race," "The Elimination of Defectives," and "Sterilization and Segregation."[37] Professional degree programs were part of the propaganda mill associated with eugenics.

The Pediatrics Department of Hahnemann Medical College in Chicago, for example, reported that it had sixteen third- and fourth-year students enrolled in a thirty-four-week eugenics course. Hahnemann was not unique; numerous medical schools propagated eugenic nostrums for the physical and mental maladies plaguing the body politic. An early and active eugenics supporter, Adolf Meyer appreciated Davenport's taking time out from his busy schedule to visit Johns Hopkins medical students. "I think it is an excellent thing to make it possible for those starting on medical work to have a correct and real conception of what your Institute is doing," Meyer wrote Davenport. "I am making a very determined effort to rouse a working interest . . . with quite a little response."[38]

It should be pointed out that not every school of higher education subscribed to this class and race warfare, not to mention the outright bigotry that many eugenicists regularly exhibited. As one college official candidly informed the ERO superintendent, "Allow me to say very frankly that in the opinion of the faculty of the University of Detroit, Eugenics is full of dangers. My desire is to protest against the brutal and superficial heredity terrorism with which certain modern eugenic enthusiasts advocate a regulation of human breeding borrowed from the stables and totally foreign to the human race." Moreover, it is only in the rarest cases that we find two parents who are both of them, physically and psychically, so equally and heavily tainted and defective, that anything could be safely predicted with regard to their children."[39]

There were other critics, some with national reputations, such as former presidential candidate William Jennings Bryan and influential newspaper columnist Walter Lippmann, but their pointed criticisms were occasionally lost in the enthusiastic chorus calling for implementing this new science promising a quick journey to a progressive utopia. Lippmann, for example, had numerous qualms about many eugenic tenets, including the movement's utopian vision. He often voiced his distaste for eugenics, especially its increasing devotion to I.Q. testing during and after the First World War. Expressing his dissatisfaction in the pages of the *New Republic* in 1922, he soberly argued, "The whole drift of the propaganda based on intelligence testing is to treat people with low intelligence quotients as congenitally and hopelessly inferior." He did not accept the principle that a person's capacity to learn, mature, and develop was "fatally fixed by the child's heredity."[40] Lippmann would subsequently admit his passionate disapproval of much in the eugenics hymnbook by writing: "I hate the impudence of a claim that in fifty minutes you can judge and classify a human beings' predestined fitness in life. I hate the abuse of the scientific method which it involves. I hate the sense of superiority which it creates and the sense of inferiority which it imposes."[41]

Fortunately for the eugenicists, the disapproving tone of Michigan Jesuits and political pundits were not often replicated at the collegiate level; most institutions of higher learning either fell in line and offered eugenics-based or related courses or remained silent. Many of the nation's premier academic institutions offered eugenic theory and curriculum in one form or another. Prestigious universities such as Harvard, Columbia, Cornell, and the University of Chicago had top faculty teaching such courses. Large state universities like Wisconsin were also on board; Northwestern was said to be "a hotbed of radical eugenic thought." Princeton had Harry Laughlin, a key ERO operative, teaching a course, and E. G. Conklin, Princeton's president, had beseeched Davenport as early as 1909 to "lecture before [the school's] Natural Science Club."[42] V. L. Kellogg, a noted entomologist, taught a course on eugenics and zoology at Stanford, and top academics like Herbert Jennings and Raymond Pearl offered eugenics courses at Johns Hopkins.[43]

In fact, "eugenics rocketed through academia, becoming an institution virtually overnight," according to one observer of the movement. By the start of World War I, over forty-four major universities offered eugenics courses. Less than a decade later, that number would mushroom "to hundreds, reaching some 20,000 students annually."[44] Eugenics would become so commonplace on American college campuses by the mid-1930s that Leon Whitney, secretary of the American Eugenics Society, proudly claimed, "Eugenics is being taught now in three-quarters of our five hundred colleges and universities, and in many high schools and preparatory schools."[45]

The upshot is that at least two generations of college students, the future lawyers, teachers, doctors, and medical researchers of America who had sworn to do no harm, were being imbued with an air of superiority and a condescending disdain for the weak, the infirm, and the institutionalized of the nation. However, if eradicating such appalling and burdensome elements was a national priority, their occasional use as research material for society's benefit was a worthy, even commendable act.

Some colleges became so steeped in this new quasi-religious faith in science that the campuses seemed saturated in an all-encompassing eugenic haze. The "unfit" in combination with occasional racial turbulence were often seen as the reasons for political unrest, social turmoil, and public disenchantment. America, particularly in the South, was no longer a harmonious "melting pot" but a boiling cauldron of social discontent. Some professors at elite southern schools even predicted "racial suicide" if society's best families did not reproduce more progeny and if legislative action was not taken more quickly on the social and legal front. The University of Virginia, then the largest institution of higher education in the South and an academic model for the region, was one of these bastions of hereditarianism and eugenic thought.

Appreciative of academic scholarship in the arts and sciences and the home of Jefferson's university, Virginia also had a long history of slavery, an attraction to harsh punitive measures like castration, and a tradition of enlightened elitism nurtured over many generations. It should be no surprise then that the University of Virginia became home to numerous high-powered eugenic proselytizers and a much-respected beacon of eugenic thought throughout the South. This was especially so in the case of the school's widely acclaimed medical school. Notions of racial superiority and hereditarian thinking cloaked in a comforting scientific veneer went back to Thomas Jefferson. They continued up to the 19th and 20th centuries with professors like James Lawrence Cabell and Paul Brandon Barringer, the University of Virginia's medical school faculty chairmen. When describing the intellectual environment in Charlottesville, "The promise of eugenics captivated many of the best and brightest physicians and biologists of the day," according to Gregory Michael Dorr.[46] Harvey Jordan was one of them.

A respected embryologist and dean of the medical school, Harvey Ernest Jordan was one of many prominent faculty members looking to eugenics to provide a biological explanation for various social issues. The more eugenics material he digested, the more intrigued he would become until he finally reached out to Charles Davenport and offered his services. "I have been wondering if I could be of service in this great work," Jordan inquired. "Perhaps in gathering statistics at close range . . . I should be very glad for an opportunity to help if my efforts could be of real assistance."[47] With his knowledge and association with numerous state hospitals and mental asylums—and an endless supply of subjects to study—Jordan's offer must have been music to Davenport's ears. As their relationship grew, Jordan would buy into mainstream eugenic principles regarding the environment's subordination to heredity and the essential inequality of man. Before long, he was trumpeting the importance of educating professionals, particularly physicians, about eugenic theory, instilling eugenic therapeutics into the medical curriculum, and lecturing about the importance of eugenics around the nation. "Physicians," argued Jordan, were central to the educational mission. They were the "most potent factors spreading . . . eugenic propaganda."[48]

"Eugenics and public health," according to Dorr's research, were seen as "identical" under Jordan's helm at the University of Virginia. "Sterilization was forced altruism, sacrificing the individual's right to procreate for the well-being of the American race."[49] Though maintaining purity of the race was critical to the Southern rationalizing process for buying into the eugenics choir, a similar justification was underway for those doctors searching for cures and preventatives to cholera, tuberculosis, pellagra, and the other dreaded diseases and health maladies of the day. When in need of human subjects for experimentation, why not use the half-witted, physically deformed individuals in state institutions? Hadn't they repeatedly proven a social menace and public expense? Weren't they, therefore, obligated to sacrifice something for the betterment of the community?

As Dorr explains in his account of Virginia's love affair with eugenics, a path for such research behavior had already been established: "Experimentation on imprisoned and institutionalized black men followed long-standing traditions. American physicians, particularly in the South, routinely performed experimental procedures upon people living at the margins of society. Poor, disenfranchised, and uneducated, lower-class blacks, poor whites, and women could not mount effective defenses against powerful authorities that believed they operated in the public interest. Stigmatized as diseased threats to the moral and physical sanctity of upper-class white America, doctors viewed these patients as fitting experimental subjects."[50] Eugenics only aided and abetted that process.

The threatening specter of dangerous blacks behind bars, along with an increasing number of institutionalized "defectives," made both groups more than suitable as research material for an increasingly eugenicized profession. Each had reached the highest rungs of the intolerable scale—the publics' long-standing fear of "Negroes" and "visual aversion to the unfit."[51] Cabell and Barringer would be followed at Virginia by equally stalwart eugenicists such as Harry Heck, Ivey Foreman Lewis, and Robert Bennett Bean. More would follow. Each would help "expose most of the university's scientific faculty and many of its best students to eugenics and thereby the biological differences between the races" and the normal from the unfit. By the beginning of the

Great Depression, at least seven members of the Virginia faculty were committed eugenicists. A further testament to their clout and the eugenic education imparted at the University of Virginia is that several of the top Public Health Service physicians involved in the controversial Tuskegee Syphilis Study were respected Virginia graduates.[52]

As the academic flagship of the State, the University of Virginia's embrace of eugenics was closely monitored by college administrators throughout the State and then replicated at schools like William & Mary, Virginia Polytechnic Institute, Harrisonburg State (James Madison University), Randolph-Macon, and the University of Richmond. Women's colleges such as Hollins and Sweet Briar adopted hereditarian faculty and eugenics-laden courses and textbooks. Many courses included field trips to state institutions to witness first-hand the pitiable lives of the unfortunates locked up there. In time, usually, sooner rather than later, academic institutions throughout the South would be following in Virginia's stead and embracing all manner of eugenic and hereditarian thought.

The Commonwealth of Virginia would champion the legality of sterilization during the post-World War I quandary concerning the constitutionality of the nation's many sterilization statutes. Eugenic activists hoping to take the issue to the Supreme Court believed they had found a suitable vehicle in the form of a seventeen-year-old girl named Carrie Buck. Classified as a "moral imbecile," Buck, then an inmate in the Virginia Colony for Epileptics and Feebleminded in Lynchburg, gave birth to a child out of wedlock just before her placement in the institution.

Emma Buck, Carrie's mother, was also a resident there. She had been certified a "moron" with the mental age of an eight-year-old and had developed the reputation as a prostitute and one of Charlottesville's least respected women. In addition, rumors circulated that she was a "feebleminded" alcoholic and unfit mother. Virginia authorities believed that if Vivian, Carrie's young daughter, showed signs of feeblemindedness, that would document three successive generations of mental deficiency, a perfect test case for the Supreme Court to rule. Virginia authorities consulted with Harry Laughlin, Davenport's chief deputy at the ERO, to underscore their argument. A zealous, indefatigable eugenicist, Laughlin was instrumental in the recent passage of federal legislation significantly limiting the number of immigrants entering the United States. He would be instrumental in fostering similar eugenics public policy remedies in the courts.

Though Laughlin brainstormed with Virginia authorities about legal nuances, helped plot strategy, and examined numerous documents, he never actually met any of the women involved in the case. Nevertheless, despite that glaring omission and conflicting information about the actual mental impairments of those at the center of the controversy, he enthusiastically confirmed that the Buck women "belong to the shiftless, ignorant, and worthless class of anti-social whites of the South." Other aspects of the case raised similar concerns from a scientific and judgmental point of view. Young Vivian, for example, barely seven months old at the time, was said in the testimony of one critical Red Cross worker to have a "look" about her that was "not quite normal."[53]

I.P. Whitehead, Carrie's defense counsel and a former member of the Colony's board of directors, recognized the dubious nature of the State's case and the tremendous potential for abuse. He argued that if Virginia's sterilization law is upheld, a "reign of doctors will be inaugurated and in the name of science new classes will be added, even races may be brought within the scope of such a regulation and the worst forms of tyranny practiced." Despite prophetic warnings from defense counsel and a court consisting of such renowned members as Louis Brandeis and former President William Howard Taft, the vote was 8 to 1 in favor of the Virginia statute. In the court's now-infamous opinion in Buck v. Bell, Justice Oliver Wendell Holmes wrote, "We have seen more than once that the public welfare may call upon the best citizens for their lives. It would be strange if it could not call upon those who already sap the strength of the State for these lesser sacrifices . . . in order to prevent our being swamped with incompetence. The principle that sustains compulsory vaccination is broad enough to cover cutting the Fallopian tubes." Holmes followed with the infamous line, "Three generations of imbeciles are enough."[54]

The decision would usher in a eugenic tsunami for those devalued souls already interned in state asylums. An ever-increasing number of children would be called on by the State and medical investigators for these and other "lesser sacrifices."

After several decades of persistent and pervasive eugenic propaganda and at least twenty years of intense personal organizing around the subject, Davenport had achieved considerable success, and his request to castrate a "Mongoloid dwarf" in 1929 provoked little alarm.

Davenport and his Cold Spring Harbor research facility were known to asylum superintendents around the country. C. S. Little, the superintendent at Letchworth Village in Thiells, New York, was certainly familiar with him and his group's work. The two men had been corresponding for years, and Davenport and his trained field workers were so often on asylum grounds measuring, examining, and studying various defective populations that many must have thought them regular staff members.

The opportunity Letchworth Village provided to his research team was not lost on Davenport. Like scores of researchers who would flock to such institutions in coming decades for access to test "material," he often expressed his gratitude. Davenport knew how to flatter the egos of those who were the gate-keepers of the charges he wanted to study. As he told Little in one missive, "I was glad to have [field workers] get acquainted with you and be introduced by you into the Village into which you have woven so much of your personality."[55]

Davenport's interest in feebleminded children was all-consuming. All matters related to their mental and physical nature interested him. In a 1927 letter to Little, he notes that he has collected the "physical measurements of 100 boys during three or four years" to study the "relations between physical and mental development." However, he now wanted to compare the results to those of "mongoloids in other institutions." Davenport closed by saying he would like "to spend an additional day each month for as many months as may be necessary to carry out this program."[56] As happened repeatedly over the many years of their relationship, Little wrote back to the nationally recognized eugenicist that "we shall be glad to have you come anytime if you can find material to work with."[57]

Over time, Davenport would go on to help create and lead the Letchworth Village Research Council, which would "investigate the causes . . . that prevent the full development of the individual, making him a financial and social burden to the community." The result of such a council of experts, argued Davenport, would "bear fruit eventually in lowered public expense and greater public security."[58]

Davenport told one Letchworth Village official that correcting the problem of the feebleminded depended on efforts "to dry up the springs from which they arise. The fact that from defective parents defective, offspring arise" made it necessary to implement numerous precautionary measures, including mass sterilization programs. One, in particular, was "to sterilize the girls before they were discharged from the institution." Davenport argued that the "solution seems to be the passage of a general sterilization law and its effective demonstration."[59]

Doctors and asylum bosses held equally expansive views on experimentation; many believed scientists deserved a free hand, especially in the use of the institutionalized. As medical historian Paul Lombardo states in his article on the castration of a "mongoloid dwarf," Superintendent Little "did not think it necessary to get written consent from one candidate's mother." Davenport, however, was concerned about the "law" and potential "legal" issues and preferred some form of parental consent. Deciding to take the path of least resistance, they passed on one "mongoloid" child whose parent was too "intelligent" and selected another whose mother was "less capable" intellectually to discern what was being orchestrated. Despite her agreement, it was feared "her permission would probably have no legal standing." To ensure that a "case could be made" for performing the surgery, Davenport pushed the rationale that the procedure was being done on "therapeutic grounds." The boy, they would argue, exhibited "a rather marked eroticism, and this probably bothers him some, as it doubtless does his attendants."[60] Like many other such institutions, Letchworth Village repeatedly proved itself a valuable incubator for numerous medical studies.

There can be little doubt that the American eugenics movement exacerbated an already grave, if not intolerable, situation for those with acute mental and physical challenges. Discarded, shunned, and often the brunt of pranks, jokes, and more serious criminal acts, the "feebleminded" and physically challenged were destined for compromised, complicated lives. The eugenics movement of the early twentieth century would show them no mercy. Proponents of "better breeding" wanted more than separation and institutionalization for such dysgenic individuals; they wanted finally to eliminate the unfit from the nation's gene pool: in short, to finally be rid of them.

Doctors and medical researchers dedicated to seeking answers for the numerous health conundrums confronting humankind, especially the more zealous among them, instinctively knew what to do with such a loathed and flawed population. Its members could serve humanity and science by participating in important research studies, experiments designed to increase knowledge and help solve long-standing medical mysteries. With the passage of years, children and "defective" children would prove increasingly attractive as test subjects, and those in a central repository like an asylum or an orphanage were an experimental gold mine.

The gradual but steady trend of utilizing institutionalized children as cheap and available research material would prove surprisingly easy. Recruitment of minors as test subjects for experimental purposes had long been a part of medicine. However, the practice grew more frequent with the onset of the eugenicists' sterilization and castration campaigns. Asylum children were chosen as test subjects precisely because they were isolated, out of public view, and considered less valuable than normal children. In these isolated venues, experiments that resulted in death or another unfortunate outcome could more easily be kept from the general public.

In 1895, between Drs. Sharp and Belfield's clarion calls for greater utilization of surgical sterilization. Dr. Henry Heiman notified colleagues at the New York Academy of Medicine that he had purposefully "inoculated" a four-year-old boy "suffering from idiocy and chronic epilepsy" with "pure cultures of gonococci."[61] In a similar experiment, a second boy "suffering from idiocy" was subjected to inoculation of gonococci; like the other boy, he experienced the nagging and painful symptoms of gonorrhea.

Those attending the New York medical forum were said to be "much interested" in Heiman's research and went out of their way to complement "his painstaking work." Discussants contributed numerous thoughts and comments; none concerned the ethics of using intellectually challenged, institutionalized children as test subjects. Such practices would become more common at the turn of the century. Their peers viewed those choosing to use institutionalized populations as innovative, judicious in their use of available resources, and dedicated to their craft.

Many physicians and medical researchers not only bought into this line of thinking but became vigorous proponents of it. With their elevated professional status, men of science would come to believe that their decisions on such matters as human experimentation were not only sound and prudent but also ethically unassailable. They were the gods of science, omniscient arbiters of public health, oblivious to their fierce desire to exploit new medical theories and methodologies at the expense of ethical boundaries related to patient inviolability and the line between therapeutic and non-therapeutic experimentation. Regardless of whether the doctor was at the bedside or the researcher in the lab, training combined with deeply embedded paternalistic and elitist beliefs told them they knew best. Medical journal editors celebrated their discoveries, popular media praised their heroic contributions, and the public applauded their triumphs. The few critics bold enough to protest such practices, such as the antivivisectionists, were easily marginalized. The longer those practices went unchallenged by significant community members, the more accepted and widespread they became.

The eugenics movement of the late 19th century and the early 20th century laid the groundwork for some of the most vulnerable segments of the American populace to be seen as so much detritus; human garbage deserving few rights and even less consideration. Asylum children at Letchworth Village, Vineland, Milledgeville, Fernald, Sonoma State, and many similar institutions were chosen as test subjects precisely because they were isolated, out of public view, and considered less valuable than normal children.

That pattern would continue until the 1940s when the use of the institutionalized as human guinea pigs would shift from a relatively small cottage industry to a full-blown, government-funded, university-sponsored pillar of modern medicine.

CHAPTER THREE

WORLD WAR II, PATRIOTISM, AND THE NUREMBERG CODE

"It Was a Good Code for Barbarians."

Fᴿᴏᴍ Dᴇᴄᴇᴍʙᴇʀ 1946 ᴛᴏ Aᴜɢᴜsᴛ 1947, ᴛᴡᴇɴᴛʏ-ᴛʜʀᴇᴇ Nᴀᴢɪ ᴅᴏᴄᴛᴏʀs and medical administrators were put on trial at the Palace of Justice in Nuremberg, Germany, on charges of "crimes against humanity" concerning "murders . . . atrocities, and inhumane acts." Officially known as the United States of America v. Karl Brandt et al., the landmark historical event is also known as the "Doctors Trial." Accomplished physicians and high-ranking Nazi officials such as Karl Gebhardt, Victor Bracj, and Wolfram Sievers were put on trial for orchestrating experiments on concentration camp prisoners where victims were immersed in icy water, forced to swallow seawater, enveloped in toxic gas, placed in vacuum chambers, injected with plague, and subjected to horrible bone transplantation surgery. The Doctors Trial concluded with the court tribunal handing down a list of ten principles, the Nuremberg Code, designed to formulate a universal standard for protecting human subjects involved in medical research.

Though the trial showcased German researchers' atrocities, the German legal team aggressively struck back at their accusers. Angered by what they perceived as a double standard, lawyers for the Third Reich's medical hierarchy vigorously questioned the prosecution's expert witnesses about the proper way to conduct human research. Though somewhat unusual in the "considerable latitude" given defense counsel, it provided greater historical context to the complex issues at hand. Prosecutors and justices alike were attempting to chronicle and assign blame as to "how medicine became caught up in politically messianic schemes for racial rejuvenation, and how these involved exterminations of peoples designated as biologically inferior and reservoirs of lethal pathogens."[1] As the lead American prosecutor subsequently admitted, "Curiously enough, we were educated in large part by our opponents."[2]

One expert witness who faced a lengthy cross-examination was Dr. Andrew C. Ivy, Vice-President of the University of Illinois School of Medicine and an eminent researcher. He was also the American Medical Association's official representative at the trial. While on the witness stand, Dr. Ivy repeatedly extolled the virtues of American medicine. He rarely lost an opportunity to underscore America's principled policies regarding human research, but his testimony was not without its ethical landmines and procedural potholes. There were several potentially embarrassing moments as in this exchange between defense counsel for the Nazis' and the esteemed witness concerning a series of deadly experiments in the Philippines carried out by an American researcher earlier in the century:

DEFENSE COUNSEL FRITZ SAUTER: Witness, when reading Strong's (Dr. Richard P. Strong) papers on those plague experiments, did it not strike you, too, that Strong carried out those experiments on 900 prisoners condemned to death, all of whom volunteered?

DR. IVY: No, I am not acquainted with that. I have not seen these records.

DEFENSE COUNSEL SAUTER: But it says so in the report. 900 persons condemned to death in the city of Manila—900 volunteers.

DR. IVY: I have not seen that report.

DEFENSE COUNSEL SAUTER: We have racked our brain as to how it was possible that there were 900 persons condemned to death in such a small city as Manila; how come there could be so many volunteers. But now, something else in this context. In many regions where those experiments were carried out, the Strong experiments in the Philippines and other areas such as America, there are unemployed people who are only too happy to earn something. Let us say you said the people received $100 in reward, and probably they received free food and extra cigarettes and cigars. Why were unemployed people not used? Why did you use conscientious objectors, why people under sentence, even people condemned by federal courts? Can you give me a satisfactory answer to that question, witness?

DR. IVY: To my knowledge, there were no unemployed people in the United States during the war.

DEFENSE COUNSEL SAUTER: And before the war?

DR. IVY: There were unemployed people in the United States before the war during the depression, but experiments on malaria on a large scale were not conducted then. Pharmaceutical chemists of the country had not been organized to synthesize some 80,000 compounds for testing of effectiveness in the treatment of malaria.

DEFENSE COUNSEL SAUTER: Doctor, didn't it occur to you just in America that with your splendid radio network, you could readily have received volunteers for your experiments by advertising for them by air, and if this did not occur to you, why didn't you do it?

DR. IVY: That obviously is impractical to collect people from all over the country and to bring them to one point for purposes of an experiment.

DEFENSE COUNSEL SAUTER: I am not requiring that people should be collected from all over the country, but America has such large cities that you could find thirty, forty, or fifty volunteers in one city alone. Now, why was that not done?

DR. IVY: Well, sometimes that is done.

DEFENSE COUNSEL SAUTER: But you didn't do it. You used conscientious objectors.[3]

The issue of American physicians using the imprisoned as test subjects in medical research was especially sensitive considering the Doctors' trial's purpose. Many observers in the courtroom were probably unaware that vulnerable populations in America—including those behind bars—had been used as raw material for medical research. When Robert Servatius, attorney for Karl Brandt, one of the Nazi defendants, brought up *Life Magazine*'s extensive coverage of the wartime malaria experiments at several penal institutions in America, Ivy worked to show the difference between medical research in America and the travesty of German medicine. German medicine, he would indicate, encouraged everything from gruesome high-altitude seawater, and severe hypothermia experiments to ghastly incendiary bombs, plague, and mustard gas experiments at concentration camps like Buchenwald, Dachau, and Ravensbruck. To underscore the difference, Ivy emphasized the voluntary nature of the American studies, the prisoners' "idealistic motivations," and the "great reformative value" of the experiments.

Though in actuality, he had only recently formulated a litmus test for ethical "Experimentation on Human Subjects," Ivy gave the impression that such rules had been in operation for some time. His moral framework consisting of three critical principles was not only brief; it also left some wiggle room for interpretation; a feature Ivy was keen on maintaining for the benefit of the medical community. His principles consisted of:

- Consent of the subject is mandatory; only volunteers should be used.
- The experiment to be performed should be based on previous animal experimentation.
- Scientifically qualified individuals should conduct an experiment.

Ivy argued that if those rules of investigative engagement were followed, there would be no question of an experiment's ethicality or legitimacy.

A consummate political actor and media-savvy operator who, according to one scholar, had "no qualms in being economical with the truth in order to hold Nazi physicians accountable and American medical science . . . ethical and legal," some of his claims would be considered a stretch, while others were blatantly dishonest.[4] For example, Ivy's line that those who participated in the malaria experiments discovered a new respect for the law, and their "return to criminality . . . markedly decreased" because of their involvement in medical research was based on thin, if any, evidence.[5]

On the witness stand, Ivy argued that Americans behind bars were "patriotic . . . loved their country" and sought ways to contribute to the war effort. Besides, he added that they "had no other duties to perform" with more than a hint of truth and were "fully available for purposes of experimentation." Servatius was quick to pounce as the following testimony indicates on Ivy's notions.

DEFENSE COUNSEL SERVATIUS: "If all of those persons apply for idealist reasons, why are they offered pecuniary recompense?"

DR. IVY: I suppose it is to serve as a small reward for the unpleasantness of the experience.

DEFENSE COUNSEL SERVATIUS: Don't you believe that the money was the motive for many of them—a hundred dollars?

DR. IVY: That is rather small from the point of view of prisoners in the penitentiary in the United States. A hundred dollars isn't much money.

DEFENSE COUNSEL SERVATIUS: For a prisoner, that would be quite a lot of money, it seems to me; for someone at liberty, it is not so much.[6]

Ivy remained unmoved. He was adamant that American prisoners did not volunteer to participate in medical experiments to "receive pecuniary compensation" or the prospect of a pardon. Servatius and fellow defense team members were equally rigid in pointing out what they considered examples of American ethical transgressions and misdeeds. Ivy was queried on Walter Reed's Yellow Fever experiments in Cuba at the turn of the century, using "political prisoners" in America as test subjects. Ivy testified no political prisoners were being used as test subjects. Also, he was asked about his involvement in the recently formed "Green Commission," which was tasked with examining the prison research issue.[7] The German lawyers had schooled themselves as best they could on American medical research history and practices in preparation for the trial. They even brought up "Nathan Leopold," an infamous lifer at Illinois's Stateville Penitentiary who participated in the malaria studies during the war.[8]

The lawyers for Karl Gebhardt, Major General in the Waffen SS; Joachim Mrugowski, Chief Hygienist of Reich Physician SS; and Waldemar Hoven, Chief Doctor, Buchenwald concentration camp; and the other infamous Nazi doctors hoped to underscore the point in their questioning of Dr. Ivy and other prosecution witnesses that America was no model of moral rectitude when it came to medical research and in no position to judge the practices of others. Was the incorporation of inmates sentenced to death in a prison in the South Pacific, they inquired, significantly different than the Third Reich's use of concentration prisoners as test subjects?[9] Were the hands of Dr. Strong any cleaner from an ethical point of view than Georg August Weltz, Chief of the Institute for Aviation Medicine, who was now in the defendant's dock on trial for his life? The defense tried to portray the American medical research establishment as recklessly experimentalist.[10] Moreover, the physician—researchers who did such cutting—edge investigative work were glorified in the American media. Dr. Kurt Blome, one of the Nazi defendants, specifically mentioned Paul de Kruif, author of *Microbe Hunters*, as not only a popularizer of scientific exploits and human experimentation but also someone who championed the position, "You must kill men to save them."[11]

There would be considerable courtroom jousting between defense counsel and Dr. Ivy that would place medical research in America under the ethical microscope. At one point, for example, Ivy was grilled about American test subjects receiving "small amounts" of remuneration, as well as those same individuals being encouraged to sign waivers "giving up all claims" if anything untoward should occur during the experiment:

DEFENSE COUNSEL: From the point of view of medical ethics, do you believe whether in America or in any other civilized nation that it is in accord with medical ethics to carry out experiments with a certain degree of danger on prisoners who are first asked to sign a waiver giving up all claims, even for their heirs? In your opinion, can that be reconciled with medical ethics?

DR. IVY: Yes, I believe it can be reconciled with the basic medical ethics.

Probably even more troubling to Ivy, not to mention American prosecutors, was the apparent disagreement between Ivy and Dr. Werner Leibbrand, another of the prosecution's key witnesses, on what exactly constituted ethical research. A noted German psychiatrist and medical historian from Erlangen University, Leibbrand was chosen for his "immaculate credentials" and what some considered his "denazification" potential. His participation allowed Allied authorities to show that only a minority of German doctors breached medical standards and were guilty of criminal practices.

Unfortunately, it did not play out that way. His relatively rigid and comparatively purist notions of the boundaries of ethical research proved a severe conundrum for prosecutors but a beacon of opportunity for defense lawyers. According to one scholar who has studied the trial, "Leibbrand's testimony backfired and left Allied medical science to appear almost in the same moral category as German medical science."[12] Robert Servatius, the attorney for Karl Brandt, Hitler's physician and Major General in the SS, crafted his strategy skillfully and quickly sprung to open the door that Leibbrand had left ajar.

DEFENSE COUNSEL SERVATIUS: Witness, are you of the view that a prisoner who had been in prison for over ten years will give his consent for an experiment if he receives no advantage from this; do you consider such consent to have been voluntarily given?

DR. LEIBBRAND: No, according to medical ethics, that is not the case because the patient or the prisoner, first of all, finds himself in a state of coercion, since he is in preventative custody and secondly because he is a layman and has no way of calculating the effects of an operation on himself. As a layman, he is simply not in a position to do that."

DEFENSE COUNSEL SERVATIUS: Are you of the view that eight hundred prisoners (those inmates involved in the American malaria experiments) who are detained at various places and who give their consent for experiments do so voluntarily?

DR. LEIBBRAND: No.

DEFENSE COUNSEL SERVATIUS: You are not answering that in consideration of whether or not the experiment leads to lasting or only temporary injury to the prisoner?

DR. LEIBBRAND: Even in the last case, my answer is still no.

DEFENSE COUNSEL SERVATIUS: If such persons are infected with malaria because they have declared their readiness, do you consider that possible?

DR. LEIBBRAND: No, because such a voluntary statement of consent is not right from the point of view of medical ethics. These men, as prisoners, find themselves under a state of coercion.[13]

Things would only grow worse for the prosecution as Servatius began reading from the June 4, 1945, issue of *Life Magazine* that featured an extensive section of photographs and commentary on the American malaria studies at four penal institutions, including Stateville in Illinois and Atlanta Federal Penitentiary. Servatius read passages from the article and mentioned the periodic fevers "as high as 106 degrees," the "severe chills," and regular bouts of delirium and diarrhea. In one instance, a sick inmate was allowed "to proceed to late stages before drugs were given to combat" his fever. The German attorney then turned to Leibbrand and asked his opinion "on this experiment regarding medical permissibility."

Though a witness for the prosecution, Leibbrand did not back off; he neither altered his views nor tempered his words. "I cannot change my previously stated opinion about medical ethics involved," said Leibbrand. "I am of the opinion that such experiments as these are an ill—chosen form of biological thinking." He would go on to state, "malaria is a very serious disease because it has complications" and should in no way be compared to "someone with a little sniffle" or cold. With the former, you "always may have death as a consequence. And in view of this, such experiments should be carried out on guinea pigs and not on human beings."[14]

Leibbrand's assessment of American medical research was a severe and embarrassing blow to the prosecution's case. According to Schmidt's account of the Nuremberg Doctors Trial, Leibbrand's testimony "undermined the case of the prosecution by giving the impression to the tribunal that German and

Allied medical science was essentially the same."[15] More problematic yet, this damaging testimony had come from the mouth of the prosecution's witness.

A German physician like those on trial, but someone who had suffered numerous indignities, discrimination, and persecution during the Third Reich, Leibbrand remained unswerving in his belief that "German physicians had perverted traditional Hippocratic ethics by showing a lack of morality and reverence for human life." He compared it to a person being seen as a "mere object like a mail package" in the Nazi's dystopian view of the world. In his mind, the Nazis had established a pure "biological state." People had become things.

For Leibbrand, "human experimentation was only permissible if the person had given voluntary informed consent, was mentally capable of giving consent, and was not forced or in any way coerced."[16] In his opinion, experimentation on vulnerable populations such as prisoners, children, and the disabled was forbidden. Under no condition, he insisted, should vulnerable populations be used for research. He believed America had committed similar sins to the Nazis was a large hole for the American prosecutors to climb out.

However, they wasted little time trying to extricate themselves from the ethical quagmire and brought Dr. Ivy back to Europe, in June 1947 to rebut their own witness. "I do not agree with that statement of Professor Leibbrand," Ivy told the Tribunal. "First, the prisoners, the experience with our prisoner volunteers in the United States is a fact showing that that does not hold, and secondly, he assumes that prisoners cannot be motivated to take part in medical experiments by humanitarian incentives. This is contrary to our experience."[17]

Pressed for time—or possibly to rescue the prosecution from an unsettling conundrum within its ranks—the Tribunal's chief justice intervened and cut off further debate on the issue. "It appears from the testimony of the witness," said the presiding judge, "that he does not in all respects agree with the opinions of Dr. Leibbrand, who testified here on behalf of the prosecution. The fact that there is a difference of opinion, of two expert witnesses on behalf of the prosecution, is clearly before the Tribunal now."[18]

The critical philosophical debate between the two key witnesses for the prosecution struck at the heart of using vulnerable populations in medical research. That debate has continued to spark periodic examination and controversy in the scientific community. Dr. Werner Leibbrand proffered that prisoners are incapable of free will and free choice by the very nature of their confined and constrained status. Due to the circumstances of their confinement, they are limited in gathering independent information about an experiment and what may be in store for them as test subjects. The upshot for Leibbrand was that prisoners, as well as other at-risk populations such as children and the mentally ill, were in coercive or "forced situations" and could never be genuinely volunteers.

As Ivy listened to Werner Leibbrand on the witness stand at Nuremberg, his worst fears were coming to fruition; American jurists may be so appalled by the Nazi experiments and the American medical community's use of prison inmates that the Tribunal may decide to end human research altogether. A prohibition of medical research on humans was a "worst-case scenario" for Ivy and central to quickly developing a viable, "pragmatic instrument" that could help separate ethical from unethical research practices. The threat of such far-reaching sanctions propelled him to create the Green Commission, prod the AMA to adopt his principles, and shape his participation at the Doctors Trial.

According to most examinations of the trial and its main actors, the protection of human subjects and the role of informed consent were secondary to Ivy's prime interest: maintaining human experimentation as a critical element of scientific inquiry well into the future, and with as few constraints as possible.

Given the rather slim nature of his three principles of ethical experimentation: subjects must be volunteers, animal studies before using humans, and the involvement of scientifically qualified investigators, there was much room for interpretation. As one reviewer of the trial argues, "There was no mention of what consent meant, how it would be obtained and by whom, or what kind of information the subject was entitled to receive. There was also no reference to vulnerable groups like the mentally challenged and children, nor did the rules explain what for the good of society meant."[19]

There were additional unresolved questions, but that was Ivy's goal. To keep any guidelines "deliberately vague in order to allow room for interpretation and discretion for medical scientists in the future." By claiming that his three principles had been long established and long accepted by "civilized societies," Ivy hoped to derail government intrusion by showing that conscientious doctors had always been faithful to issues of consent and safety. It was the Nazi version of medical research that had gone astray, not traditional medicine. It has been argued, "Ivy's main priority was to ensure that the public would not lose confidence in the medical profession. The world's medical profession, above all, had to be protected from coming into disrepute. This would include manipulating the outcome of the Doctors' Trial as a whole."[20]

As Ivy told the organizers of the forthcoming Nuremberg Trial, "It is recommended that the official in charge of the publicity of these trials should be cautioned to release the publicity in such a form that it will not jeopardize ethical experimentation on human subjects. " In addition, he added, ". . . the publicity should be pointed to emphasize the contrast between the unethical and illegal experimentation of the Nazis and the ethical experimentation conducted in Allied countries, and even in Germany before the war."[21]

Ivy also recommended that a "code of ethical rules for human experimentation" be drafted with the "idea of preventing recurrences of Nazi crimes" in the future. There can be little doubt that Ivy lobbied assiduously to have his short-list of principles incorporated in any code the Tribunal contemplated creating.

Along with Dr. Leo Alexander, another prosecution investigator and medical expert, Ivy was instrumental in crafting the ten principles of medical research on humans that American jurists delivered after the Nazi Doctors' Trial. In addition to the critical "voluntary consent" provision, the first principle also underscored the need for the subject's "free power of choice," the absence of "force, fraud, duress," and any "other ulterior form of constraint or coercion" that may influence his decision. The fact that the authors emphasized the need for test subjects to have "sufficient knowledge and comprehension" of the experiment in order "to make an understanding and enlightened decision" not only highlighted the egregious acts of the defendants in the docket but was probably intended as a recommended roadmap for future scientists contemplating experimental work with humans.

Though often receiving less emphasis and comment than the "voluntary consent" principle, the other nine principles were equally significant for protecting the rights and health of test subjects. Principles that include that an experiment is "based on the results of animal experimentation" and striving to "avoid all unnecessary physical and mental suffering" to the involvement of "scientifically qualified persons" and the subject's right to "end" an experiment if they feel they cannot continue. The Nuremberg Code further protected test subjects than any medical, moral, or legal ethical directive to that point in time.

As a noted medical historian and ethicist Jay Katz observed, "The Nuremberg Code is a remarkable document. Never before in the history of human experimentation, and never since, has any code or any regulation of research declared in such relentless and uncompromising fashion that the psychological integrity of research subjects must be protected absolutely."[22]

Regrettably, for the entire document's unique historical import and steadfast concern for human subject protection, its impact was less than its authors intended. Though occasionally given lip service and cited in books and journal articles by medical historians and ethicists, the code was shelved for all practical purposes soon after it was delivered or, in the words of one knowledgeable historian, "relegated to history almost as soon as it was born."

Most medical professionals in industrialized nations, particularly those in America, considered the Nazi experience a medical aberration, an anomaly not indicative of how the rest of the civilized world practiced scientific research. For example, Columbia University medical historian David J. Rothman has argued that "madness, not medicine, was implicated at Nuremberg." The "prevailing view" at the time and after, according to Rothman, was that those on trial at Nuremberg were "Nazis first and last; by definition, nothing they did, and no code drawn up in response to them, was relevant to the United States."[23]

Moreover, argues Rothman, Nazi medicine was interpreted by some as an example of the evils of state intrusion. The Third Reich's "atrocities were the result of government interference in the conduct of research. Science was pure," these critics claimed. "It was politics that was corrupting." The upshot for the 1947 Nuremberg Code was clear; rather than being seen as a model for the regulation of human experimentation, it was increasingly becoming viewed as an argument against "socialized medicine" and in favor of the position that "the state should not interfere with medicine."[24]

Interviews with numerous physicians have confirmed that the Nuremberg Code was rarely mentioned as part of their medical education during the 1950s and 1960s. It certainly was not the centerpiece of any ethical training regarding the limitations of research with humans. An argument can be made that those few aware of it were concerned about the code's numerous restrictions on human research. The most knowledgeable, it would appear, were searching for ways to loosen, if not jettison, the many limitations that the code's ten principles imposed on scientific investigators. According to Yale professor and ethicist Jay Katz, it was because of this entrenched and uniform opposition that "the Nuremberg Code did not become the guiding code for the conduct of research" in America and worldwide.[25] In less than a decade and a half, those disaffected elements became a concerted movement that resulted in a competing set of principles, much more to the liking of physician-investigators.

The Declaration of Helsinki adopted by the World Health Organization in 1964 was a document drafted by doctors, for doctors, and with doctors' interests in mind. "Medical progress" now superseded the "interests of the subject" in the hierarchy of principles. Gone was the Nuremberg Tribunal's harsh language prohibiting "force, fraud, deceit, duress, overreaching, or any ulterior form of constraint or coercion," as was an earlier Helsinki draft provision stating that "prisoners of war, military or civilian, should never be used as subjects of experiment." Thought injurious to the unfettered research arena that physician-researchers desired, the document's more restrictive provision was excised. The new Helsinki Code trumpeted "the advancement of science" over "the integrity of the individual."[26]

Further bolstering this philosophical shift in emphasis were the U.S. government's rules and regulations for protecting human research subjects, which confirmed the medical profession's efforts to distance itself from Nuremberg. The result, not surprisingly, was a postwar research landscape littered with the damaged bodies and embarrassing ethical transgressions of physicians and institutions that felt comfortable taking liberties with a code of research conduct never genuinely embraced by the nation that formulated it. Widely known cases of unethical medical research, such as the Tuskegee syphilis study and those occurring at the Jewish Chronic Disease Hospital in Brooklyn, the Willowbrook State School on Staten Island, and Holmesburg Prison in Philadelphia, are just four examples of vulnerable populations being exploited in the aftermath of the Nuremberg Trial. Still, many others will be identified in the coming chapters. If tenets of the Nuremberg Code had been respected, there would be far fewer instances of unethical medical research in America.

The seeds of this abandonment of the Nuremberg Code were sown early on and signaled that entrenched interests comfortable working under an unwritten but well-established utilitarian and paternalistic framework would not be blithely pushed aside.

The first prominent example of America's muddled, if not schizophrenic, perspective on war crimes, as well as its flexibility regarding the importance of medical research standards, was the decision to not replicate a doctor trial in Japan. One scholar refers to them as "deals with the devil." The U. S. Military's decided to forgo a trial of Japanese military doctors for their brutal and equally horrible medical experiments before and during the war. Lieutenant General Ishii Shiro's medical research operation, Unit 731, orchestrated an array of deadly biologic and chemical warfare experiments on a wide swath of Chinese and Russian citizenry from 1932 to 1945 that killed and maimed thousands of innocent civilians. However, he and his confederates were dealt with far more generously than Karl Brandt and the Nazi doctors at Nuremberg. This lack of legal action is shocking considering the United States did not share control of the defeated Japanese nation as they did with the Soviets, British, and French in Germany. The U. S. could have unilaterally called for a trial of Japanese doctors if they had so chosen. Believing that "the interests of national security overrode any consideration of war crimes prosecution," American military leaders in the Pacific theater scuttled the notion of replicating a Nuremberg-like trial in the Far East.[27]

The critical decisions to prosecute Nazi doctors, but not Imperial Army physicians, underscores America's lukewarm commitment to rules of ethical medical research. When one examines the laundry list of research horrors performed by Japanese scientists that included experiments with anthrax, botulism, brucellosis, cholera, smallpox, tuberculosis, typhus, and a dozen or two other deadly microbes and diseases, there is reason to question America's decision to trade freedom for scientific information.[28] At the time, however, there seemed to be little questioning, much less opposition, to the wide disparity in the treatment of enemy scientists. Seven Nazi doctors received death sentences and were executed; nine others received either life or long terms of imprisonment. On the other hand, Japanese doctors walked; they were never even tried. A public trial was the last thing American authorities desired.[29]

More problematic yet, was Operation Paperclip, a postwar program to import hundreds of German scientists into the U. S. to exploit their expertise in a range of scientific disciplines such as nuclear fission, radioactivity, and aeronautics.[30] Some, like Hubertus Strughold, were leaders in aviation medicine. However, there were also high-ranking members of the Nazi medical elite like Walter Schreiber, chief of the Department of Science and Health for the German High Command, who it is said had both knowledge and influence over human experiments at Dachau, Buchenwald, and other camps. Cleared by American authorities, they and others like them were brought to America to make significant contributions in space medicine and infectious diseases.

However, trumping all the others is the recent revelation that an American-led research mission in Central America during the trial of the Nazis' doctors deliberately infected over a thousand Guatemalan citizens with an assortment of sexually transmitted diseases. There should be little doubt if such egregious medical research were found to have been practiced by Drs. Gebhardt and Hoven at Buchenwald or Ravensbruck concentration camps would have been included in the formal list of charges by the International Military Tribunal. The fact that American jurists were haranguing German physicians about the proper way to conduct medical research and eventually sentencing seven of them to death while at the very same time purposefully infecting Guatemalan prisoners, soldiers, people with a mental health condition, and commercial sex workers with syphilis, gonorrhea, and chancroid is nothing short of stunning.[31]

A 2011 investigation by a Presidential Commission into the nefarious goings-on in Guatemala confirms that what took place was "unconscionable" and that American doctors were "morally blameworthy." Though they represented some of the nation's top researchers at the time, including the Surgeon

General of the United States, doctors chose to jettison any concerns they may have had about the ethical nature of such research in favor of garnering scientific knowledge they could not have gained any other way, at least, not in America. Cautionary notes amongst the doctors involved in the syphilis experiments in Guatemala are replete with surreptitious warnings to each other. They noted to limit information to those "who can be trusted not to talk," conduct your affairs "so that as few people as possible know the experimental procedure," and "it is unfortunate that we have to work in such a guarded, even subterranean way, but it seems to be very necessary."[32]

How could American doctors, presumably the best and brightest of the medical profession and according to Nuremberg medical expert Andrew Ivy, the most ethical, have committed such egregious acts on vulnerable populations in other countries at the very same time that representatives of the profession were lecturing Nazi doctors about how medical research should be conducted? Such hypocrisy is not surprising; American researchers had been incorporating vulnerable subjects in their work for some time. That practice had accelerated as World War II placed an increasing burden on doctors to discover a raft of cures and preventives for a host of diseases and medical conundrums. A slippery slope of research convenience and opportunism had been created where need and immediacy trumped ethics. Reining in such an institutional culture would take more than a distant trial of "barbarians" and creating a novel but unwieldy code of ethics. The last thing researchers wanted was a code of ethical conduct unsuited to a supercharged American medical community that was about to flex its institutional and entrepreneurial muscle further than anyone could have anticipated.

During the early years of the war, American medicine and human research took the giant step from a laid-back cottage industry to a well-funded, high-powered machine. As medical historian David Rothman writes: "The transforming event in the conduct of human experimentation in the United States, the moment when it lost its intimate and directly therapeutic character, was World War II."[33] A landscape dominated by unsophisticated, underfunded, and solitary practitioners striving to solve medical riddles quickly evolved into well-funded, highly coordinated scientific campaigns geared toward helping troops on the front lines. The mission's success dominated the campaign; the war's urgency subordinated all other factors, including consent. Test subjects were increasingly at risk.

Embroiled in a life-and-death struggle with ruthless totalitarian powers across the globe, the threat of annihilation dictated a unified effort, individual self-sacrifice, and contributions by all, even those on the home front who were sequestered in custodial institutions. Criticism regarding the use of institutionalized citizens as subjects for research was nonexistent. A war had to be fought and won, and all were expected to contribute to the effort.

Those warehoused in state institutions, from penal facilities to mental asylums to orphanages, were sought after by researchers needing subjects to test new medicinal potions. Letters between doctors that began "I am writing to you with regard to our conversation about the possibility of using patients of certain institutions as subjects for trial of new vaccines against . . ." were commonplace during the war. [34] War Department officials concerned about U.S. service members contracting everything from measles, dysentery, and influenza to more exotic biological threats such as sandfly fever, dengue fever, and scrub typhus fever were desperate to discover appropriate treatments and preventives as quickly as possible. However, that required experimentation; integral to any successful research effort was the ability to procure a sufficient number of test subjects to produce a disease-fighting elixir.

For example, the Army's Board for the Investigation of Epidemic Diseases had become increasingly concerned about the jump of equine encephalomyelitis from animal to man in 1941. At that time, North Dakota was forced to grapple with a medical emergency, "5,000 cases and about 500 deaths from equine encephalomyelitis of the western type" had settled on the land. The sudden "epidemic" led to concentrated efforts to discover a vaccine. It included "a large-scale experiment" in Canada using 3,000 farmers and the scientific contributions of the "Lederle Company," which eventually resulted in a successful vaccine.

The Army, however, was quick to "point out that other types of epidemic encephalitis such as St. Louis encephalitis and possibly Japanese encephalitis might appear in epidemic form in areas where our troops might be quartered. For this reason, it is highly desirable to prepare vaccines against these two specific diseases." Fortunately, Dr. Albert B. Sabin had recently developed vaccines for both. Each was "tried experimentally on about 50 students at the University of Cincinnati" with some success. But before giving it to our fighting men overseas, it was thought best "if this vaccine was administered to about one thousand individuals" to examine further its effectiveness and the possibility of "severe local reaction."

Research physicians were always on the hunt for test subjects. The acting director of the Commission on Neurotropic Virus Diseases, for example, sent out numerous missives stating, "I am inquiring whether it might be possible to find 1,000 to 1,500 candidates in the various State institutions with which you are familiar." The letter went on to underscore that the "problem . . . is intimately and directly associated with the War effort," and the government would be most "grateful indeed if there is anything you can do to help us in this matter."[35]

The letter was sent to, among others, Dr. Joseph Stokes Jr., a highly regarded physician and pediatrics researcher at the University Hospital of the University of Pennsylvania and the Children's Hospital of Philadelphia. With access to those warehoused in state institutions, Stokes and many top medical scientists like him complied with such requests. Long familiar with the drill, Stokes tested new theories and perfected medical remedies years before the war began. A longtime advocate of the immunity-boosting properties of gamma globulin, Stokes was absorbed by the latest developments in fighting childhood diseases. Everything from influenza to polio was of interest, and he did more than his fair share of investigational research. Nevertheless, with each new frontal assault on a particular malady came the need for test subjects. Stokes knew where to go for cheap and available "material."

As Stokes informed medical writer Paul de Kruif, "permission has practically been granted for an extensive experimental study . . . in an institution of 700 inmates, ranging (in age) from five years upwards." Such facilities, Stokes assured de Kruif, were not in short supply, "and if we fail to get permission from this institution, there are other groups which we can use."[36]

Institutionalized children were not necessarily researchers' first choice as experimental subjects. However, complications anywhere along the research paradigm could short-circuit a project or speed up an investigation before its time and quickly find its way into a school, orphanage, or facility for "feeble-minded" youngsters. For instance, in a subsequent series of correspondence, Stokes would inform de Kruif that he was "getting much disturbed about the situation . . . with the monkeys," whose cost was rising precipitously. "The price of monkeys," he complained to his colleague, was once again "going to be increased." He warned that if "additional funds" were not procured from some source, work would stop. Alternatively, in some cases, researchers would either resort to using less sophisticated animals, such as mice, or would move aggressively forward with human trials.

Regarding the latter, Stokes informed de Kruif that "we are greatly pleased with our results at the New Jersey State Colony" regarding the influenza studies. The institution was once known as the New Jersey State Colony for the Feebleminded. The microbiologist-turned journalist was apprised of an additional "experiment" at another "large New Jersey State Colony, which the state allowed [them] to use." However, Stokes decided it would be best to discuss that experiment, quite possibly a more sensitive one, when the men met in person.[37]

Dr. Strokes' dealings and investigative work with military and private/public sector organizations were typical of the top physician/researchers during the middle decades of the twentieth century. Geared by nature and training to fight disease, preserve life, and advance scientific knowledge, that mission was only heightened by an international political conflict whose human devastation was all too obvious and omnipresent. Not surprisingly, the war resulted in jettisoned rules, principles being abandoned or at least skirted, and some vulnerable populations being taken advantage. "The desperate push for victory amid the bloody mess that was World War II," according to medical ethicist Jonathan Moreno, "eased the way for expedience to run roughshod over high-toned principle."[38]

The research push caused by the war began, at least organizationally, months before the attack on Pearl Harbor. In the summer of 1941, with the prospects for peace looking increasingly slim, President Roosevelt signed off on a new governmental office designed to coordinate the development of both weapons research and medical research. The Office of Scientific Research and Development (OSRD) and the equally new Committee of Medical Research (CMR) were, in the words of one physician at the time, "a novel experiment in American medicine, for planned and coordinated medical research had never been essayed on such a scale."[39]

The CMR recommended over 600 research proposals to the OSRD for funding and many involved human experimentations during the war. The OSRD responded with 135 contracts awarded to many institutions, including universities, hospitals, research institutes, and industrial organizations, to conduct scientific investigations. Over 25 million dollars was expended for the research, a minuscule amount by today's standards, but a significant sum during that era.

According to Rothman's findings, the CMR was less interested in basic research than "immediate clinical payoffs." The prime concerns were keeping fighting men combat-ready and in action as too many were lost, not to enemy bullets, but disease and the elements. Dysentery, influenza, measles, mumps, and other communicable diseases sent soldiers from the front lines to hospital wards. With just about all of these medical conundrums, test subjects would be needed to solve the riddle of developing viable preventatives and effective treatments.

One CMR operative knew just where to go when laboratory work had been completed, animal data collected, and field-testing with humans now in order. "Institutions such as asylums," he suggested, were prime repositories for orphans and the developmentally disabled; throwaway people who never questioned authorities followed directives, rarely wandered away, and had few ties to the outside world.[40] What few pangs of conscience there may have been were outweighed by the ominous threat facing the nation, the urgency of solving numerous medical challenges, and years of eugenics propaganda that had attenuated the country's moral fiber and devalued entire classes of people.

According to Moreno, "the authorities had very little time to sort out these issues and precious little guidance from existing codes or conventions. They were also operating in a national and international emergency." The result, says Moreno, were "wildly inconsistent" policies and practices concerning the use of vulnerable populations in medical research, but the delicate task of whom to use and when to use them, as Rothman argues, was "deftly managed" by program administrators who understood the explosive nature of their experiments.[41] One such research project that went public was not lost on the Nazi defendants and their attorneys. America's malaria research, and those chosen to participate in it, became of particular interest to the Nuremberg defendants.

To reclaim territory lost to the Japanese after the attack on Pearl Harbor, the United States sent thousands of fighting men to a seemingly endless string of South Pacific islands only to be felled by malaria, "an enemy, even more, to be feared than the Japanese."[42] It would eventually be determined that "between 1942 and 1945 American forces lost some eight million man-days to malaria."[43] The loss of soldiers to illness constantly perturbed military leaders. In 1943 General Douglas MacArthur reportedly said, "Doctor, this will be a long war if for every division I have facing the enemy I must count on a second division in the hospital with malaria and a third division convalescing from this debilitating disease."[44] To make matters worse, Japan controlled the production of quinine, one of the few effective anti-malaria potions available.

In an urgent effort to address the situation, the CMR initiated a program to conquer malaria, but test material would be required with all such ventures. That was especially so in this case since, as the experts found, "*vivax malaria* would not take in a monkey;" humans would be needed. However, where does one go to find humans willing to be exposed to a debilitating and often deadly tropical disease? For a general society and medical community, spoon-fed a large serving of eugenic thought over several decades, the answer was simple: prisons and mental asylums.

Under a CMR grant, Dr. Alf Sven Alving, a respected nephrologist at the University of Chicago, "purposely infected" psychotic patients at Manteno

State Hospital in Illinois with malaria through transfusions and then put them through a series of antimalarial therapies. According to Rothman, Alving "made no mention of any effort to obtain their consent, but the very choice of psychotic inmates demonstrates how irrelevant such concerns were."[45]

However, it soon became apparent that more significant numbers would be needed. Once again, the answer came in the form of the institutionalized. This time those languishing behind bars in the nation's vast prison system. Four prisons were selected for the malaria trials, the two largest being Atlanta Federal Penitentiary and Stateville Penitentiary in Joliet, Illinois. Alving would once again coordinate the Stateville trials that began in March 1944. He would be working with the Chesson strain of *Plasmodium Vivax malaria,* a particularly potent and lethal strain of malaria. It is doubtful that the hundreds of prisoners who volunteered for the experiment were informed of this or, for that matter, that the strain was more debilitating than what the Nazi doctors were currently using in their experiments on concentration camp prisoners. More troubling yet, actual *Anopheles Quadrimaculatus* mosquitoes raised at Manteno State would be biting the Stateville volunteers, a form of infection much more dangerous than transfusion.

One of the best accounts of the wartime malaria experiments comes from an inmate—test subject who graphically chronicled the government's campaign to conquer the vexing tropical disease and the incarcerated men who offered themselves up as human guinea pigs. Nathan Leopold was a 19-year-old child prodigy, accomplished ornithologist, and University of Michigan *Phi Beta Kappa* when he attained infamy in the "thrill killing" of Bobby Franks, a 14-year-old neighbor. Along with his equally rich, brilliant, and self-absorbed co-conspirator, Richard Loeb, the boys set out in 1924 with an air of privilege and intellectual superiority to commit the "perfect crime." Though both were accomplished academics, Leopold was fluent in a half-dozen languages and had just entered the University of Chicago Law School while still a teenager. The two men were decidedly amateurish in their criminal escapades and quickly captured after the kidnapping, bludgeoning, and burying the young Franks boy in a cornfield culvert. The crime garnered national notoriety, and their widely presumed death sentence was only staved off by the brilliant argumentation of their defense attorney, Clarence Darrow.

By the time Alving and his team of medical researchers entered Stateville, Leopold had been a prisoner for nearly twenty years and the malaria project provided not only a diversion but also a physical and intellectual challenge of remarkable proportions. Though he repeatedly volunteered to be bitten and become a test subject, doctors would not allow it; Leopold was too valuable as a medical technician and all-around prison aide-de-camp. Eventually, however, his wish was granted, and he became a malaria patient. The entire experience was so momentous that Leopold would devote several chapters of his prison memoir, *Life Plus 99 Years,* to telling the story of the incarcerated wanting to do their part during the war, and thereby suffer through raging fevers of 106 degrees, constant headaches, vomiting, blackouts, and the occasional heart attack. Despite all that, Leopold said it was the signal "event" of his life and proudly called his hospitalized fellow convicts "good soldiers" to fight against both disease and Fascism.[46]

News organizations were quite taken with such stories, especially photojournalism periodicals like *Life* Magazine that could graphically capture on film the instant malaria-carrying mosquitoes bit the stomachs of prison volunteers. The June 1945 four-page photo spread, "Prison Malaria: Convicts Expose Themselves to Disease so Doctors Can Study It," resonated with the reading public.[47] Almost all approved of the inmates' courage and wartime contributions; no one seemed concerned that the men were captives, modestly paid, or given scant information about the short and long-term ramifications of their participation.

It is interesting that although the CMR was willing to inform the public about its prison malaria trials, it was less disposed in doing the same regarding human experiments using other targeted populations such as conscientious objectors. As Jonathan Moreno asks, "Were sensitivities about the use of conscientious objectors greater than with regard to prisoners"?[48] Even more sensitive were the many secret experiments that used children and the developmentally challenged, which will be covered in subsequent chapters. Government officials understood it was one thing to allow news coverage of criminals participating in medical research; it was another for experiments on children in orphanages and schools for the feebleminded to be exposed for public consumption. Even the average mental defective and prison inmate was deemed off-limits to the news media during the war.

For example, no one in the public arena was aware that during the war years, Dr. Sabin (who had the rank of major in the Army) was using "human volunteers from the New Jersey State Prison . . . as subjects" for the "experimental production in man . . . of Sandfly fever and Dengue Fever." The research, which was accomplished with the cooperation of the Rockefeller Institute and the New Jersey Department of Institutions and Agencies, had received the blessing of the Neurotropic Virus Disease Commission and a government grant of $17,000.[49]

Across the river in Pennsylvania, the Army was busy testing myriad theories and concoctions, including "an investigation of the possible relation between the status of nutrition and infestation of lice." Scientists wondered could "vitamins" have an impact on this problem? The military wanted to know as well and decided to fund a study. "Securing the cooperation of one of the Pennsylvania County Prisons," they believed, was the last critical piece of the project if they hoped "to obtain the human volunteers for this work."[50]

Further north, the Yale University School of Medicine coordinated a $12,000 study at the Connecticut State Hospital concerning the "Experimental Production of Infectious Hepatitis in Man." The inmates were "conscientious objectors" recruited "to determine whether the virus is excreted in the urine and feces of man."[51] Though there may have been physicians with ethical concerns regarding such experimental initiatives, the necessitude of war eased the pangs of conscience and allowed the use of prisoners and conscientious objectors, lightly regarded groups that had a social debt to repay. An additional incentive might have been the prospect of a journal publication, not a minor item in the career of an ambitious academic hoping to make a name for themself.

The Army's medical corps was proud of its accomplishments in tackling dreaded diseases around the globe. In addition to the "practical benefit to the Army" of keeping fighting men in the field was the "increased scientific knowledge," which they were sharing with "numerous agencies concerned with the study and control of infectious diseases among civilians and military forces." Underscoring the point were the "52 articles . . . published in medical and scientific journals and 30 additional manuscripts" published in the press or submitted to journals. Moreover, those numbers were just for the period 1941-1943.[52] It was not uncommon for doctors in the forefront of these investigational studies and publications to note that "experiments [with] human subjects are required, as lower animals are not susceptible." Often, "studies were gotten underway" using a pool of "volunteers," which could mean any combination of soldiers, conscientious objectors, the incarcerated, the feebleminded, or institutionalized children.[53] Update reports would subsequently be submitted stating, the "disease has been transmitted experimentally to human beings."

Like Major Sabin and other doctors involved in investigational research, Dr. Stokes coordinated a similar arrangement between the Army and the New Jersey Department of Institutions and Agencies during the war for test material. It was not unusual for the state prison system to supply the bodies while state mental asylums provided the testing site. As Stokes informed the Director of Medicine for New Jersey, "Because of the seriousness of the disease (infectious hepatitis) in the armed services and the fact that it has become worldwide, including large numbers of civilians, the Epidemiological Board, U. S. Army, has requested the Commission on Measles and Mumps, . . . to extend the studies on human volunteers as rapidly and as effectively as possible. Animals have not been found susceptible, and for this reason, human volunteers must be used for studies on the prevention and treatment of the disease."[54]

A system was established where "15 to 20 volunteers (prisoners)" would be "transferred from time to time" from a state prison "to a ward arranged for the care and study of these men at the New Jersey State Hospital" in Trenton. Critical issues such as "consent," the inmate "selection" process, and the length of time they would be at the state hospital—usually three months—was at "the discretion" of penal authorities.[55]

Occasionally, the human resources drain on one institution such as Trenton State Penitentiary would be so great that authorities were asked to consider a "similar transfer" arrangement with other institutions such as "Rahway and Annandale" that generally handled juvenile offenders. Like most researchers dependent on a steady supply of test subjects, Dr. Stokes thought that to be "an excellent idea."[56]

It would appear that New Jersey's Trenton State Hospital was a hotbed of military-related research during the war. Not only were prison inmates imported from the nearby state penitentiary for experimental purposes, but the mental hospital's patients were also routinely incorporated in studies. The institution's superintendents seemed to have been very supportive of most, if not all, experimental projects proffered to them. For example, in the fall of 1944, the Surgeon General's Office was informed that the Army had been "requested to participate in a collaborated study of the effect of induced malaria on liver function . . ." scheduled to take place at the hospital. It was said that studies like this were "carried out with ease at the Trenton State Hospital," and the director of the institution "delighted to cooperate" in such scientific exercises.[57] Army medical personnel were equally "delighted to hear" that there would be "no objections to the investigation" at the hospital.[58]

Due to cooperative arrangements such as this, the entire state system of institutions in New Jersey seems to have been mobilized for wartime scientific research. At the same time, for example, that Trenton State Penitentiary and Hospital were involved in malaria research, a "feebleminded group of humans at the New Jersey State Colony" was taking part in "dysentery vaccine" trials. The CMR-directed project incorporated at least "40 subjects.[59] A similar dysentery study had incorporated "60 feebleminded males" just a few months earlier.

Documents disclose that the "subjects were bled prior to immunization" and "the possibility of toxic reactions such as temperature rise, vomiting, diarrhea, and local reactions"—a common reaction to dysentery—were to be "watched for in each group." If the experiment proved successful, doctors planned to move forward with additional trials since "a study is being planned for normal humans who will be the same as the experiment" with the feebleminded."[60]

During these years, it became increasingly common for the "feebleminded" to be viewed as that intermediate step in the research process between mice and "normal humans." Moreover, and tragically documented in CMR files, state facilities for such special populations were considered the equivalent of frontline battlefield conditions. As one government document underscored, "In certain civilian institutions, where outbreaks of dysentery are not uncommon, opportunities have been furnished to observe the effect of the vaccines under approximately field conditions."[61] Those doctors with access to such facilities found themselves sought after and much prized by the military, the academic community, and the private sector.

Dr. Stokes developed good relations with both the scientific community and the administrators who ran the large state institutions in southeastern Pennsylvania and southern New Jersey. Such relationships often made him the go-to guy for medical investigators seeking suitable "test material" for their experimental endeavors. One letter to Stokes, for example, was a request for access to mental institutions in Philadelphia or New Jersey. The writer needed subjects for trials of new encephalitis vaccines. The individual making this request was a doctor from the Yale University School of Medicine who required "1,500 candidates, male or female, preferably between the ages of 17 and 40 years."[62]

By the last year of the war, New Haven, Princeton, San Francisco, and New York City had become hotbeds of experimental activity on hepatitis, poliomyelitis, and encephalitis. One of "the most important findings" of the experiments on hepatitis, for example, was that "the disease can be produced by feeding feces from a case of infectious hepatitis." To do so, however, required "human volunteers." These transmission studies "repeatedly reproduced" the feeding of feces laced with "infectious hepatitis" to test subjects. The key players in this drama, which "inoculated" dozens of subjects, included the Yale University School of Medicine, the Middletown and Norwich State Hospitals, and the Federal Correctional Institution of Danbury, Connecticut.[63] Their effort to demonstrate that "gamma globulin will protect injected individuals against infectious hepatitis," this time "a girls' school in Providence, R.I. and a Catholic Institution for children in New Haven," were the subjects of the study.[64]

Facilities for mentally and developmentally disabled children, such as the New Lisbon Developmental Center and the Skillman Center for Epileptics in New Jersey and Pennhurst State School and hospital in Pennsylvania, became frequent travel destinations for doctors working under the auspices of the Army Epidemiological Board.[65] Some investigators' institutional connections and travels, such as Joseph Stokes Jr., could be easily tracked by their statements of appreciation after journal publications. For example, one thank-you note concerning a series of measles studies by Stokes, Elizabeth Maris, and several other doctors offered these words of appreciation:

> Our thanks are due to all who have made these studies possible, particularly to Commissioner William J. Ellis and to Dr. Ellen C. Potter of the Department of Institutions and Agencies of the State of New Jersey; To Dr. Albert W. Pigott, Superintendent of Skillman; to Miss Ruth Jones, Superintendent at Mount Holly; to Mr. E. L. Johnstone, Superintendent at Woodbine; to Miss Marie S. Winokur, Superintendent of the Homewood School; to Drs. C. T. Jones and James Q. Atkinson, of New Lisbon; to Sister Mary Clare, Superintendent, and to Dr. Morris H. Schaeffer, physician of St. Vincent's Hospital; to Mr. E. Arthur Sweeny, Secretary of Welfare, State of Pennsylvania, and to Dr. James Dean, Superintendent at Pennhurst School. Also, we wish to acknowledge the technical assistance of Mr. William P. Jambor in the preparation of the virus, and the assistance of Dr. Samuel X. Radbill in obtaining fresh clinical material.[66]

Those receiving the authors' thanks had allowed children from their institutions to be incorporated in a series of measles experiments that included a challenge inoculation, in which "blood from children with active cases of measles" was injected into healthy children along with the forced "nasopharyngeal secretions from children with active cases of measles."[67] The several dozen children receiving the "challenge inoculations" resided in institutions such as New Lisbon, Pennhurst, Skillman, and the Homewood Orphanage in Philadelphia. Interestingly, most of the trials were not initiated due to the urgency of war: they occurred before America entered World War II.

Not all investigative work took place in institutions. Army Epidemiological Board physicians could find themselves in remote locations if the medical puzzle or scientific opportunity were deemed valuable enough. For example, in the summer of 1943, scores of young campers at Camp Akiba, a summer camp for children in the Pocono Mountains, had fallen seriously ill. The culprit was soon determined to be infectious hepatitis of epidemic proportions. The Army considered it their "good fortune to investigate an unusual and very interesting epidemic" in which "68 of 160 girls and approximately 40 of 170 boys had come down with the illness" that would continue to spiral into the hundreds.[68]

Believing the camp health crisis an "extremely interesting" event as well as an "opportunity to study the epidemiology of the disease in a closed group and to test the protective effect of the human immune serum globulin (gamma globulin) under natural or field conditions," army physicians traveled to the mountain region of northeast Pennsylvania. They injected dozens of children with the serum, a blood derivative that Stokes had been trumpeting for years as a highly effective elixir for a host of infectious diseases.[69] As Stokes proudly informed the surgeon general's office, "The sudden cessation of all cases of jaundice in the injected group is the striking finding" and one that merits "larger field experiments."[70]

Medical investigators, however, did not need to tramp into the woods to wage war against infectious hepatitis and dysentery. They had the economic wherewithal and political clout to take over buildings for their studies, as they did at Stateville (Illinois) and Atlanta Federal Penitentiary for sophisticated malaria studies. Structures on college campuses could be seized, as happened in Philadelphia during the last months of the war. In their ongoing effort to conquer infectious hepatitis, doctors recruited fifteen conscientious objectors to be quartered for "60 days" in a "fraternity house on the University of Pennsylvania campus." During that time, different preparations were tested on the men after they were given the disease; some acted as a control group. Concerned about sick men living close to one another, not to mention in a congested college neighborhood, the government claimed that its "chief objective is to prevent transmission of the disease to other persons in the unit and to persons outside the unit."[71]

The hepatitis study on the Penn campus was deemed so necessary that the army brought in environmental engineers to spray the DKE house on South Thirty-ninth Street with a potent insecticide to ensure that mosquitoes did not interfere with the research during the coming summer months. However, the order to spray a stunning "240 gallons of DDT" on "the walls, ceilings, and window screens of the building" in "six treatments" leads one to suspect that the researchers may have been testing more than hepatitis remedies.[72]

More common than the isolation-type study on the Penn campus were the many "transmission" studies in which diseases were passed on to "volunteers" by "feeding feces preparations" to them. The Akiba strain of hepatitis from the Pocono Mountains children's camp incident became a source of future experimentation.

In addition to medical research emerging as a "well-coordinated, extensive, federally-funded team venture," the impact of the war years on human experimentation was not only "transforming" but also made for a "curious mixture of high-handedness and forethought" regarding the use of vulnerable humans as subjects for experimentation. In some areas, such as research into dysentery, malaria, and influenza, there was "a pervasive disregard of the rights

of subjects. There was a willingness to experiment on the mentally and physically disabled, prisoners, ward patients, soldiers, and medical students without concern for obtaining consent." However, as David Rothman argues, research in other realms, such as survival under hardship conditions and the sensitive area of sexually transmitted diseases, were more "formal and carefully considered."[73]

The discrepancy, he argues, was the result of decision makers' navigating a course of moral brinksmanship: "When they sensed the possibility of an adverse public reaction, they behaved cautiously." However, they took liberties when they sensed that no one cared or was watching. Specifically, giving American citizens, even criminals behind bars, gonorrhea "might have raised a storm of protest from a variety of sources." The prospect of a controversial protocol appearing on the front page of a newspaper or in a courtroom was a worst-case scenario for researchers in general and CMR directors in particular.[74]

In his excellent work on the history of bioethics in America, *Strangers at the Bedside,* Rothman argues that this display of prudence contradicts the claim that investigators in the 1940s and 50s were "working in an ethical vacuum." Recent revelations, however, have shown that assessment to be quite wide of the mark. Less than a year after the war's end, researchers for the Public Health Service would enter Guatemala and embark on a two-year program that would expose thousands of soldiers, prisoners, mentally ill, and children to various sexually transmitted diseases. Performing research on syphilis and gonorrhea in America would remain problematic; however, but it did not preclude government physicians from leaving the country and orchestrating their "unconscionable" research in a foreign land.

Our ever-increasing knowledge of World War II-era scientific research gives credence to the argument that the research community was confident their decisions would not be second-guessed. Nor would they be opposed to using the orphaned, the incompetent, and the incarcerated as test subjects. A national emergency made this first "widespread use of human subjects in medical research" more palatable. If we could conscript and force thousands of citizens to confront the enemy and "face death" on the battlefield, we had every right to conscript those on the home front, including those behind bars, in mental asylums, and those below the legal age limit to sacrifice for their country too. As Rothman argues, "Some people were ordered to face bullets and storm a hill; others were told to take an injection and test a vaccine."[75]

Those calling the shots in this rapid expansion of human experimentation would seem to have been unaffected by the dramatic license they were assuming. The personal correspondence between research physicians, doctors, and institutional superintendents during this period illuminates little doubt or handwringing regarding the moral and ethical implications of consigning children or the mentally challenged or the imprisoned to the national pool of "research material." Their concerns were availability; how many subjects could be obtained, and how quickly would they be available?

This teleological mindset of the ends justifying the means permeated both the medical establishment and the general public and was aided and abetted by years of eugenics propaganda and a more recent appreciation of physicians/ researchers as heroic figures and gods of science. The confluence of those events and movements practically guaranteed smooth sailing for those microbe hunters advocating an open-door policy to the nation's custodial institutions. The war's triumphant conclusion confirmed America's vast strength, a noble cause, and scientific superiority. The medical and research establishments had undergone a tremendous transformation and witnessed unprecedented advances, much of it through unfettered access to the nation's bulging warehouses of "hopeless and useless" people. Medical experimentation, however, had transformed those "useless bodies" into "useful" commodities with a value they formerly lacked.[76]

The Nuremberg trial and code were considered a historic anomaly; they had little application to the American medical experience and scientific arena. Doctors and researchers had grown comfortable using vulnerable populations for experimentation; they were not about to give up the freedom and luxury of mining a vast and relatively inexpensive resource. Members of the profession would not allow that valuable resource to be cordoned off or circumscribed by an idealistic document designed for Nazi savages in a German courtroom.

Moreover, they would not have to because no one seemed to care.

CHAPTER FOUR

IMPACT OF THE COLD WAR ON
HUMAN EXPERIMENTATION

"There Weren't Any Guidelines as I Can Recall."

KAREN ALVES REMEMBERS THE INCIDENT AS IF IT HAPPENED YESTERDAY, but the traumatic event was over a half-century ago. It was late May 1961, and she and her family were returning home from an enjoyable day picking fruit and vegetables on a nearby farm when they heard the phone ringing as they pulled into the driveway. Karen scampered out of the car first, her two sisters were trying to catch up, and her mother urged them to answer the phone before the caller hung up.

When Karen picked up the phone and said hello, she heard an unfamiliar woman's voice say, "I'm calling from Sonoma State Hospital. Is Rosmarie Dal Molin there?" Karen was just ten years old at the time, and her heart sank.

She dropped the phone and bolted. "I ran and ran and ran," Karen recalls. She instinctively knew the message was bad. "I knew my brother, Mark, was dead. I don't know how I knew, but I knew. I ran to a secret hiding place and stayed there for hours. When I finally returned home long after dark, my sisters were crying, and my mother was locked in her room talking in hushed tones to friends and relatives on the telephone. It was the worst day of my life."[1]

"My parents were told he had been sick. That he had been running a high fever, and that led to a seizure and his death. But we were never told he had been sick, and he never had a seizure before. We didn't understand what happened. It was so unexpected."

Mark Dal Molin was born in 1955 with cerebral palsy.[2] "He couldn't talk or walk," says Karen, "but we loved him just the same. He communicated with his eyes, and we knew when he was happy or sad when he wanted something from us or just wanted to play. He'd laugh and giggle and swing his arms and legs just as if he were playing with us."

The strain of raising a severely handicapped child became an increasing burden on the Dal Molin family. Bill Dal Molin felt that Mark's care and needs deprived the three girls of their mother's time, attention, and affection. Discussions about the situation between Karen's parents grew into debates and the debates into intense arguments. As she would subsequently learn, doctors encouraged her father to have Mark committed to a state facility. They said it would be best for Mark and the family.

"Mark was a vegetable in their eyes, but he wasn't a vegetable. He connected with us," says Karen. "We had fun with him, and he laughed with us when we played together." Bill Dal Molin, however, told his wife that Mark's care and increasing needs were hurting the family. It was time the state took care of him.

Three years old at the time, Mark was turned over to the state to be cared for at Sonoma State Hospital in northern California. That emotionally wrenching decision would haunt the Dal Molin family for decades. It would also leave lasting fissures between Karen and her parents and deep regrets for all.

Karen remembers coming home from school one day in late 1958 and finding the house eerily still. Mark had been taken away. "It profoundly affected me," recalls Karen. "I don't think I ever got over it."

Rosmarie Dal Molin had committed three-year-old Mark to Sonoma State Hospital, the largest institution for children in California. Over 3,500 children, many with severe congenital disabilities, were housed there. Created in 1883 after two mothers crusaded for a suitable institution, the California Home for the Care and Training of Feeble-minded Children changed its name by 1953, and its mission emphasized medical treatment over training.[3]

Unlike many parents who gave up their children to state institutions and forgot about them, Rosmarie Dal Molin visited her son every Wednesday during the summer. Mark's sisters would visit on occasion, although Karen got the clear impression that institutional authorities were not enamored with the idea of young children visiting the hospital. "They thought we might be carrying the flu bug and wouldn't let us visit him. We'd play on the grounds outside like three monkeys doing all sorts of crazy things hoping to entertain him," recalls Karen. "We wanted to perform for him and make him laugh." Karen also recalls the "quiet trip home after every visit to Sonoma State. No one said a word."

According to Karen's sister Gail, their brother's death "pretty much blew the family apart. I believe that Dad did what he felt was best for the family. I know that is true. But the impact of it on each of us and the family was devastating."[4]

"The whole family was impacted by the decision to institutionalize Mark," says Karen. "Mark was a subject we didn't talk about. The family had problems. My parents became alienated and finally divorced. And I didn't know how deeply it had affected me until someone told me after observing my behavior, 'You're grieving. What are you grieving about?'"

Decades later, Karen was still haunted by her family's decision to give her brother to the state. His sudden and unexpected death under what she considered suspicious circumstances only heightened her guilt. Sonoma State authorities told her parents that Mark had run a high fever and choked on whatever had lodged in his mouth. But Karen was dubious.

"I needed to know what happened, no matter what it was. I just needed to know and began looking into the case in 1993," she says. "I went to the recorder's office, but there was no death certificate. I talked to a clerk there, answered all his questions about when Mark died and where, and he thought for a moment and finally said, 'You might want to take a look at Sonoma State. Some strange things happened there during that time.'"

She read a news article describing how thousands of Americans, including children, had been used in radiation experiments spurred Karen's investigation. "The article," she said, "mentioned patients in state hospitals being used in medical experiments. I said to myself, 'That's it. That's what happened to Mark.'"

The search for documentation was slow and filled with bureaucratic roadblocks, organizational subterfuge, and lengthy delays. Karen persisted; she was determined to find out what had happened to her brother.

About that time, President Bill Clinton ordered thousands of secret federal documents released detailing the government's involvement in human radiation experiments from World War II to the present day. The material only confirmed Karen's suspicions that her brother had been involved in dangerous medical experiments. In her pursuit of relevant documents, Karen discovered one study that verified that 1,100 cerebral palsy patients at Sonoma State had been incorporated in experiments between 1955 and 1960. One document mentioned her brother; he was also identified as "LPNI 8732."[5]

The July 1961 neuropathology report gave Mark's clinical diagnosis as "mental deficiency with athetoid quadriplegia due to hypoxia." In addition, the information described various aspects of his brain, from its weight to the "symmetrical atrophy of the thalamus and putamen." Karen was unacquainted with the medical jargon, but she was determined to learn every aspect of her brother's condition and the events leading to his death. She would become particularly familiar with a doctor's name at the bottom of the report: "N. Malamud, Chief, Neuropathology Service."[6]

The report confirmed a deep fear she had harbored. Mark's brain had been removed after his death and never returned to her brother's corpse. She recalled her mother saying at his cremation in the summer of 1961 that he didn't feel right when she touched him. The removal of his brain explained the mystery. His autopsy report, completed three days after his death, noted the probable cause as "a terminal type of aspiration pneumonia." It also stated that "the brain will be separately reported."[7]

Karen's hunt for additional documentation would continue. Much of what she learned showed that Mark and many other children at Sonoma State were inextricably linked to the research machinations of Dr. Nathan Malamud. A graduate of the University of California and its medical school, Malamud was a neuropathologist and director of the Langley Porter Clinic in San Francisco. He had become interested in the etiological origins of cerebral palsy and in 1953 applied with the National Institutes of Health (NIH) "to investigate the various causative factors operating in the production of cerebral palsy."

In his application, Malamud stated that "biochemical, pneumoencephalographic, angiographic, and electroencephalographic" diagnostic tools would be used and that "a large sample of patients with cerebral palsy from Sonoma State Home [would] be studied intensively." Karen shuddered at the thought of young children being put through diagnostic tests such as pneumoencephalograms, excruciating procedures in which air is injected into the spinal cord and through the brain in coordination with a series of X-rays. "Imagine puncturing someone's spinal cord, drawing fluid out, and putting a foreign substance in there like gas," she says. "When they trap air in your body, you're in pain, excruciating pain, for days."[8]

Another feature of Malamud's proposal not only allowed for such children to be "thoroughly studied during their lives" but added the prospect of a "greater number of individuals coming to postmortem examination." Malamud went on to estimate that during "a period of five years a potential group of 1200 cerebral palsied individuals would be studied historically, genetically, and clinically. Based on our experience of the past six years," argued the doctor, "it might be expected that approximately 150 of these cases would come to postmortem examination."

Malamud's proposals filed with the NIH during the 1950s disclose that "toxic solvents" and "noxious gases" would not be employed in any research endeavors. However, the same could not be said for "radiation," which was checked off on application forms as an integral aspect of the study. And it is a certainty, at least according to Karen Alves, that her brother was negatively impacted, if not killed, by radiation poisoning.

"Dr. Malamud injected radioactive material into Mark's spinal cord," Karen declares. "It wasn't designed to help him; it was just a tool for researchers to learn more about cerebral palsy. He and the other children were just used as guinea pigs to attain more knowledge about the disease."

Malamud and his team of researchers would write several journal articles about their findings. One 1964 publication summarized their work between 1955 and 1960: "During this time, a total of 4,843 patients were screened of whom 1,1184 or 24.5 percent, were classified as having C.P. Of these, 508 cases were selected as the final group Approximately 20 percent of the selected group have thus far come to autopsy, and this preliminary report is based on an analysis of 68 of consecutively autopsied cases."[9]

The loss of her brother and her long investigation into what occurred at Sonoma State and the Langley Porter Institute have dramatically impacted Karen's opinion of science and the doctors who practice it. "The researchers were a very cavalier group," she says. "They were arrogant and had an ability to disregard those who were suffering. Just like the victims of eugenics years earlier, people like my brother had no say in what was being done to them. They had no voice. And the doctors' need-to-know mentality drove them to do things that they shouldn't have. They were able to shield themselves from ethics, conscience, and compassion."

Her study of the era also colored her view of the politics that produced and encouraged such risky scientific ventures. "The fear of an all-out nuclear war," argues Karen, "drove the research community to look deeper into the effects of radiation and the treatment of radiation injury. I believe Malamud was doing cerebral palsy studies for the Manhattan Project. They were into gathering data, and national security outweighed concern for the public or compassion for patients and research subjects. Back then, doctors were seen as gods; you didn't challenge them."[10]

Despite the passage of decades, the many emotionally charged family discussions, and the years of historical research, Karen continues her search for information about Malamud's work, the relationship between Sonoma State and Langley Porter, and the whereabouts of her brother's brain. "They took Mark's brain without ever asking my parents' permission," says Karen. "Malamud's obituary said he had one of the largest brain collections in America, hundreds, maybe thousands of children's brains. I'll look under every stone until there are no stones left. I want my brother's brain back."

There were many like Mark Dal Molin, children with various physical disorders or mental challenges who were sequestered from society only to be further exploited in the name of science. Like Karen Alves, many families are becoming aware of past medical practices and learning how loved ones were conscripted into nontherapeutic experimental research during the Cold War.

Ironically, many of these recently discovered instances of medical abuse occurred after we had proudly trumpeted our abiding devotion to the highest standards of research ethics at Nuremberg. The unilateral decision by the United States to prosecute the Nazi doctors for their brutal experiments and junk science was meant, in part, to highlight America's principled stand regarding human research. Unfortunately, America's track record, then and now, is less than exemplary, and our post-Nuremberg record on research abuse would grow more problematic with each passing year.

To further the medical community's knowledge of hepatitis, an experiment was initiated in the early days of the Cold War. Five volunteers were inoculated with the Akiba strain of the virus. When all five volunteers showed "suspicious findings," including "hepatic disturbance," it was decided to do a follow-up experiment using additional subjects. The protocol called for nine volunteers ages ten to fifteen in three separate groups to receive tainted Akiba stool serum. Not surprisingly, "mild clinical illnesses and definitely positive laboratory results were noted in one or more volunteers of each group."[11]

The "volunteers" in these experiments were children at the Pennhurst School in southeastern Pennsylvania, an institution built in the early 1900s to house the "feebleminded." One child, a ten-year-old boy, was now suffering an assortment of ills, including malaise, nausea, vomiting, constipation, and liver inflammation, not to mention a variety of other maladies.

The other volunteers, as they were euphemistically called, were given hepatitis-laced feces to eat and emerged with many similar symptoms.[12] After the experiment, seven of the nine children were diagnosed with either "liver tenderness" or "abnormal liver function."[13] There is no mention that parental permission for the children's participation had been secured.

The Pennhurst transmission study was completed in August 1947. The date is significant. This research was occurring while an American tribunal in Germany was prosecuting Nazi doctors for violating accepted research standards. The timeline was also consistent with American-inspired experiments in Guatemala that were transmitting various sexually transmitted diseases to soldiers, prison inmates, and children.[14]

However, most Americans were ignorant of both the hypocrisy at play and the many unethical and dangerous experiments occurring in the research arena. Institutionalized children would become increasingly popular as test subjects. Joseph Stokes Jr. of the Children's Hospital of Philadelphia and the University of Pennsylvania School of Medicine had long-established relationships with institutional officials and could quickly locate test subjects. His research on hepatitis after the war would continue, with Pennhurst providing a seemingly endless supply of "research material." Transmission studies whereby "pooled feces" suspensions were given to children through their allotment of milk was just one of many "challenge" studies and jaundice experiments at the Pennsylvania institution during the summer of 1947.[15]

Physicians' reports and personal communications disclose a relatively seamless transition between wartime and postwar scientific endeavors from this period. Human experimentation continued unabated and would increase in scope with an ever-larger number of vaccines and products under investigation, research sites being utilized, and subjects participating in clinical trials. Many medical historians have aptly referred to the era they were entering as the Golden or "Gilded Age of Research" in America.[16]

"Many scientists and political leaders," according to medical historian David J. Rothman, found it unthinkable that so critical an activity as public health and scientific research would be "permitted to regress to prewar conditions of limited and haphazard support by private foundations and universities."[17] Collective effort and solid financial support had produced unprecedented medical triumphs during the war years. Longtime threats such as smallpox, typhoid, tetanus, yellow fever, and various infectious diseases had finally been conquered. Medical science was thought to be at the threshold of even more significant discoveries. It would be foolish for government support of science to be withdrawn when such significant breakthroughs beckoned.

It was a position that was hard to argue. "Miracle drugs" and those who discovered them had won the day. Penicillin alone was widely hailed as a life-saving wonder drug that had tamed if not wiped out numerous maladies and sparked the imagination of scientists and nonscientists alike. Potential elixirs that might cure polio, cancer, and other dread diseases might be next. Alexander Fleming, the British scientist who had documented the medicinal powers of a simple mold and transformed it into penicillin during World War II, became an international celebrity and a role model for legions of aspiring microbe hunters around the globe.

With both politicians and the public agreeing that government investment in research should continue, it was quickly decided that the NIH would replace the wartime Committee on Medical Research as the vehicle for conducting an all-out campaign against disease. Over the coming years, NIH would be the recipient of a tremendous infusion of cash. During the last year of the war, it received less than $750,000. Over the next ten years, that sum would grow to $36 million; it was well over ten times that by 1965; and by 1970, it reached

$1.5 billion with some 11,000 grants being awarded to enterprising researchers and institutions. A third of those grants required some form of human experimentation; infants and children were often part of them.[18]

Not surprisingly, the greater value was placed on scientific triumphs and the attainment of knowledge than on the welfare of those incorporated as test subjects in the research. As Rothman states of the operations of NIH's own Clinical Research Center, "the hallmark of the investigator-subject relationship was its casualness, with disclosure of risks and benefits, side effects and possible complications, even basic information on what procedures would be performed, left completely to the individual investigator."[19] This laissez-faire approach to scientific investigation would dominate the research arena from the end of the war until the mid-1970s.

The Nuremberg Code, it would appear, had little to no impact on the American research community's growing prominence and operations. It was as if the trial of Nazi doctors and the subsequent establishment of a code of research conduct had not occurred or just pertained to those who practiced medicine like Nazi "savages." The result was the same; the event had little consequence for American medical practitioners. Granted, the American Medical Association (AMA) mentioned the Nuremberg Trial in its journal, but one would be hardpressed to say the organization stressed its importance. One brief account of the proceedings published in November 1947 under the heading "The Nuremberg Trial against German Physicians" listed both Nazi medical transgressions and the new code's principles. However, a careful reading of the code shows that it was already being played down, especially those clauses journal editors might have construed as overly restrictive.[20]

In the article, the code's first principle, for instance, was 180 words short of its original formulation. The key voluntary consent provision was mentioned, but critical passages concerning the test subject's capacity to exercise free power of choice were expurgated. So, also would be exclusionary factors such as force, fraud, deceit, constraint, and coercion, not to mention the subject's ability to make an enlightened decision. Protective mechanisms designed to safeguard a subject's health were thought unimportant. That the bulk of the first principle's contents were deleted mere months after the code was created was an omen of what was to come.

The AMA wasn't alone in deemphasizing important ethically related subjects; medical schools were equally complicit in underplaying the importance of such issues. As the Oral History Project of the Advisory Committee on Human Radiation Experiments discovered during historical research for its final report, none of the physicians interviewed recalled receiving formal training in medical ethics during their medical training. In addition, few recalled any formal institutional review of research protocols being required before the early 1960s.[21]

Our research confirms the Oral History Project's findings that "the Nuremberg Code had little salience for American biomedical researchers. Few recalled any discussion relating to the Code at the time of its issuance. However, they certainly remember the atrocities of the Nazi doctors and the war crimes trials in Nuremberg."[22]

Numerous interviews we conducted with renowned medical researchers who received their medical training in the 1950s and 1960s corroborated the absence of the Nuremberg Code and any semblance of serious ethics instruction in their course work. "I was unaware of the Nuremberg Code and its code of conduct," admitted Dr. Chester Southam. "I had no awareness at all."[23] Others offered similar recollections, "There was no training in medical ethics at the time," admitted Dr. A. Bernard Ackerman. "No one ever brought up the Nuremberg Code."[24]

Researchers weren't oblivious to moral and ethical concerns despite the lack of formal coursework on ethics-related subjects. The Nuremberg Code may have been perceived as a distant and ideological construct, but individual physician-investigators faced various ethical problems on this side of the Atlantic. They frequently debated among themselves a cross-section of ethical puzzles and moral quandaries running the gamut from who could be used as an experimental subject and whether remuneration for volunteers was in order to the challenge of keeping controversial research from the public and the "yellow press."

An examination of the activities of one busy and strategically situated physician-investigator illuminates the postwar moral and ethical landscape regarding human research and the difficulties inherent in plotting an acceptable course between unfettered experimentation and the newly formulated but overly restrictive Nuremberg Code. Dr. Joseph Stokes Jr. would make his mark as one of America's leading viral and vaccine specialists during the middle decades of the twentieth century. An ardent champion of human research as the best way to relieve and prevent childhood diseases, Stokes was no Nazi and can in no way be compared to the physicians consigned to the gallows for their horrendous crimes. But he was willing to use vulnerable populations as volunteers where others advised greater caution and a less vigorous path to new vaccines. Stokes's correspondence with research colleagues during the middle decades of the twentieth century reveals the complexity and subtleties of high-risk, high-reward medical research in postwar America.

Though a staunch advocate of medical research, Stokes was not blind to the possibility of unexpected consequences or the sacrifices of test subjects. He often expressed his concern for prison inmates involved in research. Stokes thought their involvement in clinical trials essential and voiced his concern about those negatively impacted by experiments gone wrong. He felt that reimbursing volunteer prisoners who might be disabled due to the studies was only just. He knew that the "viral agents" under investigation were potent enough to cause lasting injury. As he wrote in one letter, "Our viruses have not apparently been very virulent strains, and we do not feel particularly worried about permanent disability; there is always, however, a bare chance."[25] Finally, Stokes noted in another letter that such research "might raise a point of ethics" and that reasonable compensation was in order.[26]

Unremarkably, self-interest usually won the day. Colleagues of Stokes urged him "to protect himself . . . by means of the usual waiver" in order "to release the experimenter from any liability." Though the doctors themselves did not know whether "such a waiver would really be of value in case of a suit or death or disability at a later date," it was considered a good idea.[27] The original issue, payment for injured test subjects, became of secondary interest; the more significant concern was physician liability.

Adding his sentiments on the moral and legal issues confronting them, the director of the Commission on Virus and Rickettsial Diseases of the Army Epidemiological Board (on which Stokes served) agreed that "ethics" was very much at issue. He offered caution since they were navigating through uncharted waters. Wrote Dr. John R. Paul:

> At this stage in the world situation, one should proceed cautiously, until standards are set up by whatever body is in 'authority.' I am not sure just what the rules are, but I understand that Dr. Ivy at the University of Illinois has been on some type of vigilance committee which has laid down certain principles about volunteers in order to protect this country from the criticisms brought up in Germany during the Nurnberg [sic] trials. The Russians in Japan have also accused U.S. scientists of experimenting on humans. During the war, we more or less made our own policies on this, but I am not sure that that is possible today, and if there are to be official policies, I believe we have to know them before any official statements could be made.[28]

Despite his interest in the economic welfare of injured prisoners, Stokes had no such concerns regarding his use of children in studies across the country. In defense of his work, he repeatedly argued that no research was begun that would not benefit the individual chosen for the investigation. From Stokes's point of view, "a planned exposure to a known MILD virus under nursing care during incubation" was superior from a health perspective to "an unplanned exposure to possibly a more virulent virus strain at a more dangerous age period after puberty."[29] In the coming years, Stokes would repeatedly fall back on this line of argument as critics questioned his use of institutionalized children as test subjects.

Such a rationale would appear rather lame in light of some of his research. Consider his work with an Illinois physician doing epidemiologic studies of infectious hepatitis in children at a Chicago orphanage. The project, which ran from July 1951 to July 1952, set up a "special ward where non-immunes [could] be exposed to active cases" and thereby test Stokes's theory regarding the disease-prevention attributes of gamma globulin. There is no mention of parental permission, but it can be assumed that the facility's superintendent had no objections to exposing the young wards in his care to a dangerous liver disease if it would foster the advance of science. Further control studies were to be carried out on "infants with a variety of infections" at another hospital.[30] While proximity between healthy and sick children seemed lacking, "stool preparations obtained from 2 children in the St. Vincent's [Chicago] orphanage study who were suspected of being chronic carriers for 6 and 16 months respectively [were] administered orally" to research subjects, thereby insuring "fecal-oral spread" of the disease.[31] Research physicians frequently took such liberties with their test subjects.

Stokes would be a key player in the government's establishment of medical policy on the use of test subjects. As the chair of the Sub-Committee on the Allocation of Volunteers on the Commission on Liver Disease of the Armed Forces Epidemiological Board (AFEB), the successor to the Army Epidemiological Board, Stokes was at the heart of many debates and decisions on what populations could be used in human research. His sub-committee colleagues included some important names in American research.[32] The army, which had targeted three dozen diseases requiring further investigation by AFEB physicians and divided them into categories of military importance, understood the need for human subjects as test material.[33] "Without volunteers, however," stated Stokes in one missive to an AFEB colleague, "the obstacles at times seem insuperable, and I hope . . . every effort to obtain them" is made. He didn't believe they could expect much success without them.[34]

Communications between committee members illuminate the personal and political fallout from their disagreements. Stokes was assured of his stand on using volunteers, including children, in his research initiatives, but other equally accomplished scientists occasionally voiced their doubts. When a colleague upheld a New York City "Sanitary Code" precluding children in one study, Stokes expressed his dismay and notified his superiors that such rules should be fought.[35] He argued that it was "a moral obligation to lift" the ban. He said the opposition to his experiments on children was misguided and added, "I have exposed my own children and aided my physician son in the exposure of his first child as the opportunity arose."

Undaunted by those advocating a go-slow approach, Stokes believed, "There is no reason to beat a retreat on these problems but to face them positively and at the same time with the greatest deference to the value of human life and welfare."[36]

Stokes was not just concerned about his research endeavors; he was also irritated when experiments of other investigators were blocked. He remained steadfast in his opposition to the imposition of overly restrictive guidelines and regulations on using children in medical research. When Dr. L. Emmett Holt, for example, had his request for funds for a study of infants' amino acid requirements rejected, Stokes was miffed. "Here again," he wrote to a colleague, "it seems clear that a single member of the original Committee, which considered Holt's application, quite unreasonably injected ethical considerations into a matter which is of the utmost importance to human nutrition . . . and can be of no harm to the infants."[37] Stokes went on to say: "Once the Nuremberg specter (and I am in agreement that the Nazi work was inexcusable and despicable) is raised, it appears at times that all rational approaches to such matters are obscured."

Stokes saw the Nuremberg shadow as an impediment to medical research and equated it to ethical "bullying," a tactic he thought particularly prevalent in New York City. Since Holt's investigations in Galveston were like Stokes's, he had hopes that the "medical bullying which our major metropolis seems to occasionally nurture" would not occur in Texas and that Holt's application would receive the dispassionate consideration it deserved.

Interestingly, Stokes was a Quaker who saw the benefit of conscientious objectors' offering themselves to science instead of succumbing to bullets on the battlefield. Recognizing the continuing need for volunteer subjects after the war, he advocated continuing the program. In addition, he encouraged the American Friends Service Committee to consider "using some of the . . . available 18-year-old group on a draft deferred basis as experimental subjects."[38] Stokes was not alone in believing that "pacifists" could best serve their country and science by becoming test subjects.

It was estimated that over 1,000 men had participated in such work, and the presence of a group of healthy, cooperative subjects was a "stimulus to scientific investigation and a quite unusual opportunity for the investigator."[39] Advocates of continuing the program believed that the experiments were a "service to mankind as a whole, with potentialities for the saving of lives which can hardly be over-estimated." But there was also a downside. Some test subjects developed psychiatric problems, and doctors increasingly felt the need to get legal waivers from participants and permission slips from parents.

The Quakers had every right to be cautious when allowing their young men to participate in human research; experiments were dangerous, and some had proved fatal. Stokes's volunteer allocation subcommittee members were unnerved after three prisoners died and a fourth became very ill. But any hiatus would be fleeting; there were many more reasons to continue the research than to terminate it. One reason was that those enduring the health risks were some of the least valued members of society: incarcerated criminals, psychiatric patients, and the developmentally challenged. Many of the latter group were children, a population without political influence or social capital. As one observer noted, "If it is true that the progress of medicine has been over a mountain of corpses, one objects to its being one's corpse. If it is also true that in medicine 'nothing risked, nothing gained,' one prefers to have the gain to humanity made at the expense of somebody else."[40]

The "somebody else" was often a disabled child at a place like Vineland, Pennhurst, Fernald, and Sonoma State. Hardly the institutions with the same social cachet as schools for so-called normal children. Besides, as Dr. Colin M. MacLeod, the president of the AFEB, informed a New York State Health Commissioner, such studies had "military significance." From a national defense perspective, the fight against epidemic hepatitis and serum hepatitis needed to be successful. MacLeod would point out that "it had not been possible to transmit" infectious agents to experimental animals despite their best effort. The upshot was clear: The use of human volunteers was obligatory if diseases were to be conquered.[41] He admitted to being concerned about the risks involved in human experimentation, but the advance of science was critically important to solving "crucial military problems." And "access to human volunteers" was essential to the system's success.[42]

Stokes had no doubts about that; he understood the value of test subjects and was sensitive to attitudes or initiatives that limited their availability. He drafted a confidential memo on the "question of Ethical Responsibility in the Exposure of Human Beings to certain Infectious Agents." The February 1953 document focused on the medical risks of exposure to epidemic disease and also on the criticism that "conscious exposure of volunteers or children is morally or ethically wrong."[43]

Stokes believed researchers should not adopt "a defensive attitude" or feel "vulnerable on moral or ethical grounds" due to their occasional criticism. Despite the rare mistake, they had every reason to stand by their work and continue their essential mission with "candor and forcefulness."

What may be most noteworthy about the six-page, 1,000-plus-word memorandum is not what is included in the document but what is missing: Stokes made no reference to the Nuremberg Code. The code had no import or relevance for Stokes. Yet, he was a significant figure in medical research at the time and was central to shaping AFEB and government policy on the use and allocation of test subjects for military and university-sponsored study during the Cold War.

The use of prisoners in research was a comparatively easy call for Stokes; other vulnerable populations were harder to justify. As he admitted in his memo, "a special problem arises in the case of children."[44] Stokes defended the practice by arguing that permission had been obtained from their parents or guardians whenever children were used in studies. Still, he conceded that "the notion lingered that the children are being used involuntarily and that this is somehow wrong." Though he thought this aspect "the nub of much of the present criticism," he believed that it had already been addressed through commonly accepted practices such as immunization programs for children. In other words, children don't give their "consent to inoculation against diphtheria, tetanus, and whooping cough." Still, the effort to minimize "loss of life, illness, or permanent injury from these diseases has been felt far to outweigh any disadvantage to a child's rights."

Was Stokes confusing therapeutic measures with experimentation? That would seem too simplistic an answer for a man of his experience and sophistication. However, he and undoubtedly many of his colleagues doing viral research believed that knowledgeable, well—trained infectious disease specialists knew what was best for both the patient and the subject. The real problem, according to Stokes, was "one of medical advisability and not ethics." Stokes was adamant on the subject; he recognized that "differences of opinion exist, but the problem is not one of ethics." In his mind, protective codes that tied the hands of researchers and restrictive regulations "in the name of ethics were actually self-defeating." The formal establishment of such a "concept of ethics," argued Stokes, "is not only mistaken but harmful." In the end, he repeatedly urged his colleagues to move forward aggressively. It is obvious that medicine, he advised them, "can be no more static than in any other field of investigation."[45]

Though many of the top researchers at the time shared Stokes's opinions on these questions, not all were as strident in championing the cause. Most desired an unfettered research arena but also wanted to leave the public debate to others. For instance, Dr. Roderick Murray of the National Microbiological Institute cautioned Stokes that little would be gained by bringing the issue of volunteer studies to public attention. "By any active action," he argued, "we might be put in the position of protesting too much."[46] In his message to Stokes regarding the uphill climb lying ahead of anyone attempting to explain the nobility and importance of their mission, Murray cited the "recent speech by the Pope on the subject of medical experimentation."

The papal reference was concerning a September 1952 speech by Pope Pius XII titled "The Moral Limits of Medical Research and Treatment." In it, the pontiff paid homage to science, "the bold spirit of research," and the researcher's zeal to follow "newly discovered roads." But he also identified some cautionary signposts, moral landmarks he thought men of science occasionally chose to disregard.

The quest for new knowledge is essential, argued the pontiff, but that didn't legitimize every method designed to attain it, especially if it could not be accomplished without injuring the rights of others or violating some moral rule of absolute value. Science is not the highest value that all other values should be subordinate. Though the speech did not refer to the Nuremberg Code, the pontiff's intention was clear; there are "many values superior to scientific interest."[47]

The speech, which would emphasize "*bonum commune*," or interests of the community, over the "interests of science," was a papal warning shot across the bow of a rapidly growing and increasingly robust research establishment. But as in the case of the Nuremberg Code, no one of substance and no organization with influence was willing to support the cause and campaign for reform. Most did not hear calls for a more ethical research culture; those who did tend to forget about them.

A high-powered, financially rewarding, and celebrity-oriented template for success had taken hold. Martin Arrowsmith was no longer an outlier; Paul de Kruif's solitary and poorly funded microbe hunters had evolved into a much admired and potent professional force. Periodic calls for greater restraint and concern for subject safety by a few jurists in Germany or a religious figure in Rome would not stem the tide. Change would eventually come, but it was still decades off.

Medical research during the Cold War years would become more sophisticated, lucrative, and imposing. Research using prisoners, for example, witnessed a geometric increase, and researchers like Dr. Stokes were not shy about defending the practice. As he wrote in one memo, "It cannot be emphasized too strongly that such work with volunteers in prisons conducted under the Armed Forces Epidemiological Board has no element of compulsion. The objectives of the work, its exact nature, and the possible dangers entailed are fully explained to the prisoners." Moreover, "no promises of earlier parole or release from prison or other inducements" were tendered to procure volunteers.[48]

Such a belief would appear to be willfully ignorant that prison "volunteers" were behind bars, and constraint, coercion, duress—key elements of imprisonment—were specifically identified in the first principle of the Nuremberg Code as disqualifiers for participation in human subject research. Dr. Werner Liebbrant, a German physician and prosecution witness at Nuremberg, vigorously argued that prisoners should be precluded from participating in human research. Stokes, and most of his research associates, did not see it that way. They did not view confinement behind concrete walls and steel bars as coercion. And despite his claim that no inducements were offered to the prisoners, the twentieth-century history of such operations is one of inmates expecting and receiving remuneration, such as money, early release, or better living conditions in the institution.[49]

Prison research was becoming big business. And prisoners kept in the dark about the dangers of such work but too quick to see the benefits, "volunteered" as human guinea pigs in impressive numbers. So many that researchers had the luxury of winnowing out those who might not possess the ideal public profile of a test subject.

For example, in December 1952, both the AFEB and the AMA adopted a resolution that expressed "its disapproval of the participation in scientific experiments of persons convicted of murder, rape, arson, kidnapping, treason or other heinous crimes."[50] Becoming a test subject behind bars had accrued some degree of status and prestige; it was now a privilege that researchers didn't want to be sullied by violent felons.

Stokes and his colleagues on the AFEB were very conscious of the explosive nature of their studies, the constant threat of negative publicity, and the importance of what the public learned about their research. They usually had other board members review statements, journal articles, and other items regarding using "retarded children" and "psychotic criminals" in studies. Stokes was constantly on the alert for "yellow press publicity." He believed some print media rarely missed an "opportunity for criticism."[51]

Stokes was not alone in his concern. When journalists expressed interest in doing a story on their research endeavors, collective unease precipitated. In early 1953, for example, the AFEB president received a letter from a *Washington Post* reporter requesting information regarding the use of prisoners in medical research. Though the reporter, Nate Hazeltine, said that his account would be factual and objective regarding the use of prisoners as test subjects, alarms still went off at AFEB headquarters.[52] Members of the AFEB voiced their concern about the prospect of an unflattering newspaper story, a potential "hornets [sic] nest," in the words of one army physician. They did their best to dissuade the reporter from writing a story.

If the prospect of a news story about prison research unnerved them, one could imagine their angst if a reporter had gotten wind of their experiments using "defective children."

During the early fifties, investigators continued their many research projects. Correspondence between them discloses the particulars of their craft and advice on navigating government bureaucracy, obtaining research grants, and putting the best possible public face on their investigative endeavors. An example of the latter is one Stokes draft on "the use of human volunteers in the study of hepatitis," which drew considerable comment, including that of Dr. Colin MacLeod, President of the AFEB. MacLeod believed "one must be extremely careful with statements of this sort lest it be said that 'me thinks she doth protest too much.'" Stokes tended to underplay the dangerous aspect of research endeavors and was gently cautioned by his comrades that some changes might be in order. MacLeod, for example, offered several suggestions, including, "I would also question very seriously at the end of the last paragraph the implication that mild strains of the disease only are used. That this is far from the truth is indicated by the unfortunate experiences that Dr. Murray has had in the case of the two fatal experiences during the past year."[53]

Stokes could provide editorial comments as well. For example, in a three-page letter to a colleague regarding a proposed article on "infectious hepatitis," Stokes offered 18 suggestions, including, "it would be better to replace 'feeding experiments' by 'giving oral preparations of stools to adult volunteers' leaving out human. The word 'feeding' is unfortunate since stools are not food nor are they fed." In another line, he suggested, "the term 'experimental feeding' should be changed to 'by oral administration' or some such phrase."[54] The Stokes correspondence underscores the sophistication of physician-researchers regarding the sensitive nature of their investigations and how it should be framed just in case the public got wind of it. They were conscious of being politically correct decades before the term were popularized.

The correspondence between doctors and their research associates illuminates some of the occasionally deceptive practices and cavalier decision-making involved in the endless search for "test material," the identity of the actual study sponsors, and the health risks involved. A prime example of such subterfuge occurred in the summer of 1954 when Harry Von Bulow, the superintendent of a South Jersey institution formerly known as the Woodbine Colony for Feeble-Minded Males, wrote Stokes about some growing concerns with "our little project." The project was an experiment to test a new poliomyelitis vaccine, "an active virus vaccine by the natural route, the mouth."[55]

Von Bulow and the Woodbine board "were not too happy" that the project was initially broached and agreed to over the telephone and that key concerns about children's safety never received a proper hearing. A further problem was that information about the oral vaccine experiment was misleading and might "destroy any confidence" the institution had established with parents over the years.[56] As letters demonstrate, researchers and administrators held different notions on just how much information parents were entitled to receive regarding their child's participation in a potentially dangerous polio study. In one revealing admission, Von Bulow wrote Stokes, "I am sure you can understand my administrative anxiety and my desire to inform parents as completely as we can without actually telling them what is taking place."[57]

Von Bulow was no administrative novice. To win support for the project from the Woodbine board, he requested that Stokes write a letter to them that said: "there were no risks involved either to the children concerned with the project or with the others in our Colony."

In another revealing message concerning the same piece of research, Stokes notified a Lederle Laboratories division head that the proposed letter to parents informing them of the experiment had been altered to omit "the name of Lederle." Instead, substituting "the supervision by University of Pennsylvania physicians" since they "did not wish the parents to obtain the impression that this is primarily a commercial venture."[58]

Not surprisingly, the Lederle Corporation was "heartily in accord" with Stokes's actions. The viral research director wrote him a thank-you note stating: "We both feel it a course of wisdom to not mention the name of that reputable industrial company which will prepare the vaccine. I think that it is only smart because of the legal entanglements that might ensue should our participation in this program become general knowledge."[59] Once again, the fewer parents knew about what would be done to their children, the better.

With all the research projects that were underway, it is no wonder that concerned parents occasionally became skeptical and wrote to an institution's superintendent or medical director to learn if their child had become an exper-imental lab rat. On at least one occasion, Stokes felt obligated to inform an outraged mother, "I am writing to let you know that the children at Woodbine are not being used as guinea pigs."[60] In letters of this type, he would explain the purpose of such studies and attempt to mollify strained relations, but some parents remained dubious.

For the rest of the 1950s and beyond, audacious medical researchers would proceed with the fervor of evangelists. Whether motivated by altruism, career advancement, or the attraction of old-fashioned fame and fortune, all manner of scientific quests, intellectual puzzles, and baffling health concerns became grist for the research mill. Medicine and medical research during the postwar era witnessed phenomenal growth. The number of people working in some field of medicine grew exponentially, climbing from 1.2 million people in 1950 to 4 million in 1970. Health care expenditures rose even higher: from $12.7 billion to $71.6 billion during that same period.[61] As its esteem and respect grew, medical science was accorded unprecedented approval by an appreciative public, and its role in protecting the nation became a widely accepted fact.

As Harvard medical sociologist Paul Starr has written, "medical science epitomized the postwar vision of progress. . . . All could celebrate the value of medical progress," take pride in the creation of "the latest wonder drugs," and be thankful that "life was getting better." *Time* magazine was now devoting a page in each issue to medicine, where Americans could learn of newly dis-covered "wonder drugs" and miracle treatments from contemporary microbe hunters and sophisticated laboratories.[62]

And during this period, an era ominously known as the Cold War, science assumed a symbolic and practical function in maintaining America's position as the unrivaled leader of the free world. It was not some honorary role requiring little concern and even less work; the threat from the Soviet Union was real, and its scary portent leached into every aspect of American life. As Federal Bureau of Investigation chief J. Edgar Hoover repeatedly counseled his countrymen, every American home was making a sacrifice to keep our defenses strong against the worldwide advance of Communism.[63]

Though he may have been one of the more ardent and outspoken Cold War warriors calling for constant vigilance and preparedness, Hoover was not alone in his fear of the growing "Communist menace." Americans had gradu-ally come to view our World War II ally as our greatest postwar threat. A quick succession of events underscored the looming conflict. The Soviet blockade of Berlin in 1948, the Soviets detonating their atom bomb a year later, and the start of the Korean War in 1950 all confirmed Winston Churchill's specter

of an "iron curtain" separating the free world from the enslaved and contributed to the increasing prospect of violent engagement. Adding to the dark
diplomatic developments was the equally ominous domestic threat of internal
subversion. Names such as Alger Hiss, Whittaker Chambers, Elizabeth Bentley, Harry Gold, Klaus Fuchs, and Ethel and Julius Rosenberg, among a host
of others, confirmed the Soviet Union's evil intent. Rarely a day passed when
newspapers did not carry a story dealing with House Un-American Activities
Committee (HUAC) hearings, new charges of subversion and espionage, and a
rising number of Americans building underground bomb shelters. At the same
time, their children practiced duck-and-cover drills in schools throughout the
land. By January 1951, the Federal Civil Defense Administration (FCDA) had
already published manuals about the dangers of biological warfare; they warned
of agents such as botulism, plague, smallpox, cholera, and anthrax that might
be sprayed over cities in deadly aerosols or put into supplies of food and water.[64]

The outbreak of a new war between the United States and the Soviet Union
wasn't the creation of a novelist or Hollywood screenwriter. Many Americans
anticipated a cataclysm that was fostered by a quasi-religious belief that "the
Communists were Satan's army on earth."[65]

And the feeling was mutual. Soviet leaders uniformly agreed that the
United States—a bulwark of capitalist enslavement—was "the USSR's main
adversary."[66] As Richard Rhodes aptly said of the era, the encroaching Cold
War cast an apocalyptic specter for serious men and women on both sides of
the Iron Curtain.[67]

Medical researchers were not oblivious to the ever-worsening political
climate. "Although it was not a shooting war," Dr. James Ketchum, a highly
trained and competent psychiatrist and psychopharmacologist for the U.S.
Army during the 1950s and 1960s, has written, "the stakes were every bit as
high as in the World War that had only recently ended. Most ominously, each
nation could launch megaton nuclear missiles sufficient in number to annihi-
late the other. Popular novels and films trafficked in visions of Armageddon and
apocalypse. The phrase 'mutual assured destruction' became linguistic currency
among journalists and commentators."[68]

The upshot, according to one comprehensive government study of the era,
was the "likelihood that atomic bombs would be used again in war and that
American civilians, as well as soldiers, would be targets, [which] meant that
the country had to know as much as it could, as quickly as it could, about
the effects of radiation and the treatment of radiation injury."[69] The search for
knowledge and answers to critical military and public health queries required

scientists and medical personnel to confront once again questions of risk and what actions need be taken to protect Americans. Physicians who had been educated during the heyday of the eugenics movement and went on to perfect their medical skills during World War II when ethical concerns were subordinated to national security interests were once again finding their "commitment to prevent disease and heal" subverted by the government's immediate needs. It would also prove an "opportunity for gathering data."[70] As one Central Intelligence Agency (CIA) physician informed a classroom of recruits in the 1960s, "Our guiding light is not the Hippocratic oath, but the victory of freedom."[71]

"There was the definite feeling of the threat of war with the Soviets," recalls Ketchum.[72] Ketchum, a graduate of Dartmouth and Cornell Medical School, clarifies that the threat was not created out of boredom or the lust for war; concrete events and intelligence signaled potential strife. He says it was clear that the United States had fallen behind the Soviets concerning its chemical warfare capability and the immediate need to come up to speed in preparation for some future enemy attack. It was equally clear to Ketchum and his military superiors that research scientists "could not fulfill this mission by animal experiments alone."[73] Human test subjects would be needed; fortunately, most experienced researchers already knew where to look for volunteers.

Physicians working for the military would prove particularly adept at testing innovative theories on isolated test populations while maintaining a strict code of secrecy. Spurred on by patriotic fervor, the prospect of discovering medical breakthroughs, and provided with more than adequate funding, doctors on the government payroll blazed a trail of vigorous experimentation that explored everything from truth serums and incapacitants to mind control. Once again, concrete results would be the coin of the realm, and abiding by codes of ethics was a luxury they couldn't afford. Many historians and numerous physicians would point to the Cold War atmosphere as the excuse for the multiple code violations, medical excesses, and instances of potential, if not actual, criminal behavior committed during the postwar era.

One of Ketchum's army medical colleagues, Dr. Enoch Callaway, recalls "the very lax research atmosphere" during the postwar years. There were "no codes stressed back then or any mention of the Nuremberg Code." Callaway graduated from Columbia Medical School in 1947 and subsequently spent many years exploring offensive and defensive weapons, including nerve gas. "When I wanted to try a drug at a state hospital," recalls Callaway, "I went around with a cart and syringe and asked patients if they would mind if I could try something on them. There was no paperwork involved. Some doctors did not even bother asking permission. That's just the way things were done. It was lax concerning research practices."[74]

Medical research had a manifest offensive and defensive focus. John D. Marks, whose landmark book *The Search for the Manchurian Candidate: The CIA and Mind Control,* exposed the CIA's longtime attraction to the black arts, including medical experimentation. He argues that the agency "quickly realized that the only way to build an effective defense against mind control was to understand its offensive possibilities. The line between offense and defense—if it ever existed—soon became so blurred as to be meaningless." According to Marks, every CIA document stressed goals like "controlling an individual to the point where he will do our bidding against his will and even against such fundamental laws of nature as self-preservation."[75]

Through highly secret code-named projects, the agency explored a raft of mind-control and mind-altering potions and techniques. Under the direction of the enterprising Sidney Gottlieb, the CIA's Technical Services Staff would experiment with various chemical and biological agents. Hypnotism and LSD would get a thorough workout. Different funding agencies provided cover for CIA financing that greased the skids for elite professors and renowned academic institutions to embark on some hair-raising experimental endeavors. Nearly seven dozen institutions took CIA money, many of them to ply American citizens with hallucinogenic cocktails and more.[76]

Robert Hyde, Carl Pfeiffer, and Harold Abramson are just a few academic heavyweights who signed research contracts with the CIA. Some of their projects were cruel, if not criminal. Dr. Harris Isbell, for example, the director of the Addictive Research Center at Lexington Federal Prison, had a large stable of subjects to choose from and a steady supply of bufotenine, rivea seeds, scopolamine, and other concoctions to explore.[77] One of his CIA-funded experiments kept prisoners on daily doses of LSD, the crown jewel of the mind-control treasure chest, for over two and a half months. The Lexington experiments are as shocking a display of cavalier and dangerous research as one is likely to find. The fact that Isbell's test subjects were all incarcerated black drug addicts sent to prison by American courts for daring to use illicit drugs adds a poignant note of irony to the situation.

Dr. Ewen Cameron, the godfather of Canadian psychiatry and the president of the American Psychiatric Association and the World Psychiatric Association, concocted some of the most chilling and dangerous psychological experiments in the name of science with the encouragement and support of the CIA. Supposedly motivated by a desire to find a cure for schizophrenia,

Cameron orchestrated a hellish potpourri of depatterning techniques that left his patients, victims is a more apt description, in what he referred to as a state of "differential amnesia." One of his critics likened the process to the "creation of a vegetable."[78]

Cameron's smorgasbord approach of LSD, electroshock, sensory deprivation, and psychic driving may have left subjects bereft of their sanity and mindless. Still, both he and the CIA, which funneled him monthly checks, were pleased with the "direct, controlled changes in personality" he could elicit at McGill University's Allan Memorial psychiatric institute. As Marks concludes of the famed doctor who left no tool unused in his devilish physician's bag, "By literally wiping the minds of his subjects clean by depatterning and then trying to program in new behavior, Cameron carried the process known as 'brainwashing' to its logical extreme."[79]

Despite witnessing the devastating results of Cameron's "treatments" on his father at Allan Memorial Institute, Dr. Harvey Weinstein entered the psychiatric profession with a purpose: to better understand what his father had endured and discover "what kind of man would experiment on vulnerable patients?" *Father, Son, and CIA*, his vivid account of a parent's tortured existence as a human guinea pig and the physician whose "missionary zeal" knew no bounds, is a sobering look into the Cold War era's medical excesses. Weinstein's book also explores how a medical profession designed to do no harm could occasionally partake of "evil undertakings when the motivation can be reframed so that the outcome is couched under the rubric of 'for the greater good.'"[80]

Another iconic figure in American psychology, Henry Murray also fell victim to Cold War research exuberance. Viewed by many as the conduit for accepting European personality and clinical theories into the American academy, Murray did biochemical research at the Rockefeller Institute before abandoning the hard sciences for psychology. Prior to World War II, he would go on to develop the Thematic Apperception Test, which was used to assess people's personalities, and became a consultant to the Office of Strategic Services (the CIA's predecessor) after the war to further perfect a methodology that would test "a recruit's ability to stand up under pressure, to be a leader, to hold liquor, to lie skillfully, and to read a person's character by nature of his clothing." His system would become a fixture in the OSS—and "the first systematic effort to evaluate an individual's personality in order to predict his future behavior."[81] Years later, during the Cold War's climate of fear, Murray would embark on related personality studies that would intentionally stress his Harvard student volunteers. See chapter 9 for a discussion of his results.[82]

Equally unsettling is that many Americans were unwittingly incorporated in postwar radioactive material studies designed to gauge plutonium's health effects, a dangerous radioactive element with which hundreds of weapons scientists and Manhattan Project personnel were coming in contact. Shockingly, approximately 4,000 human radiation experiments would follow over the next few decades. Most would involve radioactive isotope investigations that tagged certain elements, such as iron, calcium, and iodine, used as measuring devices in an assortment of uptake, metabolism, and blood studies. In addition to hospital patients, test subjects included soldiers, prisoners, psychiatric patients, and average citizens. Researchers sought infants and children as desirable test material.

The research establishment received a long-overdue wake-up call in 1966 when a Harvard anesthesiologist named Henry K. Beecher published an article in the *New England Journal of Medicine* titled "Ethics and Clinical Research." The six-page broadside detailed nearly two dozen research experiments that endangered the health or life of their subjects and that had been done without informing them of the risks involved or obtaining permission for such endeavors.[83] As medical historian David J. Rothman subsequently wrote, the Beecher article became "a critical element in reshaping the ideas and practices governing human experimentation."[84]

Beecher was no radical; he had no desire to cripple the medical profession or damage the reputation of his colleagues. But the real "disservice to medicine," he argued, would be to remain silent and allow the "continuation of the practices" that could prove far more injurious to the profession's reputation.[85] According to Beecher, most of those used as test subjects in the problematic protocols he cited were institutionalized and, in one way or another, unable to give informed consent. Newborns, mentally disabled children, charity patients, and soldiers in the military were easy prey for zealous researchers. The lives of many of the subjects were put in harm's way for the convenience of investigators.

Though his article did not identify the doctors involved, the institutions that employed them, or the funding agencies over the years, other scholars would piece that information together. Elite medical schools such as Harvard, Emory, Duke, New York University, and Georgetown comprised the bulk of the twenty-two protocols he described. Funders included the Atomic Energy Commission, the Public Health Commission, Parke-Davis, and Merck.[86] With this article, the best, the brightest, and the most influential researchers and training grounds had been put on notice.

Beecher's article didn't precipitate instantaneous reform, nor did a more extended treatise by British physician and healthcare ethicist Maurice

Pappworth the following year. Still, they were clear and widely heard warning shots for an ethically lax and comfortable profession that had been imbued with a self-congratulatory, utilitarian spirit.[87] The change would come slowly, then quicken in 1972 with revelations about the Tuskegee syphilis study. Still, the new safeguards would be too late for the vulnerable American "volunteers" who had already been victimized.

CHAPTER FIVE

VACCINES

*"Institutions for Hydrocephalics and
Other Similar Unfortunates."*

I
T WAS FEBRUARY 1973, AND THE MONTHLY MEETING OF THE PENNSYLVANIA
Association for Retarded Children (PARC) at a Harrisburg hotel had just
ended. Pat Clapp, the president of the statewide group, was shaking hands with
board members and discussing potential issues for the next meeting when a
woman with a look of concern approached her. Clapp introduced herself and
welcomed the unknown woman only to be met with a pointed question, "How
could PARC have condoned using retarded children as test subjects for medical
experiments?"

Clapp was aghast at the accusation. As the mother of a child with Downs
Syndrome and a dedicated advocate for those with disabilities, Clapp had risen
to a leadership position through hard work, fighting for institutional reform,
and calling for change whenever possible. She was not one to blithely okay the
use of disabled children as raw material for experimentation.

Clapp listened carefully and was stunned by the woman's story. Visibly
upset, tears beginning to stream down her cheeks, the woman claimed her child
had been used as a laboratory guinea pig in an experiment at Hamburg, a resi-
dential center for the mentally disabled near Reading in Berks County. "They're
injecting live virus into children up there," she said. "My child was injected with
a meningitis virus, and no one asked my permission or informed me what was
going on." Distraught and desperate for help, the woman described the situation in Hamburg. She remained adamant that she had not been asked for nor
had she given her permission for her child's participation in any such research.

When Clapp asked if she had any proof of her charges, the woman showed
her a letter she had just received from Dr. Weibel in Philadelphia. Incredibly,
the letter stated her child had been used in an experiment, and they were now,

after the fact, asking for her permission. Equally shocking was a statement in the letter claiming PARC had approved the investigational exercise.

"That's when the lid flew off," recalls Clapp. "I was appalled. I had never heard of medical experiments on children in these state centers, and I knew the PARC Board had never discussed such an issue, much less given its blessings. I immediately started to inquire if the allegations were true and what was going on at Hamburg."[1]

Clapp had no personal knowledge of the facility. However, she was not unfamiliar with large underfunded and understaffed state institutions that held a motley collection of what was referred to at the time as "retarded," "feeble-minded," and "defective" individuals. She would learn that Hamburg had once been the Charles H. Miner State Hospital, a sanitarium that cared for people with tuberculosis. With the advent of medical science conquering the disease, the hospital was closed in 1959 to re-open as the Hamburg State School and Hospital. More than 900 patients with myriad physical and mental maladies now resided there.

The following day back at her home in Pittsburgh, Clapp got on the phone and would be there until well into the evening, calling everyone she knew in the mental health community, state government, the advocacy arena, and the media. Now she had her list of questions. Was the woman accurate in her claims? Were children being used as test subjects at Hamburg without researchers gaining parental permission? Were other institutions in the state system doing similar medical research without parental consent?

"I was on the phone at 8:30 A.M. and talked to Eleanor Elkin, our national president, explaining what I had just learned," recalls Clapp. "She was horrified, as was everyone else I talked to. I stayed on the phone the entire day calling people like Helene Wohlgemuth, Pennsylvania's Public Welfare Secretary; Gunnar Dybwad, a noted expert in retardation issues; and Henry Pierce of the *Pittsburgh Post-Gazette*. Many people were outraged and energized by what had occurred. Parents were being taken advantage of, and children were being used." Recalling what eventually grew into a multi-faceted campaign to end experimentation in Pennsylvania's institutions many years later, Clapp told us with a hint of pride, "We really went after the thing."

Within days, Pat Clapp led an effort that would become a much-followed political juggernaut and result in numerous changes in Pennsylvania's mental health system. As she and her colleagues accumulated information, they were further horrified to learn that Hamburg may not have been an isolated incident. Other institutions such as Whitehaven and Laurelton were equally guilty of turning their charges over to researchers perfecting new vaccines for various diseases such as pneumococcal pneumonia, influenza, and meningitis. Furthermore, the parents of the children in those institutions and the PARC Board were in the dark about it.

One of Clapp's more revealing conversations was with Dr. Robert Weibel, the University of Pennsylvania pediatrician behind the Hamburg vaccine studies. "Weibel admitted he was doing research," recalls Clapp.

> He never denied it. He said 20 children were being tested with a new vaccine. I asked him how he could do this to children—most of them between three and ten years old. However, Weibel saw nothing wrong. He defended his actions. He said another doctor linked to PARC had permitted him, and he did not feel it was necessary to notify the children's parents. I continued to press the issue and asked how he could do this to defenseless children with an assortment of mental and physical disabilities, and he replied, 'This makes their lives worthwhile. They will be making a contribution to society.' I was a little bit taken aback by his answer and then asked him how he could tell if the child receiving the vaccine was in pain or danger? He calmly said, 'We take their temperature.' That really burned me up. That is when the fire was ignited.

Pat Clapp was no novice, a citizen-activist who had worked her way into a statewide leadership position in the mental health arena. She understood the community and issue organizing as well as the levers of power in state politics. She also understood how doctors and institutions had taken advantage of the parents of children with disabilities. "Parents had no place to turn," recalls Clapp in a recent series of interviews.

> There were not many places or programs where you could place your child. Women were afraid to say they had a child with a disability. It was an embarrassment, and most parents were incapable of taking care of a child with severe disabilities. You were usually told to put your kid in an institution. This was the best alternative you were often told. It was the medical model at the time, and parents had little choice. They had no voice. Everyone accepted things as they were back then. Parents were desperate. They needed institutions to take care of their children. If a doctor told you something, you believed it. You did what he said. No one doubted doctors; they were authority figures. No one challenged the medical profession back then.

Times were changing quickly, and activists like Pat Clapp were at the forefront of the movement. The startling revelations of the controversial Tuskegee Syphilis Study were only months old, and a firestorm of similar but less well-known instances of medical exploitation was being unearthed in cities, towns, and hamlets across the country. Disclosures of vulnerable populations incorporated in clinical trials were making headlines regularly. Clapp and her coalition colleagues helped foment Pennsylvania's contribution to this growing list of medical infamy. Public protests, letter-writing campaigns calling for a state ban on research tests, and the demand for legislative hearings were all put on the organizing agenda.

Newspapers in the Keystone State devoted considerable space to the controversy. Pennsylvanians discovered unethical medical experimentation was not just an ugly story from the Deep South; abuse was occurring in their backyard. "PARC Panel Asks Drug Test Probe," "Experiments on Humans Denied Here," "State Kills Testing of Meningitis Shots," and "State Halts Use of Retarded as Guinea Pigs" were just a few of the newspaper headlines readers were confronted with during the spring of 1973.[2] "Once it hit the newspapers," said Clapp, "Things really blew up."

"The state will not allow Dr. Weibel, University of Pennsylvania pediatrician, to resume tests of a meningitis vaccine on a group of retarded youngsters before June 18—in effect killing the project," wrote Henry W. Pierce, one of the *Post-Gazette* reporters Clapp had contacted.[3] The article went on to state, "Edward Goldman state commissioner of mental retardation yesterday, said the state would insist that Dr. Weibel adheres to a ban on human experimentation in all state institutions."

Though Weibel would vigorously appeal the decision, the state authorities were not about to relent; Governor Milton Shaap's administration was caught napping, and unaware their facilities were being used as clinical test sites. The flood of negative newspaper stories and critical public comments was embarrassing.

As the *Post-Gazette* framed it, "Dr. Weibel's meningitis vaccine, which he was testing under contract with Merck, Sharp & Dohme laboratories, was one of several being tried on retarded children at White Haven and Hamburg State School and Hospital in Eastern Pennsylvania." Weibel admitted others were being "tested by doctors at Rockefeller University and the National Institutes of Health," and that they had previously worked on a variety of measles vaccines. The current vaccine, said Weibel, "already had been tried on military personnel . . . and large-scale trials" were now necessary "before it can be approved for general use."[4]

Encouraged to opine on the legality of such an activity, the Justice Department admitted, "there is no statutory law against doctors conducting such experiments, with or without parental consent."[5] That assessment did not sit well with some knowledgeable observers.

One medical expert brought in to weigh the pros and cons of the case was Cyril Wecht, the nationally recognized coroner of Allegheny County in Pennsylvania. Adamantly opposed to testing vaccines on institutionalized children unless it was designed to benefit the child, Wecht went on to argue, "Even if parental consent is provided, it still violates the individual rights of the mentally disabled. Parents do not own their children." The bottom line for Wecht was the child's welfare: unless the experiment were "clearly to the benefit of the child, parental consent would not make it legal."

Wecht had earned both law and medical degrees and understood the implications of human experimentation from both perspectives. He suggested, "the Pennsylvania Medical Society appoint a special committee and along with other scientific groups to begin thinking about policies involving human experiments." According to Wecht, "laypeople should also participate in the review with the aim of drawing up guidelines." [6]

Though the government's investigation of PARC's charges was designed to focus on human research, a litany of other abuses occurring at state mental facilities was exposed as well. Residents at Hamburg and other institutions were being "kept heavily drugged," making it impossible for some even to move. Some were said to act more like "robots" than humans. According to one defender of the practice, the institution was so overcrowded with "severely or profoundly retarded" individuals that using "psychotropic drugs" was the only way to keep the facility functioning.[7]

Equally disturbing revelations were unearthed at the Polk State School in the Northwest part of the state, where during the 1950s, Jonas Salk conducted his first polio vaccine trials. When Helene Wohlgemuth, the state Welfare Secretary made a surprise visit to Polk, she was confronted with a host of unsightly and unseemly practices. One of her more unpleasant discoveries was the presence of "five-by-five wooden pens used to cage disorderly patients."[8] It was explained to Clapp that a previous superintendent instituted the "playpens" as a control mechanism. Some were "12-by-12 feet, five times the size of those used with slats but without a top."[9] Whatever the size of the cages, however, Wohlgemuth was so disturbed by the institution resorting to such devices, especially when the entire system was under such public scrutiny, that she sent the superintendent packing. On April 16, 1973, just three days after her visit, she wrote James H. McClelland, the physician in charge of Polk, "I regret to inform you that you are hereby removed from your position as Superintendent. . . ." Amongst the reasons given for McClelland's dismissal were "cruel, degrading, and inhumane conditions" along with "severe and chronic deficiencies" concerning the training of professional staff.[10]

Pat Clapp and her associates learned several vital lessons from the Hamburg battle. "You can make an impact. People willing to fight can make a difference," said Clapp with an air of pride. PARC's successful and heavy media-covered campaign to end unauthorized medical research in Pennsylvania's mental institutions was a significant victory for health advocates and critical for establishing principles such as parental permission for the protection of underage test subjects. The triumphs were coming late in the day. Over a quarter-century had passed since the Nuremberg Code was drafted. During that time and indeed for many years before 1947, mentally challenged children residing in institutions were routinely used in various experimental ventures. During that time, they would be viewed by many in the research community as that cheap and convenient step between chimpanzees and humans in the vaccine discovery process. Many could claim participation in some of the greatest scientific quests of the twentieth century.

In the early part of the twentieth century, two diseases that took a significant toll on children were tuberculosis (TB) and polio. Though TB, known as "consumption," was a disease among adults, children were also highly susceptible to the fatal bacteria. On the other hand, polio was a significant disease primarily among children and young adults. To conquer both diseases, researchers conscripted vulnerable children and considered them excellent research material to find cures.

These early 20th-century disease-fighters used an array of diagnostic techniques and methodologies to assess the health of their patients and determine what specific malady was the source of their problem. Tuberculosis, a particularly incapacitating and deadly disease in the early decades of the last century, was for many years detected using tuberculin, a glycerinated extract of the tubercle bacillus that some believed might be a cure for the disease. Three different methods, each named after the physician who invented them, incorporating tuberculin as the analytical diving rod, were used to detect tuberculosis. The Calmette test dropped a solution filled with tuberculin into the patient's eyes, the Moro test injected the tuberculin into the patient's skin, and the von Pirquet test injected the tuberculin solution directly into the patient's muscle.

It was not long before the Calmette test was confronted with a growing chorus of concern, if not outright opposition. As one medical observer wrote, "the alarm had been sounded by several oculists of note," resulting in "a growing distrust and fear among ophthalmologists" about the "use of the conjunctival test." Increasingly, doctors "declined to make use of the Calmette test . . . because they considered it dangerous."[11]

As the medical community debated the strengths and weaknesses of Calmette versus the other two TB tests during the first decade of the 20th century, several researchers at the William Pepper Clinical Laboratory at the University of Pennsylvania decided to examine the merits of the three diagnostic tools. Their experimental test site was a natural for such an undertaking: the St. Vincent's Home for Orphans, a catholic orphanage along the banks of the Delaware River in Northeast Philadelphia. As medical historian Susan Lederer describes the event, the Penn physicians applied the tests to over 130 young orphans resulting in significant discomfort and "serious inflammations of the eye."

Antivivisectionists were some of the first to take note of the growing practice of using children in research and used the controversial accounts of children being subjected to experimentation in their efforts to harness the aggressive methods of researchers. Their leaflets and newsletters dramatically described the suffering orphans endured at the hands of heartless tuberculin-dropping physicians. "The little children would lie in their beds moaning all night from the pain in their eyes. They kept their little hands pressed over their eyes, unable to sleep from the sensations they had to undergo," according to one anti-vivisection activist's account.[12] Accompanying photos of sweet, little girls no more than five years old in identical dresses with colorful bows in their hair only added to the powerful message that university doctors were routinely exploiting society's least advantaged members.

Despite the criticism, other doctors were equally interested in adding their thoughts to the Calmette, Moro, and von Pirquet debate. For example, Louis M. Warfield, a St. Louis physician, published an article in the *Journal of the American Medical Association* on his findings after using the von Pirquet test on over 100 children, 55 of them infants. Another 51 subjects between the ages of 5 and 14 were found in an "orphans' home."[13]

Warfield's numbers were downright puny compared to Dr. L. Emmet Holt's stunningly large sample of "one thousand tuberculin tests in young children" at New York City's Babies Hospital in 1909. A noted professor of pediatrics at Columbia University's College of Physicians and Surgeons, Holt was aware of "the possible dangers connected with the eye test" and potential "scarification" from skin tests but moved ahead undaunted. He proudly claimed in a journal article the reports that "young infants do not respond to the eye test . . . was not our experience."[14]

Holt admitted "considerable experimenting" before he settled on a proper dose for the children, most of whom were under a year, and some said to be "dying" or "extremely sick." He further admitted the children's "prolonged reaction sometimes occurs which is not pleasant to see" and often necessitates "the hands of the children [being] confined during the first twelve hours to prevent any rubbing of the eye."[15]

While researchers attempted to tame the TB scourge, other researchers began to concentrate their research effort on poliomyelitis, more commonly termed "polio." Polio or infantile paralysis was a crippling and devastating disease primarily afflicting children. Polio research would begin during the 1930s, and earnest attempts to find a vaccine and cure began after World War II and through the early part of the Cold War during the 1950s.

Physicians in the 1930s were working under the mistaken belief that polio was an airborne disease and "the nasopharynx as the common portal of entry of the virus."[16] An assortment of uncomfortable nasal sprays and painful nasal injections were explored as possible preventatives. Paul de Kruif suggested when the discussion at a Baltimore meeting of scientists gravitated to the "difficulties of immunization" and potential test populations for trial runs. He inquired, "Could there not be a test set up where half of some age group would be given picric acid and then control some colored material. . . ." Suddenly, another doctor interjected, "I do not think we should discuss it here."[17] So important was this endeavor that the notes and minutes of this meeting were sent to the sixth Surgeon General of the United States, Thomas Parran. This interest in polio by Parran is unsurprising since he was appointed Surgeon General by President Franklin D. Roosevelt, diagnosed several years earlier with polio himself.

Though the unsavory practice of using vulnerable populations was not uncommon—the infamous Tuskegee Syphilis Study was in its infancy at the time—boldly suggesting such an idea at a public meeting was not encouraged. De Kruif's embarrassing comment was far from the only problematic statement or suggestion uttered at the high-level medical conclave. One doctor ruminating over the need for a poliomyelitis trial openly wondered about the possibility of using two different test groups and "two different solutions and using them alternately," an experiment he even thought might lay bare "questionable ethics?"[18]

The Baltimore brainstorming session demonstrated other utilitarian bias and blatant self-interest regarding large-scale experimental polio vaccine trials.

The most egregious was the lengthy discussion as to where large numbers of test subjects could be found and the creative suggestion "to get up an experiment" that would target the nation's many "Infant Welfare Clinics." As Dr. Freeman forcefully stated, "We have 2,000 children in our own welfare clinic between two weeks and six years of age. Throughout the country, there are hundreds of thousands of children in this same relation." The logic was incontrovertible, and researchers needed children as test subjects, and welfare clinics had them in abundance.

When Rivers offered a cautionary note about such an initiative and expressed a fear of the public learning about a dangerous experiment involving their children, Dr. Freeman replied, "The group of people with whom we deal in the Infant Welfare Clinic would not be affected by this advance publicity, and of course I would not encourage any of them. We will tell them, now is the time to take your baby for a tuberculosis test, diphtheria test, etc." Artful use of deception and outright mendacity with uneducated and economically disadvantaged people was not a problem for some medical group members. Acquiring convenient and sufficient "material" was the critical thing.

As Dr. Donald Armstrong said in support of the economic advantages of using Welfare Clinic children, "It is a group easy to handle, already corralled, who could be treated with 1/12 of the expense of the population that you could go out and set up for yourself."[19]

In a race to be the first to conquer the dread disease, several doctors with visions of joining the pantheon of great microbe hunters had begun vaccinating children with their new anti-polio concoctions only to discover what had always frightened Dr. Isabel Morgan; instead of protecting humans from disease, they were giving it to them. Paralysis and death were the results.

In 1935, Dr. John Kolmer, a pathologist at Temple University in Philadelphia, and William H. Park, a highly respected bacteriologist at New York University and his protégé, Maurice Brodie, claimed they had discovered safe and effective vaccines for infantile paralysis. Brodie, a "hard-driving and ambitious" young man determined to make a name for himself by discovering an effective polio vaccine, had convinced his esteemed mentor that he had done so through a "virus-containing emulsions of infected monkey spinal cords and inactivated with formaldehyde." After successful trials with his killed virus on monkeys, Brodie, Park, and a few lab assistants inoculated themselves with the vaccine and survived. Dispensing with further trials and not shy about his presumed success, Brodie went to the press and extolled the significance of his accomplishment. Eager to exploit news of the triumph, newspaper headlines sang the praises of the doctors for providing hope to millions of anxious parents fearing for the safety of their children. The scourge had been conquered.

Kolmer was also in a boastful mood. Unlike the Brodie/Park version, his vaccine was a "live but devitalized" virus that had been further attenuated using sodium ricinolate.[20] Moreover, it had been tested on 22 children in addition to himself and his two children. Newspapers were quick to announce the breakthrough: "New Infantile Paralysis Vaccine is Declared to Immunize Children" and "Will Give Children Paralysis Vaccine."[21] The press was in a feeding frenzy with the twin discoveries and "whipped up the rivalry to the point where newspapers carried frequent progress reports resulting in antics in which each tried to outdo the other."[22]

Not everyone was caught up in the excitement, however. Thomas Rivers of the Rockefeller Institute remained unconvinced. By October of 1935, Brodie's vaccine had been given to about 8,000 people and Kolmer's to another 12,000, but definite signs of concern had surfaced. Some children had contracted polio where no outbreak had occurred, but vaccines trials had. Rivers believed the vaccines had never been proven safe, and some individuals—at least eight by his counting—may have contracted polio from the inoculations. As he told the press, "Information in my hands about the time and circumstances of these eight cases make it imperative that Dr. Kolmer show his vaccine is safe."[23]

Other eminent medical scholars would weigh in on the looming controversy, such as Dr. Simon Flexner, a medical legend and the top man at Rockefeller. Flexner strongly criticized both methods, considered both unsafe, and urged caution. He argued, "No adequate evidence exists to support the claims" that the Kolmer and Park/Brodie vaccines "were effective agents against infantile paralysis."

Drs. Park and Brodie fired back aggressively, and they were not intimidated by Flexner's warnings. "We are giving definite immunity with our vaccine treatment," argued Brodie. "The fact that our . . . virus of infantile paralysis is killed by formalin obviates any possible danger of giving the disease to any child who might not be susceptible to it. There is absolutely nothing to lose and everything to gain by continuing our tests."[24]

However, evidence was quickly mounting and proving contrary to what the doctors were claiming. Instead of protecting people, the vaccine experiments were giving people polio. Confirmed data showed "at least 12 vaccine-associated cases and six deaths."[25] By the end of the year, and after much professional embarrassment, the race for a new polio vaccine was seen as a "foolhardy venture" that destroyed lives. Medical researchers in general, and certain doctors, were taken to task for "lack of restraint, poor judgment," and using innocent citizens as laboratory test subjects. More newspaper headlines were now bellowing a similar message, "Paralysis Vaccine Discontinued Here."[26] The research debacle left the once esteemed William Park with a damaged reputation and Drs. Brodie and Kolmer considered *persona non grata* amongst their peers in the profession. Furthermore, the research community took a severe hit; ego and the pressure to be the first with a polio vaccine led to mass vaccinations before it was determined safe to do so. Moreover, after it was all over, infantile paralysis was still out there: an ominous shadow annually crossing the American landscape, leaving thousands of paralyzed or dead as it passed.

Years later, two institutions for the intellectually and physically challenged in Pennsylvania—the D. T. Watson Home and the Polk State School—would play a critical role in discovering a long-sought vaccine to combat infantile paralysis. The Watson Home on the outskirts of Pittsburgh was a small, upscale facility for children with polio. Formerly the country estate of a successful Pittsburgh lawyer who handled the accounts of area robber barons and became America's ambassador to Great Britain, it opened in 1920 as a residence for "crippled or deformed" children.[27] The Polk State School, situated 80 miles north of Pittsburgh, was opened in 1897 and was initially known as the State Institution for the Feebleminded in Western Pennsylvania. Located just outside the town of Franklin, in Venango County, the facility would grow and provide care for both mildly and profoundly mentally challenged children and adults.

As one of a growing list of virologists and microbe hunters seeking to conquer the dreaded disease, Dr. Jonas Salk was anxious to further explore "the prevention of poliomyelitis by immunologic means." Though one of the younger and lesser-known investigators in the polio vaccine posse, Salk had already spent considerable time experimenting with living and killed poliovirus, various adjuvants to shock the immune system, and different methods to inactivate the virus such as formaldehyde and ultraviolet light. In all these experiments, monkeys were exclusively used as the test material. Much was learned, but "the next step" for Salk, according to historian David Oshinski, "was the big one: human testing."[28] However, where does one go to test a new potentially dangerous potion that could result in paralysis and death?

Salk was introduced to the answer just a few years earlier while doing influenza research. The Ypsilanti State Hospital in Michigan was home to a wide assortment of mentally ill and challenged patients. Salk, along with several other inquisitive researchers, took over a 96-man ward and injected half of them with an experimental vaccine before being "exposed to infection by inhalation of a strain of Type B influenza virus. . . ."[29] The exercise proved successful and resulted in a journal publication with Salk as the lead author, an academic sign-post that his work possessed scientific rigor and intellectual gravitas. It would not be the last time Salk used such institutions.

Described by Oshinski as "eager, confident, aggressive," traits not uncommon to the great microbe hunters. Salk, in 1950, informed one colleague who was aiding him in the quest for a viable polio vaccine, "I think that the time has come for these experiments to be carried out in man." Representative of both the era and his profession, Salk immediately knew where subjects could be rounded up for risky experimental work and attract little fanfare or interruption—"institutionalized children" or "inmates of prisons." Salk informed his colleague that he had already laid the groundwork for such a venture. "I have investigated the local possibilities for such an experiment and find . . . there are institutions for hydrocephalics and other similar unfortunates. I think we may be able to obtain permission for a study."[30]

Salk had specific institutions in mind and an idea of which superintendents would be amenable to using inmates as test subjects. One of them was Dr. Gale H. Walker, the headman at Polk. He also knew how to appeal to men like Walker and sometimes had intermediaries intervene to bolster his case. It was only slightly surprising then that Superintendent Walker would become an avid supporter of the Pittsburgh virologist's request.[31] As he began his letter to Pennsylvania's secretary of welfare, Walker frankly stated; "During the past six months I was approached by several prominent practicing physicians who were anxious for me . . . to meet with Dr. Jonas E. Salk, Research Professor of Bacteriology, School of Medicine, University of Pittsburgh, and the Director of Bacteriology, School of Medicine, University of Pittsburgh, and the Director of the Virus Research Laboratory there." Walker would go on to admit that he had had two "long discussions" with Salk and was now requesting permission to enter into a "collaboration" with the University of Pittsburgh School of Medicine and the National Foundation for Infantile Paralysis in a proposed field study at the Polk State School dealing with the administration of poliomyelitis vaccines to patients in our institutions."

Sounding more like a personal agent than the headmaster of an under-staffed and overcrowded state institution, Walker would go on to illuminate Polk's attributes as a test site; its stable, "long-term" population, controlled "diet," and "relative isolation from the general community." He admitted his "intensely favorable" reaction to the request and firm belief that "in no manner could the charge of using institutional patients for guinea pigs be leveled at us. . . ." Walker also informed his boss that he had "already taken the liberty of approaching several patients' parents" with the idea and received positive feedback.

A few weeks later, the Pennsylvania Commissioner of Mental Health gave Superintendent Walker his answer. He admitted the commonwealth had a "vast resource of clinical material on hand" for these types of "research projects." He had "frequently" acceded to the research requests of "the superintendent of Pennhurst" and "University of Pennsylvania pediatricians." However, the commissioner was clear that no such endeavor should place patients at risk. None could be "considered an assault upon a patient" nor any patient put "under jeopardy of health."[32] In the end, Salk would gain access to the pitiful wards of an overburdened state facility and initiate an experiment that was not dissimilar from what Drs. Brodie and Kolmer had attempted in 1935 in their polio experiments. Risk was undoubtedly involved, but it would not be the cherished and pampered students of elite Pittsburgh area prep that would shoulder the dangerous burden of testing a new vaccine; it would be those who were still occasionally referred to as "feebleminded," "morons," and "mental defectives."

The leap from animal experimentation to clinical trials with humans was a chasm that only the most driven and single-minded investigators hurdled without some degree of trepidation. However, the jump was made that much more palatable by knowing that near-humans—the insane, "mental defectives," criminals behind bars, and other lesser members of society—would be used as test material. Still, some were perpetually nervous about exposing institutional flotsam and jetsam to potentially paralytic and deadly diseases. Polio was not the flu; it could quickly destroy one's life.

Isabel Morgan, for example, a talented Johns Hopkins researcher and the daughter of accomplished biologists, one a Nobel Prize winner, was further along than Salk in developing a killed poliovirus in the late 1940s but jettisoned the effort when she married and became a housewife and stepmother. However, it was well known to close friends that more than marriage impeded Morgan's progress in the laboratory. She had often expressed a decided reluctance to use humans as lab rats. As Oshinsky writes in his award-winning account of the race to discover a polio vaccine, Isabel Morgan was fraught with fear; she never felt "completely confident about her vaccine."[33] She was concerned she might end up paralyzing test subjects rather than discovering a viable preventative.

However, others were always willing to take that extra step, ready to expose another human being to a potentially harmful germ, dangerous substance, or painful procedure. Hilary Koprowski was such an individual. As a young and aspiring Polish scientist who fled Europe after the Nazis invaded his homeland in 1939, he and his wife, Irena, also a scientist, first settled in Brazil. He was able to procure a job working for the Rockefeller Foundation researching yellow fever. By the end of the war, he had migrated to America. He had accepted a position with Lederle Laboratories as a researcher at their spacious Pearl River campus in New York. One of his first assignments was the development of a live-virus polio vaccine.

Possessed of old-world charm, a connoisseur of gourmet cooking, and an accomplished musician, Koprowski was also bright, creative, and bold. He was a definite risk-taker; no one had ever accused him of lacking self-assurance. His research game plan at the time was quite simple. He "decided to first attenuate (weaken) poliomyelitis virus, then to find out whether it was possible to develop a vaccine that would replicate in the human gut without causing signs of disease, and then to immunize people by feeding them this vaccine." Koprowski planned on his creation being the world's "first oral vaccine."[34]

After several years attenuating the virus in mice and rats, he decided to test it in rhesus monkeys. Koprowski was elated; "not a single monkey became paralyzed." Better yet, they "developed antibodies and were resistant to challenge with a virulent strain of the virus." Further experiments on chimpanzees successfully followed, resulting in Koprowski believing he had discovered a viable and effective polio vaccine. Following in the tradition of some of the great medical researchers who abided by an unwritten code that dictated scientists should be the first to test a new and potentially dangerous elixir, Koprowski and his loyal assistant, Thomas Norton, imbibed a "polio cocktail" consisting of ground-up rat spinal cord and mashed brain tissue. Both survived the unappetizing beverage.

Two years later, Koprowski confronted what he referred to as their next problem; "whom we would vaccinate." According to our interview with Dr. Koprowski, the answer came in the form of a timely request from Dr. George A. Jervis, a physician at Letchworth Village, a state institution for "abnormal children" near Lederle's Pearl River campus. In the traditional sense, these were "not experiments," claimed Koprowski, but a response to "a plea by authorities of the institution. Children were eating feces and throwing feces all over the place and at each other. There was contamination throughout the entire facility, and they believed the children were at risk of contracting polio." Dr. Jervis, whom Koprowski called" a close friend," pleaded with us, "Please try the vaccine at Letchworth."[35]

In his account of that first human trial, Koprowski realized he would "never get official permission from the State of New York," so he decided to forgo state authorities and just "ask permission from the parents of these children. On February 27, 1950, the first human subject was immunized with poliomyelitis virus by drinking an emulsion of cotton rat brain and cord. . . ."[36] Oshinski's account of the historic incident leaves open the question whether "Jervis got consent from the children's parents or simply took on the responsibility himself." That first subject, a young "boy [with] no antibodies," was chosen, and after several weeks, Koprowski, Norton, and Jervis "increased the number of children to 10, and ultimately ended with 20 children."

That promising first step was not revealed until March 1951, when Koprowski attended a National Foundation for Infantile Paralysis conclave in Hershey, Pennsylvania. A collection of elite and highly accomplished academic and university hospital researchers was in attendance including, Joseph Stokes, Jr., David Bodian, Thomas Francis, Jonas Salk, and Albert Sabin. The little-known Lederle researcher was the low man on the totem pole, but his presentation quickly captured the attention of the august members in attendance. Being the first to use a live poliovirus on children was noteworthy.

Most of the attendees were stunned. Albert Sabin, the University of Cincinnati virologist, was apoplectic. According to Koprowski's account, "Sabin was quite vociferous at the meeting. Sabin questioned my daring. How did I dare to feed children live poliovirus? I replied that somebody had to take this step. Well, he turned round and round, saying, 'How do you dare to use live virus on children? You are not sure about this, and you are not sure about that. You may have caused an epidemic.' Even kind Dr. Stokes ". . . asked whether I had checked the possibility that the Society for Prevention of Cruelty to Children would sue me for what I had done."[37]

Over six decades later, Koprowski chuckled at "the great polio war" and the intense competitiveness of his peers in the virology community as to who would be the first to claim the title as the microbe hunter who bagged polio. He ruminated over every scientist's dilemma;" doing something when you do not know the outcome." He said, "there was a fight over everything," and believes Sabin's attack at Hershey had more to do with "jealousy" than any ethical rules he may have breached. Sabin "was not a nice character," says Koprowski. "He was a fine scientist, much better than Salk, but human nature is not nice. We are jealous of each other, and that motivates us to do things. It was an unethical family" He wonders why they jumped all over him and paid little to no attention to "Dr. Stokes vaccinating female prisoners" in a New Jersey penal facility and using their "newborn children as research subjects."[38]

As for ethical restrictions during the early postwar years, Koprowski says there were few. "I had no idea of the Nuremberg Code. I guess I did not read enough newspapers. I was not aware of the code." Others at the time may have been equally uninformed, but they still had some strictures or guidelines concerning who could be used as test subjects.

Thomas Rivers, one of the most senior and respected scientists at Rocke-feller and a shocked participant at the Hershey meeting, would frankly address the Koprowski/Letchworth Village experiment a decade-and-a-half later. He was not a fan of the commercial scientist or his methods. "First," recalled Riv-ers, "I did not think that the safety tests that Dr. Koprowski had done were anything to write home about, and second, I personally did not approve of using mentally defective children for such a test with inactivated vaccine, and what Koprowski wanted to do was not unusual. You might even say that it was standard practice."[39]

Rivers, a significant figure in 20th-century virology, held strong views on using institutionalized children as research material and was out of step with many of his colleagues at the time on the issue. Referring to the early Cold War years, Rivers said,

> Some people at the Public Health Research Institute of New York wanted
> to test what was then a new typhus vaccine on some mentally defective
> children in Letchworth Village, and they found me bitterly opposed . . .
> I think that if someone wants to use adults as volunteers to try out a new
> drug or vaccine, that is perfectly all right, provided that the adult had been
> told about the nature of the disease he is exposing himself to, has been
> completely informed about the nature of the agent he is to receive and been
> told the chances for success or failure.

Further commenting about human volunteers, Rivers believed there were "two classes" of research volunteers, "prisoners in some state or federal institu-tions or they are scientists," but he admitted,

> I do not even know that you can actually call a prisoner a volunteer. I believe
> that although prisoners are usually told that they will get nothing out of
> volunteering as guinea pigs, deep down when they believe that they may get
> a commutation or reduction of their sentence, that it is perfectly all right: the
> point is prisoners are generally adults who can weigh the pros and cons of
> submitting to a test, and if they arrive at a decision to participate in a test it is

a decision or judgment that they have made. It's not made for them. An adult can do what he wants, but the same does not hold for a mentally defective child. Many of these children did not have any mommas and papas, or if they did, their mommas and papas did not give a damn about them.[40]

Despite the ethical reservations of Rivers and others who shuddered at Koprowski's use of mentally disabled children as "volunteers" in the battle against polio, his Letchworth Village experiments would be viewed as a "turning point" and "courageous" step in the problematic campaign to conquer the dreaded paralytic disease. Time and events seem to have been speeded up in these early days of the Cold War. Salk would soon be doing experiments at Watson and Polk. However, his research at those institutions would not attract the negative criticism Hilary Koprowski's had received. In 1952, for example, the British journal *Lancet* chided the Lederle scientist for suggesting the mentally disabled Letchworth children in his studies were actually "volunteers."[41] Salk managed to avoid such snipping commentary. Even Sabin, one of Koprowski's most ardent challengers that day at Hershey—and someone who, like many others, had been influenced by Paul de Kruif's *Microbe Hunters* in their youth—would go on to push the ethical envelope.

Instances of cavalier research would become increasingly common during the mid-twentieth century fight against polio. In December 1951, at a meeting of polio researchers in New York City, for example, Dr. Howard A. Howe, a distinguished virologist, presented a paper on the need for additional immunology studies and suggested a "pilot experiment" that would inject 50 to 100 children, "presumably mentally deficient," with a trivalent vaccine. If that exercise proved successful, the test population would be enlarged "to include 1,000 normal children in the age range of 1-3 years."[42] A year later, Howe would write a journal article on the "Antibody Response of Chimpanzees and Human Beings to Formalin-Inactivated Trivalent Poliomyelitis Vaccine." The humans for his study were procured at the "Rosewood Training School" in Owings Mills, Maryland, and would consist of "11 bedridden children in the second to fifth years of life." According to the author, they "were low-grade idiots or imbeciles with congenital hydrocephalus, microcephaly, or cerebral palsy." Howe went on to assure journal readers that "despite these handicaps, their physical condition was . . . good," thereby making for acceptable test subjects.[43] There is no record of opposition at either the New York gathering or from journal editors regarding Dr. Howe's belief that "defective children" were the chimpanzee's closest relative, at least from a clinical trial perspective.

As Rivers candidly observed, "defective children" and other disadvantaged populations were so often sought as test subjects that it became "standard practice" among medical researchers. For decades, similar refrains had been heard at scientific meetings as researchers planned their next investigative steps in the war on polio and other troubling public health maladies. At one 1936 high-level meeting of the President's Birthday Ball Commission Infantile Paralysis in Baltimore attended by both Rivers and Paul de Kruif, the group's secretary, a dozen influential doctors discussed everything from tannic and picric acids as potential polio preventatives to the belief that only "through studies on children" would a victory finally be achieved.[44]

During the 1950s, however, recollections of that terrible medical faux pas had begun to fade, but the siren call of personal success and scientific triumph was as strong as ever. Koprowski and Salk may have been at the forefront of a new generation of young and aggressive microbe hunters, but the quest was the same. The scourge of polio was still omnipresent, and they both seemed to know where experimental vaccine trials could be cheaply and quietly tested.

Researchers would also take on other childhood diseases. Many infectious diseases such as influenza, measles, hepatitis, and rubella were now in researchers' crosshairs. Unfortunately for vulnerable populations, such as mentally and physically challenged children, they would be in the crossfire of these battles.

In the early years of World War II, researchers at the University of Pennsylvania School of Medicine and the Children's Hospital of Pennsylvania became preoccupied with "inhalation experiments" and the "effectiveness of vaccination for the prevention of epidemic influenza." They hoped that research in this area and experiments on "vaccinated and non-vaccinated human beings" would provide some "additional information about the value of these vaccines."[45]

In one experiment, a vaccine consisting of "allantoic fluids infected with PR-8, WS, and Melbourne strains of influenza A virus" was manufactured, inactivated with formalin, dialyzed against buffered saline solution, and preserved with phenylmercuric nitrate with the assistance of colleagues at Sharp and Dohme. Before any test subjects underwent vaccination or inhalation, they were routinely" bled" two weeks before and two weeks after each procedure. After receiving intramuscular injections of two different vaccines, test subjects underwent an influenza inhalation procedure. A viral fluid was directed through rubber tubing that entered "aviation oxygen masks" that fit tightly over the faces" of the test subjects. Six atomizer units were operationalized simultaneously through an "electrically driven air compressor" where a "very fine mist was formed and passed through the tubing of the mask." Each subject was "exposed for 4 minutes" to the vaporized fluid which represented "approximately 1.8 million fifty percent mouse mortality doses of virus" to each subject. The massive dose of influenza germs was due to the fear that the attenuation process had weakened the vaccine, thereby lessening its effectiveness.

The subjects for this non-therapeutic experiment were selected from a "cottage of a large state institution in New Jersey." The "72 occupants" ranged from "6 to 14 years of age" and did not have the flu. After being quarantined for some time, 11 out of 72 children came down with clinical influenza. Their signs of infection include "flushing of the face, malaise, aching of the back, arms and legs, dryness and redness of the throat, dry cough, leucopenia," and several other symptoms including 100 to 104-degree temperatures.[46]

In 1943, doctors at Penn and the Squibb Institute for Medical Research experimented to determine if an egg passage vaccine in children would effectively protect them in chance exposure and challenge inoculations of a measles virus. The authors of the study noted in their subsequent article on the project that "immunity or susceptibility to measles" studies have "been possible only using the relatively scarce and costly *Macaca mulatta*" monkeys and the use of convalescents, which was deemed "seldom practicable for experimental studies."[47]

However, investigators knew precisely where to find suitable test subjects for their study. In addition to nine children from their backyard at Children's Hospital in Philadelphia, they blanketed orphanages and institutions for the feebleminded and epileptics in the area. Their experimental dragnet resulted in three children from Skillman, five children from Mt. Holly, six children from New Lisbon in New Jersey, ten children from the Homewood Orphanage in Philadelphia, and 11 children from Pennhurst. Half of the children in both groups developed measles from the experiment.

There were educational institutions closer to the Penn and Children's Hospital campus than Skillman in central New Jersey and Pennhurst in Southeastern Pennsylvania. However, the doctors behind this study were fully cognizant of where certain types of medical research were off-limits and where it was condoned. Orphans at Homewood, epileptics at Skillman, and the mentally disabled at New Lisbon proved ideal as test subjects. Useless and devalued bodies had become useful bodies, at least to researchers. They had become that critical intervening step between monkeys and humans. Often cheaper than chimps and less problematic to deal with than adults and children of the well-to-do, institutions for children played a significant role in developing many vaccines during the last century.

In November of 1950, Dr. Richard Capps of the Liver Research Laboratory at St. Lukes Hospital in Chicago wrote Dr. Joseph Stokes, Jr. a letter laying out an experimental game plan and concluding with the optimistic line, "It seems to me that this is a very neat little project, and if it works, we'll really have something."[48]

The "neat little project" Capps was referring to be an experiment testing the ability of gamma globulin to prevent the onset of hepatitis. The initiative grew out of a hepatitis epidemic at Chicago's St. Vincent Orphanage and Hospital during the 1940s. St. Vincent's was a five-story structure that served about 200 infants and children. There was also a small ward for expectant mothers who, after delivery, often worked in the orphanage. Oddly enough, new student nurses were particularly hard hit with hepatitis. Dr. Stokes in Philadelphia was sought out for his knowledge of the disease and his assistance in eradicating it. Stokes recruited a team of Chicago liver specialists for assistance, and they began mapping a strategy to test their hypothesis.

They decided to "set aside a special ward of approximately 25 beds. Approximately 20 normals" would be housed there, "1/3 of whom will have received gamma globulin." They would then "introduce . . . two of our old chronics who still seem to be active" and then "fresh cases" sometime later. An added feature of the experiment would be by "special arrangement with the Sisters . . . poor nursing technique in this one ward which, of course, is essential." An added component would be "repeated skin tests" of the experimental participants and 25 additional nurses and children in the building.

Capps, the primary designer of the "neat little project," was buoyed by the fact that, "I have already talked to the Sisters, and the . . . plan is definitely feasible." He was excited by the prospect of testing gamma globulin's power to thwart infection and further determine whether "skin test material produces active immunity."

Dr. Stokes wrote back that the plan was "in accord" with their earlier discussions. They had been discussing the situation at the orphanage for nearly a year. In addition to the St. Vincent's project, the liver virologists theorized about "methods for permanent active immunity" and submitted a scientific paper on the subject for some time. Now that Capps was ready to begin the actual experiment and expose children to hepatitis, Stokes offered a few cautionary notes. He was concerned about an excessive number of skin tests. He commented that "the new test material will not be ready until January (1951) because we want to be sure the new test material will not produce hepatitis." Stokes went on to underscore the point, "I think you can understand why we must be careful."⁴⁹ He did not want to be the reason for any hepatitis epidemic at the institution by underlining it.

A few years after Koprowski and Salk entered Letchworth Village and Polk in the fight against polio, Dr. Saul Krugman was invited into the Willowbrook State School on Staten Island in New York for another battle. The large, perpetually overcrowded institution was home to over 4,000 children with various mental and physical disabilities and was suffering from an outbreak of infectious hepatitis. Krugman, a pediatrician at New York University Medical School, could not help but connect the scores of children acquiring liver disease with the facility's horrid sanitary conditions and the children's propensity to languish in their filth.

Krugman would perform experiments at the institution and continue to do so for well over a decade. His research would significantly contribute to science and increase our understanding of the infectious disease. However, those Willowbrook studies would also become some of the most controversial human experiments of the last half-century. For decades, defenders and detractors of Krugman's research would square off at forums, in journals, and on op-ed pages to illuminate what was right or wrong with "feeding virus-laden stool to mentally retarded, indigent children on the wards of a state mental hospital." At stake, the ethical issues were so complex and convoluted that some ardent opponents found themselves over time, becoming equally enthusiastic champions of Krugman's work.

Though the NYU pediatrician went unnamed, Krugman's research, example #16, was cited in Henry Beecher's controversial 1966 *New England Journal of Medicine* article that drew uncomfortable attention to 22 dubious clinical studies that were said to put patients and test subjects at risk. The issue of whether it was morally right to infect a human being with hepatitis virus purposefully was only heightened by the fact that the human beings in question were children; specifically, mentally challenged children. Many of which, according to Krugman, was "the most severely retarded, the most handicapped, and most helpless of those being cared for in the New York State System."⁵⁰ Moreover, their numbers ran into the hundreds.

Many medical community members felt such research could be justified. No less than Dr. Franz Ingelfinger, for example, the esteemed editor of the *New England Journal of Medicine,* argued: "How much better to have a patient with hepatitis, accidentally or deliberately acquired, under the guidance of a Krugman than under the care of a zealot who would exercise intuitive management, blind to the fact that his one-track efforts to protect the rights of the individual are depriving that individual of his right to good medical care."⁵¹

Such arguments proved unconvincing to Krugman's detractors. His outraged opponents were less concerned with Krugman's credentials as a serious-minded investigator or the results of his research than the "ethics of his studies." As Dr. Stephen Goldby wrote in *The Lancet*, "I believe . . . the whole of Krugman's study, is quite unjustifiable, whatever the aims, and however academically or therapeutically important are the results."[52] Goldby would go on to voice his amazement that such ethically flawed work would be "actively supported editorially by the *Journal of the American Medical Association* and by Ingelfinger." In Goldby's opinion, it was "indefensible to give potentially dangerous infected material to children, particularly those who were mentally retarded, with or without parental consent, when no benefit to the child could conceivably result."

That was the heart of the issue for Goldby and many others, "Is it right to perform an experiment on a normal or mentally retarded child when no benefit can result to that individual?" Their answer was "no." As the Willowbrook Study opponents believed, "it was the duty of a pediatrician in a situation such as exists at Willowbrook State School to attempt to improve that situation, not to turn it to his advantage for experimental purposes, however lofty the aims."[53]

That was the point that Beecher tried to make when he first mentioned the issue of increasingly problematic research appearing in American medical journals. He was not out to lambaste or embarrass doctors, but the incidence of unethical research was becoming ever more frequent and increasingly troubling. It was critical in his estimation for the profession to understand the importance of ethics. He wanted all to know that "A study is ethical or not at its inception. It does not become ethical merely because it turned up valuable data."[54]

Krugman responded to the attacks at various forums and in writing. He usually replied that the ethics of a situation could "not be divorced from the time and place in which these studies were conducted." Willowbrook in the mid-1950s, Krugman argued, was an exceptional and troubled place. Unsanitary, overcrowded, and experiencing a rapid increase in infectious hepatitis and jaundice cases, newly admitted children to the institution were likely to become infected within six to twelve months. According to Krugman, the answer to this growing problem was acquiring new knowledge that would lead to an effective immunizing agent. This vaccine would protect children how the Salk and Sabin vaccines had recently protected children from infantile paralysis.

As Krugman would subsequently write of that initial decision to tackle the Willowbrook hepatitis problem, "It was essential to acquire new knowledge about the natural history of this disease—knowledge that might lead to its ultimate control." After three decades of both praise and scorn over his work at the institution, Krugman remained convinced his studies were both "ethical and justifiable."[55]

In their initial "Plan of Study" for tackling the Willowbrook hepatitis conundrum, Krugman and his NYU medical colleagues sought answers to two questions: "Would gamma globulin stop hepatitis . . . in the same manner as reported by Stokes and his associates working in a similar institution," and "Could passive-active immunity be experimentally attempted in human subjects who would later be tested for protection?"[56] The results of their early studies on Willowbrook children showed, "There is nothing to suggest a protective effect from gamma globulin." The second question led to "inducing passive-active immunity by simultaneously injecting gamma globulin and feeding virus-containing material. "The material was made from the stools of six patients with hepatitis and jaundice, and put through complicated heating, testing, and manufacturing process leading to Krugman's team to believe the product "was deemed safe to feed."[57]

According to the NYU team, "permission was obtained," and "newly admitted children 3-10 years of age" were "kept in separate isolation wards of the same building." The children were "gingerly" given the infected "suspension in chocolate milk." One of eight children "came down with typical hepatitis with jaundice on the 30th day." None of the other children "exhibited anything suspicious during the period of observation." A second trial resulted in five of 11 children developing "typical jaundice with confirmatory liver tests. . . ." Desirous of "producing jaundice in a larger proportion of the recipients, 13 children were fed" and increased dosage of suspension. "This resulted in hepatitis with jaundice in 12 of 13" children.[58]

There is little doubt that Krugman and his research team produced some valuable information about "serum phosphohexose isomerase," "glycolytic enzymes," and other valuable data concerning bodily fluids and processes. However, the experimental results probably provided little solace for the once hepatitis-free children now confronted with "fever, vomiting, diarrhea, enlargement of the liver, and equivocal liver function tests."[59]

The hepatitis experiments would go on for years. They did help establish two clear types of the disease, paving the way for successful active and passive immunization. The studies would withstand the criticism emanating from the 1966 Beecher article and proceed into the 1970s. However, did those triumphs negate the shock of feeding infected serum to mentally challenged children? Even as far back as the fifties, when a lone dissenting voice commented on "disturbing" research practices at Willowbrook, Krugman was quick to defend his program and reply, "We, too, are keenly aware of our moral responsibilities. This study was not undertaken lightly."[60] He would then usually mention "our sponsors," supporters, and those who knew about the research effort. A formidable list of organizations included the Armed Forces Epidemiological Board, NYU's School of Medicine, the New York State Department of Mental Hygiene, and the *Journal of the American Medical Association*. All knew about the research program; not one had a problem with it.

New allegations arose in 1964, claiming that the parents of Willowbrook students had been coerced into signing their children over to the researchers. Due to intense overcrowding at the institution, new admissions had been curtailed unless, of course, one was willing to have their child become a test subject in Krugman's Willowbrook research unit, where spots were still available.

Lost in the long-running debate over the hepatitis experiments are other interesting aspects of the research program we believe deserve comment. Just as had occurred in other institutions holding vulnerable populations that opened their doors to scientific investigators, the wealth of test material combined with the presence of other health maladies, and the freedom and convenience to explore potential remedies, presented researchers with a rare opportunity, an investigatory gold mine that allowed experimentation to their heart's content. For example, in early 1957, not long after the NYU team started work at Willowbrook, Dr. Robert Ward, Krugman's associate, wrote the school director "about the possibility of enlarging the scope" of the research program. In a four-page letter, Ward proffered a continuation of the hepatitis research that would explore numerous maladies and treatments. Everything from additional stool studies and "Thorazine's" relationship to infectious hepatitis to polio's relationship to various neurological disorders and a measles vaccine trial. Also, a study of "amino acids in the blood and spinal fluid; and research on "new types of inborn errors of metabolism which might be correctible by diet."[61]

Ward believed such an expanded research program requires "separate isolation units," additional "laboratory space," and more staff "to care for the patients and conduct the studies." Ward had already done his homework; he suggested "the second floor of Building 2" as the ideal location for the new, enlarged program. In closing, Dr. Ward thanked the director for his cooperation. "Medicine, "he wrote, "have profited enormously by their experiences with rubella, pertussis, tuberculosis, and hepatitis at Willowbrook." It was "in the spirit of continuing this happy relationship" that the researchers now asked for more space, more freedom to explore other scientific pursuits, and more test subjects."[62]

The state school for the mentally challenged had been transformed into an attractive investigative gold mine for NYU researchers. Documents from the 1950s and 60s repeatedly disclose Dr. Krugman or one of his associates writing Dr. Harold Berman, Willowbrook's director, for permission to conduct an additional piece of research at the institution. For example, in the spring of 1959, Krugman informed Berman that "Dr. John Enders of Harvard Medical School has investigated a strain of live attenuated measles virus. After preliminary studies in monkeys and adult volunteers, he recently administered the vaccine to a group of susceptible children in a Massachusetts institution." Krugman went on to write that "It occurred to me these studies could be extended at the Willowbrook State School." In other words, the state school for the developmentally disabled had evolved into a supermarket of investigatory opportunities for NYU researchers.[63]

Dr. Krugman was also helpful to the U.S. military when circumstances allowed. In 1960, for instance, one Army medical investigator wrote Krugman, "It occurred to me that pre-inoculation sera from participants in the Willowbrook Volunteer Studies who responded with hepatitis and jaundice, would probably constitute the best such controls which could be devised at present."[64] The Army medical officer wanted "any prebleed sera" from the Willowbrook "volunteers" for the military's experiments. Unfortunately, Krugman claimed a "limited supply" of his own since "our subjects are children" and therefore "difficult to obtain large quantities of blood."[65] We do not know what added pressure such requests presented for the NYU researchers to increase test subjects or hepatitis experiments.

By the mid-1960s, Krugman was a significant name in research circles with several notable firsts to his credit and a pivotal role in developing vaccines to prevent mumps and rubella and the trivalent mumps-measles-rubella vaccine. He would often write the Willowbrook directors "thank you" notes for their "cooperation" in permitting the "many outstanding Willowbrook studies" and assuring them that "the name Willowbrook [had achieved] a permanent place in the world's medical literature."

Such letters often were followed by others requesting permission for another clinical trial. For example, in the summer of 1965, Krugman asked permission to "conduct a Diphtheria Immunity Study" that would require at least "360 individuals, and preferably 480 individuals."[66] Less than twelve months later, Krugman was back asking permission to do another vaccine study as the "Merck Institute for Therapeutic Research" had made some advances with "lines of the live measles vaccine" and were looking to build upon "preliminary clinical studies that had been "carried out in the Philadelphia area."[67]

The institution's directors usually endorsed these initiatives, but documents disclose that the medical research program could often cause administrative problems for the underfunded and understaffed Staten Island facility. In fact, on one occasion in 1967, Dr. Jack Hammond, the Willowbrook director, requested Krugman inform an associate of the increasing burden new research projects imposed on his custodial operations. "The additional administrative and paperwork," said Hammond, "that such a [proposed] project will place on my already over-worked staff, in view of the need to obtain informed parental consent for the administration of the para-thyroid extract on an experimental basis." Hammond wanted the doctors to appreciate his organizational bind and "the great problem of insufficient staff to ensure urine collections when I have perhaps two attendants at night for wards holding anywhere from 50 to 80 patients." Hammond was justly sensitive to "complaints of over-work by either my ward staff or stenographic staff to arise because I am involving them in too many research projects conducted at the request of other agencies." In short, Director Hammond was a supporter of Krugman's research program, and was willing to endure the "sensational accusation[s] concerning research and experimentation" that he was periodically confronted with, but the "additional administrative" burdens it presented were a recurring headache.[68]

For Krugman, however, Willowbrook was a career-maker, a vast, unfettered laboratory that allowed him to explore the hidden mysteries of viral disease to his heart's desire. With a neglected and devalued population of over 6,000 residents living in close quarters and devoid of any say in the matter, Krugman and his fellow investigators had a vast repository of cheap and available human test subjects that exceeded what he had with rodents in the NYU laboratory.

Great things would come of Krugman's human experiments at Willowbrook. New knowledge, groundbreaking vaccines, a river of honors and awards including the Lasker Award and the Gold Medal of the Robert Koch Institute, and front-page *New York Times* headlines that solidified Krugman's reputation as a microbe hunter in the best tradition of Walter Reed, Theobald Smith, and Joseph Goldberger.[69] There can be little doubt that children in succeeding years at Willowbrook and schools and institutions around the country were better off for Krugman's many discoveries. For the thousands of children from the 1950s to the 1970s who were volunteered for hepatitis, measles, mumps, rubella, and other experiments, there would be no awards nor headlines, nor Paul de Kruif to chronicle their story.

The Willowbrook controversy stimulated considerable debate and consternation over the years. Letters attacking Krugman and his research generated an equal number of missives defending his scientific contributions. It was not uncommon to find combative letter writers targeting each other on occasion. One 1972 letter accused a Krugman critic of "know-nothingism." It informed the unschooled Krugman basher who had taken it upon himself to become both "judge and Jury" of a dedicated doctor's career that Krugman had "produced more information about hepatitis . . . than anyone else in the world."[70] The annoyed writer was Dr. Stanley A. Plotkin, Associate Professor of Pediatrics at the University of Pennsylvania.

Plotkin was no research novice or blindly loyal Krugman supporter; he was an established microbe hunter in his own right and would spend 31-years as a member of the research faculty at Wistar Institute. He was not only remarkably familiar with doing serious clinical research but doing it in state institutions. Plotkin had done some groundbreaking vaccine work of his own, and his studies were not too dissimilar to Krugman's. Plotkin had invested considerable time studying rubella or German measles, a mild disease in children but far more dangerous when a pregnant mother became infected. A child born with rubella could be beset with a range of serious, incurable maladies. Plotkin's discoveries would go a long way in helping to eradicate rubella in the United States.

In 1964 and 1965, America would become part of a rubella pandemic like much of Europe. It was estimated that there were over 12 million cases in the United States, and the numbers of therapeutic abortions stretched into the thousands. Plotkin would spend years researching the disease.

One of his more provocative pieces of research concerned a series of rubella vaccine trials orchestrated at an orphanage and an institution for the mentally disabled in the mid-1960s. Those critical vaccine trials grew out of a personal tragedy; a pregnant woman became infected with the rubella virus and was encouraged to have an abortion. "The fetus was surgically aborted . . . and dissected immediately," according to a subsequent Plotkin publication, and "explants from several organs were cultured and successful cell growth was achieved from lung, skin, and kidneys. All cell strains were found to be carrying rubella virus."[71] After being put through a refinement process and several passages, the potential vaccine was tried on "adult mice" and "African green monkeys." Plotkin and his lab partners now believed the vaccine was ready for human trials were now ready for human trials.

According to one of his rubella publications, Plotkin chose to do his first human trials at the "Hamburg State School and Hospital" in central Pennsylvania in addition to "volunteer families living in Philadelphia." He would also claim to have attained "full written informed consent of parents, guardians, and relevant authorities." Children in the study were said to be "moderate to severely retarded" and ranging from "4 to 13 years of age." It was further revealed in subsequent rubella studies that Plotkin gained access to "St. Vincent's Home for Children," a Catholic orphanage in Philadelphia. His test subjects at the orphanage ranged from "1 1/2 to 3 years in age." The children were either given injections of the new vaccine or kept in a confined space with those that had received the rubella vaccine where "contact between subjects was promoted."

Neither institution was a stranger to doctors knocking on their door requesting to incorporate inmates in some bit of medical research. Both had a history of cooperation and hosting clinical trials. The choice of a Catholic orphanage is interesting; however, considering the Plotkin's rubella vaccine was derived from an aborted fetus, something church officials would typically frown upon. How much of that "Sister Agape," the Mother Superior of St. Vincent's, was informed of is open to question.[72]

Throughout the century, examples of such research would become more frequent and varied. No disease was off limits for a clinical study. In addition, researchers knew where to acquire the "fresh clinical material" needed for their studies, whatever the scientific quest or medical mystery under investigation.

For example, in 1946, doctors at the Bowman Gray School of Medicine of Wake Forrest College in North Carolina were concerned about "an unrelated disease process altering the reaction to the trichinella skin test." They decided to initiate an experiment "to determine whether a biologic cross-reaction detectable by skin test might be demonstrated in human beings."[73] Designers of the experiment determined it would be desirable to "choose one institution in which only children were in residence and one institution where only adults were confined" as their test populations. According to the designers, "an orphanage and a prison, both under close medical supervision, most nearly met the requirements."

The orphanage was the Methodist Children's Home of Winston-Salem, North Carolina, and 285 children "varying in age from 6 to 19 years were tested" for trichinella and tuberculosis reactions after being fed killed trichinella. Approximately 20% of the children eventually tested positive after being exposed to trichinella.

Another example, in 1953, Dr. Johannes Ipsen, Jr. traveled to Wrentham State School in Massachusetts, an institution formerly known as a custodial facility for the "feebleminded" and "defective boys." Ipsen performed a "series of experiments" on humans after he had performed similar tetanus potency studies on mice and guinea pigs. Ipsen's experiment was designed to determine if different manufacturers' tetanus vaccines produced different potency and effectiveness when injected in humans. According to a subsequent journal article on the project, "about 150 young men aged 15-25 years were selected" to follow mice and guinea pigs in receiving "four tetanus toxoid" injections.[74] Ipsen unlikely gave any serious thought to conducting this experiment at other educational institutions like the elite Boston Latin School and Harvard University.

Interestingly, in his account of his tetanus project, Dr. Ipsen mentions the actual "cost of organizing, injecting, and bleeding volunteers, can hardly be estimated. Such studies are usually a matter of opportunity, and the costs were, in this case, on the low side because all 128 individuals could be injected in a few hours. The measurable costs are those involving mice."[75] Though it was widely understood that institutions holding mentally and physically challenged individuals were a tremendous asset and could often supply human subjects for less cost than laboratory animals, not every researcher was willing to state it so frankly in a medical journal publicly.

A year after Ipsen's experiments, in 1954, Chicago-based doctors Louis W. Sauer and Winston H. Tucker used a total of "213 infants" in a series of dosing level studies. "132 [were] Evanston Infant Welfare children attending the Evanston Health Department Immunization Clinic," and the "remaining 81 infants [were] orphans at St. Vincent Infant and Maternity Hospital."[76] To determine the safety and efficacy of "immunization procedures against diphtheria, tetanus, and pertussis," the doctors selected healthy children from a Chicago institution that had not suffered an outbreak of any of the diseases under investigation. Dr. Sauer was an emeritus professor of pediatrics at Northwestern University, and Dr. Tucker was the commissioner of health in Evanston, Illinois. The study was paid for by a grant from the Parke, Davis Company.[77]

Researchers were far less forthcoming about their research and the reasons they chose one test population over another to participate in clinical trials. For example, in a somewhat similar non—therapeutic exercise in 1960, "26 children between the ages of 2 and 12 years of age" were given canine "distemper virus" to see if there was an immunological relationship to measles virus. After injecting the children with the dog virus, "no clinical reactions were observed." The authors would subsequently state in a journal article, "In the absence of a significant rise of measles antibody in distemper virus vaccinated children," investigators questioned, "the likelihood that significant measles protection is conferred by attenuated distemper virus."[78] It is not surprising that their article on the experiment made no mention of where the children in the study were obtained or whether parental consent was granted for the study.

During the 20th century, it did not take much convincing medical researchers to look toward vulnerable children as test subjects. With each successful discovery, researchers would become heroes while the children would soon be forgotten, a pattern repeated all too often in medical research.

CHAPTER SIX

SKIN, DIETARY, AND DENTAL STUDIES

"The Kids in These Institutions Are So Desperate for Affection."

A S A FLEDGLING DERMATOLOGY STUDENT AT THE MEDICAL SCHOOL of the University of Pennsylvania in the early 1950s, Margaret Grey Wood was mesmerized by her young, vibrant professor. Equal parts scholar, showman, athlete, and accomplished raconteur Albert Montgomery Kligman was a medical rarity. A physician-research who could entertain an auditorium filled with adoring students and wax eloquent on everything from his departmental colleagues' comedic acts and personality traits and the best restaurants to dine while in Philadelphia. Moreover, all from a man who could churn out textbooks and medical journal articles with the best of them. In addition, he was a much sought-after clinical operative for the government and pharmaceutical industry, which only enhanced his reputation as a scientific wunderkind. "His lectures were very interesting and well attended," recalled Dr. Wood.

> Kligman was very entertaining. There was always a lot of laughter in his classes. He'd make fun of everything and everyone. He could make the most serious subjects sound humorous. I remember one day he was telling us about his research at Vineland, a school for mentally disabled children in South Jersey. He was doing ringworm studies there. He'd tell us about abrading the scalp of the kids and then how he rubbed tinea capitis into the wound to create a fungus. Some of the students in the class were taken aback by Kligman's unemotional account of how he used the children for his research, but most were unfazed. I don't think he realized or cared how it all sounded. He thought it was fine using these kids this way. To further underscore his point, he told us, 'The kids in these institutions are so

desperate for affection, you could hit them over the head with a hammer, and they would love you for it.[1]

Wood, who would go on to a lengthy career in dermatology and become the first female chair of Penn's dermatology department, admits to being "quite impressed by Al Kligman" upon first meeting him. However, her veneration of the *infant terrible* of Cold War era dermatology would eventually dissipate. Though most would remain in his corner and boast of their association with one of the great minds in postwar dermatology, and some would try to replicate the master's work in their careers, others quietly withdrew from the large and passionate Kligman fan club. However, even his detractors admit to being initially impressed by his "pizazz" and "brilliance" only to be alienated by his cavalier treatment of people, his self-aggrandizing personality, or his perversion of medicine's true mission.

"I believed everything he said as a student," said Dr. Paul Gross in medical school in the late 1950s. "Kligman was brilliant and tremendously creative. He was a genius, one of the very few that is creative and original. He should have had a foundation to discuss new ideas and ways of doing things."[2]

However, another side was the often ingratiating, fun-loving medical professor who often took young, aspiring dermatology students under his wing and exposed them to the finer things in life. At a moment's notice, he could turn on you, make you the brunt of jokes, and ridicule you until you felt like a fool and outcast. However, as Dr. Wood observed, retaliation was out of the question. "He was not somebody you'd want to tangle. He had power and knew how to use it. Kligman always did what he wanted to do. He would often claim that superior people did not have to abide by the rules and regulations that most people have to live by."

"He thought he could do and say anything and get away with it," said Dr. Gross. "He was superior to the average fellow and deserved greater freedom. That was certainly the way it was in the classroom and the laboratory. Students did not question his tactics or methods. On the contrary, they were all in awe of him."

Gross concedes Kligman was an outstanding salesman for Penn's program. He was outgoing, had a million interests, and told prospective students, "You will have 10 to 15 papers published by the time you graduate. I believed everything he said as a student. He was wonderful. He took me all over, introduced me to important people, showed me how things worked." But later, Gross got wise to the act and "realized that a lot of what Kligman said was self-serving and ridiculous." Kligman wanted to impress people, entertain them, and show how brilliant he was.

Dr. Gross recounted one incident that he believed underscored Kligman's approach to research and cavalier treatment of test subjects. "I was just a med student in 1958, and Al told me to use this drug for an experiment. I had not even had pharmacology yet. Later I found out how dangerous the drug was and the fact that it was never marketed because of its dangerous qualities. Paritol causes renal toxicity; it was an experimental drug like heparin, an anti-coagulant that could really do some damage. But I did not know any better at the time. I could have killed someone."[3] Looking back at such events after the passage of several decades, Gross explained, "It was a different era then. Ethics were different. Views of such things changed as time passed."

Even more critical of Kligman than Drs. Wood and Gross is A. Bernard Ackerman, one of the world's leading dermatopathologists and a former student and protégé of Kligman's. Ackerman's path from admiring acolyte to ardent critic is well documented. "When I first met him, I believe it was at a medical conference in Miami in the mid-1960s," recalled Ackerman. "He invited me and some other prospective dermatology residents up to his suite to discuss the Penn program and its opportunities. I went up later and knocked on the door. He invited me in, and I told him what I would like to pursue. Within a few seconds, he cut me off and said, 'Come to Penn. We have acres of skin.'"[4] Ackerman did just that but soon grew to regret his decision.

Dr. Ackerman readily admits to being impressed with the Penn professor. "By virtue of his eccentric character and style," said Ackerman, "he commanded attention and respect. In the sixties, Kligman was the most interesting man in dermatology. Nobody was as dashing or as exciting. He was the figure, and he had pizazz." Ackerman admits he was "dazzled" by Kligman. Everybody was. "I was a big Kligman fan. He was famous and had a lot of style. I was prepared to go along with his line. Kligman was entertaining, fun, smart, and there were ideas."

However, it was not long after coming to Penn when another dermatologist took Ackerman aside and counseled him that all was not what it seemed. He was told his esteem for Kligman would be short-lived. "It is not going to last," Paul Gross told his young colleague. "He uses people and then discards them. Eventually, you will be quite disillusioned by your experience." Thus, it turned out, Ackerman began to detect whiffs of crass commercialism, showmanship trumping substance, and "crap" in place of true scholarship. "He did not prepare lectures," Ackerman said of Kligman, "It was all extemporaneous, right off the top of his head. He never prepared himself to teach a class. It was all made-up. All the numbers in his studies were phony. He made them up, and they were fake."

Ackerman says that what finally threw him over the edge, causing him to rethink his values and priorities, and depart Penn for Harvard was Kligman's prison operation. By 1966, when Ackerman became a resident in dermatology at Penn, Kligman directed a wide-ranging clinical research unit in the Philadelphia Prison System for fifteen years. Arguably the largest human research operation of its kind in the country, hundreds of inmates at any given time at Holmesburg and the city's two other jails were testing a wide array of commercial products including, toothpaste, detergents, deodorants, athletes foot medication, hair dyes, chocolate, diet drinks, and scores of other lotions, creams, and drugs for the pharmaceutical industry.[5] More ominous yet, was Kligman's work on behalf of chemical companies and the military.

It would eventually be discovered that in addition to his myriad clinical pursuits, Kligman was injecting inmates with radioactive isotopes, coordinating cancer studies for the tobacco industry, and applying dioxin to the faces and backs of inmates for Dow Chemical. In addition, his research was putting hundreds of prisoners through a series of debilitating mind control experiments for the U.S. Army's Chemical Corps and CIA. Yet, during his near quarter-century run as a captain of prison labor, no request seemed too outrageous, no protocol too drastic for consideration and implementation.[6]

Though young medical residents like Ackerman could not imagine the depth and breadth of Kligman's experimental ventures, what they did see was an extraordinary human laboratory where about anything could be undertaken with the approval of their ambitious and dynamic leader. Moreover, though the use of vulnerable populations for medical research was not uncommon, medical investigators rarely have carte blanche opportunity to explore the impact of dangerous substances on humans, test innovative theories, and be handsomely paid for non-university extra-curricular activities as they did at Holmesburg.

Like others before him, Ackerman was assigned an area of study, in his case dandruff, and regularly traveled from the Penn campus in West Philadelphia to Northeast Philadelphia, where the prisons were located. He gave little thought to the dramatic transformation before him; a prison turned into a medical research factory. Instead, he was focused on his studies and learning as much about skin pathology as possible at one of the nation's preeminent schools of dermatology. It was not until Ackerman took his brother, an orthodontist and dental professor, for a tour of Holmesburg that he was confronted with the harsh reality of which he had become a part.

After walking through the institution that was opened in 1895 and observing the jail's primitive condition, the tremendous overcrowding, the 1,200 poorly educated, mostly black prisoners, and the many studies underway in the Penn research unit on H-Block, Ackerman's brother soberly inquired, "Have you ever heard of the Nuremberg Code?"

That question and the serious re-evaluation it provoked of Kligman, Penn, and his goals in life resulted in what Ackerman called a "soul-searing" experience. "I had not the slightest idea what I was doing. I was new to the setup and just followed directions uncritically. There was no training in medical ethics at the time. It did not strike me at the outset, but it had a definite impact on me after time and considerable thought. I have a different view of the cosmos now."

Within months, Ackerman would abandon Penn for Harvard. It would also foster a life-long commitment to maintaining and encouraging ambitious standards of medical ethics in the practice and teaching of medicine. More importantly, when instructing his students, he would strive to be the antithesis of Albert Kligman, the entertaining "showman" and indefatigable "hero" to so many impressionable students who chose "to model themselves after Kligman."

"He pandered to an individual's worst instincts, self-interest," said Ackerman. "He turned an honorable mission, medicine, into a business. Holmesburg was the model for all to follow. Kligman orchestrated the program, rationalized its excesses and the subterfuge that surrounded its operation." Ackerman would forever educate his pathology students that "If a person is not a volunteer, really a volunteer, one cannot use them in research. It is impossible to get informed consent in a prison; the whole thing is wrong."[7]

What Ackerman and many others did not realize at the time is that the inmates of Holmesburg Prison were not the first institutionalized inmates that Albert M. Kligman found so convenient to use as test material. Even the geriatric patients he incorporated in his skin experiments at Philadelphia's Riverview Home for the Indigent came years after discovering a gold mine of research opportunity in Southern New Jersey.

Kligman had graduated from Penn State University in 1939 and went to the University of Pennsylvania, where he earned a Ph.D. in mycology. He quickly developed a reputation as an expert in fungus, and farmers in the mushroom industry began noting a new but knowledgeable name behind a series of informative journal articles. Whether due to the lack of status or money or just plain ambition, Kligman decided to jettison mushrooms and go back to school and become a physician. Graduating medical school in 1947, he quickly shifted his research interests from plant fungus to human fungus and found some ideal locales to perform his skin studies.

The State Colonies for the Feebleminded in Vineland and Woodbine, New Jersey, had a long history in hosting scientific projects and a generous spirit when researchers came calling and requested "material" for their studies. Dr. Kligman would neither be the first nor last microbe hunter to travel from New York or Philadelphia to the grim institutions in rural South Jersey. However, the studies he performed there and the journal articles that followed would launch him to the next and most lucrative phase of his controversial career.[8]

As an expert on fungus and at the time in search of "effective fungicides," Kligman recognized that institutions for "congenital mental defectives" presented "experimental circumstances [that] were ideal" for such research initiatives. Moreover, the institutions represented an opportunity for "large numbers living under confined circumstances [that] could be inoculated at will and the course of the disease minutely studied from its very onset." Furthermore, as he frankly boasted about the children's facilities, "Biopsy material was freely available."[9]

In one set of fungus studies designed to measure "the effect of severe trauma" and supported by a U. S. Public Health Service grant, Kligman took "8 children between the ages of 6 and 10" and rubbed infected hairs over an area of their scalp. On the opposite side of the child's head, "a corresponding area was first vigorously scraped with a dull knife until there was a copious exudation of serum mixed with blood. Ten infected hairs were then applied to this abraded area. These readily stuck to the site of deposition and were trapped in the crust which formed." In total, Kligman took either a "dull" or "blunt knife" to the scalps of dozens of mentally disabled children and then proceeded to anoint them with ringworm. To add insult to injury, and eerily like the infamous untreated Tuskegee Syphilis Study, "The experimentally produced lesions were not treated." Instead, he preferred to observe the fungus run its course, to the detriment of children already burdened with a horrifying set of circumstances. It should also be pointed out that Kligman did not mention gaining parental permission for the experiments or notifying the superintendent precisely what he was doing to the children.

The journal article that subsequently described this bit of medical mischief also included the comments of various medical experts. Regrettably, not one discussant objected to the fact that the study's investigator had rubbed "millions of spores" of *Microsporum Audouini* into the "traumatized" heads of numerous mentally disabled children. On the contrary, one much-respected Ivy League dermatology professor was so pleased with the experimental exercise that he commented, "The employment of human test subjects is ideal" and admitted that he, too, had once applied "fungicidal agents" to inmates at two institutions. He then advised his fellow investigators, "We have not been alive enough to the wealth of test material" in the nation's custodial institutions.[10] In addition to his position at Penn, the reviewer, Frederick Deforest Weidman, was a former president of the American Dermatological Association and vice president of the American Board of Dermatology and Syphilology. His views and endorsements carried weight.

In another ringworm experiment that tested various chemical preparations as potential treatment modalities, Kligman applied "various strengths of formalin solution to the scalps of ringworm patients." In one trial, "a tightly fitting rubber bathing cap was placed over the head of the patient and a three-inch incision made into the dome of the cap. Through the hole was inserted about six four-inch gauze squares. One hundred milliliters of formalin were poured onto the gauze. The hole was sealed with adhesive." In several cases, the "strength" of the formalin, a substance like formaldehyde considered toxic and carcinogenic, was increased. "In six cases," according to Kligman, "the individuals were exposed to full strength formalin for one hour." Regrettably, Kligman was forced to admit, "In none of these was a cure effected." However, and as a surprising admission considering the painful nature of the procedure, Kligman stated, "One child in a state mental institution was able to tolerate the formalin treatment for five hours."[11]

Once again, discussants chose not to question Kligman's choice of subjects or his questionable methods. The opposite occurred. One reviewer wanted to "congratulate Dr. Kligman for conducting this excellent study" and further stated that such research had "been overdue for many years." Not only had Kligman's work not been criticized, but it had also been held up as an "excellent" model for all to follow.[12]

During the late 1940s and early 1950s, Kligman would perform other experiments at what he termed "schools for mental defectives." These included everything from the "effect of x-rays on sebaceous glands" and inoculations of "molluscum lesions" to the probability that he had also included Vineland and Woodbine residents in a series of nail stress studies that applied "caustic agents" to children as well as "punch biopsies," and the surgical removal of children's nails."[13]

In one large study during the 1950s that utilized inmates at "prisons, mental institutions, the Army, and the general population," Kligman applied Rhus radicans and Rhus toxidendra to 2000 subjects ranging in "age from 4 to 70."[14] His quest for a preventative for poison ivy and poison oak would ultimately prove unsuccessful, but the campaign did result in a three—page spread in *Life* Magazine.[15] Furthermore, though he may have been the most prolific of his Penn colleagues concerning journal publications stemming from his research, other dermatological students and faculty traveled to various Philadelphia area institutions to practice their craft and take advantage of the "morons and imbeciles" warehoused there.[16]

Kligman's reputation would soar during the Cold War years, and he would become something of a dermatological celebrity, known for his innovative and varied research interests, his lucrative relationships with major pharmaceutical firms, and his discovery of such popular skin creams as *Retin-A* and *Renova*. Several of his peers and students came to believe he was the most famous dermatologist in the country and someone who had single-handedly turned a minor medical sub-specialty of "pimple-squeezers" into a profitable, respected profession. However, to a certain few, his critics, Albert M. Kligman represented the worst of the medical profession: physicians who were motivated by commercial and economic interests and willing to use everything and everyone to accomplish their goal.

Regardless of one's views on Kligman's career and contributions, he is arguably one of the best representatives of an unfettered research atmosphere during the 1950's, 60's and 70's that allowed medical investigators to use mentally disabled children, geriatric patients, and prison inmates as docile, unquestioning test subjects. Scholars can debate how essential elements like eugenics, economic self-interest, and utilitarianism shaped Dr. Kligman's view of human research. However, few can doubt his indefatigable, freewheeling approach to scientific investigation and the acquisition of "research material." As Kligman nostalgically said of that era, "Things were simpler then. Informed consent was unheard of. No one asked me what I was doing. It was a wonderful time" to do research.[17]

Although Kligman would perform a wide array of skin experiments, not to mention a broad spectrum of other clinical trials on prison inmates and indigent geriatric patients in coming years, he was certainly not the only physician/investigator performing skin experiments on institutionalized children. He and others were just following a long-established tradition of taking advantage of the "material" in custodial institutions to test new theories on prevention and treatment and practice various aspects of their chosen craft.

Before Kligman, researchers would use institutionalized children for a myriad of skin studies. During the 1920s, Dr. Botho F. Felden came upon the risky notion that thallium acetate, a highly toxic agent and suspected carcinogen, would be an effective treatment for ringworm in children's scalp. So, to produce alopecia to combat the fungus, Felden went to the Children's Hospital on Randall's Island in New York City and targeted 47 children with trichophytosis of the scalp. Forty-five of them were between 2 and 13 years of age.[18] "All of the children," according to Dr. Felden, "had various degrees of feeblemindedness. They consisted of morons, imbeciles, and idiots between 2 and 19 years."

Thallium acetate's toxic impact was no secret. Those who cared to read the medical literature had long known of its potency. As Drs. Swain and Bateman commented, based on their experiments in 1909, "thallium deserves to be classed among the most toxic of the elements, progressing in its physiological action with remarkable certainty and definiteness." Moreover, the authors noted, it "ranks very close to arsenic."[19]

Another doctor wrote of his investigations, "The effect of a single dose of thallium acetate is well known; about the seventh day, the hair begins to loosen, and by the fourteenth day, it comes out most dramatically. By the nineteenth day, depilation is complete."[20] Though pleased with such results, the downside for patients was many, including "joint pains," "loss of appetite," "irritability," "damage to the thyroid gland," and "achlorhydria." Some doctors, however, believed young children were "more tolerant of thallium" than older children. "My youngest patients have been one year old," boasted one physician.[21]

Felden was pleased with his results as well, though toxic symptoms did occur in his test population. Undeterred, Dr. Felden considered his experiment satisfactory and informed doctors that "thallium acetate is a valuable drug in producing epilation in children." However, he further warned them, "The indiscriminate use of thallium by those not thoroughly familiar with its indications, contraindications, and its grave toxic qualities is warned against emphatically."[22]

Years later, another physician who would claim to be concerned about healthy skin traveled to the Laurel Children's Center in Maryland and gave 50 patients with mild to severe acne the drug TriA or triacetyloleandomycin. Opened in the 1920s as Forrest Haven, the institution gradually suffered budget problems, fell into disrepair, and routinely abused and neglected residents. Many were sought out as test subjects for medical research. One doctor who traveled to the facility was Howard Ticktin of George Washington University Medical School. In "an attempt to determine the incidence and type of hepatic dysfunction relatable to the administration of TriA," Ticktin determined that after two weeks of treatment, "more than half the patients showed hepatic dysfunction."[23] Eight individuals had to be transferred to the hospital for treatment as six showed anorexia and abdominal aching symptoms, and two became jaundiced. Though that level of hospitalization should have confirmed the doctor's fears, his decision to double down and give a "challenge dose" of the medication to four of the recovering patients, and a "second challenge dose" to one subject was at the very least risky, if not wildly imprudent even by the lax medical standards of the day. However, such actions against physicians were a rarity at state facilities. That is a crucial reason doctors gravitated to such institutions to perform clinical trials. There was little fear that an untoward result or serious injury would result in legal complications.

Early in the twentieth century, doctors were befuddled with the problem of spontaneous hemorrhaging or bleeding in some newborns. As a result, medical researchers came up with some bizarre ways to remediate this dilemma. One of the "remedies" attempted consisted of the subcutaneous infusion between the shoulders and some oral doses of a gelatin solution. In one chilling case, a doctor tried to inject the gelatin into the child's rectum. Not surprisingly, the children often got very sick with toxemia-type symptoms, including fever and an increased pulse and respiration rate. The mixed results, some children died while others recovered, seemed to confirm that gelatin did coagulate the blood, but "the ineffectual use of gelatin in case 12 (where a child died) led us to do some experimental work on normal children with gelatin."[24] Those subcutaneously infused with gelatin were hospitalized for assorted reasons though they were not said to be bleeding. This small sample included a 4-year-old "feeble-minded" malnourished child, a 9-year-old, ill boy, and a 22-month-old infant. All three became quite ill from the gelatin infusions. In addition, the infant suffered "alarming symptoms of prostration and collapse, with an elevation of temperature and an acceleration of pulse and respiration."[25]

Interestingly, Dr. Isaac Abt, the innovative theorist behind this dubious project, then grew slightly defensive about the quality of the sterilized gelatin in the study. He admitted, "It was not deemed wise, however, owing to the grave symptoms of toxemia which resulted, to carry on the work any longer with children, and therefore, a few rabbits were injected." Unfortunately, the animal experiments turned out as poorly as the human trials; some rabbits died, leading Abt to believe "the explanation of the toxemia produced by the gelatin is not very far to seek when one recalls that the gelatin is manufactured from the bones of animals." In other words, Abt believed "the decomposition which takes place in these bones gives rise to cadaveric poisons . . . and these ptomains are contained in the gelatin. . . ." Incredibly, despite his admission that "it would be difficult to state what a safe dose of gelatin should be," he still "warmly recommend[ed] the gelatin treatment for the newborn infant."[26] We cannot be sure that Dr. Abt first tried his gelatin concoctions on animals before moving to humans or at least "feebleminded" children. However, he proceeded to move forward far before all the data was tabulated and his gelatin therapy had been proven safe.

Slightly more than a hundred years ago, one of the greatest plagues gripping America was pellagra. An ugly and much-feared skin disease particularly prevalent in the Deep South, the disease was characterized by the four D's—dermatitis, diarrhea, dementia, and death. During the first half of the 20th century, there were an estimated 3 million cases, with 100,000 culminating in death.[27] In 1914 alone, there were an estimated 50,000 cases, with 15,000 just in Mississippi alone. At least 10% of those resulted in death.

The medical establishment was at a loss as to pellagra's origin and treatment. The dreaded disease was characterized by a horrible red rash that would cover the face, hands, and feet and turn dry and scaly over time. Victims became physically weak, easily disoriented, and eventually suffered acute diarrhea and pronounced mental aberrations. Most doctors thought pellagra an infectious disease, while many eugenicists argued that the disease demonstrated long-standing hereditary defects aggravated by poor personal hygiene and inadequate sanitation. Frustrated by the lack of progress, one prominent public health official from South Carolina who was wedded to ancient myths and eugenicist notions described the disease as "the greatest riddle of the medical profession," and "a sphinx of which we have asked a reply and gotten none, for nearly two hundred years."[28]

The intractable scourge finally met its match in Dr. Joseph Goldberger. A wise and dedicated U.S. Public Health official drawn to science, skirted myth, and disdained eugenic propaganda, Goldberger took an extended tour of the South in 1914 to better observe the disease. He visited some of the locales that appeared most victimized and specifically examined the operations of public institutions that seemed hotbeds of pellagra. His observations were both sound and revolutionary. Most importantly, he forcefully argued, pellagra was not a contagious disease. First, institutional residents with the disease never gave it to staff members. Secondly, the disease was not directly due to poverty or defective hereditary traits, as eugenicists suggested.

So, what was behind the age-old pellagra dilemma? Goldberger targeted a dietary connection; an individual's diet made all the difference. From his travels across the South and particularly in state institutions where the disease usually ran rampant, he could not help but notice how some foodstuffs were plentiful while others were non-existent. If the disease was to be stamped out, theorized Goldberger, the first and most crucial remedial measure was to ensure that everyone had access to a complete and balanced diet. He argued for the "reduction in cereals, vegetables, and canned foods that enter to so large an extent into the dietary of many of the people in the South and an increase in the fresh animal food composition such as fresh meat, eggs, milk."[29]

However, he admitted to a "grave doubt" that his curative prescription would be taken seriously without a "practical test or demonstration" for community leaders that his theory was sound. Since pellagra did not occur in animals, human trials would be required. Goldberger knew just where to begin his studies. The Mississippi Orphans Home of the Methodist Episcopal Church South in Jackson, Mississippi, had over 200 inmates. At any given time, a quarter to a third of the institution's children displayed the red rash of pellagra across their faces and bodies. Once the facility's superintendent granted permission for the experiment based on assurances that the Public Health Service would pay for the additional foodstuffs. Goldberger went to work. He ensured the children's regular diet was augmented with supplementary items, especially fresh meat, milk, and eggs.

Not only did the orphanage's residents much appreciate the dietary changes, but their health also improved dramatically. As Goldberger would write of the historical event and scientific puzzle, "the thing works out with almost the precision of a mathematical problem." Dr. Goldberger had indeed solved the riddle of an age-old disease, but a backward, racist region of the country steeped in eugenics lore resisted his conclusions and refused to implement the necessary changes. It soon became clear that the eradication of pellagra would not come overnight. Goldberger would have to repeatedly explain and demonstrate "that animal protein in the diet cured pellagra." His most famous experiment came at the Rankin Prison Farm. Over months, "volunteer" prisoners had items withdrawn from their diet until the repugnant "red flame" of pellagra appeared across the inmates' bodies. Some nearly died in the process, but Goldberger had established that the disease was of dietary origin. Furthermore, for all his brilliance and originality, it should be underscored that even Goldberger felt comfortable using institutionalized children and prisoners as test material to prove his theories. Enlightened and intuitive when it came to medical conundrums, he fell back on the age-old practice of using the devalued to solve problems.

However, for the children of one Mississippi orphanage, a doctor's innovative medical experiment had proven both enjoyable and life-affirming. Unfortunately, not all such children in custodial institutions across the country would be so fortunate.

Doctors were not averse to incorporating the very young in clinical trials too. In Detroit in 1932, researchers working on rickets turned to the city's newest and poorest members to learn about the disease. They chose three and four-month-old infants from Detroit's Child Welfare Clinics—199 of them in total—and "all . . . free from rickets clinically."[30] They were then divided into three groups and given various combinations of evaporated milk, pasteurized milk, and cod liver oil to determine what was most and least effective in combatting rickets. In addition, the infants received monthly x-rays of their legs, a radiation regimen that doctors in the 1930s must have known was not recommended for young children.

A decade later, during the Second World War, doctors initiated several non-therapeutic dietary experiments on youngsters. One such study on young males at an institution supported by the Mead Johnson Company was designed to induce thiamine deficiency. Subjects were fed granular dough three meals a day for more than 18-months. There was no other source of nourishment. Though the investigators admitted the diet was "monotonous," they told others, "The subjects soon became accustomed to this food and ate it with every appearance of relish."[31] In addition to the extreme "diet," test subjects were repeatedly put through blood, urine, and fecal tests, plus periodic EKGs. Not surprisingly, the desired end, thiamine deficiency, did develop and anorexia and vomiting. Nevertheless, they were pleased with their results, Drs. Victor Najjar and L. Emmett Holt of Johns Hopkins moved from thiamine to riboflavin. They did a similar deficiency experiment with twelve 10 to 16 years old in an undisclosed institution for three months.[32]

During the Korean War, researchers from Texas State College and Penn State went to three orphanages to put children through a series of bread enrichment studies. The subjects ranged from 6 to 14 years in age and were fed four or five slices of bread daily that contained various enrichment levels of thiamine, riboflavin, niacin, and iron. During the 36-month study, the children were examined to gauge the impact of enriched bread being repeatedly added and discontinued from their diet. This shifting diet impacted the children's health as determined the numbers resulting from their blood, urine, and other tests.[33] Interestingly, now knowing the positive effects of enriched bread, the doctors made no great plea or effort to ensure that children would have enriched bread as a regular part of their diet.

During the 1960s, doctors at the Long Island Jewish Hospital were determined to establish if lactic acid milk products produced acidosis in newborn infants. Acidosis, the presence of excessive amounts of acid in bodily fluids, including blood, urine, and tissues, can be dangerous and cause weakened body systems, a dilemma for infants, especially those born prematurely. To assess this problem and satisfy their curiosity, they intentionally administered lactic acid to healthy premature infants to see if they did worse than other babies. Not only were various formulas given to the infants to produce acidosis, but infants also had their femoral veins punctured for blood analysis. Over seven days, 18 infants were experimentally fed lactic acid evaporated milk.

Doctors then examined how acidosis impacted the infants' carbon dioxide, plasma, blood, and lactate levels. Adding to the risky venture, doctors gave four infants intravenous injections of sodium lactate over two hours to determine if lactate levels in blood were increased. Not surprisingly, the infants proved vulnerable to acidosis. In the authors' words, "many were not capable of handling this relatively small acid load and developed acidosis."[34] Such studies were occasionally replicated, putting newborns, some as young as two days old, at risk. The surprising conclusion of all these studies: "It would seem advisable that lactic acid milks should not be used in the nursery for premature infants."[35] Moreover, the article never mentioned parental permission, a dubious prospect at best if parents understood what their babies would endure.

Putting infants through non-therapeutic ordeals for the sake of acquiring new information was far from an unusual practice. Adding to the corpus of medical knowledge was a respected pillar of the academy. Researchers gained in all manner of ways when attaching their name to an article in a respected medical journal. The rewards from such an exercise seemed so much more important, not to mention attractive than not moving forward with an exciting project due to the potential harm inflicted to the study's subjects. For example, the authors of a gastric emptying study in the early 1960s gave various solutions, including "barium sulfate" to 148 premature infants to take abdominal "roentgenograms."[36] The experiment resulted in a journal article and increased knowledge of the gastric tract. However, it is questionable if the twelve-dozen infants benefited from having their systems flushed with chemicals, not to mention the unnecessary and dangerous exposure to radiation.

The Cold War era was also a period of intense experimentation for members of the dental profession. Dentists initiated numerous studies on everything from "the effect of fluoride-containing dentifrices" and the "effects of various ions on enamel solubility" to the impact of "refined sugar" on cavity development. Consistent with the practice of their medical colleagues, a disproportionate share of these studies was undertaken at orphanages and schools for the "feebleminded."[37]

For example, one 1951 study "recognized the need for a well-controlled, long-term, individualized study of caries progression in children's teeth under conditions which would permit control of as many variables as possible."[38] When the opportunity allowed, admitted the authors, they jumped at the chance "to use subjects already living under conditions of limited regimentation. The most appropriate group for our purpose was that to be found in one of our state schools for the mentally disabled."[39]

The study, which the Sugar Research Council sponsored, included 200 children between the age of 13 and 20 whom they believed had the "capacities for adequate cooperation." To ensure they would disrupt institutional operations as little as possible, the doctors admitted the "subjects had received only minimal amounts of dental repair before the beginning of our study, and during its course, only emergency reparative services were given. Cavities initially present remained untreated and unfilled throughout the study. . . ."[40] Interestingly, the authors found the diet of the children "so deficient" that they had to alter it dramatically. While one group avoided all refined sugar, the other was "provided not less than three ounces of sucrose daily, usually as a constituent of foods, sometimes as candy which would be eaten at the table with the meal." The result of the two-year study found "no significant difference" among adolescent children when the ingestion of refined sugar was arbitrarily prohibited or was given daily in large amounts."

Other dental studies from the early postwar period till the 1980s continued to use "regimented" institutions that provided cheap and easy access to their inmates. Dental studies measuring everything from sweetened to unsweetened "ready-to-eat cereals" to "chewing gum" were commonplace during these years. A careful examination of the articles on these experiments shows that those noting parental permission and less severe confines tended to be studies that reduced cavities and gave children a choice of foods. At the same time, those in grim custodial institutions and without parent involvement conducted studies that risked producing cavities and offered a far less attractive diet to the participants.[41] The articles also occasionally disclose the corporate sponsors of the studies, such as *General Mills* in the "ready-to-eat cereal" study.

An example of another detrimental diet study that harmed children occurred in 1972 at the Lincoln State School in Illinois, where 567 institutionalized children eight and older with an IQ of 20 or more were incorporated to determine the effect of carbonated beverages on the incidence of cavities.[42] The Lincoln State School and its mentally disabled residents merged with the Illinois State Colony of Epileptics to form an inviting, if not irresistible, pool of potential test subjects. In his acknowledgment section of a subsequent article in the *Journal of the American Dental Association*, Dr. A. Steinberg, a periodontology professor at the University of Illinois College of Dentistry, gave thanks to the superintendents of the Lincoln State School, the Illinois Soldiers and Sailors Children's School, and the Glenwood School for Boys for their cooperation in allowing the studies at their institutions.

The upshot was clear; regardless of whether they were dermatologists, dentists, or nutritionists, researchers understood where to conduct clinical trials. An abundance of "test material" was available at the many children's homes and schools for the disabled. The approval of hospitable superintendents made for a cheap and convenient scholarly enterprise for those physicians interested in doing research.

Charles Davenport was the founder of the Eugenics Record Office and an indefatigable champion of the better breeding movement. Consumed by the goal of ridding society of "defectives," Davenport regularly journeyed to Lechworth Village to study abnormal inherited traits. He would initiate the castration of a "mongoloid dwarf" to augment that research. Photo courtesy of the National Library of Medicine.

Over-crowded and under-staffed state institutions for the cognitively impaired and developmentally disabled, such as this one in New Lisbon, NJ, were often inviting research sites for those physicians desirous of performing a wide range of clinical trials. Photo used with the permission of Philadelphia Inquirer Copyright 2013. All rights reserved.

One year old Mark Dal Molin with his sisters: Chris (3), Karen (4), and Gale (2). Born with cerebral palsy, Mark was placed in Sonoma State Hospital in 1958. He would die there in 1961, according to his sister's investigation of the case, after being used as a test subject in radiation studies. Photo courtesy of karen Dal Molin.

Dr. Jonas Salk, the celebrated University of Pittsburgh virologist who developed the first effective polio vaccine, coordinated some of the vaccine's early trials at the D. T. Watson School for Handicapped Children and the Polk State School. Photo used with the permission of Philadelphia Inquirer Copyright 2013. All rights reserved.

Dr. Hilary Koprowski tested his live-virus vaccine on children at Letchworth Village in 1950. Koprowski's actions shocked many of his colleagues and his use of the term "volunteer" to describe young test subjects drew critical comment from the The Lancet. *Photo used with the permission of* Philadelphia Inquirer *Copyright 2013. All rights reserved.*

Saul Krugman was an accomplished NYU virologist whose research on hepatitis from the 1950s to the 1970s would break new ground in understanding and fighting the disease. His research on retarded children at Willowbrook would also become some of the most controversial experiments of the last half-century. *Photo courtesy of the National Library of Medicine.*

When Albert M. Kligman earned his MD, he moved from plant fungus to human fungus. Much of his clinical research in the late 1940s and early 1950s incorporated children at the Vineland and Woodbine Institutions for the Feebleminded in southern New Jersey. *Photo courtesy of Allen M. Hornblum.*

Roman Catholic confirmation of Austin LaRocque and his sister Rosie at the Fernald State School in the early 1950s. Archbishop Cushing of Boston presided over the service, a rare event for the children who were provided little education but made to perform an array of menial tasks. Gordon Shattuck is at the streme right. Photo courtesy of Austin LaRocque.

Dr. Clemens Benda emigrated from Germany during Hitler's rise to power in the 1930s. He would become the Medical Director of the Fernald State School from the late 1940s to the mid-1960s. During that time he would helpt MIT establish the "Science Club" at Fernald and Pursue the causes of "mongolism." Photo courtesy of the private archives of Rev. Dr. Doe West, from her work and studies in disability rights.

Shy, withdrawn, and the son of an institutionalized paren, six-year-old Ted Chabasinski was placed in Bellevue Hospital, declared schizophrenic, and subjected to a battery of electro-shock treatments.

Lauretta Bender was one of America's leading neuropsychiatrists during the middle decades of the twentieth century. In her quest to combat childhood schizophrenia, she would become an ardent advocate of putting institutionalized children on electro-shock and LSD regimens. Photo courtesy of the National Library of Medicine.

Walter Freeman, a George Washington neurologist, would become the nation's foremost lobotomist. A disciple of Portuguese physician Egas Moniz, Freeman never lost an opportunity to proselytize the attributes of lobotomy in the fight against a wide range of psychological maladies. He once performed lobotomies on 25 women in one day. Photo courtesy of the national Library of Medicine.

Former "State Boys" Charlie Dyer, Austin LaRocque, and Gordon Shattuck reunite on the grounds of the Fernald School. As childrensix decades earlier, they were inmates of the institution, forced to work for their keep, and used as unwitting test subjects in medical experiments. Photo courtesy of Allen M. Hornblum.

CHAPTER SEVEN

RADIATION EXPERIMENTS

"The Littlest Dose of Radiation Possible."

WHEN GORDON SHATTUCK WAS BROUGHT DOWN WITH APPROXIMATELY twenty other children early one morning in 1950 for a special meeting in the boys' dormitory, there was an air of excitement and expectation in the room. Dr. Clemens Benda, the medical director of the Walter E. Fernald State School, was there along with several other people. Most of the adults present were unfamiliar to the boys, but they all looked official, important, and referred to each other as doctor or professor. They had smiles on their faces and seemed eager to talk to the boys. The Massachusetts Institute of Technology (MIT) guests were about to offer the kids at Fernald a rare treat, an opportunity few would turn down.

"This was something new and really out of the ordinary," recalls Shattuck, who was barely twelve at the time. "Most of us never had visitors, not even our parents came to see us, and to be brought down for a meeting with strangers was really unusual. It was exciting. They told us they were starting a new club, a special Science Club that would be involved with some interesting experiments."[1]

A curious and handsome boy who displayed natural leadership qualities, but not always for the best of endeavors, Gordon Shattuck had difficulty containing his enthusiasm for the new program.

Shattuck, who is now in his mid-seventies, does not recall much being said about the scientific experiments the doctors had in mind at that initial meeting. However, he and all the other boys clearly remember the mention of special events and fun-filled excursions. "We all got excited," says Shattuck. "We never got out of Fernald; we never left the institution. It was terrible in there, and now they were offering us trips to Fenway Park to see the Boston Red Sox and the Boston Braves and go to MIT for parties and tours of the college. Everybody agreed; it sounded great. I remember them saying it was going to be something like the 4-H Club. We all thought it was wonderful."

It would not remain wonderful for long. Quickly, Shattuck and many of his friends in the Science Club would come to loathe the scientific studies they were now part of, and the few incentives that were being tossed about did not come close to ameliorating their fear of the project. That feeling would only intensify over time, especially when they finally learned the truth about the Fernald medical experiments.

The Shattuck household in Marblehead, Massachusetts, was a crowded, raucous, challenging environment. There, one did not grow up as much as struggle to survive. Though it was good preparation for what Gordon and several of his siblings eventually would have to endure at Fernald and other institutions, there can be little doubt that the children would have much preferred to have grown up in a healthy, loving home.

Gordon was born on September 9, 1937, to Henrietta and Gordon C. Shattuck Jr. His father was a big, intimidating, hard-drinking man who ruthlessly ruled his ever-growing roost and did his utmost to make everyone there miserable. A six-foot four-inch, 250-pound short-order cook who worked in a series of Massachusetts diners when he was sober enough to do so, he was cursed with an addiction to alcohol, a terrible temper, and little regard for his wife and children. When he was not spending his modest wages on beer and liquor or pummeling his wife in recurring and violent domestic disputes, he managed to father a staggering twenty-two children. Gordon's mother, a besieged and occasionally bloodied homemaker with her own alcohol problems, was a baby factory. Gordon felt neglected and abused as the oldest boy in a rapidly growing and unruly household and was ever searching for parental affection.

"My father beat me all the time," Gordon says matter-of-factly. The few good times are hard to remember and pale compared to the many tough times, especially when he witnessed his mother getting physically abused. "He would come home drunk, they would argue, and then he would beat her up." Eventually, she would succumb to the pummeling and pervasive hopelessness and try to take her own life. Gordon, a young child at the time, watched in horror as his mother took a kitchen knife to her own throat. Shattuck recalls, "Blood was on her, on the floor, it was everywhere. It was terrible. She nearly died. They had to give her five transfusions."

Not long after that Gordon was first taken away from his family. The state determined that the Shattuck home was a dysfunctional, dangerous environment and no place for young children to be raised. "State ladies came," recalls Gordon, "and took six kids away. I was about five years old and went to a series of foster homes. I hated them. There was only one that was any good, most were terrible, and I often ran away. Then they would capture me, and I would be returned to the same foster family or some other people. I must have been in a hundred homes over the years and ran away as often as I could. I missed my brothers and sisters."

After many foster homes and a few institutions such as Boys Haven, a Catholic shelter for troubled boys, the Massachusetts Division of Child Guardianship decided that some of the Shattuck children needed a more rigid and structured environment. Brother Bobby and sister Dottie were sent to Wrentham State School, and Gordon was sent to Fernald.

When Gordon entered Fernald in the spring of 1947, he was just nine years old. Frightened, lonely, and desperately missing his siblings, he was about to embark on as painful and troubling a journey as one can imagine a young boy taking in postwar America. Over the next half-dozen years, Gordon Shattuck would be subject to constant verbal and physical abuse, repeated sexual assaults, and extended periods of forced labor. He contemplated escape daily.

Fernald was a large state institution housing 2,000 children and adults with a stunning array of afflictions and disabilities. The size of the place and the many severely impaired people warehoused there alarmed and frightened the boy. The institution struck him as a combination of prison and human zoo, making him miss his mother and siblings even more. Initially, he underwent a battery of physical examinations, interviews, and tests. Documents were collected from his family and various state agencies. The papers disclosed much about his life. He had weighed "9 pounds at birth . . . began to walk at 18 months . . . and talk at one year." He had the typical childhood diseases, such as whooping cough, measles, chickenpox, and German measles, and was declared healthy and sound of body. However, his psychological state and educational status were other matters.

His "peculiarity" was first noticed "when he was unable to compete in public school." Gordon spent two years in the first grade and shortly after that was "placed in a special class where he accomplished very little," and his classroom effort was described as "poor." He was further said to be "egotistical, selfish" and prone to "run away from foster homes if he is not occupied" with something he enjoys doing. It was recommended that he needed direction and a "firm hand."[2] The leadership of Fernald planned to give him that and much more.

Said to be the oldest institution serving developmentally disabled people in the Western Hemisphere, the Walter E. Fernald State School was founded in Boston in 1848 by Samuel Gridley Howe, the antebellum philanthropist, physician, and social activist. Originally known as the Massachusetts School for the Feeble-Minded, Howe was a reformer and well-known abolitionist who had previously founded a school for the blind. He was determined to establish a similar type of institution for the region's high-functioning disabled youth who were "condemned to hopeless idiocy" as they were "considered idiots by their neighbors" and destined for a life of "brutishness."[3]

Howe believed there were "between twelve and fifteen hundred" of these wretched souls in the Commonwealth of Massachusetts and actively advocated "that measures be at once taken to rescue this most unfortunate class from the dreadful degradation in which they now grovel." Howe's appeal for legislative action was based on more than sympathy and altruism; there was also an economic component. He wrote that "idiots" were "dead weights upon the material prosperity of the state," that some "were worse than useless," and many of them required "a good deal of watching to prevent their doing mischief." In the end, argued Howe, "the moral evils" of so many such people in one community was too much to disregard. "The spectacle of human beings reduced to a state of brutishness and given up to the indulgences of animal appetites and passions, is not only painful but demoralizing in the last degree." Massachusetts, he reasoned, "liberally provided for her more favored children" and even "provided education at great cost to the blind and deaf." Why, he then asked, "will she longer neglect the poor idiot—the most wretched of all who are born to her?"

Howe's remarkable campaign increased public support, and the legislature provided funds for "training and teaching ten idiotic children."[4] As time passed, the school would grow in both size and recognition. In its early years, the institution provided housing and classroom training for juveniles that included everything from music therapy, dancing, and basic housekeeping to weaving, rug making, and shoe repair. The school's success added to its problems. By the last quarter of the century, the school was under increasing pressure to accept older individuals with more severe disabilities and in need of long-term custodial care. To do so would require a larger institution and more space, so the school decamped from Boston to the distant countryside.

By the turn of the century, the school was situated in a pastoral setting along the rolling hills of Waltham and would witness a tremendous growth spurt both in terms of students and reputation under its third superintendent, Walter E. Fernald. Dr. Fernald's long tenure (1888-1924), solid and scientifically-based opinions, and growing status as an internationally recognized expert on mental illness and mental retardation placed the institution firmly on the educational map.

Walter E. Fernald, the school's third superintendent, was an internationally recognized expert on mental illness and mental retardation and placed the institution firmly on the educational map. After Fernald died in 1924, the institution would adopt his name, maintain its allegiance to a eugenics movement and philosophy that dominated a good portion of the intellectual arena in the early decades of the twentieth century, and become home to a cross-section of people with developmental disabilities.[5] It would also increasingly become home to those without physical and psychological disabilities: orphans and other children from poor, broken, or dysfunctional homes, delinquents, and people with epilepsy. Even those who scored low on IQ tests found their way to Fernald. Many of this group would become part of the free labor pool that sustained the institution when state funding did not keep pace with its ever-growing population and responsibilities. As Ransom Greene, Walter Fernald's successor as superintendent, readily admitted regarding his financial constraints, he "needed a mix of 30% morons to keep the school operating."[6] "The upper level of mental defect," Greene went on to explain, "helps in the care of those less able to care for themselves, or we would have a very much larger employee roster."[7]

Gordon and many boys like him during the 1940s, 1950s, and 1960s, such as his friends Charlie Dyer and Austin LaRocque, would become the backbone of Fernald's "inmate labor" system and representative of the "powerful financial incentive" to keep normal children on the premises. Stigmatized with the classification of "moron" after achieving a 74 in his Fernald entrance examination, Gordon, and other State Boys, as they were known, with below—average IQ tests, became the mid-twentieth century version of indentured servants, non-paid laborers critical to the institution's upkeep and performance. Every new "moron" sent to Fernald meant one less painter, one less postal messenger, and one fewer gardener overseers needed to hire.

Case records of children at Fernald meticulously charted the results of medical examinations and changes in each child's behavior. They even noted masturbation rates, weight gain, and those with whom each child associated. Gordon, for example, was described as a "pleasant, serious, attractive little boy" who was in "good health" and competent at "braid weaving and brush weaving," skills that every Fernald resident was expected to learn. However, assessments of his interests and moods would take on a darker cast as the months and years passed. He would be described as "very stubborn and sly," possessing a "very mean disposition," and "an inveterate liar" who thought "himself better than the other boys." His "habits," such a "running away," getting into "fights," and exhibiting a "saucy and defiant" attitude was regularly noted. The fact that the other boys held him in high regard—" hero worship" in the opinion of administrators—was of increasing concern.

Interestingly, for all the scrupulous attention to Gordon's "sneaky" ways, "troublesome" attitude, and displays of "antagonistic" behavior, there is no mention in his case folder of the harmful impact Fernald was having on him. The school's personnel and unforgiving practices were taking their toll. Sexual assaults by staff were practically every day, or, more accurately, every night occurrences for him and other boys. "I do not know how many times I was raped," Shattuck admits. "They would grab you out of bed at night and take you to the dayroom. Sometimes they would bribe you with candy while other times they would beat the shit out of you if you did not do what they wanted."

Gordon says attendants, many of whom turned out to be sex offenders, would pick out one of the thirty-six boys in the dormitory, take him to an unoccupied room, and then sexually assault him. "I was beat up really bad one night, "recalls Gordon. "I did not do what he wanted. It was in the winter, and he opened all the windows, made me take off my nightgown, and threw a bucket of cold water on me." Gordon says he and the other boys told Fernald officials about the assaults, "but they would not believe me. We were considered idiots, morons, and retards. No one listened to us. They knew it was going on, but they did not do anything about it. That is why I would run away. I hated that place."[8]

In addition to the sexual assaults, Gordon and most of the others designated as "morons" were forced to work in an assortment of physically demanding jobs that grown men usually did in the free world. "They put me on a weaving machine when I was nine years old," says Gordon. "I would work on it four, five hours at a time, sometimes all day. In the summers, I worked on the Fernald farm, weeding crops. We would be out in the hot sun a full day. I was not much more than nine years old, and I was working from eight in the morning until five in the afternoon. Then they would march us back to our dormitory as we held each other's hand, and then they would feed us."

The boys were treated like unpaid field hands during the growing season and performed other complex tasks the rest of the year. Charlie Dyer was thrown in the kitchen and scullery at twelve and informed he would be a meat cutter. Before that, he was a mattress maker and also spent time running a weaving machine.[9] Austin LaRocque was assigned the mailman job and spent his days going from building to building delivering letters, packages, and messages. The school had an extensive library, but boys like Gordon, Charlie, and Austin were never taught to read. Even if they had mastered the language, it is unlikely they would have been interested in reading works that Fernald had in abundance—titles such as *Eugenics*, *Safe Counsel* or *Practical Eugenics*, and *The New Eugenics*.

If the sexual assaults, work assignments more reflective of the nineteenth-century convict labor system, and abysmal living conditions were not bad enough, the institution had one more thing in store for its young, devalued residents: participation in the exciting new Science Club.

Initially, Gordon was thrilled with the notion of the club. Only a handful of special students were selected, and it seemed like an excellent opportunity to join the real world. "It sounded great," recalls Gordon, "we all got excited. It was a chance to get out of the institution."

Austin LaRocque is in total agreement. "I spent five years looking out a window waiting for somebody to visit me, waiting for somebody to come and take me on a trip. You would not believe how important that was to us at the time. When you are in a place like that, you respond to anything that you perceive to be to your benefit. Trips outside the institution were a real inducement."[10]

Their enthusiasm would not last long, however.

"They put us in a separate unit, and we were no longer allowed to associate with the other kids," says Gordon. "They kept us apart from everyone else and made us eat special foods. They made sure we ate everything on the plate. They gave us oatmeal for breakfast every morning and made sure we ate all of it. Worse yet were the needles. I hated the needles. Every morning before breakfast, they would give us a needle, take a vial of blood, and make us piss and crap in glass jars while nurses watched us. I really hated it."[11]

The boys enjoyed the occasional outings but became increasingly petrified of the needles, an everyday occurrence. Whether the doctors were extracting blood or injecting them with some unknown concoction, the entire exercise had lost its appeal. Gordon finally told the doctors and nurses he had had enough; he wanted out of the Science Club.

To Gordon's alarm, he would not be allowed to drop out of the program. "I refused to take another blood test," he says. "They told me if I did not let them take blood, they were gonna put me in seclusion. I said I did not care; I did not want any more needles."

True to their word, the doctors and Fernald administrators put Gordon in Ward 22, a building with six special punishment cells in the basement known to Fernald residents as the jail. "They put me in a little room with bare walls and an old ratty mattress and a can to piss in," says Gordon. "There were no windows except for a little pane of glass in the door so people could look in and check to see what you were doing. For the first few days, they just gave me bread and water. Then they came and asked me if I was ready to rejoin the Science Club, and I told them no. I was not going back; I did not want any more needles."

Gordon spent several more days in seclusion. By the eighth day, however, he had been worn down. When the authorities again asked if he was willing to rejoin the program, he conceded. The doctors sweetened the pot by promising to take him and the other club members to a baseball game.

"I did not want to do it," Gordon says regretfully of his decision, "but I said okay. I was just a little kid. What could I do?" Study organizers may have downplayed the burden on participants, but children quickly recognized the time, isolation, and discomfort associated with it. Eventually, documents showed that a test subject would have to endure six blood samples and four urine samples between early morning and two-thirty in the afternoon.[12]

Gordon Shattuck was not the only State Boy to demonstrate defiance regarding participation in the Science Club. Others lost their enthusiasm for Fernald's version of the 4-H Club. One of these boys was Gordon's friend Charlie Dyer. Also, with a below-average IQ and from a broken home, he was just entering his teenage years, and the new club seemed like a welcome diversion from the tedium and routine of institutional life. "I jumped at the chance to get in the Science Club," Dyer readily admits. "I would do anything to get out of Fernald, even for a day."

However, his interest in the program quickly waned, and it soon became something he feared and despised. Like Gordon, he wanted to leave the club. He told the doctors and administrators that he wanted to return to his original ward and end his association with the Science Club. Dyer was stunned and angered when told he could not withdraw; he had signed on and would have to remain involved until the program concluded. The next time the doctors and nurses went to take his blood, Charlie would not let them. They, in turn, would not let him leave the building and continued to chase after him for a blood draw. The battle of wills resulted in something no one at Fernald had ever seen before: Dyer climbed up a support column toward the ceiling and shimmied across a crossbeam high above the floor. Doctors, nurses, school attendants, and institutional residents pleaded with him to come down, but Dyer refused. He was determined not to go back to the Science Club. Dyer said that even though he feared heights, he "climbed up there to get away from those needles."[13]

The standoff lasted for hours, and with each passing hour, the staff grew more frantic. Finally, after four excruciating hours, Dr. Malcolm Farrell, then superintendent of Fernald, was brought in and talked Charlie Dyer down.

Visions of a twelve-year-old boy falling thirty feet to his death shot through everyone's mind, but for all their threats, promises, and words of encouragement, Charlie refused to climb down. Moreover, just like Gordon Shattuck, he was forced to remain in the Science Club, eat his morning oatmeal, give blood, and continue to do his business in glass jars.

Eventually, many State Boys would put the Science Club and the Fernald Training School behind them. After their release from the institution—usually in their late teens and early twenties—they made their way in life by getting jobs and earning a living, getting married and having children, and doing the best they could after being dealt a bad hand by their parents and the state. Recognizing that they had lost any semblance of a normal childhood and bore the stigma of being officially declared morons was not easy; nor was the challenge of going through life unable to read, but many persevered, and their struggles paid off. They became contributing members of society, and few who met them could ever imagine the horrors they had endured. The acclimation process was far from easy, however. The famous century-old state institution had not prepared its graduates to enter society.

"When I finally got out of there at the age of twenty," says Charlie Dyer, "I could not read and had a hard time functioning. They never taught me anything. I did not even know what money was. I had worked all my life but never got paid for anything." He was not alone. "I did not know what to do," says Austin LaRocque of his release from Fernald. "I never rode on a bus before. I did not know how to use money. I did not know what money was. I was totally unprepared to make my way in the world."[14]

But Charlie, Austin, and Gordon did make their way in the world only to receive one last shocking blow, a blow that harked back to their days in the institution in Waltham. On the day after Christmas in 1993, the *Boston Globe* published a front-page story that shocked local citizens and reverberated throughout the country. The banner headline, "Radiation Used on Retarded," and the subtitle, "Postwar Experiments Done at Fernald School," would jumpstart a media frenzy that would last many months, launch both state and federal investigations into the origin and reasons behind the experiments, and spark a national debate about medical research in America.[15]

"In the name of science," the lengthy article began, "researchers from MIT and Harvard University [had] retarded teenage boys" at the Fernald School "eat cereal mixed with radioactive milk for breakfast or digest a series of iron supplements that gave them the radiation—equivalent of at least 50 chest X-rays." News of the studies funded by Quaker Oats and the US Atomic

Energy Commission sparked headlines, widespread debate, and a good bit of moral outrage. Some argued that the experiments exposed the true "face of evil," people in authority who were "infected by opportunism and arrogance" and cavalierly exploited defenseless children. Others claimed that the experiments "yielded important information about nutrition" and that no one was harmed "because the radiation levels were so low."[16]

Almost immediately, the State Boys themselves were inundated with media requests. The former neglected New England waifs were now media celebrities. "I started getting calls and visits from the *Boston Herald* and the *Globe*," said Gordon Shattuck. "All the North Shore papers wanted to talk to me as well as the radio and TV stations. Even *People Magazine* wanted to talk to me. They all came to my house and asked what I thought about the revelations now coming out concerning secret medical experiments at Fernald. I told them it was pretty shocking, and I was beginning to wonder how long I had to live. That stuff is in your body, and you do not know what it can do."[17]

During the coming days and weeks, investigative stories, editorials, and lengthy op-ed articles on the Fernald story would become de rigueur for news gathering agencies across the country. The public interest would continue to build as the media became preoccupied with "retarded boys" being used as "human guinea pigs" in dangerous "radiation tests."[18] The *Boston Globe* underscored the inexcusable "wrongness and arrogance" of MIT and Harvard, two of the most influential educational institutions in the country, using "retarded children" for a series of questionable medical experiments.[19]

A couple of months earlier, the Albuquerque Tribune published revelations concerning eighteen unwitting hospital patients injected with plutonium in the late 1940s. With this new report, relatives of the victims and average citizens became aware of scary stories concerning strange Cold War scientific experiments and official investigations that were now being initiated to discover the truth.[20] Phillip Campbell ordered one such investigation, the Massachusetts Department of Mental Health Commissioner, who admitted to his "shock and horror" on reading the initial *Boston Globe* story of the Fernald experiments. He immediately decided to establish a task force to "fully disclose and research activity at any [DMR] facility that involved the use of radioactive substances."[21]

The fifteen-member Task Force on Human Subject Research, which included lawyers, academics, and a member of Congress as well as two former members of the Fernald Science Club, set to work. They established an 800-telephone line to enable individuals to request information, comb documents and archival material in Fernald's extensive library, and seek and receive

the full cooperation of Harvard and MIT in their search for relevant information. In its effort to answer the question "How could it have happened?"
the task force examined the history of guardianship and wards of the state
during the middle decades of the twentieth century and the development of
the concept of informed consent during those same years. It tried to build a
narrative of the Fernald experience from the actual individuals, the residents
themselves.[22] The narrative proved both illuminating and depressing as former
Fernald residents spoke of emotions running the gamut from disillusionment
to moral outrage. Charles Dyer, for example, recounted for the investigative
committee that when he first entered the school, he thought he would "learn
and maybe better myself." As the days and weeks turned to months and years
"with little understanding" as to why he was there, he realized that "it wasn't a
school for learning but in fact an institution for the mentally retarded." He said
he witnessed abuse routinely perpetrated on residents and provided numerous
examples, such as "an employee burning a mentally retarded child with a lit
cigarette." The experience did not leave him unaffected. "My bitterness then
turned to rebellion," Dyer admitted.[23]

In fact, for most Fernald residents, particularly those who were profoundly
disabled and intellectually challenged, life was much worse than it was for the
Science Club boys. Neglect and abuse were a way of life, and graphic eyewitness
accounts of the institution's appalling practices rightfully disturbed task force
members. One distraught mother who took her severely mentally disabled five-
year-old daughter to Fernald in 1947 spoke of her great regret "and wondered
how I ever parted with my only child."

She told of her daughter being so heavily medicated that she could not
hold her head up. "The bare rooms with cement floors" were routinely "hosed
down to remove the urine and feces," and overcrowding resulted in "very large
ward-like rooms with many beds only inches apart." More troubling by far were
her daughter's recurring injuries: "skin tore off both sides of her face, neck, and
back;" being found "bloody each morning;" and a "head wound" that resulted
in a skull depression requiring several stitches without the mother getting an
explanation about what had happened.

Another guardian spoke of his care for a young girl with Down syndrome
and was placed in Fernald in the mid-1960s. One of the many indignities,
injuries, and examples of indifferent care the young girl was subjected was the
decision of the institution's medical staff, without informed consent, to "extract
all her teeth" so she would "not be bothered with tooth decay and cavities." For
the rest of the girl's life, she would be forced to "eat pureed or ground food."[24]

Commission members heard many additional stories, such as one of "the girl found at the bottom of the pool because someone neglected to take a headcount; the girl who wandered out of her building and died in a culvert from hypothermia; and the girl who received blows to the head from a male caretaker" because she soiled herself and then smeared her feces on the school's floors and walls.[25] Such personal stories underscored Fernald's miserable living conditions, overall neglect, and dubious decision-making. They may have provided the answer to why Harvard and MIT chose to do their experiments there.

The association between Fernald and the two elite Boston academic institutions began after World War II when the National Biochemistry Laboratories at MIT sent a detailed letter to Dr. Malcolm Farrell, superintendent of the state training school in Waltham. In the letter, Robert S. Harris, an associate professor of nutritional biochemistry, said they were interested in conducting a clinical study at Fernald on the role of "phytates upon mineral metabolism."[26] Phytates are stored forms of phosphorous found in grains, seeds, nuts, and many cereals, and "considerable disagreement" had arisen regarding their impact on nutrition. Harris explained that some nutrition experts advised against using large amounts of cereal products in the diet because their phytates interfered with calcium metabolism. Harris wanted to establish the effect of phytates on iron metabolism.

He explained that earlier measuring devices were too crude for such delicate and precise scientific detective work, but the "recent production of radioactive materials by cyclotron bombardment offers a new tool for the study of materials." It would now be possible "to tag iron atoms, combine the iron into a compound, feed it and follow its metabolism in the body."

Recognizing the potential harm of radioactive material as well as the heightened concern about such matters just a few short months after the atomic bomb blasts in Hiroshima and Nagasaki, Harris assured Farrell that "very minute quantities of a radioactive substance are required, and the radioactive emanation from this substance is also extremely small." It would be no more harmful than "the cosmic rays continually bombarding people living at the altitude of Denver, Colorado," he explained. To further underscore that there was nothing to worry about regarding the quantities of radioactive substances the scientists planned to use, Harris cited experiments involving "more than 100 medical students." He indicated it had proved harmless over a two-year study period and similar results in "clinical investigations at Rochester Medical School" where much more significant quantities of radioactive compounds were being used.

Harris explained that they had planned to use rats in their experiments, but rodents differed radically from humans in how they metabolized iron and phytates. Researchers thus believed that it would be necessary to use humans for the experiments, preferably subjects during active growth. Additional constraints, such as the need for the subjects to remain in the study for its entirety and the need for a uniform diet, provided further advantages of Fernald as a test site. Its proximity to MIT's labs, where the blood would be analyzed, was also in its favor.

Harris then described each of the five experiments occurring over eight weeks and the need for ten or fifteen subjects. He also mentioned in passing that if there were any way to reward the subjects, they would be glad to do so.

Over the next several weeks and into the early days of 1946, letters were exchanged between MIT, Fernald, the Massachusetts Department of Health, and the latter's Committee on Psychiatric Education and Research, which had oversight responsibilities for such a venture. Clifton T. Perkins, the department commissioner, had already signed off on the scientific exercise, stating, "I see no objections to your selecting the fifteen or so patients" in preparation for the research project, which would start in early February 1946.[27]

By midsummer, MIT scientists had concluded that phytates impair iron absorption and that this interference is much greater when phytates are administered in solutions as opposed to food. The data had been collected using eighteen children between the ages of ten and fourteen who were fed equal amounts of iron at breakfast. It was also mentioned that their milk, oatmeal, and water were "laced with radioactive material."[28]

Harris went back to Fernald in 1949 and entered discussions with Dr. Clemens E. Benda, the institution's new medical director, requesting permission to replicate the exercise, this time experimenting on radioactive calcium metabolism. As with the earlier study, Harris explained that metabolic investigations of this sort were "difficult to conduct on human subjects," but that radioactive calcium now made it "possible to obtain information on calcium retention promptly at little inconvenience to the subject."[29]

Harris explained that "radioactive calcium (Ca 45) will be administered to adolescent children" in their oatmeal and milk at breakfast. He believed "at least 20 normal subjects will be necessary," but there was "no limit on the number of abnormal subjects that may be studied." By "abnormal," he specifically meant a class of children and adults who were in abundance at Fernald: "cretins, mongoloids," and others with rare developmental maladies whose calcium metabolism was believed to be abnormal.[30] Each subject would participate in two test periods, possibly more. Each test meal would contain the minimum amount of radioactive calcium required to test the hypothesis.

Consistent with gaining authorization from the Atomic Energy Commission (AEC) to acquire radioactive material, the Walter E. Fernald State School established an Isotopes Committee to oversee handling the material and the nature of the research. The five-member committee consisted of five physicians, four employed at the school. The fifth and lone outsider was an instructor at Harvard Medical School.[31] No one on the committee had concerns about the nature of the experiment, who the subjects would be, or the level of radioactive material the subjects would receive.

Without question, the one person on the committee who should have had the most concern about the proposed MIT study's nature and potential health impact was Fernald's medical director, Clemens Ernst Benda. The son of a German pathologist, Benda was born in Berlin and studied philosophy and medicine at the Universities of Berlin, Jena, and Heidelberg before receiving his medical degree in 1922. He spent his early years as a medical practitioner in clinics in Berlin and Heidelberg. In 1935, Benda and his wife, also a physician, and their two young sons, immigrated to America because of Hitler's rise and the growing political instability in Germany.[32]

Benda settled in Boston and became director of the Wallace Research Laboratory for the Study of Mental Deficiency at the Wrentham State School. In 1947 he would become the director of research and clinical psychiatry at Fernald and remain there until his retirement in 1963. Benda held several academic appointments at respected institutions, including Harvard Medical School, Clark University, Massachusetts General Hospital, Tufts Medical School, and Boston University School of Theology. He would also serve as president of both the American Association of Neuropathologists and the American Academy of Mental Retardation. Benda's research interests focused on Down syndrome (commonly known as mongolism at the time), cretinism, mental retardation, neuropathology, and existential psychology, and psychiatry.

During their time at Fernald and for many years afterward, the State Boys would speculate about Benda's numerous research projects and recount stories of strange experiments, secret autopsies, and unmarked graves in cemeteries filled with former Fernald patients. Lurid anecdotal accounts of dozens of dissected brains in glass jars and Benda in photographs with Nazi uniformed officers would only increase after the 1993 Science Club revelations.[33]

Though Benda and his colleagues quickly approved the MIT protocol and saw little concern, the AEC sought revisions. The AEC's Subcommittee on Human Applications expressly stipulated "that only one dose of Ca 45 be administered to each normal child used in the study" and "no subject will receive more than one microcurie:"[34] the study had proposed two microcuries, which was equal to two grams of radium isotope. S. Allan Lough, the chief of the Radioisotopes Branch of the Isotopes Division, passed on the news of that restriction to Robley Evans of MIT and Clemens Benda of Fernald: The radioactive material was dangerous, and exposure to too great a level of the material could harm "normal children." Those deemed "abnormal" did not warrant the same level of concern, and restrictions on their involvement in the studies were loosened.

Correspondence between the AEC and Benda during the fall of 1949 would underscore that point and illuminate the inexperience of Fernald's medical personnel in handling radioactive substances. Lough would be forced to emphasize that normal patients would receive radiocalcium "one time only."[35]

Lough stated that the Fernald experiments should use the "minimum amount of Ca 45 which would provide significant scientific data in each test" and that no subject should be administered more than "one microcurie" of the radioactive material. The only leeway Lough was willing to grant concerned the number of tests in which individual subjects could participate. "Normal control subjects" could "be used in one test only with the minimum possible Ca 45." According to Lough, others, meaning "mentally deficient subjects," could "be used in more than one test" as long as the other guidelines were followed.[36]

Robley Evans assured Dr. Paul Aberhold of the AEC that the level of radiation exposure each child would receive could be accomplished "without going above trivial dosage levels." He then explained four simple approaches to the experiment to ensure that the doses would be harmless to subjects.[37] Evans's letter of support helped win AEC approval for the project and begin the next phase of the operation. Eventually, seventeen children would take part in the iron study.

Letters that went out to parents from Superintendent Malcolm J. Farrell notifying them of the forthcoming MIT research study emphasized that the Fernald School was interested in nutrition and that only some brighter patients would participate in the project. Farrell went on to underscore the enriched diet that study participants would receive and noted that each child would exhibit "gains in weight and other improvements, particularly in the blood." He concluded his pitch for parental permission by stating: "Rest assured that I feel this project will be of great importance [and] eventually will be of considerable benefit to mankind."[38]

As time passed and the human research program grew to become an established part of Fernald operations and culture, additional experimental requests would be submitted and granted. For example, in the spring of 1953, Harris would inform Benda that the Department of Food Technology "planned to conduct a study of five different calcium compounds in human subjects" and requested access to "fifteen subjects." Ten subjects had already been secured, but thorny problems still needed to be resolved. Three of the subjects "objected to being included in the study," and five others had already been used in experiments and dosed with radioactive calcium, so they could not be utilized. Harris and his medical colleagues were seeking "fresh subjects" for tests in which "each subject [would] receive one microcurie on each of five experimental tests."[39]

The request and the protocol are troubling; three years earlier, the AEC had stipulated that no subject should receive more than one microcurie and that only the mentally deficient could participate in more than one test. Either the rules had changed, and no such written record can be found, or physicians were taking liberties with the protocol.

Harris went on to impress upon Benda the importance of the study and his hopes that test subjects could be obtained. He appealed to Benda, asking that the "three subjects who objected to being included in the study can be induced to change their minds."[40] Such inducements for vulnerable children meant verbal threats and institutional pressure. If that did not work, punishment, doing time in the Fernald "jail," isolation from their friends, and a bread-and-water diet were imposed until they agreed to join the program.

The fact that subjects were opting out and boys now needed to be induced to participate reminded Harris that they had "neglected the Fernald Science Club." Harris suggested a baseball game excursion and a follow-up assembly to explain the doctors' work to get the boys "to feel satisfied their small pain is really worthwhile."[41] Unfortunately, many of the boys now viewed an increasingly rare trip to the ballpark as too modest a reward for the onerous burden of participating in the Science Club.

It is an open question about how many of the boys' parents knew about the experiments; fifty-seven subjects participated in the calcium studies, most taking the radioisotopes orally while several received injections. According to Gordon Shattuck, his parents were never informed and were unaware of his involvement in a science club or his use as an experimental test subject. Nor was his name on documents representing those whose parents had signed off on their child's participation in the project. Records do show, however, that some parents were sent notices from Benda informing them that the "nutritional department of the Massachusetts Institute of Technology" was performing "some examinations" designed to "improve the nutrition of our children."[42]

Though the one-page letter cast a positive spin on the enterprise, the test was nontherapeutic and would not benefit the boys in the study. Benda completely omitted some crucial aspects of the study, such as the use of radioisotopes, and altered other aspects of making the exercise appear either less threatening or directly beneficial to the boys. For example, according to the letter, "volunteers" would give "a sample of blood once a month for three months." In truth, blood was drawn from the test subjects far more frequently.

Benda's letter cast the research project in an innocuous, if not valuable and festive, light. Study participants would receive such privileges as a "quart of milk daily," trips to baseball games, the beach, and outside dinners. In short, according to the letter's author, the participants "enjoy it greatly." Benda told parents to rearrange their vacation plans so that test subjects would not leave the institution during a critical stage of the research.[43] Fernald medical personnel-maintained files on each research subject, including whether parental permission for their child's participation had been received. Some documents identified who had granted permission, and others disclosed personal information about the test subjects.[44] In several cases, "no relatives" was handwritten after a subject's name, meaning he was declared a ward of the state. This designation gave the superintendent total control over a boy's fate.

As Benda became more confident of his authority and more experienced in his position as Fernald's medical director, he expanded his scope of research. He embarked on some projects that would give considerable pause today.[45] One of the more ghoulish projects was Benda's desire in September 1953 to use a very sick child for a calcium metabolism experiment. This would require giving "a dose of 50 uc Ca 45 to a moribund gargoyle patient." (The terms "gargoyle" and "gargoylism" were commonly used in the medical community during the first half of the twentieth century to describe Hurler-Hunter syndrome, a degenerative disease of the nervous system associated with dwarfism, extreme disfigurement, and death by the age of ten). In his request letter to the AEC, Benda claimed that the ten-year-old boy had "suffer[ed] from this severe metabolic disorder since birth but [was] going progressively downhill at present." The patient was considered to have only a "few months" to live, and Benda urged "prompt consideration" of his request so his research could begin without further delay.[46]

He bolstered his argument by reminding the AEC of his three-and-a-half-year experience of conducting calcium metabolism studies with MIT researchers and noting that permission had previously been granted to other medical investigators "for the use of higher doses administered to moribund patients."[47]

The study was never completed due to the patient's death on day 16 of the study. Interestingly, despite injecting the boy with a significant amount of radioactive material, the authors of the journal article detailing the study expressed their "appreciation to the staff of the Walter E. Fernald State School who nursed this patient with skill, self-sacrifice, and patience."[48] Though one cannot be sure, it is unlikely that Benda or anyone else at Fernald informed the young boy's parents what they had in mind for their terminally ill son.

The level of knowledge government officials had regarding medical research projects at Fernald and throughout the rest of the commonwealth's mental health system is unknown. However, there are some indications that they periodically sought out such information. For example, in 1956, Dr. Jack R. Ewalt, commissioner of the Massachusetts Department of Mental Health, informed institutional superintendents throughout the state that "the Governor and some members of the legislature expressed interest in the kinds of research going on in our institutions." Eighteen months had passed since the last information had been provided, and Ewalt was requesting another accounting.[49]

Outside of the handful of former State Boys who are around to tell their story, few witnesses or researchers are alive from the early years of the Fernald experiments clinical trials that would eventually stretch over three decades. One of the very few who was present at the program's inception and has remained steadfast in his conviction that the experiments were unassailable scientifically and safe from a health perspective is Dr. Constantine Maletskos. Widely sought out by the media at the time of the Fernald revelations in 1993, Maletskos assured everyone, "I feel just as good about it today as the day I did it. The attitude of the scientists was we are going to do this in the best way possible." Those chosen as test subjects would receive "the minimum radiation they could possibly get and have the experiment work."[50] Little has occurred since those remarks to alter his view that MIT's research at Fernald was ethically sound, of scientific merit, and done with the utmost care.

In a series of interviews with the authors of this book in 2011, Maletskos underscored his chief concern at the time—that the test subjects receive "the littlest dose of radiation possible" to ensure that no one was harmed, but still sufficiently large to accomplish the goals of the study. The issue was to "better understand young kids and digestion" was the crux of the study.[51]

Maletskos was a graduate student researching at MIT's biology department when Robley Evans selected him to help coordinate the Fernald study. Maletskos felt honored to be chosen to work on a project of significance. It was an exciting time at MIT. Many scientific investigations were underway, and human experimentation was part of it. On the advice of Karl Compton, another giant in the nascent field of nuclear physics and the president of MIT, Evans was recruited after the war to head up MIT's nuclear physics department and oversee constructing one of the nation's first cyclotrons. There was an "explosion of interest," says Maletskos, in nuclear issues, its implications for science, and how it would affect humankind in the postwar years.

And test subjects were not misused. "We treated the kids great," said Maletskos, recalling his interactions with the children. He would spend many years in scientific research, train doctors to use radioactive material, and eventually do similar isotope studies on the elderly. Maletskos remembers Clemens Benda as more than competent; "he was a smart cookie," somebody who knew his business. "We wanted to know how people metabolize certain minerals like iron and calcium. We needed a controlled population for the study," said Maletskos, describing a group that could be confined, monitored, and fed quickly, and one in which urine, feces, and blood could be regularly collected.

"Everybody was trying to do the job right," recalls Maletskos of the mindset that pervaded the study. "I did not know the Nuremberg Code. The Code had little to no impact. I do not recall it being taught in school or mentioned in classes. There were no rules at the time; I had to make my own rules as I went along. I had to set my standards and believed the littlest you can use [radioactive isotopes] to gain the information you want, the better. I did it just that way; I was measuring very low amounts of radiation. But it worked, and we got some nifty numbers."

However, after many decades, Maletskos admits yester-year's standards do not measure up to contemporary rules and expectations regarding clinical research. "I can see in retrospect it was not right," he now says. The research from Maletskos's early nutrition studies at Fernald would eventually be published in four scientific journal articles in the early and mid-1950s.[52] If anyone reading the articles thought there was something objectionable about using institutionalized, mentally challenged children as test subjects in experiments incorporating radioactive material, there is no record of it. As Maletskos says, it was an era that downplayed or was oblivious to rules, regulations, and ethical constraints; researchers had wide latitude in crafting and orchestrating their research protocols.

More than a decade would pass before Henry Beecher published his groundbreaking piece in the *New England Journal of Medicine*, illuminating colleagues' ethical lapses in the conduct of their research.[53] During much of that time, the Fernald Training School and Wrentham, its nearby sister institution, would continue to host medical experiments using their wards as accessible and compliant research material.

Throughout the 1950s and 1960s, thyroid studies focused on researchers' interest in the two institutions. To better understand how the thyroid gland functioned, a series of experiments was initiated incorporating radioactive iodine as a tracer to track and monitor the passage of iodine in the body. Interestingly, the studies utilized Fernald residents and their parents and residents of Wrentham. Studies that focused on one specific congenital disability were not unusual. In the mid-1950s, for example, researchers from Harvard Medical School and Beth Israel Hospital traveled to Fernald to administer "70 microcuries of . . . radioactive iodine" to "21 mongoloid subjects" ranging in age from five to twenty-six.[54]

However, the Massachusetts Commission investigating the Fernald experiments discovered that "the amount and type of tracer materials used went beyond the minimal tracer levels of the earlier nutritional research studies" and demanded immediate follow-up examinations of the former test subjects.[55]

The Massachusetts Investigative Task Force found one study particularly troubling. The 1961 study of children at Wrentham was designed to determine the amount of regular iodine that had to be added to children's diets to block the radioactive iodine uptake they might be exposed to from nuclear fallout after a nuclear attack or accident. This study had definite military overtones and was subsequently referred to as a "Cold War experiment." The task force also learned that "the results of this study were actually referenced at a 1989 European conference after the nuclear accident at Chernobyl."[56]

Seventy young children at Wrentham participated in this study, all between one and eleven years of age. According to task force findings, over sixty of the children were given daily dietary supplements of sodium iodide, and others received separate doses every two weeks for three months. In total, each of these subjects received eight microcuries of radioactive iodine. The task force members assumed that other subjects in the study had received similar doses. According to the task force, the study's designers "chose this population of children because it was desirable to secure children living under constant conditions of environment, diet, and iodide uptake."[57] The Wrentham study was coordinated by researchers from Harvard Medical School, Massachusetts General Hospital, and the Boston University School of Medicine. It was supported by the Radiological Health Division of the US Public Health Service.

Subsequent studies at Wrentham during the mid-1960s included dozens of children between the ages of one and fifteen who had Down syndrome and other forms of mental retardation. One study was designed to test the thyroid function in children with Down syndrome and compare it with normal children.[58] Additional studies were undertaken at Fernald and Wrentham that measured thyroid function in both myotonia dystrophica, a severe chronic neurological disorder, and Down syndrome. Benda, who spent years exploring the cause of "mongolism" and its relationship to thyroid dysfunction, was the lead author of the myotonia dystrophica study with Constantine Maletskos.[59]

The task force collected the opinions of several experts regarding the short- and long-term health effects of exposure to radioactive tracers. Calling them "minute amounts (less than one-billionth of an ounce) of radioactive iron and calcium" and often comparing radiation exposure levels to those of people living in different geographic locations, flying in airplanes, and having diagnostic medical and dental X-rays, the experts agreed that the likelihood of any of the test participants developing cancer was minimal. However, the most significant risk of leukemia resided with those young children who were part of the thyroid gland studies.[60] The experts did, however, have serious reservations about the "informed consent" aspect of the studies and agreed that the experiments would "not be permitted today even with the low radiation doses that were used and informed consent of parents or guardians."[61]

Regardless of the reassurances from the health experts, many of the former State Boys who were part of the Science Club remain distrusting of the medical community, concerned about the fair chances of long-term health damage from the experiments, and convinced that much more went on at Fernald that was never uncovered. "The report said we were not hurt by the study," said Joseph Almeida, who spent his youth in Fernald and is outspoken in his denunciation of its treatment of children. "They worked for the state. What do you expect them to say?"[62]

"There were people buried out there in paupers' graves beyond the farm," said Gordon Shattuck. He continues to decry the institution's cavalier use of children in various medical experiments over the years. "They just put 'em in the ground in a pine box. They killed them. Benda was working on them all the time. They died from the medical experiments."

As Austin LaRocque told us, "Fernald ruined a lot of kids' lives. They were the worst years of my life. They stole my childhood."

"We were told we were morons and idiots all the time," said Charlie Dyer. "Nobody wanted us or cared about us. They just used us for whatever they wanted or needed done."

The state investigative task force issued its final report in the spring of 1994. However, it received decidedly less media coverage and public interest than Fernald's original abuse allegations.

Surprisingly, the report omits any questions regarding the scope of the investigation. The commission only examined medical research incorporating radioactive isotopes. Was no one curious about the possibility of other types of medical research occurring at Fernald over the years? During the era of unrestrained research, institutions housing vulnerable populations were a treasure trove of investigative opportunities for medical researchers and pharmaceutical companies. One trial invariably led to a second, and then a third, and soon, a cottage industry of medical research was in full bloom with too many players benefiting the practice to be curtailed. For Fernald to have escaped this typical pattern would be unusual.

Sandra "Sunny" Marlow, the librarian at the Howe Library at Fernald who is credited with discovering the papers disclosing the school's long association with medical researchers and the radioactive tracer studies, said she was not impressed by the commission's data collection effort. In short, "They were not particularly aggressive in collecting information."[63]

More damning yet is the account of Dr. Doe West, a former chaplain at Fernald and the Massachusetts Task Force report coordinator. She expressed reservations and regrets the parameters placed on the investigation. West believes she had discovered evidence of "earlier studies at Fernald," more than rudimentary diet research incorporating radioactive isotopes. "There was clearly more going on than Cream of Wheat versus Quaker Oats," says West.[64] However, she was informed in no uncertain terms that nutrition studies and the use of radioactive material as tracers would be the focus of the investigation. Anything other than that was to be jettisoned. Curiously, no one, neither lawmakers, citizens, or members of the task force nor even patients' relatives, protested the narrow scope of the investigation.

Three decades have passed since West performed the many daily duties of coordinating a state-authorized investigative commission. However, she still expresses regret that a more comprehensive study was not undertaken. "There was massive proof that Fernald was ground zero for a wide spectrum of maladies," says West. "The researcher/doctor role was blurred, and doctors used the school as a training ground" for students and research projects. "Doctors wanted to come there to do their research. It was convenient," and it also had "affiliations with top schools and parents who were desperate or disinterested. They did not challenge authority."

Though the Fernald story is one of the more poignant and better-documented cases from the Cold War era, it pales compared to many other experiments that placed institutionalized children at even greater risk. By deceiving parents with incomplete and misleading claims, pitching seductive offers to disadvantaged and affection-starved children, and punishing those who chose not to participate, physicians circumvented moral principles for the sake of convenience and their conception of the greater good. Eugenics and the Cold War had contributed significantly to developing a flexible moral landscape that rewarded utilitarian action over ethical restraint.

Regardless of whether clinical trials during the Cold War were designed to learn more about radiation or the nature of the disease, institutions holding impaired and orphaned children often became the epicenter for investigational studies. The Manhattan Project and the extraordinary campaign to build the world's first atomic bomb during World War II touched off a frantic effort to learn the secrets of new science and weapons that had never existed before. Decades earlier, scientists had known that radiation was dangerous. Proximity to X-rays by early investigators had confirmed their threat, and most knew that women who ingested liquid radium while painting watch dials were subject to premature and painful deaths. During the last years of the war, Manhattan Project doctors raised the alarm about potential problems. Enriched uranium and plutonium were necessary for the project's success, but they were both problematic from a health standpoint. As one scientist counseled his colleagues, plutonium, even at low doses, should be regarded as "extremely poisonous." Additional research was needed, and that required human experimentation.

In national medical journal articles, the subjects of the research were often described as those "institutionalized for mental inadequacy," "mental defectives," "juvenile delinquents," and "abnormal children." For example, one study measuring thyroid activity in children using radioactive iodine (I-131) at the dawn of the Cold War in 1949 incorporated both "normal" and "abnormal" children. Not surprisingly, the abnormal group formed most of the subjects and consisted of a cross-section of children, including a "cretin," a "pituitary dwarf," and others who were said to possess characteristics of "mongolism" and "gargoylism," terms that eugenicists decades earlier had helped to popularize.[65] Also, a month-old infant described as a "Mongolian idiot" was presumed to be one of the first with that malady to be injected with radioactive iodine. The research was conducted at the University of Michigan Medical School and funded, in part, by the American Cancer Society.

Radioactive studies were conducted on young subjects throughout the United States. At the University of Tennessee College of Medicine in 1954, Dr. Van Middlesworth experimented on seven newborn boys: "six Negroes" and "one Caucasian," just two and three days old and weighing between seven and nine pounds.[66] Middlesworth believed that no such studies had been reported on newborns. Realizing that "the use of radiation in the very young organism is open to some question," he decided to consult a local group of advisors. The group, including a radiologist, a radiation physicist, two internists, two pediatricians, a physiologist, and a pathologist, decided injecting I-131 into newborns was acceptable and "not expected to be harmful." Middlesworth stated that he described the procedure to the mothers of the infants and received their consent. What mothers, black or white, in the South in the early 1950s understood about radiation uptake studies and the half-life of certain atomic particles is another issue. However, doctors were hopeful that the exercise would "prove useful in diagnosing thyroid abnormalities in infants" in the future.[67]

A year later, doctors at a Michigan hospital increased the number of infant test subjects receiving radioactive iodine to sixty-five. Most of the infants were less than two weeks old. "The possible danger of using I-131 on a premature infant" was debated among the director of research, the chief of the Radiology Department, the director of the Radioisotope Laboratory, the director of the Pathology Department and the chief of the Pediatric Division. The consensus was that oral administration would not be harmful.[68]

The accumulation of knowledge was a powerful incentive, and radioactive isotopes' availability to foster that goal spurred excitement. Thyroid gland investigations proved attractive and were much replicated, despite potential health risks from radiation exposure. As doctors in one journal article soberly stated, "A calculated risk is taken in performance of any irradiation examination, but the potential benefits may outweigh any hypothetical dangers whenever such an examination is indicated."[69] The question naturally arises of the potential benefit for whom. The subjects in this study were normal newborns from 72 to 180 hours old. Radiation exposure at this early age could only do them harm.

Even into the 1960s, researchers were still traveling to custodial institutions to access test subjects. The attraction was not a secret; doctors freely admitted it in subsequent journal articles. As one doctor frankly wrote, "We chose this population of children living under constant conditions of environment, diet, and iodide uptake."[70] The investigators interested in the impact of atmospheric radioactivity from nuclear explosions and desirous of conducting a study on the suppression of the thyroid function to prevent radioactive iodine retention could have just as easily conducted their experiments in their backyard. There was no shortage of schools with the controlled environments the researchers sought. Wrentham and Fernald and others like them had something else: throwaway children who had been given up by their families and severed from society. If something untoward should happen during a study, there was far less chance of hearing from an outraged parent, dealing with an embarrassing news story, or encountering any uncomfortable legal entanglements.

Gordon Shattuck, Charlie Dyer, and Austin LaRocque eventually learned of their history as human guinea pigs during the Cold War and the Golden Age of Medical Research. However, many of such subjects would never discover how they had been used and conscripted as "volunteers" in the campaign to benefit medical science.

CHAPTER EIGHT

PSYCHOLOGICAL TREATMENT

"Lobotomy . . . Is Often the Starting Point
in Effective Treatment."

SEATED ALONE AND TERRIFIED IN A COLD AND GLOOMY HOSPITAL CORRI-
dor, six-year-old Teddy Chabasinski tried to remain calm, but everything
about New York City's Bellevue Hospital frightened him. Unlike the other boys
his age housed on one of the hospital's wards, he was relegated to a bed in a
bleak, lonely hallway. The dreary ceilings seemed as high as the sky, and the vast
windows were covered in urban dirt and grit. The smelly, filthy mattress he was
forced to sleep on disgusted him, and an old, heavily stained olive drab blanket
left him nauseous and shivering throughout the night.

It was winter 1944, and young Ted's life had taken a terrible turn. A bright
boy who loved to read and listen to the news on the radio, Ted knew about the
surprise Japanese attack on Pearl Harbor, victory gardens, and the war against
the Axis powers. As he sat alone and shivering in a hospital corridor, he would
now be involved in his own life-and-death struggle, a struggle so severe that on
occasion, he wished he were dead.

After being snatched from his foster parents, Ted had been taken to Bellevue by Miss Callaghan, an officious social worker. She thought he displayed
all the characteristics of someone with a severe mental illness. He was smart and
had learned to read much earlier than other children his age, but Ted always
seemed withdrawn, he cried easily, and he ran away from older children. He
also fought with his younger sister. Ted's mother was schizophrenic, unmarried,
and institutionalized, which resulted in his being sent to a foundling hospital
when he was just ten days old. Five months later, he was handed over to foster
parents. "They were nice but not strong," Ted says of his foster parents. "They
didn't know how to stand up to the social worker." Miss Callaghan, according
to Ted, figured that if Ted's mother had schizophrenia, he must have it too.[1]

Ted was deposited in the children's ward of the psychiatric division of Bellevue Hospital in Manhattan. He awaited his fate fretfully as children his age were probed, prodded, and examined for the cause of their psychological disturbance. Ted never understood why he was there or why no one came to his rescue at night when he screamed for help while being sexually assaulted by a hospital attendant. No one seemed to care, not even the female doctor, whom everyone appeared to be in awe. Dr. Lauretta Bender occasionally came down the hallway with her entourage of aides and acolytes. "They seemed to worship her," Ted would write years later, though he believed some might, like him, have been in fear of her. "Sometimes she would pass very close to me," he would write, "but never acknowledge me. It was if I didn't exist. She seemed to just look right through you."[2]

Ted remembers being taken to a room down the hall where attendants forced him to lie on a gurney. A rag was shoved in his mouth and down his throat till he nearly choked. It was then that Ted saw Dr. Bender, the person who had labeled him as suffering from childhood schizophrenia. He recalls little else of that first electroconvulsive therapy (ECT) session.

He would wake up in a dark room, dizzy, disoriented, with a terrible headache and little memory of what had happened. Sometimes he would not even remember his name. Sometimes another boy, Stanley, would be in the room. Stanley was a large boy about thirteen years of age who never talked or moved. Ted became terrified of him though he did not know why. He referred to his lost memory as a "black hole that the shock had created." He focused on his name each time he was dragged into the ECT room to combat the memory loss. "I'm Teddy, I'm Teddy, I'm here in this room, in this hospital," he would tell himself over and over as he was being strapped down. The pain, the disorientation, the seemingly endless sessions of being shocked and then trying to remember who he was and why he was being punished this way would go on until May of that year.

During that long, harsh winter, Ted learned the system well. On those mornings he was not given breakfast, he would begin to cry; he knew he could expect another shock treatment. He would then be dragged screaming into the room where Dr. Bender or one of the other doctors would shock him with electricity. Though Ted resisted with all his might, he was no match for the three or four attendants who were always there to restrain him and secure him with leather straps. Then bolts of electricity were shot through his brain until he was unconscious. ECT patients, usually adults, were strapped down, a rubber object was forced between their teeth so they would not bite the tips of their tongue off, and electric coils were attached to the patient's temples. When the switch was thrown and the current shot through the patient's brain, a series of violent convulsions would begin. It was not uncommon for patients to leave the gurney with a broken bone or dislocated joint along with a tremendous headache and loss of memory.

Ted often wished he were dead. Ironically, he and the other boys were frequently "marched across the hall to the girls' ward where they were supposed to sing and show how happy and normal, they were." Ted rarely complied, a sign, he was told by nurses and attendants, of his illness. If he wanted to get better, he had to sing. Often tears would streak his face as he did so.

Though he was only six years old, intelligent, and never violent or disruptive, Ted was given the usual complement of twenty ECT treatments. He would never understand what crime he had committed, what he had done wrong, or why he had to receive such a horrible and oft-repeated punishment. As he would write many years later: "And so, in May 1944, after being raped and killed over and over, I finally was released from Bellevue. The little boy who had been taken there to be tortured did not exist anymore. All that was left of him was a few scraps of memory and a broken spirit, and the rest was ashes in a giant dark pit, mixed with the ashes of the hundreds of other children who had been tortured and burnt alive by Doctor Bender, a leader of her profession."

Ted was returned to his foster family in the Bronx, but he was not the same boy the authorities had taken away just a few months earlier. Terrified, he rarely left his mother's side. For a while, Ted refused to go outside. When reintroduced to his tricycle, which earlier he had confidently ridden through the neighborhood, he was apprehensive. Where he once knew every block and every house on the street, he was now dumbfounded. "Suddenly," Ted would later write, "I realized that I didn't know where I was, and I panicked. I used to have a sense of freedom, that I was a big boy and could ride my bike anywhere, but that was gone now."

Geography and familiar physical landmarks were not the only things the shock treatments had stripped from Ted's brain; people had also been cut out of his memory bank. Karl, one of his closest friends who lived just two houses away, was unfamiliar to him. "I didn't know who he was. Miss Callaghan said this was a very bad sign. It meant I wasn't getting better. She told my foster parents my memory loss was due to my malady, not the shock treatments."

Once again, Ted was taken from his foster parents. This time he was placed in Rockland State Hospital in Orangeburg, New York, where there were both children, some who were forced to wear football helmets because they banged their heads against the wall, and adults whom he realized were "crazy." Many seemed dazed and delusional, while others required restraints. Ted would no longer be confronted with ECT, but he was still a prisoner and fearful of his new surroundings and the people there.

Classified as a schizophrenic at seven years of age, Ted would remain at Rockland State for ten years until he was seventeen and deemed cured. During that time, he would observe all manner of personal degradation and institutional abuse. Incredibly, he survived his ordeals. After many years in a mental institution, adjusting to the free world was not easy, but he managed to make a life for himself.

Though he never earned a high school diploma, he enjoyed reading and learning. Subsequently, he matriculated at New York University, where he accumulated thirty-eight credits before dropping out due to a lack of funds. City College of New York presented an attractive economic alternative, so he enrolled there and eventually earned a GED and a bachelor's degree in psychology in 1961. His excellent grades also earned him a Phi Beta Kappa key. He then went on to take graduate courses at Columbia and New York University. Years later, he would move to the West Coast, enter and graduate from law school, and help lead a campaign in Berkeley to stop the use of ECT. The municipal ballot measure passed by a 62 percent to 38 percent vote.

Over a half-century after being diagnosed with childhood schizophrenia and having to endure nearly two dozen shock treatments, Ted Chabasinski is as adamant as ever about the destructive scientific impact of doctors caught in the wake of novel cures and professional ambition. Not surprisingly, he is especially critical of Dr. Lauretta Bender. Her attachment to the latest but unproven medical techniques and potions had earned her tremendous recognition and honors, but no doubt at a high cost to those who became her patients and experimental subjects. "Doctors were an elite group," says Chabasinski, "and as one of the rising stars in the field, Lauretta Bender was shocking sub-humans, mental patients, people who were not of the same value as real or regular humans."

Though he knows she is still respected in many medical and psychological circles, Chabasinski roundly criticizes Bender for her inhumanity, elitism, and attraction to untested therapies that often did more harm than good. Devalued, institutionalized children and adults were grist for the exploratory mill Bender established, and professional colleagues who should have known better praised her or remained silent about her misguided ventures.

"Bender is comparable to the Nazi doctors," argues Chabasinski. "I was helpless, and nobody in society cared about me. I was a shy, somewhat withdrawn kid, but I wasn't crazy or schizophrenic or in need of institution-alization. However, Bender needed ECT subjects. They were able to do what they wanted with no thought or care of the consequences." Chabasinski blames much of the laissez-faire atmosphere in the medical arena that allowed Bender and people like her to exploit the "disenfranchised" on the nation's fascination with the eugenics movement earlier in the century. "The attitude that some people were subhuman took hold," says Chabasinski, "and a campaign began to get rid of them. And if people are declared subhuman, you open the door to all sorts of stuff. It's not a very large step from there to human experimentation."

Born in Butte, Montana, in 1897, Lauretta Bender faced her own struggles as a child. The fact that she repeated first grade three times led some to believe "she was mentally retarded." Her habit of reversing letters when reading and writing was due to dyslexia, it turned out, a handicap she overcame along the way to becoming her high school's valedictorian.[3] She would earn degrees at the University of Chicago and Iowa State University and specialize in psychi-atry. Bender quickly came to believe that "learning disorders were determined neurobiologically and were related to delayed maturation of brain function that were required for language."[4] Though she may be best known for creating the Bender-Gestalt Test used to examine personality and emotional problems, she also gained acclaim for work and theories regarding language development and reading disability. Her much-used diagnosis of childhood schizophrenia gained her increased fame, and her fervent attraction to questionable remedial devices and potions to harness those maladies is what many find troubling today.[5]

Bender joined the staff of Bellevue Hospital in New York City in 1930. She was the senior psychiatrist in charge of the Children's Services for two decades before moving on to other influential positions. During those early years of the Great Depression and into the 1940s at Bellevue, Bender was associated with innovative hospital programs like puppet shows and music therapy. Her ardent championing of ECT and her routine and cavalier over-use of it with children cries out for critical comment.

As Bender repeatedly wrote in journal articles, "Childhood schizophrenia is an early manifestation of schizophrenia as it appears in adolescents and adults," emphasizing its "inherited predisposition," "noxious or traumatic events," and their impact on "maturational lags or embryonic immaturities."[6] Unfortunately, particularly given her growing status and influence in the medical and psychi-atric community, she tended to see schizophrenic characteristics in an over-whelming number of the children she examined. Ted Chabasinski was one of them. Chabasinski might have been timid, insecure, and in need of counseling, but it is doubtful that psychiatrists today would have labeled him schizophrenic and placed him in an institution. Nor would various forms of shock treatment be prescribed for him today.

Bender was an early and zealous devotee of all manner of convulsive treatments. The 1930s, a period that coincides with her early years working with children at Bellevue, would be a fruitful period for creating and using such treatments. She and other doctors struggling to diagnose and treat a wide range of mental problems with a small armamentarium of cures eagerly welcomed whatever new therapies came along. According to medical historian Joel Braslow, "The shock therapies provided the first new remedy since the introduction of malaria fever therapy in the 1920s." Hailed by the press as "wonder cures of modern medicine," these new practices acted directly on the body.[7] Doctors became enamored of them; that was particularly true of Lauretta Bender.

Manfred Sakel, a Viennese physician, invented insulin shock therapy in 1933 when he realized that massive insulin doses would precipitate hypoglycemic shock. Sakel discovered that when large insulin doses were given to psychiatric patients, some showed dramatic improvement. Though he would never completely understand why a low blood sugar shock would return some psychotic patients to normalcy, Sakel's new technique quickly drew converts, despite occasional failures in which patients died on the table of heart failure and cerebral hemorrhage.

Metrazol convulsive therapy came along a year later and proved an even more powerful but hazardous form of shock therapy. Metrazol patients often suffer injury and leave the table with broken bones and dislocated joints. Patients had a deathly fear of it and pleaded with doctors to be taken off Metrazol regimens. Pentylenetetrazol, the generic name for the drug, was discovered by Ladislas J. Meduna in Budapest. He realized that intramuscular injections of camphor-related drugs caused intense convulsions. Quicker acting, cheaper, and requiring less staff than insulin, Metrazol therapy soon rivaled insulin therapy at many hospitals. There would be a tidal wave of complaints, however.

In 1936, two Italian physicians produced another method to induce seizures using electricity. Ugo Cerletti and Lucio Bini had been electrifying animals—and killing a respectable number of them—before they perfected their machine and learned where the electrodes should be placed. By the end of the decade, psychiatrists had three different shock techniques to treat melancholic patients, depressives, and psychotics. But they also used them on many others whose symptoms and maladies made them improbable candidates for convulsive therapy.

Doctors and hospitals, overrun with people with a mental health condition, quickly bought into one or the other or all three methods of shock therapy. In 1941, according to Braslow, "42% of institutions surveyed had electroshock machines just three years after the first human electroshock trial."[8] By the end of the 1940s, ECT would be the backbone of therapeutic care at asylums and mental hospitals across America. At Stockton State Hospital in California in 1949, for example, "patients receiving electroshock increased fivefold over the previous year to 7,997. Doctors were shocking over 60% of the patients at Stockton."[9]

Lauretta Bender was one of the earliest and most enthusiastic proponents of the new shock-therapy regimens, especially when prescribing such treatment for children and publishing articles on her studies. However, assigning young children to "convulsive therapy" could easily strike objective observers as torture rather than treatment.

Granted, insulin and electric shock were less physically jarring than Metrazol. They resulted in patients having less need for orthopedic attention, but each method had its drawbacks, and none was guaranteed to produce a cure. Nevertheless, Bender believed that such measures were safe and highly beneficial to patients. As she wrote in one article, the "treatment does give a spurt to lagging maturation; it stabilizes the functions of the autonomous nervous system and the electroencephalogram." In addition, shock therapy broke up "bizarre schizophrenic patterns in body image . . . improved level of intelligence, gestalt drawing," and "personality improvement." In short, Bender believed, "The pre-puberty child is more normal" with the use of shock therapy.[10]

Bender became so enamored of convulsive treatment that she argued that ECT was appropriate for young autistic children. This treatment would perhaps still strike today's therapists and psychiatrists as bizarre. More confounding yet, especially from the perspective of young subjects like Ted Chabasinski, who experienced Bender's treatment firsthand, is her statement that "a close personal relationship with a physician during the period of recovery from the insulin, while the child is fed sweets, may encourage a child to talk and it may be generally therapeutic."[11] Chabasinski's recollections of Bender revolve around her "cold, imposing stare," her indifference to him as she quickly marched through the corridor during hospital rounds, and her "throwing the switch" that caused him to convulse and lose consciousness. He has no memory of being given candies, watching puppet shows, hearing a kind, reassuring word, or receiving a cold compress for his throbbing, sweaty brow.

Bender's fondness for shock therapy in all its forms, "it stimulates appetite and general well-being," was not shared by the children Chabasinski knew at

Bellevue and Rockland State Hospital. It was Dr. Bender, however, who was writing the journal articles and trumpeting the technique's perceived success stories. In one 1947 article titled "One Hundred Cases of Childhood Schizophrenia Treated with Electric Shock," Bender discussed the results of giving "grand mal seizures" to children whose IQs ranged from 44 to 146. All were diagnosed schizophrenic and suffered no lasting negative effect from the treatment on subsequent psychometric tests. As she unscientifically proclaimed about ECT therapy, "the children were always somewhat improved by the treatment inasmuch as they were less disturbed . . . more mature . . . happier."[12] Chabasinski would undoubtedly disagree with that assessment, and likely so would a good portion of today's pediatric community.

Shock therapy was fraught with controversy from its earliest days, and opposing camps argued the new remedy's strengths and weaknesses. Sound, unbiased, and controlled studies of shock therapy were few and far between. Anecdotal tales of dramatic recovery seemed to rule the day. Such stories only encouraged greater use of the new remedy. Before World War II, a US Public Health Service survey disclosed that three-quarters of 305 public and private institutions used insulin therapy.[13] Lauretta Bender needed no encouragement; she was a devoted advocate of shock therapy from the beginning and went farther than most in prescribing it for young children she considered schizophrenic.

At the time, there was little direct criticism of Bender's penchant for sending electricity through children's brains, but the opposition would soon grow, and Bender would come under direct attack. In a report for Karl Menninger and a group of psychoanalysts, Bellevue Hospital's ECT program for preadolescent children with schizophrenia was called "promiscuous and indiscriminate."[14] The report argued that shock therapy showed some effectiveness with depression but not with other mental diseases such as manic depression or schizophrenia. More important, the report said that brain damage was an inevitable consequence of ECT. "Abuses in the use of electroshock therapy are sufficiently widespread and dangerous to justify consideration of a campaign of professional education in the elimination of this technique, and perhaps even to justify institution of certain measures of control."[15] The American psychoanalytic community had spoken, but it would back off in coming years as those supporting a physical/biological school of thought mounted considerable counterpressure.

Bender did not escape the sting of criticism. Her decision to subject children as young as four years old to a battery of twenty ECT sessions was questioned, as was her unsubstantiated belief that children "had become much more sociable, composed, and able to integrate in group therapy as a result of the daily ECT."[16]

It is difficult to say with certainty how Ted Chabasinski and the many children like him with minor behavioral issues who were labeled schizophrenic, institutionalized, and given ECT, would have done if they had escaped the clutches of doctors and institutions with their agendas. Some might have outgrown their problems as they approached adolescence. Others might have required counseling and medication. But shock treatment for young children should have been a last resort, if an alternative at all.

Insulin, Metrazol, and electric shock therapies were not the only new remedies for damaged minds emerging from Europe in the 1930s. Egas Moniz was a Portuguese physician, and like many of his medical colleagues, he decried the slim armamentarium of effective weapons in the fight against mental illness. They treated patients suffering a range of phobias, delusions, weeping fits, lack of self-restraint, and various forms of depression for years. Cures were hit or miss and usually only temporarily effective. Moniz believed something more radical was needed to address the problem, which would dramatically shake up the brain cells that fostered bizarre behavior. After returning from the International Neurological Congress in London in 1935, he decided to attack the problem directly. He created a scalpel-like metal instrument in the shape of an apple corer and instructed his colleague, surgeon Almeida Lima, to cut into the brains of nearly two dozen anxiety-ridden and insane patients.

The results, according to Moniz, were nothing short of miraculous; hypochondriacs were no longer preoccupied with contracting cancer and polio, the depressed jettisoned notions of suicide, and those in fear of imaginary pursuers no longer suffered from persecution complexes. Granted, most of the long-documented cases of dementia praecox, an early term for schizophrenia, seemed intractable. However, there were enough significant changes in other patients to capture the medical community's attention. Some were willing to concede, Moniz was on to something; perhaps his concept of "psychosurgery" was the medical breakthrough they had been waiting.

Despite initial skepticism and vigorous debate about boring holes in the skull and cutting delicate brain tissue, one American physician, in particular, was taken by the Portuguese doctor's methodology and results. Dr. Walter Freeman, a neurologist at George Washington University, was fascinated with the idea that individual peculiarities, bizarre notions, and unattractive behaviors could be excised by simply cutting the connecting fibers between the thalamus and the prefrontal lobes. By 1936, less than a year after Moniz had invented his surgical procedure, Freeman had brought the radical technique to American shores. Freeman considered Moniz "a scientific Renaissance man impervious to criticism, whose strikingly original arcs of thought would bring him international acclaim despite his location outside the world's most prestigious centers of neurological research and learning."[17]

With Freeman as the intellectual driving force and his partner, George Washington University surgeon James W. Watts, as the physician holding the scalpel, they would transform lobotomy into one of the most controversial types of human surgery of the last 200 years.

The procedure would amplify Freeman's medical and public profile to the point that one biographer argued, "Aside from the Nazi doctor Josef Mengele, Walter Freeman ranks as the most scorned physician of the twentieth century."[18] Though Moniz was lobotomy's creator and would receive a Nobel Prize for his achievement, it was Freeman who would travel, ice pick in hand, from institution to institution, aggressively advocating the surgery's unique attributes and sterling triumphs. During the 1940s, 1950s, and 1960s, lobotomy would become a key and often—used treatment by psychiatrists from Europe to America and Africa to Asia. In hindsight, the procedure's quick adoption by Moniz's and Freeman's acolytes and its widespread use for over a generation underscores a sad example of the psychiatric profession's irresponsibility when prudence and sound judgment were most in need.

Freeman was both committed and indefatigable. A potentially deadly combination of characteristics when possessed by a man with a knifelike instrument in his hand who frequently cut into the brains of individuals with little more than anecdotal tales of success to guide him. Freeman once wrote an ode titled "The Religion of Science" that included these revealing lines: "When a man can stand on his feet and say to his fellow man 'I know' and say it with the conviction that comes from observation, can defend his knowledge by a statement of actual happenings or conditions, then his faith in that proposition is unshakable."[19]

Freeman would soon come to believe that "lobotomy, instead of being the last resort in therapy, is often the starting point of effective treatment."[20] That religious-like fervor combined with his eager attitude was prodigiously productive. During one three-week period in midsummer 1952, Freeman operated on 228 West Virginia patients in institutions throughout the state. On one day alone, he operated on twenty-five female patients. Freeman's daughter was so impressed with her father's mass production capabilities that she began to refer to him as the "Henry Ford of Psychiatry."[21] Even Watts was in awe of his partner's peripatetic nature. "The worst thing about Walter Freeman," said Watts, "was that he never got tired. . . . That was what made him the most difficult."[22]

Freeman's decision to abandon hospital surgery made his assembly-line schedule possible. He believed that he was the equal of any surgeon, that anesthesia could be replaced with ECT, and that nurses, sterile garb, and the other accouterments of contemporary surgery only cluttered up and needlessly extended the length of the procedure. Contributing to even greater efficiency in time and money was Freeman's decision to adopt a new, revolutionary procedure: the transorbital lobotomy. Freeman believed he could more easily cut through the neural pathways between the frontal lobes and the thalamus through the eye sockets with an ice pick-like instrument. The new technique could accomplish in seven minutes what the standard Freeman-Watts lobotomy required hours to do. All he needed now was an ice pick, a portable ECT machine, and an automobile to get him from site to site.

By the late 1940s, Freeman was traveling the length and breadth of the United States, performing transorbital lobotomies like a traveling salesman. One critic referred to him as a "one-man medicine show traveling across the continent."[23] His travels and the procedure's growing popularity alarmed more reasonable members of the psychiatric community. They believed that too many lobotomies were taking place, preliminary psychiatric examinations were discarded, and postoperative analyses did not support advocates' claims.

Dr. Nolan Lewis, the director of the New York State Psychiatric Institute of Columbia-Presbyterian Medical Center, was one of the more outspoken opponents of lobotomy. "The patients become rather childlike," said Lewis in 1949. "They act like they have been hit on the head with a club and are as dull as blazes. It does disturb me that so many lobotomies are given without any psychiatric control . . . and it does disturb me to see the number of zombies that these operations turn out. I would guess that lobotomies all over the world have caused more mental invalids than they've cured. I think it should be stopped before we dement too large a segment of the population."[24]

Even Freeman's friends became alarmed at the stories they were hearing. "What are these terrible things I hear about you doing lobotomies in your office with an ice pick?" wrote John Fulton, a respected Yale researcher. "I have just been to California and Minnesota and heard about it in both places. Why not use a shotgun? It would be quicker!"[25]

It was Fulton who was out of step, however. The scientific community had embraced lobotomy as an effective and fashionable way to deal with a

Psychological Treatment   187

wide range of mental diseases. That was confirmed when the Nobel Prize was awarded to Egas Moniz in 1949. Over the next four years, 20,000 Americans would undergo lobotomies, at least a third of them of the transorbital variety. Moreover, at least half of the public psychiatric institutions in the United States were now performing psychosurgery. Though knowledge of the intricacies of the brain and the workings of the mind was still in its infancy, cutting into the brain had become de rigueur for doctors and institutions that wanted to be seen as up-to-date and competent in the latest techniques to combat phobias, manic depression, and schizophrenia. Even children had become fair game for brain surgeons.

Freeman attempted his first lobotomy on a child in 1939. The nine-year-old suffered terrible temper tantrums and symptoms of schizophrenia, but the severing of neural pathways did not end well; the child was forced to return to a psychiatric hospital. Freeman next tackled even younger children: a four-year-old boy and a six-year-old girl. The girl, who had "stopped talking, tore her clothes, smashed dolls, and used toys as weapons," had been diagnosed with encephalitis by her family physician. However, Freeman and Watts thought her bizarre behavior was due to childhood schizophrenia. They performed a lobotomy in August 1944 only to conclude that her "chewing her clothing and fingers, incontinence, and sitting alone gazing into space [with] no affection for anybody" was a sign of relapse and the need for a second surgical procedure, which was performed. Such failures, not to mention Freeman's liberal diagnosis of childhood schizophrenia, "dogged him throughout his career."[26]

Walter Freeman had definite thoughts on the cause of seriously troubled children and how prefrontal lobotomy could help them. He believed schizophrenia in childhood was a form of psychosis that would progress until it destroyed the individual's personality. "Seclusiveness," according to Freeman, characterized a slide into schizophrenia, and this critical emotional milestone could manifest itself "before the age of two." Freeman claimed that he could detect an infant turning away from other children at nine months old. Not long after that, he warned all who took the time to listen, the child in question would "stop playing with toys" and use them as "weapons or as objects to be torn apart or otherwise destroyed." From that point, there would be a direct path to increasingly serious problems; the child would reject both "praise and blame," lack "warmth or affection," and display "sullen hostility and exaggerated tantrums."[27]

Psychotic children, argued Freeman, were "ritualistic . . . to an extreme" regarding their "playthings, clothing, washing," their "personal habits disorganized," and feelings like "happiness" did not exist in their world. Facial expressions usually bore this out. Such disturbed children had "a dreamy, far-off look, a sullen . . . attitude, and self-absorbed appearance." In addition, they were prone to "sluggish[ness] to the point of immobility," were generally "poor sleepers," and were subject to periods of "prolonged wakefulness and fantasy."[28]

Freeman believed he had an answer for the prayers of concerned parents. If lobotomy could improve adults with serious mental problems, it could do the same for children. By 1947, Freeman and Watts had performed hundreds of prefrontal lobotomies on a vast array of patients, including "11 individuals whose schizophrenia developed before the age of ten." Some had been institutionalized, and others were still at home in the care of families that "had not sent their loved one off as a matter of convenience." Freeman believed that lobotomies would be instrumental in terminating the child's fantasy life and reducing the expenditure of emotional energy. More importantly, he argued, "the aim has been to smash the world of fantasy in which these children are becoming more and more submerged."[29]

Freeman had no hesitation applying a radical methodology that seriously challenged adults to formative young minds. He seemed to argue that the younger the diseased mind, the more destruction the surgeon's scalpel needed to do. As he stated, "a great deal of frontal lobe tissue has to be sacrificed in children in order to obtain any more than temporary improvement. The younger the age at which the psychosis has begun, the more posteriorly the incisions have to be made, with resulting greater disability." Besides, Freeman went on to argue, "The loss of frontal lobe tissue is better tolerated by children than by adults."[30]

Comments such as these should have signaled Freeman's compatriots in the neurological community that he was on thin ice both medically and factually, but he and others carried on unimpeded. Freeman and Watts even admitted, "Our experience in the surgical treatment of childhood schizophrenia had been rather disappointing." Two children "died shortly after the operation," and one had undergone "three operations" and was now hospitalized with little hope of "relieving the disturbed behavior." As the doctors were forced to admit, none of their patients could function like normal adults. They were now "childlike and dependent on institutions for their survival."

Nevertheless, Freeman and Watts remained wedded to lobotomy as a viable answer to everything from anxiety and manic depression to schizophrenia. "In view of the wretched prognosis in all these cases without operation," they went on to argue, "modest results indicated in the case reports have encouraged us to continue with prefrontal lobotomy in certain patients whose schizophrenia has developed in early childhood."[31]

The grim results occasioned Freeman and Watts to sometimes double down on their bets. Several children had the outrageous misfortune of being subjected to multiple lobotomies. One child had endured two operations by the time he was six; a seventeen-year-old child had received three lobotomies. The doctors' unadorned results for some young patients seemed to confirm the devastating effects of invasive brain surgery. Some succinct postoperative reports read as follows: "No change, institution" for one nine-year-old; "profound inertia after second operation" for a fourteen-year-old; and "operative death" for a twelve-year-old.[32] It was terrible enough that Freeman, Watts, and the other lobotomists surgically induced childhood in thousands of adults; it was even more troubling that they were willing to ensure permanent childhood in so many preadolescents who were caught up in their research dragnet.

Even fourteen years later, when the controversial procedure had precipitously declined in popularity, Freeman and Watts were still resolute champions of psychosurgery. In a 1961 letter to a skeptical administrator of a California hospital, James Watts wrote, "Lobotomy is an ethical and recognized method of treatment of emotionally disturbed children." Watts, a graduate of the University of Virginia Medical School, a known hothouse of eugenic thought at the time of his matriculation, wrote that the "operation [is] most effective in reducing hostility, aggressiveness and destructive tendencies."[33] No surprise there. If one carves through enough gray matter, one is left with an inert, mute, stupefied half-human, something that hospital attendants, caretakers, and even some parents might have found a decided improvement.

By the late 1950s and early 1960s, Thorazine and other antipsychotic medications had come on the scene. Acting like chemical lobotomies, they tended to relax patients, calm them down, and even eliminate delusions and hallucinations. Doctors who used these drugs no longer needed as many straitjackets, locked cells, and psychosurgical procedures to end the screaming, crying, and wild ravings that once dominated the psychiatric wards. Some inmates referred to the new drugs as "brake fluid."[34]

Walter Freeman, however, refused to mothball the tools of his magnificent obsession. He continued to travel, preaching the gospel according to Moniz and performing lobotomies. In 1961, for example, "he performed a series of transorbital lobotomies on seven adolescents at the Langley Porter Clinic" in San Francisco.[35]

At one of his Langley Porter presentations in 1961, Freeman proudly brought several transorbital lobotomy subjects with him for a show-and-tell session. The three children he had performed surgery on included Richard, sixteen, Ann, fourteen, and Howard, just twelve. As Howard Dully writes in *My Lobotomy*, his graphic account of his unnecessary psychosurgery, "When Freeman said I had just turned twelve, the doctors were shocked. Only twelve? It was outrageous. The doctors started shouting and yelling. Freeman shouted back. Soon the whole place seemed out of control."[36]

Dr. Freeman was no shrinking violet and shouted back at his accusers but was eventually "booed off the stage." The tide had turned on risky surgical procedures like prefrontal lobotomy, but not soon enough for children like Howard Dully. He was said to have been a "normal, happy baby" at birth, but his new stepmother considered Howard a problem. They did not get along, fought often, and she believed he stole items from the house. Everything about him frustrated her. From her standpoint, he was just "impossible to control." She took him to a series of psychiatrists, but the sessions proved unsatisfactory; they considered Howard's behavior "normal." She was then referred to "a doctor named Walter Freeman."

Freeman listened to Mrs. Dully's list of grievances and thought them "sufficiently impressive." The more he heard, the more he came to believe the boy had "childhood schizophrenia." Meetings with Howard's father and four with Howard himself went well. A careful reading of Freeman's notes would suggest that nothing more than counseling was in order, but Mrs. Dully was determined to do something more drastic. Eventually, Freeman acceded to her wishes and wrote in his notes: "The family should consider the possibility of changing Howard's personality by means of transorbital lobotomy."[37] The decision was made on Howard's twelfth birthday.

The boy was taken to a small general hospital in San Jose. He came out of the relatively short operation, which included an electric shock to knock him out and a prefrontal lobotomy with black eyes, a severe headache, a stiff neck, acute sluggishness, and a 102.4-degree fever. Freeman prescribed a "spinal puncture" and hefty doses of penicillin as postoperative therapy. Howard's heartrending return home was captured by his brother Brian who would later write, "You were sitting up in bed, with two black eyes. You looked listless. And sad. Like a zombie. It's not a nice word to use, but it's the only word to use. You were zoned out and staring. I was in shock. And sad. It was just terribly sad."[38]

Howard Dully now wonders how his life would have been different if he had not met Dr. Walter Freeman. He also wonders, "Where were the authorities? Freeman wasn't a licensed psychiatrist. How could he determine on the basis of a couple of visits with me that I had been schizophrenic since the age of four? And why would anyone accept his diagnosis anyway without insisting that I be seen by someone with the proper training? Was there no medical standard for giving someone a lobotomy, especially a child?"[39] Apparently not.

In his history of psychiatry during the twentieth century, Edward Shorter argues that "In retrospect, frontal lobotomy was indefensible for ethical reasons. While results were dramatic, many of these patients may have eventually spontaneously recovered. And the irreversible damage to their brain and spirit must be weighed against the months or years with which they would have encumbered the institutional system."[40]

Though Shorter recognized the limitations of lobotomizing thousands of American citizens given the medical community's scant knowledge of the complexities of the brain and the fact that the procedure was irreversible, it was more egregious for the profession to subject young children to the same draconian crucible magnified the collective error in judgment.

Psychosurgery would forever after have a particularly ominous and chilling aura. As doctors learned more about the intricate workings of the mind, they seemed less willing to disturb delicate brain tissue, which led to fewer instances of invasive brain surgery. Popular novels such as Ken Kesey's *One Flew Over the Cuckoo's Nest* only added more baggage to an already suspect medical procedure. However, a few doctors were not intimidated by the negative newspaper articles, salacious magazine pieces, and growing patients' rights movement that opposed such nefarious undertakings.

Dr. O. J. Andy was one of them. The director of neurosurgery at the University of Mississippi continued to perform a wide variety of brain surgeries into the 1970s. Like Walter Freeman, he found it equally acceptable to perform such surgery on children. Andy was interested in treating abnormal behavior, which did not respond to psychotherapy or medication, including emotional instability, aggression, hyperactivity, and nervousness. All of these symptoms of abnormality, according to Andy, had "become manifest in children."[41]

Like Walter Freeman before him, he saw little reason to wait until the patient reached adulthood to address the symptoms. W. B., for example, was a twelve-year-old "mental defective with seizures, repetitive movement and behavior disorder." Andy believed a thalamotomy (a procedure where a portion of the thalamus is destroyed) was in order and performed one on the left side on February 13, 1964, and on the right, later that same year on December 17, 1964. Andy considered the surgery a success; "the rocking, self-beating, regurgitation, and destructiveness had ceased," and the boy was "up and around with other mentally retarded patients."

Another boy to receive the procedure was J. M., a nine-year-old who "had seizures and behavioral disorder" that included "combative" and "destructive" behavior. Andy performed a "bilateral thalamotomy" on the left side in January 1962 and a similar procedure on the right in September, only to witness many negative behaviors return a year later. A fornicotomy (surgical destruction of a bundle of fibers in the brain that carry signals from the hippocampus to the hypothalamus) was then performed in January 1965, resulting in the boy's having an "impaired memory" and greater "irritability and combativeness." Undaunted, Andy dug into the child's brain once again, performing a "simultaneous bilateral thalamotomy." He thought this fifth operation a success; the child had "become adjusted to his environment and displayed marked improvement in behavior and memory." Less optimistically, however, Andy admitted that the patient was "deteriorating intellectually."[42]

After so many invasive procedures to destroy brain tissue in such an abbreviated period, it is a wonder the child could function at all. The one discussant to the journal article offered comments regarding several technical issues but did not mention Andy's inclusion of children in such irreversible surgery. Nor did the article mention parental permission to conduct the surgery.

One physician at the time was willing to speak out about the use of children in such devastating surgery and Andy's cavalier history of repeatedly performing such surgery. Dr. Peter R. Breggin was a reform-minded psychiatrist active in national antipsychosurgery campaigns. He believed there might have been a political agenda behind Andy's research, which explained the inordinate number of African Americans and criminals used as psycho-surgery subjects.

Breggin began researching the resurgence in psychosurgery in the early 1970s and came upon the work of O. J. Andy. Andy had published surgical reports on approximately three dozen young children, ages five to twelve, diagnosed as aggressive and hyperactive. Breggin contacted a civil rights attorney in Mississippi who determined that most of the children operated on were housed in a segregated black institution for the developmentally disabled. Nurses told the attorney that Andy had a completely free hand picking children for psychosurgery.[43]

A few years earlier, Breggin had made similar statements when he testified in Washington at congressional hearings on "human experimentation" after the Tuskegee syphilis study revelations. Andy was there to testify as well, along with a number of the nation's top surgeons and medical administrators. Senator Edward Kennedy, who chaired the hearing, asked Andy a series of questions, including how many patients he had practiced psychosurgery on, their ages, and when he had started performing such surgery. Andy admitted to doing brain surgery in the early 1950s on "30 or 40 patients," of which "13 or 14" were children. He claimed the youngest was between "6 or 7 years of age."[44]

Where Andy was the model of brevity when questioned, Breggin was far more expansive in his comments. Dissatisfied with the laissez-faire approach to medical research, Breggin said, "The reliance on professional ethics and medical control over these issues leaves the physicians in charge of the situation. It creates for themselves an elitist power over human mind and spirit." Under questioning from Kennedy, Breggin went on to declare his opposition to psychosurgery, a procedure that "destroy[s] normal brain tissue." The practice "opens up a Pandora's box of possible approaches; men like Dr. Andy invent diseases to operate on."

In addition, said Breggin, there was no oversight or peer review. He claimed that when he asked Andy's superior at the University of Mississippi, the chairman of the Department of Psychiatry, whether he knew Andy was doing surgery on children, the man replied, 'Oh, my God, no."[45] Breggin went on to castigate both the procedure and the doctor performing it.

Decades later, psychiatrists and medical ethicists admit that doctors still do not know much about the circuits they are tampering with or what will result from their intervention: "Some people improve, others feel little or nothing, and an unlucky few actually get worse."[46] Institutions today conduct ethical screening to select candidates, insist that potential subjects must have disabling maladies, and disclose in informed consent instructions that the operation is experimental. Surgical precision is emphasized today, but "there still remain large gaps in doctors' understanding of the circuits they are operating on." That surgeons—and in Walter Freeman's case, non-surgeons—were wielding scalpels and icepicks and "slashing into the brain" during frontal lobotomies on thousands of patients and "blindly mangling whatever connections and circuits were in the way" is a perfect example of the well-intended doing great harm. They chose to perform this risky procedure on children, only magnifying their flawed judgment and self-serving approach to research and medicine.

"Faced with profound clinical problems," writes medical historian Joel Braslow, "doctors saw lobotomy as a humane solution."[47] From the perspective of frustrated and overworked doctors, the situation is not difficult to understand. The number of asylums increased, yet psychiatric wards were overflowing, and effective and lasting remedies were exceedingly rare. Doctors confronted with a laundry list of mental diseases and inexhaustible caseloads remained desperate for cures, as did patients themselves. Any new theory, technique, or drug that showed promise sparked an interest. Some would become wildly enthusiastic promoters of a particular treatment regimen and forever be strongly associated. Perhaps not to the extent of the association between Walter Freeman and the transorbital lobotomy, but devout champions of a particular elixir or procedure. And Lauretta Bender was one of them.

As mentioned, early in her psychiatric career, Bender had believed shock therapy was an effective treatment for a full range of mental problems, even for young children. Initially at Bellevue and later at Creedmore State Hospital in Queens, she assigned a childhood schizophrenia diagnosis to an inordinate number of young patients. A regimen of twenty shock-therapy sessions would usually follow. For children like Ted Chabasinski, who was troubled but not schizophrenic, the ECT sessions were more punitive than therapeutic.

Two decades later, Bender would discover a new medicinal elixir, LSD, and utilize it aggressively. As a zealous enthusiast of the controversial hallucinogen, she saw no bounds in its potential application.[48]

In 1943, Dr. Albert Hofmann, a Swiss chemist for Sandoz Pharmaceutical Company, accidentally ingested a chemical he worked with in the laboratory. He quickly noticed dramatic physiological and psychological changes; it was his first psychedelic trip. The substance he was working with was an ergot fungus, and its bizarre hallucinatory impact captured his curiosity. He called the chemical derivative lysergic acid diethylamide 25 (LSD), and it would quickly become the most sought-after and controversial hallucinogen in the world. Within a few short years, many believed LSD was the long-sought potion that held the keys to unlocking the universe.

During the war, Nazi doctors at Dachau and other concentration camps used prisoners for a host of experiments, including mescaline studies. They were searching for mind-control techniques, or incapacitants, that would help immobilize and defeat an enemy. American authorities also were exploring new chemical concoctions that would have wartime utility.

However, they had not progressed much past truth serums using various forms of marijuana. Hofmann's psychedelic creation was more potent. Interest in LSD was enhanced during the early years of the Cold War with numerous, inexplicable incidents of soldiers, citizens, and political leaders in Europe and Asia confessing to crimes they could not have committed. Cardinal József Mindszenty in Hungary captured American troops in Korea, and several other disturbing examples of individuals under someone else's control alarmed American leaders. The new threat of mind control and brainwashing frightened everyone and exacerbated fears of the Soviet Union and the rise of Communism.

Members of the defense establishment, particularly those in the newly established Central Intelligence Agency (CIA), quickly recognized that mind control had both defensive and offensive capabilities. "Nearly every Agency document," according to author and former State Department official John Marks, "stressed goals like controlling an individual to the point where he will do our bidding against his will and even against such fundamental laws of nature as self-preservation."[49] In 1950, the CIA initiated a top-secret plan called BLUEBIRD to monitor Soviet developments in the behavioral field and explore America's potential regarding mind control. A year later, it would be renamed ARTICHOKE, and the following year rolled into MKULTRA. Those and the many other incarnations that followed were secret government programs designed to investigate everything from novel chemical substances like LSD to sensory deprivation, brain electrode implants, and hypnosis. Human experimentation would be the methodology that determined which of these clandestine efforts showed the most promise. "We lived in a never-never land," said one CIA doctor, "of unceasing experimentation."[50]

Techniques as varied as ultrasonics, high and low pressure, poison gases, radiation, extremes of heat and cold, and changing light were all explored. Marks even discovered evidence that in 1952 the Office of Scientific Intelligence considered giving a doctor $100,000 to study "neurosurgical techniques," which meant lobotomy and electric shock.[51] The memory of Hitler was still fresh, Stalin had taken his place in the pantheon of evildoers, and the global threat of Communism was increasingly apparent. Apologists for the scientific excesses that were about to be committed quickly underscore "the fear, even paranoia" that gripped the American political and social landscape. Just as World War II provided an excuse for various ethical transgressions in the medical arena, the toxic Cold War atmosphere of the 1950s and 1960s provided cover for similar excesses.

Some embarrassing episodes were kept secret for decades not to expose America's own questionable, if not criminal, behavior. The deaths of Harold Blauer, a former professional tennis player, and Frank Olson, a biological weapons expert, in 1952 were caused by dedicated but reckless government operatives pursuing greater knowledge about hallucinogens and mind control.

Blauer was diagnosed with clinical depression and transferred to the Psychiatric Institute (PI), another well-known city hospital operated by Columbia University. Unbeknownst to Blauer and other patients at PI, the hospital had a secret contract with the US Army's Chemical Corps to investigate the impact of hallucinogens on humans. Blauer was progressing well with psychotherapy sessions, but at some point, he was informed that doctors wanted to try an experimental drug on him. Though dubious, Blauer acceded to the request, but he was never told the drug was not intended to improve his health. He was injected with five different mescaline derivatives and progressively stronger doses that caused violent tremors, apprehension, and intense hallucinations. Despite his pleadings to stop the injections, they continued until he lapsed into a deep coma.

Later that year, at a CIA Special Operations Division party in Western Maryland, staff director Sidney Gottlieb decided to spike the drinks of some fellow operatives. Gottlieb was a brilliant but erratic Cal Tech Ph.D. with a penchant for black bag weaponry. The point man in the CIA's campaign to understand and master Eastern Europe's secret brainwashing techniques, Gottlieb, like a growing number in the scientific community, believed LSD might be the answer. Unsurprisingly, Gottlieb's whimsical but unscientific and dangerous prank of spiking alcoholic drinks with LSD ended in disaster. Though many men displayed some unusual but fleeting behavior, one Fort Detrick staffer named Frank Olsen went into a severe depression. Non-communicative, paranoid, and disturbed, Olsen was taken to a series of doctors in the coming days without showing improvement. It was believed the shot of LSD had triggered a severe psychotic reaction. After a visit with a CIA-affiliated physician in New York City in November 1953, and just before being admitted to a Maryland sanitarium, Olsen fell or was pushed out the window of his 10th floor, midtown, Manhattan hotel room to the concrete pavement below.

Gottlieb had no problem spreading the CIA wealth around to physicians that may be interested in using LSD on patients.[52] One of those was an allergist, Harold A. Abramson, MD. In addition to doing his own experiments on children, Abramson would write numerous journal pieces extolling the use of LSD in children with autism, schizophrenia, and character disorders. He called those doing experiments on children with LSD "pioneers" and "with medical courage and scientific imagination."[53]

Another Gottlieb-inspired experiment took place at the Boston Psychopathic Hospital. Gottlieb hired a psychiatrist and the institution's assistant superintendent Robert Hyde to begin a series of LSD experiments. After the CIA funded Hyde, he would conduct a study using Harvard, Emerson, and MIT students. To drink "a little vial of a clear, colorless and odorless liquid," the students would receive $15. They were only told it might produce an "altered state" and left clueless of the vial's content. Several students had adverse reactions, and it is reported that one hanged themselves.[54]

Equally repugnant, though no loss of life was reported to have occurred, was the CIA's funding of respected scientists in their exploration of various and occasionally crack-pot mind-control methodologies. One of the stranger cases was that of Dr. Ewen Cameron, an esteemed Scottish-born psychiatrist at Montreal's McGill University, who used electroshock, drugs, psychic driving, and an assortment of other bizarre methodologies to depattern patients and restore them to the desired condition.

A coterie of accomplished psychologists and psychiatrists signed on as covert scientific collaborators with the CIA in exploring LSD's full potential.[55] Other doctors and academics had no formal ties to the CIA, but their research was of great interest to the agency. As some observers now believe, "it was impossible for an LSD researcher not to rub shoulders with the espionage establishment, for the CIA was monitoring the entire scene."[56] Some of these investigators during the 1950s and 1960s claimed that LSD positively affected everything, including lessening alcoholic or homosexual tendencies. One believed the new hallucinogen could make revolutionary inroads in fighting childhood schizophrenia and autism.

As an enthusiast of new groundbreaking psychological techniques, electronic gadgets, and drugs that showed promise, Dr. Lauretta Bender knew how to discard caution and skirt codes of conduct to satisfy her scientific curiosity. There is no better example of this than her dubious decision to give dozens of young autistic children daily doses of LSD. During the 1950s, Bender began experimenting on children with several tranquilizers and psychopharmacological agents. In one journal article on the subject, she tipped her philosophical hand with the off-the-cuff comment, "I am one of the old clinicians who feel that research cannot be done by pattern, it has to be done by inspiration."[57]

The inspired notion of breaking with convention and prudent decision making and giving children the most controversial psychoactive drug under investigation must have given pause to the more conservative members of the psychiatric community. The idea "that LSD could be used to treat psychological problems seemed downright absurd to certain scientists in light of the drug's long—standing identification with the simulation of mental illness."[58] Bender, however, thought otherwise.

In 1960 Bender began giving LSD and UML-491, a derivative of LSD, to children at Creedmore State Hospital. There were initially fourteen subjects between the ages of six and ten years old, though the number of participants would quickly increase. Eleven were boys, three were girls, and all were said to be either schizophrenic or autistic. Because Bender's diagnostic criteria were different from those today, it is challenging to determine the children's actual maladies. Initially, the children were given small doses that were gradually increased and divided into two daily doses. Incredibly, some children received this regimen, hefty even for adults, for a year or more.

Bender's comments about the experiment in a subsequent journal article are pretty revealing. After being given the LSD, several formerly quiet children became entirely "aggressive—pushing, biting, or pinching other children." Bender considered this an improvement over their past behavior, in which they ignored the surrounding environment.[59] Furthermore, if the LSD was not enough to break through each child's defenses, Bender planned to add ECT or insulin therapy "to take maximum advantage of the intensified" stimuli which caused physical and mental battering by any standard of measurement. Even more revealing was this comment: "Because of the extremely violent psychotic reactions described when adults were given large dosages of LSD, we were extremely cautious when first using the drug, even obtaining parents' consent."[60] Of course, the implication of such an admission is the probability that Bender routinely incorporated institutionalized children into research studies without first asking their parents' permission.

During a conference presentation and a subsequent journal article reviewing her use of Metrazol and ECT on children over the years, Bender made this strange statement:

> Now we have not determined who the sinner may be. There are many who will believe that the mother is always the sinner; is she not schizophrenic? There are others who will believe that the individual himself is the sinner since, after all, is he not the one whose behaviors and fantasies are schizophrenic? However, there will be many of you attending this fifty-second annual meeting of the American Psychopathological Association, who will judge the speaker to be the sinner, for have I not given you this wealth of clinical material without charts, graphs, or statistical evaluation?[61]

There is no indication of how those in the audience reacted to this odd remark.

In a journal article dealing with Bender's Creedmore LSD experiments, she admitted that some children, both autistic and non-autistic schizophrenic boys between six and twelve years old, were kept on a two-dose-a-day LSD regimen for weeks, months, and in some cases a year or two. Though most prudent physicians would, no doubt, shun such a dangerous experimental venture, Bender was pleased with the results: "These were mute, autistic, and schizophrenic children. And they showed a general improvement in well-being, appearance, and lift in mood."[62]

In one ironic admission, Bender said that two adolescent boys in the study "became disturbed to the extent that they said we were experimenting on them." Months later, one of these boys complained that "we were experimenting on him with the drug and trying to keep him from getting out of the hospital."

Bender said they soon after decided to end the boy's participation in the study "not because of the drug but because of the boy's attitude toward it, based on his own psychopathology."[63] The boy's awareness and sense of self-preservation lead one to believe he may not have been as autistic or schizophrenic as Bender believed.

It would be in this same 1970 article that she admitted using "LSD on 89 children from January 1961 to July 1965 . . . because we have found that it is one of the most effective methods of treatment, we have for childhood schizophrenia." Also, in this article, Bender admitted to keeping the children isolated as they went through the drug reaction. A practice that doctors even then would have opposed in both theory and practice.[64]

A half-century later, the vast majority of Americans—including most doctors—are unaware that a noted child psychiatrist conducted such unethical and dangerous psychotropic medical experiments on children. Whether it was due to Dr. Bender's firm conviction that LSD held the keys to unlocking the mind's secrets, to her desire to become the next "god of science," or just to her desire to accumulate knowledge, the research went on without comment or opposition. The practice is a sad commentary on how concerted action by influential people can cow intelligent, sophisticated members of an esteemed profession. Lauretta Bender was not the only person to provide LSD tablets and injections to scores of children over the months and years the research project was in operation. Why did no one in authority speak up? Why didn't another doctor, nurse, or medical administrator say stop, this is wrong? Did no one recognize the harm that was being done?

Walter Freeman had a dangerous fascination with performing lobotomies on as many mentally ill people as he could; Bender was also a passionate propagandist of illusory nostrums. As an avid enthusiast, first with shock therapy in the 1930s and then with powerful hallucinogens twenty-five years later, she was convinced that she had the answer to a series of long-troubling mental mysteries. That she repeatedly trampled on the rights of patients, violated professional codes of conduct, and carried out her experiments on society's most vulnerable members and was still honored by her colleagues says more about the medical profession than do glossy brochures or expensive television commercials that hype the heroes and accomplishments of the medical establishment.

CHAPTER NINE

PSYCHOLOGICAL ABUSE

"I Call That Brainwashing."

WENDALL JOHNSON ARRIVED ON THE CAMPUS OF THE UNIVERSITY of Iowa in 1926 with lofty expectations. With Sinclair Lewis's *Arrowsmith* and Paul de Kruif's *Microbe Hunters* garnering national recognition at the time, skillful writing and important scientific research were helping to make serious scholarship a promising and exciting venture. Johnson was a fine athlete and a good student. He set his sights on accomplishing two goals in college: becoming a writer of consequence and improving his speech.

For most of his youth and adolescence, Johnson had been plagued with a severe stammer. The affliction had been a profound embarrassment that often led to teasing, name-calling, and impromptu fisticuffs. After the heavyweight champion Jack Johnson, Johnson even picked up the nickname Jack for his propensity to punch out classmates with the temerity to tease him about his stuttering habit. The University of Iowa was considered a leader in the new field of speech pathology, and Johnson often "offered himself up" as a willing test subject. "In the clinic, Johnson was hypnotized, psychoanalyzed, prodded with electrodes, and told to sit in cold water to have his tremors recorded." He even put pebbles in his mouth and placed his right arm in a cast to "equalize the imbalance of the hemispheres of his brain," some believed led to stuttering. None of the nostrums had any long-term success. Johnson wrote of his career as a test subject in his journal ten years after arriving at Iowa, "I'm a professional white rat."[1]

Johnson's preoccupation with conquering his dilemma enabled him to become an authority on speech pathology, and he gave presentations on the subject throughout the Midwest. He could talk authoritatively on the social stigma, the embarrassment, the loss of self-respect, and the "self-imposed isolation" that stutterers often faced. Thoughts of suicide are not uncommon among stutterers. As he wrote in his journal, "The stuttering child is a crippled child."

After years of contemplating his problem and the flawed speech patterns of others, by the mid-1930s, Johnson had begun to formulate his own ideas about the origin of stuttering and the best methods for conquering it. The dominant theory at the time was biological; stuttering was the result of a genetic defect. The more Johnson thought about his history and that of other individuals he interviewed, the more he realized that every person "had been labeled a stutterer at a very early age." As he would enter in his journal, "Stuttering begins in the ear of the listener, not in the mouth of the child."

Looking back at his unhappy history with speech, he believed that a first-grade teacher had exacerbated his relaminorblem with her frequent and aggressive efforts to correct him. Her recommendation that his parents do the same only compounded the problem. The more he thought about his own case and that of others, the more Johnson came to believe that "the affliction is caused by the diagnosis." Johnson believed children would naturally overcome their stuttering problem if left alone. His notion was revolutionary; it was also unsupported by any scientific data. If he hoped to confirm his "diagnosogenic theory," a term he coined, he would have to formulate and carry out an original research project that would require repeated access to children in a controlled environment. Becoming a speech professor at the university himself would be one of the things he would place on his research agenda.

The perfect test site was just an hour's drive from the campus: the Iowa Soldiers' Orphans' Home. There was precedent for his choice: The orphanage had been used previously for research by college professors. One of Johnson's students, a former professor of speech pathology, said, "They used that orphanage as a laboratory rat colony."[2] Johnson received permission to carry out his study during the fall semester of 1938. The last piece of the puzzle fell into place when he asked Mary Tudor, a graduate student, "Have you chosen anything for your master's thesis?" Her negative reply would allow Johnson to suggest one. Moreover, though that meeting would enable Tudor to get her degree and help confirm Johnson's theory, it would culminate in the most embarrassing chapter of their professional lives.

Tudor was told that she would be working with two groups of orphans from the Soldiers' Home: one of stutterers and another of normal speakers. Half the children would be assigned to an experimental group, the other half to a control group. Children in the control groups would be labeled normal speakers and receive positive therapy. Children in the experimental groups would be labeled stutterers and given negative therapy.[3]

It was imperative that Tudor point out stuttering among children in the experimental group (even when none existed) so that they would be sensitized to their speech and made conscious of their speaking habits. Tudor was to sternly lecture the children when they repeated a word, mispronounced it, or even stopped midsentence. Speaking was to be made an ordeal. If Johnson's theory proved correct, they would have created a group of young stutterers.

Tudor was told she would have to lie to the teachers and matrons of the orphanage and tell them she was there to do speech therapy. They were to follow her orders in correcting the children when she was not on the premises. She had no qualms about the experiment. Johnson was a rising star in the field, and any association with him was bound to help her career.

Tudor found the Iowa Soldiers' Orphans' Home a depressing place. She imagined how unfortunate it would be to grow up in such a cold, austere environment, but Johnson's theory made sense to her, and it was flattering to be asked to be part of such an important project of which she would be the sole author. After going through files and examining "the speech of 256 orphans, she and the other speech pathologists culled 22 subjects: 10 stutterers and 12 normal speakers. They paired the children based on similarities in age, sex, IQ, and fluency. Then they randomly assigned one from each pair to the control group and the other to the experimental group." Just that simply, Tudor and Johnson would orchestrate a human research project that would prove psychologically destructive to the lives of young children. Many decades later, it came to be known as the infamous Monster Study.

As one of the luckier children would say after learning what had happened to her friends some sixty years earlier, "There but for the grace of God, I could have been placed in an experimental group. It could have been my life that was destroyed."

Initially, children at the orphanage were delighted to be part of such a venture, much as the Fernald boys were told of the new Science Club; like the Fernald boys, they had no idea what was in store for them. Visitors were rare and to be the center of attention was unprecedented. Mary Korlaske, for example, was a twelve-year-old with an IQ of 81 who had been in the orphanage for five years.[4] The Depression had wreaked havoc on her family; her mother had sent her and two older brothers off when she was seven. On her arrival home one day, her mother quickly ushered her into a waiting black sedan with no explanation other than "You'll be safe. You'll be all right." Tender, loving care was undoubtedly not watchwords at the Davenport institution.

Young Mary Korlaske was smitten with the tall, slender college student showering her with attention. She wondered if Mary Tudor, just twenty-three at the time, was there to adopt her and become her new mother.

Mary Korlaske's first interview was on January 19, 1939. Tudor asked her if she knew anyone who stuttered. As she answered that and other questions, Tudor frequently interrupted her and told her she was beginning to stutter. She sternly warned Mary that she would go through life with a pronounced stutter if she did not address the problem quickly. Tudor would write in her notes of that day that Mary Korlaske "reacted to the suggestion immediately and her repetitions in speech were more frequent."

Tudor offered the young girl, who was enamored with her suggestions to combat her stuttering. However, they were psychological trapdoors and tricks: "negative therapy" designed to make Mary more self-conscious about her speech. "Take a deep breath before you say the word if you think you're going to stutter on it," advised Tudor. "Stop and start over if you stutter. Put your tongue on the roof of your mouth. Don't speak unless you can speak correctly. Watch your speech all the time. Do anything to keep from stuttering." The advice was the direct opposite of what Wendell Johnson truly believed ameliorated a stutterer's dilemma.

For "Case Number 11," a five-year-old who was a normal speaker but had been declared a "stutterer" by Johnson's team, the sessions were stressful from day one. Mary Tudor had asked the young girl to "tell me the story of the three bears." When the five-year-old "repeated the word 'she' three times," Tudor "called her attention to it and told her that that was stuttering." Tudor wrote in her thesis:

> I told her to stop when she repeated words and take a deep breath or to stop
> and begin again and try to say them just once. The next time she repeated,
> I stopped her, and she reacted immediately. From then on, when she had a
> repetition, she stopped, put her hand to her mouth, and gasped. Then she
> laughed and tried to do it over again. She became conscious of her difficulty
> immediately. She noticed her own mistakes, and she began to cut her words
> off precisely.

Additional "negative therapy" sessions with the girl only worsened her speaking ability. The problem grew to the point where the little girl refused to speak. As Tudor wrote of the girl's downward spiral: "It was difficult to get her to speak although she spoke very freely the month before. I asked her why she didn't want to talk. She didn't answer. Then I asked her if she was afraid of something. She nodded her head. What are you afraid of? Tudor asked. After some time, she said, 'Afraid I might stutter.' She reacted to every repetition by stopping and hanging her head. She looked down practically all of the time. She seemed inhibited, and she didn't smile."[5]

Johnson's theory of stuttering was proving correct, and Tudor's graduate thesis was moving along nicely. However, there was less reason to be cheerful for the children at the orphanage.

Tudor returned to the orphanage every week or two for additional sessions with the students. They were given verbal exercises and drills that stressed them. When Tudor was not there, matrons at the orphanage continued the barrage of criticism and destructive advice. The experimental group witnessed a steep decline that affected more than their quickly diminishing communication skills. They were made the brunt of jokes, their grades dropped, and some children began to withdraw and isolate themselves.

After several months, Tudor was also showing the effects of her emotionally exhausting work. She was not thrilled with her treatment of the children, but Johnson was delighted with her progress, and his enthusiasm recharged her occasionally flagging spirits. As Tudor would one day admit, "I didn't like what I was doing to those children. It was a hard, terrible thing. Today, I probably would have challenged it. Back then, you did what you were told. It was an assignment. And I did it."[6]

In late May 1939, Johnson traveled with his student to gauge the final product of her work. Of the key experimental groups, five of the six once-normal speakers were now stuttering, and three of the five stutterers had further deteriorated in speaking ability. As expected, the control groups were unaffected by the experiment.

Tudor spent that summer transcribing her many Dictaphone recordings and writing her thesis. Many of the pages from the 256-page document contain comments like this of "Case Number 11."

> [T]his subject showed a decrease in fluency . . . and an increase in the percent of speech interruptions. During the experimental period, her manner of speaking changed markedly. At the beginning of the period, she spoke freely and connectedly, but she was very unwilling to talk at the end of the period. She also ceased to tell stories or converse freely with her playmates.[7]

Generally said Tudor, "all of the children in [the experimental group] showed overt behavioral changes during the experiment that was in the direction of the types of inhibitive, sensitive, embarrassed reactions shown by many adult stutterers. There was a tendency for them to become less talkative." Interestingly, even though Tudor had delineated and documented how the exercise had stamped in each child's mind that "there was something definitely wrong with their speech" and "noticeably" altered their behavior, she recommended that they "repeat this study under conditions more nearly comparable to the home situation" most children live. "More extensive results might reasonably be expected," argued Tudor, if a "home situation" were the site of future research.[8] Fortunately, there is no record of Johnson or Tudor replicating the study.

Mary Tudor, in her thesis, would also include some interesting comments about the staff of the Iowa Soldiers' Orphans' Home. "Both the teachers and the matrons of the institution were very easily influenced, that is, they accepted the diagnosis given without questioning." Moreover, wrote Tudor, the staff believed "children of such 'caliber' and in such environmental surroundings could not be helped. They apparently felt that it was a waste of time to give these children special attention."[9]

By the end of that summer, Tudor's hefty research document had been submitted and approved, and she was off to a job as a speech therapist in Wisconsin. Though it was over for her, those who made up the experimental groups at the Iowa Soldiers' Orphans' Home were still receiving speech "therapy" from the institution's teachers and matrons. By now, Mary Korlaske and others were stuttering badly, and it was having a dramatic effect on their behavior, schoolwork, and relations with other children and orphanage staff. Orphanage officials contacted Dr. Johnson and expressed their concern. Could he do something to address the problem? Johnson, in turn, reached out to his former graduate student and asked if she could visit the institution during her Christmas vacation and see if some positive therapy would work.

Tudor's visit was brief, depressing, and unsuccessful; the children's speaking ability in the experimental group was significantly worse. Nothing she did improved the situation. Two additional visits proved equally futile; she could not reverse the damage she had done.

During WWII, Mary Tudor worked as a procurement officer for the navy. When the war ended, she returned to Iowa, hoping that her former mentor would assist her in getting a job in some aspect of the speech therapy field. The reunion was less than cordial. "It was clear he didn't want me around," Tudor recalled. "He was worried I'd tell somebody."

The intervening years had been instructive for Wendell Johnson. His graduate students questioned the ethics of the Iowa orphan study and began referring to it as the Monster Study. It was something that should be hidden, not celebrated. Some even compared it to what the Allies had discovered on entering Ravensbrück, Treblinka, and Dachau. The Nazi medical experiments had sensitized Americans to the misuse of test subjects, and the research project at the orphans' home could quickly strike some as similar in design and impact. "This was the kind of stuff you would think they were doing in Auschwitz, and this is why, at the time, people concealed it," said Franklin Silverman, a speech pathology professor and former student of Johnson's. "They wanted to block it out of their minds and make-believe it didn't happen."[10]

Johnson must have been on the horns of a considerable dilemma. The research had proved his theory sound, but the project also disturbed and angered people; its ethics were corrupted from the start and had caused considerable damage to innocent children, orphans no less. How does one handle such a sensitive matter in which a research project confirms a groundbreaking theory and will launch its author to the highest ranks of the profession but is so explosive and repugnant to ordinary sensibilities that it could also cause that individual to be shunned, if not jettisoned from the academy?

It is probably that quandary that prevented Johnson from sending his speech students back to the Iowa orphanage to undo what he had helped create. As one college communications professor and former Johnson student said, "He didn't know how to react to it or handle it." Instead of addressing the situation in a concerted and forthright fashion, Johnson chose to try to forget about it and hoped that everyone else would as well. In the end, he chose a prayer for collective amnesia rather than something more meaningful such as a profile in courage.

Johnson was not about to sandbag his diagnosogenic theory, however. He shoehorned it into the literature by arguing that some Indian tribes had no concept or word for stuttering from an anthropological perspective. "The Indian children were not criticized or evaluated on the basis of their speech, no comments were made about it, no issue was made of it," Johnson argued in his 1946 book, *People and Quandaries*.[11] He made no mention of his student's research, a project that documented his important, new theory and one that would subsequently transform speech therapy around the world.

When Johnson died in 1965, the few who knew of his secret were still hiding it. Through the audacious and controversial efforts of *San Jose Mercury* investigative reporter Jim Dyer, the Monster Study was finally revealed. His series on the Iowa Soldiers' Orphans' Home research project in the summer of 2001 attracted nationwide coverage. Mary Korlaske Nixon was seventy-five when she learned what had happened at the orphanage, and she was furious. After her participation in the experiment, she had been teased, laughed at, and ultimately sent to a reform school for girls. Her lawyer admitted she has "a very poor self-image. She's afraid to speak out, not very outgoing. . . . She's lived her whole life like that."[12]

Not long after, Mary Tudor, then eighty—four and living in California, received a letter from her former speech pupil, Mary Korlaske Nixon. "I remember your face, how kind you were, and you looked like my mother," the letter began, "But you were ther [sic] to destroy my life." The letter writer went on to call Tudor a "monster" and a "Nazi" for what she had done to her and the other children at the orphanage sixty years earlier.

Back in Iowa, the university was forced to apologize. Dr. David Skorton, the vice president for research, said, "This is not a study that should ever be considered defensible in any era. In no way would I ever think of defending this study. In no way. It's more than unfortunate. But this man made enormous contributions, both by his direct work with patients and with training so many practitioners and students over the years."

The former orphans brought legal action. Friends and former colleagues of Wendell Johnson were left trying to make sense of it all. "I think it's not coincidental that he chose to do it with a group of parentless kids," said Tricia Zebrowski, an assistant professor at the Wendell Johnson Speech and Hearing Center at the University of Iowa. "This was the only way he was going to get kids," she said of Johnson's decision to use institutionalized children. Though she told Dyer she disagreed with Johnson's approach and thought the study unethical, she did not consider Johnson a bad person, "I think it was just the culture of the time." Duane Spriestersbach, a former colleague of Johnson's, also argues that "it was a different time, and the values were different. Today we might disagree with what he did, but in those days, it was fully within the norms of the time." Not all agree; many argue that some rules and standards precluded causing harm to test subjects, especially children.

In 2007, the six plaintiffs who filed suit eventually won a settlement of $925,000. Hazel Potter Dornbush, eighty-four at the time of the settlement and one of the orphans chosen for the study, found it hard to forgive the study's organizers for what they did. "I call that brainwashing. I don't care what anybody else calls it; that's my language. I was wise to it right away, but I cooperated. You know we weren't in no [sic] position to argue with nobody. We had nobody to lean on to help us out."[13]

Professor Wendall Johnson's ability to stress test subjects in the course of scholarly research and divorce himself from ethical standards that he would typically advocate and abide by is, in fact, not that unusual. There is no shortage of accomplished and respected academics who breached standards of ethics when blindly pursuing a particular point of interest. Whether in the hope of confirming a new theoretical breakthrough, cementing a long-sought financial connection with a pharmaceutical company, or just trying to establish themselves as legitimate scholars and researchers, investigators took liberties they should not have taken. The attraction of the all-consuming scientific hunt was only heightened. The need to follow prescribed rules and regulations was whittled away when outside pressures, obligations, and enticements intruded to make the calculus of everyday decision-making that much more problematic.

World War II had that effect on many normally prudent scientists. The Cold War that followed had a similar impact, especially for those on the front lines of America's defense establishment. The famous Harvard psychologist Henry Murray was one of them; his psychological stress research would gain him some undesired notoriety late in life. As one commentator would write of him, "Murray was an anomaly among academic psychologists, and controversy surrounded his career."[14]

Born at the end of the nineteenth century, Murray was from a wealthy New York family and was educated at the finest private schools. He would go to Harvard and major in history, but his mediocre academic record as an undergraduate would not have predicted the remarkable things that were to come. Murray went to medical school at Columbia and earned a master's degree in biology. After teaching at Harvard for a few years, he traveled to England, earning a Ph.D. at Cambridge in 1928. Murray's eclectic spirit would lead him to spend time with Carl Jung, fostering his newfound interest in psychology and psychoanalysis and increasing his curiosity about various matters of the mind.

Back at Harvard, Murray would make a name for himself, exploring notions of latent needs, external influences on motivation, and the concept of "apperception." In the 1930s, he developed the Thematic Apperception Test. This psychological evaluation device encourages individuals to tell stories based on photographs they are shown. He would write the well—known psychology text *Explorations in Personality,* which added gravitas to his reputation as a scholar and creative thinker.

Though increasingly accomplished, Murray was hard to peg down. "Murray was trained not in psychology but rather in medicine and biochemistry. Furthermore," says one biographer, "Murray rejected reductionism in psychological theory and research, instead promoting methods derived from medicine and a theory of personality influenced by psychoanalysis and . . . biological systems theory."[15] The cross-pollination of disciplines was hard for the Harvard faculty and administration to digest. Fortunately, Murray had the financial backing of the Rockefeller Foundation, which allowed him to continue at the university and further his study of personality development.

During World War II, the military used Murray's knowledge of personality traits to select secret agents for special intelligence assignments. Much of his work was for the Office of Strategic Services (OSS), the forerunner of the Central Intelligence Agency. In addition to matching personality and character traits to military job descriptions, Murray was asked by OSS chief William Donovan to develop a personality assessment of Adolf Hitler. Murray's analysis, along with several other scholars, contributed to one of the first mergers of criminal profiling and political psychology to pursue character prediction. The team's prognostications, including Hitler's suicide, gained them and their new profiling system additional plaudits. After the war, Murray returned to Harvard but continued work as a CIA consultant. His shadowy research work for the spy agency would shock the conscience of those in the academic community who were unaware of his clandestine ventures.

In 1958, Murray began stress research with definite CIA and Cold War implications. The project, which at least one author believes had MKULTRA associations, was designed to establish an assessment scale that would collect an impressive amount of data about people's reactions under pressure. Twenty-five Harvard students were selected to participate, and the aim was to assess their reactions to stress. Murray's experimental protocol measuring personal reactions to intense sustained and highly insulting criticism was unusual but relatively simple in design. The student subjects were told they had a month to write a brief composition regarding their philosophies of life. Once submitted, an experienced lawyer would confront each subject about his respective philosophy and attitudes. Both personal and general issues were considered fair game. The subjects were informed that the debate would be filmed; they were not told, however, that the attorney's criticisms would increase in number and tone and become personally abusive.

The dialogue, designed to be highly stressful, was more a psychological endurance contest constructed to measure how much verbal abuse an individual could withstand. The students were connected to monitoring devices that charted their psychological reactions as the lawyer pointedly and repeatedly belittled aspects of their personal essay and stand on issues. Subsequently, each student was forced to watch a tape recording of the session, illuminating their impotence and rage. Students were also told to rate their feelings about the lawyer. They were required to return to watch the tape again and answer additional questions at two- and eight-week intervals.

One of the student subjects was a sixteen-year-old math prodigy named Theodore John Kaczynski; today, he is better known as the Unabomber. An excellent student from a second-generation Polish American family, Kaczynski had always been more comfortable with numbers than with people. Growing up, he had few friends but many books. He skipped several grades in the Chicago school system and graduated from high school at fifteen. At Harvard, he excelled in mathematics and was taught by some of the nation's top mathematicians, who vouched for his exceptional ability with numbers.

According to one observer, Alton Chase, and his account of Kaczynski's troubled life in *Harvard and the Unabomber,* the precocious math student was emotionally stable when he became a test subject in Murray's research project. Kaczynski's lawyers argue that some of his emotional instability is related to his participation in Murray's research project. They believe the young math student cracked under pressure.

It is further argued that, over time, Kaczynski would embrace ideas that "were products of two historical trends: a crisis of reason and the impact of the Cold War."[16] Kaczynski came to believe that only empirically verifiable statements were meaningful. The Cold War accelerated this process. The threat of Communism and the ever-present threat of war with the Soviet Union "created a climate of fear. It stimulated technological progress, provoking an anti-modernist backlash . . . by equating scientific progress with national survival. It also encouraged researchers to abuse the rights of students and others. It fed the hubris of some psychologists, encouraging them to seek ways of modifying behavior to make people better citizens. It gave birth to a drug culture and a generalized disillusionment with America and government."[17]

Kaczynski transformed his frustrations into an ideology, and his experiences at Harvard proved crucial to that ideology and his understanding of the world. Murray's experiments triggered in Kaczynski a suspicion of psychology and the system of which it is a part. Soon nightmares about psychologists followed. Ironically, Dr. Murray, an establishment figure who fancied himself a father figure to students, became a catalyst for transforming Kaczynski's anger at individuals into philosophical fury against industrial society and the significant role that psychology plays therein. "As the only leading psychologist Kaczynski knew personally, Murray represented the establishment. And this establishment, Kaczynski thought, threatened liberty and demanded submission . . . and retaliation."[18]

Kaczynski would isolate himself from society, living in a remote Montana cabin without electricity and running water, learning survival skills, and beginning a two-decade-long campaign against the modern industrial world. An interest in explosives would replace his love of mathematics, and he would mail sixteen bombs to an assortment of targets, including airlines and universities. His one-man terrorism campaign would result in three dead, twenty-three injured, and the haunting specter of the Unabomber's next target.

Some believe Kaczynski's long and convoluted political manifesto, *Industrial Society and Its Future*, shows definite indications that his time as a Henry Murray stress subject impacted him. Though others in Murray's psychological studies did not take up arms against their country, Kaczynski's youth and fragile mental state made him too vulnerable for the emotional pounding the professor's experiment was designed to deliver.

Wendall Johnson and Henry Murray were not the only psychologists who initiated experiments that heaped excessive psychological pressure on vulnerable children. Over the years, a cursory look at psychological journals discloses numerous studies that subjected already burdened children to questionable levels of stress.

In one 1969 study, researchers decided to take an eight-year-old severely mentally disabled boy who had been on tranquilizers, an eight-year-old mentally disabled girl who was forced to wear restraints, and another eleven-year-old mentally disabled boy and use various degrees of aversive therapy to disabuse them of self-destructive and psychotic behavior. Because drugs, electro-convulsive therapy, and other treatment regimens proved unsuccessful, doctors decided to experiment with painful shocks delivered to the child's leg or a 1,400-volt shock from a one-foot-long rod with spikes. The authors said the shocks were "definitely painful," similar to "a dentist drilling a tooth."[19] Later, the authors would address the perceived need to ensure that the pain threshold was severe enough to impact children who had already grown used to pain from their own behavior. "To avoid selecting a neutral shock, or a weak one to which the children could adapt quickly," the authors designed one that "smarted like a whip or a dentist drilling on an unanesthetized tooth" to ensure "the subjects gave every sign of fear and apprehension."[20] Incredibly, researchers found it more convenient to use an electrified cattle prod on mentally disabled children than to put in the time and effort it would take to help children in desperate need of assistance unlearn some self—destructive habits.

In other studies, during the 1980s and 1990s, children from psychiatric clinics between seven and thirteen years of age, many of whom were emotionally disturbed or with conduct disorders, were told to imagine being chased by a monster or being scolded for something they had not done. Their biological reactions were compared to "normal" children.[21] In one 1989 study, eighteen anxious children hospitalized for enuresis or a tonsillectomy were exposed to a supposedly mild stressor while being measured for salivary cortisol and electrodermal activity. The stressor was a series of scary, harrowing scenes from a film called *Rollercoaster*. A control group was shown ducks swimming on a small lake, and differences in biological reactivity to stress between "disturbed" children and "normal" controls were assessed.[22]

Even more recently, in another study of twenty-one young males between the ages of eight and eleven who were recruited from schools for special children, "stress was induced for 75 minutes and involved frustration, provocation, and aggression."[23] Remarkably similar to Murray's Harvard study, competition between each subject and a "videotaped opponent of similar age and sex" would compete for "best performance over the session. Frustration was induced by having the subject solve a difficult task under time pressure." The task was "made to be unsolvable," especially given the added "provocation" that took the form of constant and disparaging criticism of the subject's performance. Their biological reactions to this stress, measured by cortisol levels and cardiovascular response, were compared to thirty-one "normal" children.

Finally, from a few years ago, twenty-seven children with varying degrees of aggression and anxiety issues were emotionally challenged with a series of go/no go tasks designed to cause emotions such as sadness, anger, and frustration.[24] Their cortical activity as measured by EEG was compared to fourteen normal developing controls.

Experimental psychological studies such as these are commonplace in the academic literature. However, there are few examples of journal editors, psychological professionals, or readers voicing their concerns about the judiciousness of putting vulnerable children in such harmful scientific exercises. Where are the institutional review boards that were instituted to ensure that such abuse did not occur? Where were the journal editorial boards who might have ensured that such problem-ridden experiments were not accepted for publication? Regrettably, the literature is replete with nontherapeutic experiments that could only cause harm.

CHAPTER TEN

REPRODUCTION AND SEXUALITY
EXPERIMENTS

"They Treated Those Girls Just as if
They Were Cattle."

Though he had died decades earlier, Charles Davenport, the ardent and indefatigable early twentieth—century eugenicist, would have appreciated the gung-ho race—cleansing spirit that dominated certain parts of Alabama in the early 1970s. Nearly four decades, the U.S. Public Health Service's experiment in Tuskegee monitoring the long-term consequences of "untreated syphilis in the Negro male" was not the only research project in the Heart of Dixie that smacked of eugenics. In the state capital of Montgomery, just twenty-five miles away, another government study was underway that, in both design and practice, fostered all the principles and goals championed by America's better-breeding movement earlier in the century.

To restrain the birth rate in certain parts of the community, especially among people on welfare and residing in low-income public housing projects, the Montgomery Community Action Committee, in conjunction with the federal Office of Economic Opportunity had begun giving experimental birth control injections to women. The drug chosen was depot medroxyprogesterone acetate, which would become better known to the American public as Depo-Provera.

The drug was developed by Upjohn scientists in the mid—1950s. In 1960, Upjohn applied to the Food and Drug Administration (FDA) for its approval for endometriosis treatment. During testing in Brazil, however, it became clear to Upjohn researchers that the drug had utility as a long-term contraceptive as well. That realization led them to apply to the FDA for the drug's approval as a viable contraceptive.[1] During the 1960s, animal and human trials were begun domestically and in numerous foreign countries. The results disclosed unwanted side effects, including tumors and various forms of cancer in dogs and monkeys.[2] One large Upjohn trial in 1967 took place in the Grady Memorial Family Planning Clinic in Atlanta, Georgia, where as many as 1,000 women may have been involved.

Though the FDA had not blessed it as an approved contraceptive, more and more doctors were prescribing it off-label; they viewed it as a cheaper and more consistent alternative to other forms of contraception. States from Tennessee to Texas were incorporating it in their birth control programs. Poor black women in the South tended to be the overwhelming drug recipients. Threats, deception, and the loss of welfare benefits were recurring themes in many of these anti-pregnancy programs.

Anna Burgess, for example, was a twenty1year-old woman from Cumberland County, Tennessee, who lived in a three-room house without running water or electricity. In July 1971, she was called to her local welfare office. "The welfare lady asked me if I had signed up for family planning," recalled Burgess before a congressional hearing in 1973. "I was not on it then, and she said I ought to be taking something or other. She said they would rather feed one youngun [sic] as two. She made arrangements for me to go to the health departments. She said the shot would last 6 to 8 months. I didn't go the first two times she arranged it because I was scared a little." Burgess went on to tell the Senate Committee, "If it had not been for them, I would have not have taken it. If it had not been for the welfare people, I would not have taken the stuff in the first place. They wanted me to take the birth control shot so there would not be no more children."[3]

It became increasingly clear to her that she would be in serious financial trouble if she did not do what they wanted. "Well, it seemed the way I took it was, I thought they would take the check or something. From the impression I got, if I did not take the birth control, they would take the check."

Such stories were commonplace throughout the South in the early 1970s. It was estimated that the state of Tennessee alone had "between 1,000 and 1,500 women getting Depo-Provera each year." And girls younger than twenty were caught in the anti-pregnancy dragnet. As Jessie Bly, an Alabama social worker who was to become a key player in a landmark medical abuse case, said of the widespread, discriminatory, and coercive government practices at the time, "They had become a way of life for many in the South."[4]

One family particularly hard hit by these modern-day eugenic practices was the Relfs of Montgomery, Alabama. Unschooled field hands with various learning disabilities, Lonnie Relf and his wife struggled to raise and care for their three young daughters. They all had some degree of mental, physical, and social obstacles to overcome. Katie was the eldest, followed by Minnie and Mary Alice, who were intellectually challenged.

When the family walked through the doors of a Montgomery Department of Human Resources office in desperate need of housing in 1972, Jessie Bly was assigned to assist them. Bly was thirty years old, married to a military service member, and attended Central Texas College before her husband was transferred to Alabama. "Home visits" would become a core part of her social work duties, which included checking on the condition of the elderly, poor, and making sure their needs were met. Many would have gone without food, heat, and other necessities if she had not repeatedly gone to their residences to check on them.

Bly helped the Relf family get an apartment at Smiley Court, a public housing complex in Montgomery. While aiding them with the move and doing the paperwork that would assist them in procuring additional government services, not an easy chore considering that the Relfs could neither read nor write, she was particularly struck by the young Relf girls. Katie was just fifteen and already receiving shots of Depo-Provera. Bly suspected that Minnie, a couple of years younger, might be on them as well. She was most concerned about the youngest daughter, Mary Alice, who was twelve. She was mentally disabled and missing part of her arm, which had been amputated shortly after birth because the umbilical cord was wrapped around it during delivery. The girls had modest to no schooling, leaving them terribly behind other children their age. Mary Alice had several issues, including "a problem with hygiene," that Bly addressed.

Lonnie Relf and his wife had to be taught almost everything. Some mundane features of life were mysteries to them. The family had "huge power bills," said Bly, and she could not understand what was causing them. An investigation and a couple of visits turned up why "The Relfs had no comprehension of thermostats. They never knew what a thermostat was or how it worked," recalled Bly. "When I went to visit them, the heat was always way up; they had it blasting. And all the windows were open to cool the place off. They had no idea what a thermostat did. They were really backward and completely dependent on public assistance for food, shelter, and medical care."

Life for the Relf family had always been a struggle, but the situation grew particularly dark for the family in 1973. All three girls were receiving Depo-Provera injections by that time, and in March, a nurse took Katie to a health clinic to insert an intrauterine device. Her parents were never asked if they had any objection, and Katie certainly did not want it, but as with most poor blacks in the South, they believed they had to do what the government wanted. In June, a family planning nurse picked up Mrs. Relf and the younger girls and transported them to a doctor's office. "Mrs. Relf was told the girls were being taken for some shots. She thought the shots were the same as those all three children had been receiving for some time."[5] From there, they were transported to the hospital, where the girls were assigned a room, and Mrs. Relf was asked to sign a document. Unable to read or write but believing it had something to do with the girls getting more shots, she placed an "X" on the paper. It was an authorization form for "surgical sterilization."

At some point during their brief stay at the hospital, Minnie managed to borrow a dime from another patient on the ward and call a neighbor as the Relfs had no phone to plead for their mother to come to pick them up. Minnie was in fear for her life and believed something dreadful would happen to her and Mary Alice. Their mother said she had no means of transportation; she could not get to the hospital or get the girl's home. According to Joseph Levin, general counsel of the Southern Poverty Law Center, "the next morning both children were placed under a general anesthetic and surgically sterilized. At no point before the surgery did any physician discuss with the girls or their parents the nature or consequences of the surgery to which Minnie and Mary Alice were about to be subjected."[6]

That same morning, Jessie Bly arrived at the Relf apartment to take Mary Alice to her first day of school. Bly was intent on getting the youngest Relf girl at least a modicum of formal education and was unaware of the visits by the family planning nurse. Katie, the eldest sibling, explained what had taken place. Katie said they wanted to take her as well, but she had locked herself in her room and then ran away so they would not get her. She was scared to death of doctors and hospitals.

Bly went directly to the hospital only to be met by a shattered and terrified young girl. Mary Alice had just come out of surgery and was "scared to death," recalled Bly. "It hurt me so bad. She was so frightened and fearful. She wouldn't let me go. It was pitiful. They treated those girls just as if they were cattle."[7]

Bly was furious. "I went to the doctors, but they wouldn't tell me anything. I then went to the head nurse and demanded to know who authorized the surgery. She told me, 'They could get pregnant. There are boys hanging around them now. We don't want any more of that kind.'"

"That did it," said Bly, who was already greatly disturbed that young girls throughout the state were being injected with experimental birth control drugs. "That's what pushed me out there. It became a matter of principle for me. These people were so backward; they were easy targets. They needed somebody to speak up for them. That's when I decided to talk to a Jesuit priest who did good work in the community. I also got them a good lawyer."

Bly went to the Southern Poverty Law Center, an organization known for helping the poor and dispossessed. When Joseph Levin, the center's general counsel, heard the story, he immediately took the Relfs' case. He would later recount before a Senate subcommittee that the Relf girls had been taken to the clinic because of "new policies which prevented nurses from going into the community to administer shots and birth control devices . . . the only way to ensure against pregnancy was sterilization."

At the hearing, Senator Edward Kennedy asked Levin whether he believed they were getting Depo-Provera before being sterilized. To quote the hearings:

> MR. LEVIN: I am not familiar with the drug, but I am told that it is the only birth control injection available. So, I assume that that is the only injection they received prior to the sterilization.
>
> SENATOR KENNEDY: Did you know that that is an experimental drug, as well? Depo-Provera?
>
> MR. LEVIN: I have since been informed of that.8

Levin thought it possible that Congress's effort to deal with one problem, off—label use of a potentially dangerous drug (Depo—Provera), may have resulted in some communities taking the extraordinary step of sterilizing many poor women. Levin and many others believed young girls in Alabama were caught in a difficult situation: their choice was either an experimental drug that they had no understanding of or sterilization.

"I decline to engage in debate over the relative merits of sterilizing children," Levin testified. "I see no justification for permanently depriving any child of his or her right to conceive, regardless of the child's present mental or physical condition, nor do I believe that agencies, by committee or other means, have the right to sterilize any persons, regardless of age, unless that person, intelligently and with full and complete knowledge of the consequences, desires to be permanently stripped of his ability to create life."9

Levin described the lives of these poor women who depended on the state for food stamps, medical assistance, and the "$156 each month from the Alabama Department of Pensions and Security" for their existence. However, the trade-off was that their lives were now "under a microscope." They were constantly under supervision with almost weekly visits by some government representative. As Levin told the lawmakers, "They are surrounded by a welfare state upon which they depend for their very existence, and they are easily 'coerced' into doing what the welfare people recommend to them. It is a very sophisticated, probably unintentional, form of coercion, but it is extremely effective."

When questioned on related subjects, such as how widespread such practices were, Levin expressed doubts about whether paying customers would have been treated in such a fashion. "I believe this subcommittee will find that the children of middle America are not sterilized, regardless of physical or mental condition. The 'free clinic' patient is fair game for this most final of birth control methods. Sterilization is not 'birth control' when applied to minors and incompetents—it is mayhem, and it should be stopped now."

The early history of Depo-Provera and its misuse and overuse were due not so much to aggressive pharmaceutical company marketing as to average doctors becoming wedded to the notion of the drug as a quick, effective, and relatively cheap method of contraception. Disregarding the fact that it was an investigational new drug still under examination by the FDA, they casually prescribed it for their patients, the majority of whom were poor and black, for a good number of years during the late 1960s and early 1970s.

Even when forced to testify at Senate hearings in 1973, doctors continued to deny Depo-Provera's official status as an investigational drug. As one physician boldly stated, "We keep referring to Depo-Provera as an experimental drug. It has never been our understanding that it is an experimental drug, and our use of Depo-Provera has not been within the context or the framework of the way we would go about doing an experimental study if we did one."

Irritated, Senator Kennedy fired back, "Just to clarify our terms. Depo-Provera is an experimental drug for the purpose of birth control." Earlier in the day, Kennedy pointed out there had been testimony stating that Depo-Provera "is not to be used for birth control purposes."

The combative witness, Dr. James Brown, the superintendent of Arlington Hospital in Arlington, Tennessee, argued the point. "We were advised by our medical specialists that quarterly injections of a progestational product of the Upjohn Company, Depo-Provera, while not specifically licensed for the purposes mentioned above, would safely control menstruation and serve as a contraceptive should sexual exposure occur."[10]

Further questioning by Kennedy concerned its use in state institutions. Brown not only admitted that the drug was used in state facilities for the "retarded" but went on to argue, "The problem of providing birth control, and the problem of menstrual periods in a facility among the very severely retarded is a considerable problem. It is one we agonize over from the standpoint of the normalization principle and try to weigh the benefits of obliterating menstruation to the resident, as compared with the benefits to the staff."[11]

Kennedy summed up the situation: "It is my own conclusion that there have to be some straightforward and important protections for the individuals that are being affected by these very dramatic and in many instances constructive and others destructive experiments which are taking place."[12]

The case Joseph Levin, Morris Dees, and the Southern Poverty Law Center brought against the Department of Health, Education, and Welfare (HEW) and the Office of Economic Opportunity would address and rectify these egregious practices that had affected the Relfs and many other families in the South.

In *Relf et al. v. Weinberger et al.*, Judge Gerhard A. Gesell ruled that HEW guidelines had to be corrected, including the need for a definition of the term "voluntary," the lack of safeguards to ensure that sterilizations were indeed voluntary, and the absence of prohibitions against the use of coercion in obtaining consents.[13] On April 18, 1974, HEW published revised regulations that included Gesell's changes. Informed consent was now defined as "the voluntary, knowing assent" of any person undergoing sterilization procedures verified with a consent form that included information on the actual procedure, any possible risks or discomforts, any benefits of the operation, information on alternative methods of birth control along with an explanation that sterilization is an irreversible procedure, and a statement "that the individual is free to withhold or withdraw his or her consent to the procedure at any time prior to the sterilization without loss of other project or program prejudicing his or her future care and without loss of other project or program benefits to which the patient might otherwise be entitled."[14]

The revised regulations also dictated that every sterilization consent form exhibit prominently at the top of the form this legend: "NOTICE: Your decision at any time not to be sterilized will not result in the withdrawal or withholding of any benefits provided by programs or projects receiving federal funds."

Interestingly, one agency that was not obligated to abide by these regulations was the Indian Health Service (IHS), which performed twenty-three sterilizations of women under the age of twenty-one from mid-summer 1973 to April 30, 1974, despite the HEW moratorium on them. Thirteen more sterilizations on underage girls occurred between April 30, 1974, when HEW published the new regulations in the *Federal Register*, and March 30, 1976. It was suggested that some IHS physicians did not completely understand the regulations, and those contract physicians were not required to adhere to them.

Health care, in general, for Native Americans is something of a national embarrassment, and women's health concerns were indeed no exception. Sterilization was standard on Indian reservations in the 1970s, and in the 1990s, the use of Depo-Provera and Norplant (another chemical anti-pregnancy medication) was routine. It is estimated that up to 80 percent of women were "voluntarily" sterilized on some reservations, even women under twenty-one and even within seventy-two hours of giving birth, violating federal regulations.[15] According to accounts, two fifteen-year-old girls were sterilized during what they were told were tonsillectomy operations. Additional breaches of the regulations included parents not being informed of the procedures, coercion being used to acquire their signatures, improper consent forms, and not observing the seventy-two-hour waiting period between signing and the surgical procedure.

It was also argued that informed consent papers were worthless, as those giving their consent could not understand them. Moreover, Depo-Provera was still considered dangerous. An investigational drug was being given to Indian women long after it was no longer prescribed for women in the rest of the nation.[16]

As we pointed out in earlier chapters, sterilization and castration were once thought viable remedies for troubling reproductive issues concerning "defectives" who had just entered their teenage years. Physicians under the influence of an emerging and boisterous eugenic movement practiced various experimental procedures to rein in the explosion of defective germplasm that gradually laid waste to society. At the turn of the twentieth century, some in the profession were on a crusade to seek out and identify "degenerates" in the community. Extreme measures were occasionally utilized to neutralize their spread.[17] Many converts to the eugenic banner were proud of their work and boasted of their triumphs in various medical journals.

Disturbed by the level of masturbation occurring at his Baldwinville (Massachusetts) home for children, Dr. Everett Flood castrated over two dozen boys between seven and fifteen. He would go on to claim that the first castrations were performed with the idea of "preventing masturbation in certain cases where the habit was most constant, and the boy had no sense of shame, besides being a confirmed epileptic and, of course, somewhat feeble-minded."[18] The *Journal of the American Medical Association* editors saw nothing unethical or improper about such drastic and irreversible measures when they published Flood's article. There is no telling the impact of such messages on the profession, but colleagues must have noticed Flood's success. "Masturbation has ceased," he informed readers, and the boys were now "more manageable, less inclined to quarrel, and more capable of reasoning."[19]

Flood was a serious champion of the therapeutic effects of castration. He not only articulated its benefits when performed on oxen, horses, sheep, and, of course, humans but also came to the rescue of doctors who might have drawn the wrath of critics for performing such surgery on children. For instance, in one psychology journal article, he wrote:

> Dr. Pilcher, Supt. of the Institute for Imbeciles and Weak Minded Children, at Winfield, Kan., has been bitterly denounced by newspapers in Winfield and Topeka for castrating several boys, inmates who were confirmed, masturbators. His predecessor, Dr. Wile, had treated these boys five years without benefit, and Dr. Pilcher, taking a rational view of the subject, operated for the same reason that he would perform any other surgical operation—for its curative effect.

Another doctor who advocated for greater use of such methods was Harry C. Sharp. An ardent eugenicist and surgeon at the Indiana Reformatory, as discussed in chapter 2, Sharp wrote a paper titled "*The Severing of the Vas Deferens and Its Relation to the Neuropsychopathic Constitution.*"[20] He practiced what he preached and cut the vas deferens of forty-two patients whose ages ranged from seventeen to twenty-five to prevent the birth of criminals, cure excessive masturbation, and bring about positive results for the patient. A lobbyist as well as a practitioner of sterilization, Sharp often proposed the mass sterilization of the "feebleminded" and encouraged state authorities to sterilize the 300 girls in the state institution for the "feebleminded."

Those in the medical profession preaching greater utilization of sterilization and castration were preoccupied with other sexual dilemmas besides masturbation, or what was diplomatically referred to as the "sexual over-excitation" of delinquent boys. Those who had bought into the theory of biological determinism viewed castration as a crime preventive. Whereas sterilization served chiefly to prevent offspring, some argued that castration was a crime-prevention measure for the existing generation and indirectly for posterity.[21]

By World War II, the medical profession had, in general, repudiated castration as an acceptable option. However, it was replaced with hormone therapy in some quarters, particularly among physicians exploring the treatment of homosexuality for individuals displaying violent or criminal behavior. In one experiment with teenagers at a child guidance clinic, two thirteen-year-old males with effeminate characteristics and one fifteen-year-old with "latent and innate homosexual tendencies" received "androgen hormone treatment." Sounding much like the triumphant Drs. Flood and Pilcher, a half-century earlier, the author of the article detailing this treatment, believed that any individual given testosterone injections "became a pleasing type of aggressive male. There were no more delinquencies. His sexual life also became normal."[22]

Medical experiments on pregnant women had a dramatic impact on the health of their fetuses and children. Since Dr. J. Marion Sims, the renowned antebellum surgeon, doctors have found it convenient to experiment with pregnant women. The son of a poor South Carolina family, Sims would graduate from Jefferson Medical College in Philadelphia and return to the South to practice his craft. Sims may have questioned his competence as a physician early on, but once he commenced his career on the plantations of Alabama, he cast aside all caution. He would become quite daring. In a misguided attempt to address black infants suffering convulsions, Sims performed radical brain surgery on slave children. He blamed their deaths or permanent childlike behavior if they survived on "the sloth and ignorance of their mothers and the black midwives who attended them."[23]

To understand and treat vesicovaginal fistula, a catastrophic complication of childbirth, Sims experimented on his slaves, whose lives were considered less valuable than those of genteel Southern society. Sims spent four years experimenting on black women with new equipment and new methodologies in the hope of arriving at a surgical breakthrough and making a name for himself in the medical arena. The procedures were terribly painful, and test subjects were given little in the way of anesthetics, but Sims pushed on firmly in the belief "that blacks did not feel pain in the same way as whites." Publications on the subject by Sims resonated in the medical community, and eventually, he would become known as the father of American gynecology.

By the 1850s, Sims had relocated to New York City and become the toast of the town for his well-publicized medical triumphs, although detractors believed the good doctor had done much damage over the years. In trying to determine whether Dr. Sims was a hero or villain, one scholar has written: "It is certainly ironic that an icon of medicine like Sims could be mentioned in the same context as Nazi medical experimenters and the authors of the notorious Tuskegee study on syphilis. An exploration of the apparent paradox reveals as much about the state of medicine during Sims' lifetime as about the man himself."[24]

On pregnant women, the impact of teratogenic agents, such as thalidomide, diethylstilbestrol (DES), and radiation, is especially devastating, resulting in severe consequences for both the women and their children. The thalidomide episode of the early 1960s is one of the most unfortunate in terms of damage done. To those who lived through the period, just the mention of the word "thalidomide" draws the heartbreaking recollections of photographs showing children born with arms like flippers, legs like boat paddles, and severe eye and ear deformities. A drug fiasco and human disaster of incredible proportions, it need not have happened. By the late 1950s, science had evolved enough that it was understood that drugs ingested by pregnant women could affect the developing fetuses, even those drugs labeled as "the drug of choice for pregnant women upset by morning sickness."

As the *Sunday Times of London* said of the health calamity:

> It is a popular fallacy to assume that the thalidomide tragedy alerted the
> world to the danger that drugs can cross the placental barrier and affect the
> fetus. This was commonplace knowledge before the thalidomide tragedy,
> and before it, drugs were also tested on pregnant animals and given clinical
> trials on pregnant women. The knowledge and scientific procedures to
> give protection were available. The disaster might well have been averted
> everywhere. Unarguably, the havoc wrought could have been much less than
> that which occurred.[25]

The result of what was referred to as "a huge and disastrous scientific experiment" was untold damage to the German people and people around the world. As one appalled observer stated, "It was an experiment conducted with unusual incompetence, and its dire effects penetrated eventually to most parts of the medically developed world." Seductive advertising copy for the marketing campaign mentioned that the drug was "completely non-poisonous," "astonishingly safe," and that thalidomide could "be given with complete safety to pregnant women and nursing mothers, without adverse effect on mother or child."[26]

> Nevertheless, by 1955, if not sooner, it was scientifically quite well known
> that any substance with a molecular weight of less than 1000 could be
> expected to cross the placenta and appear in the fetal blood—and the
> molecular weight of thalidomide is only 258. A general practitioner could
> not be expected to be aware of this by 1961. Indeed Grunenthal (the
> German pharmaceutical company that produced it) should have been
> aware of it.[27]

By misrepresentation, the company had made it appear that experimental work had been successfully accomplished. In fact, such work had not been done. However, if it had, the teratogenic effects of thalidomide (teratogenic means "monster making," or the creation of significant deformities) would undoubtedly become known from 1956 to 1958. What had become evident were complaints of neuritis when used as a general sedative, but the German manufacturer, Chemie Grünenthal, actively fought those complaints as well as attempts to prevent the drug from being marketed. It squashed early adverse news reports, but by 1962 there were rapidly increasing accounts of babies born with a laundry list of appalling congenital disabilities.

Stunning physical deformities were the signature feature of a thalidomide baby. Deformities depended on the embryo's development stage when the mother took the drug. As one author mused, "It was as though the jigsaw of life had been jumbled and then the pieces forced into places they could not fit or simply left out altogether."[28]

Fortunately, a young FDA official had significant questions about thalidomide. Even though it was her first drug review assignment, she would not be bullied into granting approval for the drug to be marketed in America. A Canadian pharmacology school graduate from McGill, Dr. Frances Kelsey, understood German, and was able to read the original application forms, and understood the potential effects of new drugs on developing fetuses. Kelsey rejected the company's applications six times; she had serious reservations about the drug's safety. Unfortunately, the Richardson-Merrell Company, which had gained the right to market thalidomide in the United States if FDA approval was secured, managed to distribute many pills for investigational purposes—a custom permitted under U.S. law pending agency approval.

As one scholar has written of that loophole:

> The law also permitted pregnant women to be included as research participants after the first three months of the investigational period. Two and a half million tablets were distributed in the U.S. for experimental purposes, and nearly 20,000 patients received thalidomide, including several hundred pregnant women. The window of danger for congenital problems turned out to be relatively narrow, but the amount needed to cause problems was minimal: infants of women who took thalidomide (one tablet was sufficient) between the 20th and 36th day after conception were at risk for malformation. The result, thanks to Kelsey, was that only 17 children in the U.S. were born with thalidomide-related deformities. By contrast, in the rest

of the world, an estimated 8,000 to 12,000 infants were born malformed due to their mother's use of thalidomide and . . . only about 5,000 survived beyond childhood. Approximately 40% of thalidomide victims died before their first birthday.[29]

Another well-known example of drugs for pregnant women damaging their offspring was the synthetic hormone DES. It was given to women from the 1940s until the 1970s when physicians finally realized that the drug did not significantly prevent miscarriage and substantially increased health risks to the 6 million children born to these mothers.

In utero, the female fetus genital tract exposure to DES led to infertility and malignant transformation.[30] Adenosis, a nonmalignant vaginal problem, occurred in 50 to 90 percent of DES daughters. The relationship between mothers taking DES and daughters developing rare clear-cell adenocarcinoma of the vagina fifteen to twenty-two years later is estimated to be between 1 in 1,000 to 1 in 10,000. Other adverse effects include infertility, spontaneous abortion, ectopic pregnancy, stillbirths, early menopause, cervical cancer, and breast cancer. Sons of women taking DES are more prone to have undersized sex organs and low sperm counts, epididymal cysts, microcephalus, and testicular hypoplasia, among other health issues.[31] However, the use of the drug had not started with such bleak expectations. It was once believed that DES averted late pregnancy complications. Many doctors recommended it. As one 1940s study suggested, based on the results of 387 women at Boston Lying-In Hospital, even if women delivered early, DES protected the fetus against death since the fetuses are unusually premature for their gestational age. Researchers thought this was because DES created a better intrauterine environment for fetuses. And though there was a lengthy discussion at the end of the journal article debating various aspects of the study, not one doctor brought up the possibility that DES might have teratogenic effects on the fetus.[32]

By the early 1970s, though, doctors reported a link between vaginal tumors in daughters of mothers who had been prescribed DES. The association with clear-cell adenocarcinoma was the first instance of prenatal carcinogenesis in humans. This finding led to many animal experiments dealing with the mechanisms of transplacental carcinogenesis and the effects of exogenous hormones on developing embryos.[33]

The impact has been significant for the children of pregnant women who took DES during the quarter-century following World War II. Not long after the connections between DES use in pregnant women and problems with the genital/reproductive health of their children were dis-covered, headlines such as "A DES Victim Tells of Anger, Awareness, and Despair" and the "University of Chicago to Pay $225,000 to 3 over DES" became more frequent.[34] News of large sums of money changing hands in out-of-court settlements and offers of free exams to children of all 1,081 women given DES while maternity patients at the university's hospital followed. Similar stories played out at numerous medical institutions around the country.

However, if proper precautions had been implemented early in the drug's development, the situation could have been much different. As one reviewer has written of the DES debacle, "Ultimately . . . it serves as a reminder that though the narrow lens of today might reassure us that an intervention is safe, it is only with the wisdom of time that the full consequences of our actions are revealed."[35]

One of the more inexcusable examples of scientists cavalierly incorporating pregnant women in dangerous research and thereby putting their unborn babies at risk at the dawn of the Cold War concerns the radiation studies performed on low-income expectant mothers at Vanderbilt University in Tennessee.

As was eventually revealed, from the end of World War II in 1945 to May 1947, over 800 pregnant women were ushered into Vanderbilt's Prenatal Clinic for a thorough physical examination. The clinic patients, usually poor and not well educated, appreciated any attention by university health personnel. Invariably, the hospital visit would conclude with what was described as a nurturing cocktail. Some women wondered if a "cocktail" was a judicious choice so close to the birth of their baby. Eileen Welsome graphically captured those ominous moments in her book *The Plutonium Files*.

> "What is it?" Helen [one expectant mother] asked.
> "It's a little cocktail," said the doctor. "It will make you feel better."
> "Well, I don't know if I ought to be drinking a cocktail," she responded, her voice light and bantering.
> "Drink it all," he told her. "Drink it on down."[36]

As it turns out, the young woman who was part of this exchange, and the hundreds of others like her, might have been luckier if they had been handed a shot of bourbon. They had been given something far more debilitating and dangerous for both themselves and their fetuses: a glass of liquid containing radioactive iron isotopes. As Welsome states, "[M]any of the women were led to believe that the drinks contained something nutritious that would benefit them and their babies. But nothing could have been farther from the truth. The drinks contained varying amounts of radioactive iron. Within an hour, the material crossed the placenta and began circulating in the blood of their unborn infants."[37]

The research, coordinated by some of the top biochemists in the country, including Paul Hahn, who was bright, energetic, and described as possessing "insatiable curiosity," traits not unlike those of many other top-flight microbe hunters, had a definite scientific goal in mind. The scientists were eager to learn how a woman's diet and nutrition affected her pregnancy and delivery and the condition of her infant.

Though some of the more experienced physicians understood the implications and potential risk in giving pregnant women radioisotopes, some were just carrying out an assignment, ignorant of the damage they were causing. Dr. William Darby, for example, one of the physicians who doled out the isotope-laced drinks, as one would give "sweet[s]" to a child, admitted years later that the radioactive libations had "no therapeutic purpose" at all. The study was designed to obtain additional knowledge. He further admitted, he "didn't know much about radiology."

The repercussions of such clandestine and cavalier scientific mischief cannot be overestimated. Manhattan Project physicians may have acquired some useful information, but many Vanderbilt women and their children would suffer bizarre health complications that ran the gamut from strange rashes and bruises to unusual blood ailments, including cancer. Welsome's gripping account of one girl developing "a lump about the size of an orange on her upper thigh," whose poisonous contents gradually "spread into the child's spine, then moved up through her lungs, heart, throat, and finally, into her mouth," leading to eventual paralysis and death at eleven years of age, is heart-wrenching.[38] Other children of Vanderbilt who developed liver cancer, acute lymphatic leukemia, and synovial sarcoma and died between five and eleven years of age were poignant proof that there was an unmistakable cause-and-effect link between the covert isotope experiments and the pregnant women who were purposefully deceived for them to become raw research material.

No matter what was being tested and for what reason, doctors found it convenient to use young boys and girls as if they were nothing more than lab animals. Though there was the occasional protest, most of these egregious experiments were met with indifference by both practitioners of the healing arts and medical journal editors. It was easier to go along with moral and ethical outrages than oppose them.

CHAPTER ELEVEN

RESEARCH MISCONDUCT

"Science Actually Encourages Deceit."

IN 1998 BRITISH PARENTS OF INFANTS AND YOUNG CHILDREN WERE GIVEN a severe fright. A London researcher was making headlines claiming that the combination measles-mumps-rubella vaccine, known as MMR, was quite dangerous and precipitated the spike in autism around the globe. Panicked parents immediately began to question the wisdom of their family physician, and many decided to forgo MMR shots for their children. These difficult familial decisions would result in numerous repercussions, not the least of which were growing doubts about the medical profession and an ever-increasing number of children falling victim to measles, mumps, and rubella (or German measles).

Andrew Wakefield, the physician who had sparked the controversy regarding vaccine safety and its relationship to autism, had published a study earlier in the decade linking measles to Crohn's disease but later admitted he had been wrong. He was now confident that MMR was linked to autism and recommended that children not be vaccinated. After his report made worldwide headlines, there was a noticeable decline in children receiving the MMR vaccine. The increasing numbers of laypeople supporting Wakefield's allegations, growing consternation among physicians, and general controversy surrounding vaccine safety led to much angst, debate, and, in time, public hearings on the issue.

The son of a surgeon and general practitioner, Wakefield earned his degree from St. Mary's Hospital Medical School and became a fellow of the Royal College of Surgeons. His specialty would become tissue rejection, especially concerning small-intestine transplantation. Eventually, he would become the head of experimental gastroenterology at the Royal Free Hospital School of Medicine.

Wakefield's name would become known to his medical colleagues worldwide through his controversial 1998 *Lancet* article. Along with a dozen coauthors, Wakefield's study of twelve autistic children claimed a link between bowel disease, autism, and the MMR vaccine. "Autistic enterocolitis syndrome" was the name he gave his discovery, and he was not shy about broadcasting it. A well-attended press conference and numerous media interviews ensured maximum exposure to his theory.

Parents of autistic children were desperate for answers, and Wakefield's theory provided an explanation. Curious about his findings, doctors and medical researchers made repeated attempts to replicate a definite connection between gastrointestinal disorders and autism but could not do so. After they could not establish the critical linkage Wakefield had supposedly discovered, doubts about his hypothesis grew.

More parents, fearing the specter of autism, decided to delay regular vaccinations for their children, but serious concerns about Wakefield's research increased in the medical community. The doctor's *Lancet* article and MMR theory took a dramatic hit six years later when Brian Deer, an investigative reporter for the *Sunday Times of London,* authored a scathing article regarding Wakefield's research practices and financial motivations. Deer raised questions about Wakefield's errors. He interviewed some of the parents of the six- to nine-year-old children in the study and found that their stories did not match the doctor's claims. No case was free of misreporting or alteration. Deer was also critical of Wakefield's practice of putting children under general anesthesia, doing spinal taps, threading fiber optic scopes into their intestines, doing biopsies, and collecting large quantities of blood for testing. Moreover, according to Deer, all this was without Ethics Committee approval. Deer communicated his concerns and findings to the *Lancet's* editor in chief.

More explosive yet, Deer charged that Wakefield had received $100,000 (the actual sum was much higher) from a personal injury lawyer representing a parents' group that believed vaccines caused many illnesses. They looked for a respected medical advocate to join their cause, and the attorney found one in Wakefield. With this financial conflict of interest revealed, many of the original article's coauthors requested that their names be removed from the research. The British General Medical Council was brought in and determined that misconduct had taken place, that autistic children had been subjected to unnecessary medical procedures, and that Wakefield had never received institutional review board approval for his research.

Not long afterward, a retraction appeared in the *Lancet,* asserting that the data were insufficient to support the claim of a causal relationship between MMR vaccines and autism and that no studies could replicate Wakefield's hypothesis. The UK General Medical Council examined the charges against Wakefield and concluded that he had acted against the interests of his patients and was irresponsible in his research. In May 2010, he was struck off the medical register, which ended his career as a doctor in the United Kingdom. As one reviewer has commented on the controversial case, "Good science will be reproduced by other investigators; bad science will not."[1]

Though Andrew Wakefield's research and reputation would be seriously damaged, the *British Medical Journal* labeled his work an elaborate fraud. Both Great Britain and America witnessed a "vaccine scare" and a steep decline in MMR vaccinations. The result would be a sharp increase in measles among children and unnecessary fatalities. In 2008, for the first time in fourteen years, measles was declared endemic in England and Wales.[2] The *British Medical Journal* estimated that Wakefield's mischief has resulted in hundreds of thousands of children in the United Kingdom being unprotected and vulnerable.

Regrettably, research misconduct involving children extends far beyond Andrew Wakefield's shenanigans in the MMR/autism controversy. There are numerous examples of physicians and academics purposefully manipulating data to accomplish some grand scheme or goal. However, such unethical practices fly in the face of professional principles like fidelity and integrity and fail to consider the damage done to patients and the medical profession. The manipulation of data and the publication of false results waste precious research funds, take up journal space, and provide fictitious and misleading information. The theoretical and scientific detours are bad enough, but some may result in postponed or wholly jettisoning proven prevention strategies, leaving populations at significant risk.

Many scientific investigators have contemplated the motivation to commit fraud. Some believe it is the all-consuming desire to be first with a discovery. As William Broad and Nicholas Wade have argued in their book *Betrayers of the Truth*, "There are no rewards for being second."[3] They go on to state that, in trying to be first with a discovery, "some researchers . . . sometimes play fast and loose with the facts in order to make a theory look more compelling than it really is. The desire to win credit, to gain the respect of one's peers, is a powerful motive for almost all scientists." As Broad and Wade point out, "Massaging data in some way may help toward getting an article published, making a name for oneself, being asked to join a journal's editorial board, securing the next government grant, or winning a prestigious prize."[4]

They argue that there is an almost total absence of credible deterrents. Most cases go unreported or are kept quiet. And on those rare occasions when someone is willing to report a violation or breach of ethics, the accuser is associated with the accused. For each significant fraud they suggest, a thousand minor fakeries are perpetuated. The reward system and career structure of contemporary science are among the factors that induce fraud. Those impressive rewards overmatch the modest chance of getting caught, especially those who have long lusted after professional success and personal recognition.

The impact of Paul de Kruif's *Microbe Hunters* in the 1920s cannot be overestimated in its power to fire the imagination of generations of aspiring doctors and medical researchers. His heroic account of doctors laboring for years in the laboratory, trekking through godforsaken jungles, and battling everything from deadly mosquitoes and outdated practices to stuffy bureaucrats and lack of financial support, enhanced the reputation of a formerly staid profession and sparked widespread interest in the lives and personal crusades of the great disease fighters. There is no telling how great an influence the personal sagas of Koch, Pasteur, and Reed had on the scientists detailed in de Kruif's work.

Some aspiring scientists, for whatever reason, perpetuate scientific sins. Some misrepresent data; others practice deception, thereby placing subjects at risk. Still, others may remain silent while observing colleagues embellishing a journal article, conducting an experiment that puts an individual in jeopardy, or falsifying test results.

Some believe the level of scientific misconduct, particularly the promulgation of inaccurate data, has grown worse in recent decades. As Allan Mazur has written about dishonesty in the academy, "Since 1980 there has been an unusual number of reports of misconduct in scientific research in the United States, especially falsification of data and plagiarism." Mazer argues that such practices "represent a challenge to universities, medical schools, academic research institutes, and bodies which support research." Moreover, he asserts, "It is a plausible although untested contention that the norm and conditions of biomedical science foster more cheating than do those in other fields of research."[5]

> According to Mazur, physicians doing in-depth research operate in a more competitive environment with higher professional stakes. At least in terms of money . . . there may be more pressure to publish . . . more haste in doing so . . . with so many medical journals . . . to accrue credit for publication through 'honorary authorships,' . . . and they can always leave research to pursue more lucrative careers. These conditions may account for the higher incidence of misconduct in biomedical science than in other research areas. The path to success is so well defined that 'any lofty ideals . . . a neophyte

scientist' may have been quickly jettisoned in favor of 'being first, the need to obtain research grants, trips to exotic places for conferences, and the lure of money and prestige.'[6]

That such behavior is so pervasive and widely accepted speaks to the power of the medical profession in getting its members to rationalize and buy into the system. As one observer has commented, "When a person sees ego-inflation, monetary gain, power, or prestige as the criterion for success, engaging in fraudulent behavior will cause minimal dissonance arousal . . . an individual may proceed to reduce the dissonance through a type of cognitive reframing or rationalization (What will it hurt? . . . those would have been the results anyway)."[7]

We could cite numerous other examples of research misconduct to underscore our point regarding the prevalence and acceptance of such unethical scholarship. Here we will focus on one of the better-known examples of research misconduct, that of Sir Cyril Burt, an eminent, award-winning British psychologist whose research eventually came under considerable suspicion and was finally rejected.

Between the start of World War I and the onset of the Great Depression, a period that corresponds with the height of the eugenics movement, Burt collected an impressive amount of data to support his hypothesis that intelligence was determined by heredity. Though there may have been those who doubted the wisdom of Burt's pronouncements over the decades, it was not until the 1970s and Burt's death that detractors began to challenge his scholarship. Leon Kamin of Princeton University was one of the first to criticize missing details and false statements. "Kamin came to the conclusion that Burt has 'cooked' his data in order to arrive at the conclusion he wanted," wrote Alexander Kohn in *False Prophets*.[8] Additional critics would soon surface, leading to increased scrutiny of Burt's work and his formerly unchallenged findings. As more scholars took notice of the inconsistencies, it became more remarkable that "during Burt's lifetime, his work was never challenged despite its shortcomings."[9]

According to Broad and Wade, this phenomenon has much to do with scientists' becoming prisoners of their dogma. An entire coterie of scientists appeared ready and willing to accept and digest what was served up to them. The scientific community has too often allowed charlatans and propagandists to impersonate scientists and wave a banner of suspect and illegitimate claims— making for bad science and potential harm.

Burt was a disciple of the great eugenicists like Charles Benedict Davenport and Henry H. Goddard. He was never wavering in his hereditarian beliefs.

He was quite willing to massage his data to confirm his convictions. Early twentieth-century IQ testers argue Broad and Wade "had a hereditarian bias so strong that it blinded them to the evidence of environmental influence that cried out from their data. All they could see was the reflection of their own dogmatic beliefs, which, just like those of Samuel Morton, echoes the prejudice of their time and social class."[10] Data repeatedly pointed to the importance of environmental factors, but those administering the tests created tortuous rationalizations to preserve their hereditarian biases. The result was multifold, impacting everything from reshaping national immigration policy to changes in the military and other American institutions.

With the passage of years and still intransigent on the subject of the genetic origin of intelligence, Burt rallied both data and coworkers from his vast reservoir of prejudiced research to undergird his scientific argument and fool his fellow scientists for more than a generation. Even once-loyal Burt defenders eventually realized that he had systematically arranged and rearranged data and studies to document the heritability of intelligence. "This deception is inexcusable for a scientist," admitted Arthur Jensen, but that realization had come decades late, for the ruse had already affected educational policy throughout the nation.[11]

Patrons of the old *New York World-Telegram* were stunned when they picked up copies of the paper at newsstands on Monday, January 20, 1964. The front-page banner headline rang out with the shocking announcement, "Charge Hospital Shot Live Cancer Cells into Patients."[12]

The lengthy article began with the stunning accusation by a well-regarded and "prominent lawyer" in the city that the Jewish Chronic Disease Hospital was "conducting cancer experiments on unsuspecting non-cancerous patients." The hospital, situated in the borough of Brooklyn, served an elderly population and those in need of long-term physical care. The lawyer, William A. Hyman, who also happened to be a member of the hospital's Board of Directors, was outraged by the incident and told reporters even he was prevented from acquiring information about the experiments. "They say I am not entitled to medical records of these human guinea pigs. I don't want Nazi practices of using human beings as experimental guinea pigs. Don't want people used as human guinea pigs." Hyman went on to claim the experiments were orchestrated in collaboration with doctors at "Sloan-Kettering Cancer Center" and that live cancer cells had been injected "into patients without their permission."[13]

Hyman made the additional claim that medical staff at the hospital found the situation so egregious that "three doctors resigned because of these secret experiments." It is that critical point-the resignation of doctors in protest over unethical medical experiments and research misconduct-that we include the infamous Jewish Chronic Disease Hospital case in a book about the abuse of children in medical experiments. In addition, some of Southam's trials of injecting cancer patients, before 1963, with other viruses to fight cancer included two fifteen-year-old-old male patients.[14] One patient had osteogenic carcinoma, and the other was afflicted with embryonal carcinoma. Southam was hoping to show that other viruses could fight cancer. He injected both boys with the West Nile Virus. Additionally, he injected the mumps virus into one child and the Ilheus virus into the other. Ironically, he would go on to thank Drs. Hillary Koprowski, John Enders, and Albert Sabin for supplying the viruses.

Revelations regarding dangerous clinical trials were not unfamiliar to newspaper readers—the thalidomide episode was only a couple of years old, the Willowbrook hepatitis experiments on nearby Staten Island were a regular staple of discussion and debate, and newspaper accounts of interesting human experiments were not unusual. Just eight years later, the Tuskegee Syphilis studies would be revealed. However, it was unprecedented for doctors to take a principled stand and resign their positions to protest questionable research practices. Furthermore, though the courageous act of three physicians was mentioned in all the newspaper articles, their stand was never given the attention such a high-minded and selfless act deserved.

The Jewish Chronic Disease Hospital case is considered a significant event in America's annals of unethical medical research and misconduct. It shocked the conscience of most Americans when they learned of it. Even one of the reporters who broke the story admits to being shocked when he heard what had transpired. Selwyn Raab was a relatively new hire at the *World Telegraph* when an editor assigned him to check out a tip he had received about some research shenanigans at a Brooklyn hospital. "I was astonished," recalls Raab on his initial meeting with Bill Hyman and what was being described to him. "The idea that they would inject sick people with cancer cells was incredible to me. It struck me as abhorrent. Anyone of even limited intelligence knew you could not get informed consent from senile people."[15]

The experiment began months earlier, on July 5, 1963, with a letter from Dr. Chester Southam, a noted immunologist at Sloan-Kettering Hospital, suggesting a collaborative research project with Emanuel Mandel, director of medicine and medical education of the Jewish Chronic Disease Hospital (JCDH). Southam hoped to initiate an "evaluation of the immunologic status of patients with chronic non—neoplastic diseases, as revealed by the promptness of rejection of subcutaneous cancer cell homografts." He said the project would aid the "treatment and diagnosis of cancer." He thought it would have "equally great interest" to Mandel for understanding "autoimmune and degenerative diseases and in the budding field of organ transplantation."[16]

The project Southam was proposing was a continuation of cancer studies he had been doing for well over a decade. He mentioned in his letter that research at Ohio State University Medical School had "revealed that healthy persons reject the cancer cell homografts completely and promptly." He was now hoping to determine the reaction of "people who do not have cancer but who have chronic and debilitating diseases." In short, Southam wanted to see if the immunologic systems of debilitated individuals reacted any differently to the introduction of cancerous cells than healthy people. So non-therapeutic was this experiment, it would have usually been done on lab animals.

The procedure, according to Southam, would be simple. All it required was "simply the hypodermic injection of a suspension of tissue-cultured cells at two sites on the anterior thigh or arm. . . ." Though simple in design and practice, advised Southam, there was one "drawback;" when injecting "cancer cells" in humans, one has to deal with "the phobia and ignorance that surrounds the word *cancer.*"[17] Their decision on how to deal with that conundrum would have lasting repercussions. As Southam related to us in an interview, the patients "were thoroughly informed that they were getting human cells growing in test tubes."[18] They would not be told the solution in the syringe contained live cancer cells.

To ease any concern Dr. Mandel had about the project, Southam informed him that his studies were so "routine" at other hospitals that they no longer request "(written) permission from patients." Southam provided the interesting admission, "We do get signed permits from our volunteers at the Ohio State Penitentiary, but this is because of the law—oriented personalities of these men, rather than for any medical reason."

Southam had performed similar cancer cell experiments on well over 100 Ohio prisoners in the 1950s. When interviewed by the authors on the subject, he was assured that the human body's immunologic system would naturally reject foreign material. Pressed further and asked what he would do if his belief proved incorrect and his injections did spark cancer cell growth in test subjects, Southam replied matter-of-factly, "Well, we'd just cut it out. If anything like that happened, we'd just surgically remove it."[19] The likelihood of such an eventuality, he assured us, was quite remote.

Southam's simple experiment required one thing more customary in clinical trials at large institutions holding vulnerable populations: a cooperative staff willing to perform specific duties, in this case, the cancer cell injections. Though the mastermind of the exercise, Southam never planned on being a daily presence at the Jewish Chronic Disease Hospital. He needed regular hospital physicians to perform that critical function. It was that mundane housekeeping chore that would prove the Achilles heel of the dubious venture and seal its doom.

Historically, such a task proved simple to accomplish. Whether one examines Johnson's stuttering experiments at the Iowa orphanage, Salk's poliovirus experiments at the Polk and Watson schools, Stokes' vaccine experiments at Pennhurst, Bender's LSD studies on autistic children, Kligman's poison ivy experiments at Vineland, or any of the dozens of others including the long-running Tuskegee Syphilis Study, there was never any difficulty in acquiring loyal staff that would orchestrate the experimental protocol as directed and remain silent about its existence and implications. However, that cozy code of medical omerta would go awry at the Jewish Chronic Disease Hospital. Dr. Mandel's s search for a cooperative staff member to inject the cancer cell suspension material proved troublesome from the start. The first three doctors he approached reacted with horror and promptly turned him down, an ominous omen of what was to follow.

It was in July 1963 that Dr. Mandel approached Drs. David Leichter, Avir Kagan, and Perry Fersko with the Southam research initiative. Dr. Kagan, the first physician he approached, clearly recalled that uncomfortable moment even though it was 50-years ago. Kagan had graduated from New York University in 1952 and then went to medical school and service in the army. After leaving the military in 1962 and needing a job, he took a position at the Jewish Chronic Disease Hospital as the coordinator of the department of medicine. He was not there long when one of the hospital's top medical officials came to him with a proposal.

"Mandel came to me," said Kagan, "and explained who Southam was and what the project was about. He said that Southam had injected healthy people and now wanted to test chronically ill people." In a classic piece of understatement, Kagan went on to say, "The entire thing seemed a little bit ill-conceived to me. I couldn't understand how they could get consent and the willingness of people to go along. The issue for me was whether we had the right to do this to the patient. I decided I wouldn't do it. There was never a question. It was all so iffy. I certainly would not consider it unless we got consent. The very issue of informed consent was the key to it. I couldn't imagine approaching a patient and asking his permission to inject him with live cancer cells. It would be like telling a patient I'm going to give you a shot of anthrax."[20]

Dr. Mandel pressed Kagan further. "He tried to convince me it was okay," said Kagan. "He said we have to lead and take the forefront. Research was very important. Such a project would benefit many people and the hospital as well. They definitely had no compunction or reservations about it," recalled Kagan.[21] No matter what argument Mandel proffered, Kagan was rightfully not buying it. He refused to perform the cancer injections.

By the end of July, Mandel had also pitched the project to two other hospital physicians with similar results. Dr. David Leichter, a more senior physician than Kagan and a survivor of the holocaust, was equally put off by the proposal, considering it "immoral and illegal without the prior written informed consent of each and every informed patient."[22] Leichter also warned hospital administrators of "rumors spreading" and the "tremendous damage it could do to the hospital's reputation and its standing in society."

Undaunted by three rejections, Dr. Mandel finally found his man. Dr. Deogracias Custodio was a Philippine physician whose tenure at the Jewish Chronic Disease Hospital consisted of little more than a year of employment when he met with Mandel, Southam, and another Sloan-Kettering physician to discuss the research project. After hearing of Southam's past work and what was being asked of him, Custodio agreed to work on the experiment. He would inject the hospital patients with live cancer cells.

Dr. Custodio would subsequently admit that "before any patient was injected," they received "oral consent" from the patients. According to Custodio, "The patient was told that an injection of a cell suspension was planned as a skin test for immunity or resistance. The patient was also told that a lump would form within a few days, which would last several weeks and gradually disappear. The patient was not told that the injection would contain cancer cells. The reason for this is that we did not wish to stir up any unnecessary anxieties, disturbances, or phobias in our patients. There was no need to tell the patients that the injected material contained cancer cells because it was of no consequence to the patient."

Within short order, 18 patients were injected with live cancer cells, thereby solidifying the hospital's place in the annals of unethical biomedical history. Dr. Custodio would eventually receive $100 for his services from the US Public Health Services and American Cancer Society grant monies funded by the Sloan-Kettering research project.[23]

Initially undecided what they should do, Kagan, Leichter, and Fersko decided that if they kept quiet about the experiment, they could still be accused of being part of a conspiracy. That predicament and their agreement about the experiment's egregious nature caused them to take radical action. "We decided to resign," said Kagan. "We quit to show we were not condoning what had happened. Our jobs were not important."[24]

The three physicians drafted a letter explaining the reasons for their actions and braced themselves for some unpleasant repercussions. To their surprise, according to Kagan, "the resignations did not cause the fallout they feared, and the medical staff of the hospital accepted their resignations. They seemed untroubled by the experiment. They closed ranks around Mandel."

Dr. Kagan admits to being "befuddled by what happened." He says there was a "period of ten days where rumors floated around as to what could happen to Mandel and us, but nothing happened." Dissatisfied that business was occurring as usual and the experiment had not been stopped, the three doctors then went to a hospital board member, William Hyman, and explained what had occurred. The attorney was stunned. "Hyman jumped on it," says Kagan, and proceeded to take it to the press where it became a front-page story in the *New York World-Telegram*.

The subsequent media coverage caused the experiment to be terminated. In its place would be a lengthy and painful period of self-reflection, much recrimination, and a series of court and disciplinary proceedings. Testimony would conflict over whether the Jewish Chronic Disease Hospital patients were, in fact, senile and fully capable of understanding English. Some patients supposedly only spoke Yiddish. However, there was little doubt regarding one key element of the experiment. The test subjects had never been accurately informed about what had been injected into them. As Louis J. Lefkowitz, Attorney General of the State of New York, would declare in a post-hearing memorandum, "the salient factor remains that at no time and to no volunteer patient was information given that, in truth and fact, the cell suspension mentioned contained live cancer cells. This then is the nub of the entire case. These volunteers, the 22 debilitated patients at JCDH, were not each made fully cognizant of all that is entailed in the proposed project. There was missing, deliberately and willfully so, any statement to the effect that the injectable material contained live cancer cells."[25]

It should be noted that attorneys for Mandel and Southam argued that the research practices of the two men did not differ dramatically from those of other researchers. "If the whole profession is doing it," said one of the attorneys, "how can you call it unprofessional conduct."[26]

After much testimony and legal argumentation, Drs. Chester Southam and Emanuel Mandel were found "guilty of fraud or deceit in the practice of medicine and unprofessional conduct in the practice of medicine" by the Board of

Regents Discipline Committee.[27] The Regents went on to suspend the licenses to practice medicine of the two men for one year, but then "stayed" the suspensions and "each respondent [was] placed on probation for a period of 1 year" if they agreed to conduct themselves professionally and refrain from "any further misconduct."

Though the event had garnered Southam and Mandel unwanted publicity and an embarrassing professional suspension, they recovered from the episode. Chester Southam, for example, was elected president of the American Association for Cancer Research just four years later.

"That was hard to take," recalls Kagan.

Drs. Leichter, Fersko, and Kagan would also recover their careers and reputations, but it was far from smooth sailing. As Avir Kagan related to us, others initially called him a "whistleblower" and a "rat" at the hospital. They were "more interested in protecting the institution. They closed ranks around Mandel. Ethics was secondary."[28] Looking back, Kagan says there was "so little emphasis on ethics at the time. Ethics dealt with how you should deal with other doctors, not with patients or specific issues. In retrospect, it was not good."

Like many doctors of that era, Dr. Kagan willingly admits his understanding of sophisticated codes of medical conduct was meager in the early 1960s. He believes the Nuremberg Code, Henry Beecher's journal articles, the Helsinki Code, and the other steps to prevent the exploitation of subjects in clinical trials were of little consequence to doctors in the decades after Tuskegee. "There was so little emphasis on ethics," says Kagan. "What I did at JCDH was without knowing about ethical benchmarks. It was some innate moral stance that caused me to reject Mandel's request. What he was requesting of me was something I just couldn't do. I just felt it was wrong."[29] Kagan's instincts proved correct.

The individual decisions by the three JCDH physicians to reject participation in Chester Southam's cancer cell experiments on ill and senile hospital patients and their collective decision to answer press questions to illuminate what was occurring to unwitting patients in the name of science is all too rare in the annals of medical experimentation. In the book, we have previously mentioned the concept of "hero" worship of doctors in the early 20th century. Kagan and his colleagues are heroes, too, for following their conscience and maintaining the tenets of the Hippocratic Oath during this time.

Embarrassing incidents of research misconduct affecting children occurred in fields other than virology and genetics. Charles Glueck, for example, was a well-respected and much-published physician who oversaw the lipid unit and the General Clinical Research Center at the University of Cincinnati. He was one of the most influential and well-funded scientists at the Center; Glueck published approximately 400 articles, an average of a remarkable 17 per year since his graduation from medical school.

In 1987, however, the National Institutes of Health (NIH) found that an article in the journal *Pediatrics* was sadly lacking and called it "utterly shoddy science." The paper tackled a controversial treatment for children at risk for developing heart disease.[30] Doctors could not agree on whether a low-fat diet combined with cholesterol-lowering drugs called resins would hinder a child's physical development, causing concern that their growth could be stunted. Glueck, however, declared the diet perfectly safe.

Prior to publication, two anonymous calls were placed to NIH warning of potential problems, but those warnings were never passed to the journal editor. Though the article was published, a continuing investigation disclosed that Glueck's methods were unacceptable by any scientific standard. He had not measured the children's height, weight, and cholesterol levels, as required for such a study. Eventually, the article was retracted, but there is no record of who, under its influence, might have tried to replicate its findings, thereby placing children at increased risk. Glueck was barred from federal funding for two years and resigned from his position at the university.

In his defense, Glueck claimed that he was overworked. "When career pressures," he said, "get too great in any field, people do funny things. They work hours that would put a securities lawyer to shame."[31]

An argument can be made that Glueck's errors pale compared to what some consider the country's six-decade-long experiment with fluoridation, which violated the Nuremberg Code since people had little choice but to drink the treated water whether they wanted to or not. As the argument is presented, when the US Public Health Service endorsed the widespread addition of fluoride to the nation's water systems, no trials of its impact had been completed. But there was a strong desire to change the image of fluoride from a nasty pollutant to something harmless that children could drink. Moreover, the sugar lobby was a strong presence. There were allegations that childhood over—exposure culminated in bone fractures, lowered IQ, and lowered thyroid functioning.[32]

The field of psychology has not been spared claims of research misconduct. One of the better-known cases is that of Stephen E. Breuning, a University of Pittsburgh psychologist who developed a name for himself as an expert on the effects of behavior-controlling drugs on severely retarded institutionalized persons. Although Breuning never received a doctorate, he achieved a national reputation owing to his many studies and journal publications over the years.

Earlier in his career, Breuning had worked under Dr. Robert Sprague at the University of Illinois. Their research dealt with the effect of neuroleptics (tranquilizers) on violent, intellectually challenged patients. After Breuning departed to take a position at the University of Pittsburgh, Sprague noticed errors if not outright lies in his former apprentice's studies, particularly in Breuning's new research, which argued that withdrawing neuroleptics would increase IQ. The numbers were too good for Sprague's taste, and he feared "there was fakery."[33] Sprague notified the National Institute of Mental Health (NIMH) and the University of Pittsburgh of his suspicions. Though the investigation moved slowly, Breuning eventually admitted faking data under questioning and resigned. After the investigation, NIMH found that Breuning "knowingly, willfully, and repeatedly engaged in misleading and deceptive practices" and banned him from receiving research funds for ten years. As one observer has commented, in cases like this, the work is not just wrong, "it is potentially deadly . . . he is playing with lives."[34] Between 1980 and 1983, Breuning published twenty-four papers on neuroleptics and related topics—a full third of the literature on the subject. Coauthors claim never to have seen his raw data.

The federal court case that resulted in Breuning's pleading guilty forced the University of Pittsburgh to reimburse NIMH $163,000 in grant monies and repay over $11,000 in salary. Breuning was sentenced to serve 250 hours of community service and spend 60 days in a halfway house. One last stipulation was that Breuning cease any involvement in psychological research for at least five years.[35]

The results of the Breuning affair cannot be overestimated. According to Alan Poling, "the recognition that Breuning's work cannot be trusted has seriously eroded the database concerning psychotropic drug effects in mentally disabled people. We now know less about how psychotropic medications affect this population than we appeared to know when Breuning's data was accepted. This has implications for patients, as well as scientists."[36]

It has been argued that the greatest purveyors of fraud are not young, struggling researchers but experienced, well-published ones, and the problem will only grow worse as pressure mounts to publish groundbreaking articles that foster acclaim, status, and professional recognition. It has become increasingly apparent that science fosters deception and deceit to build a record of important publications that will earn individual personal recognition, reap honors and awards, and invite invitations to join celebrated organizations and associations. Cheating and cutting corners, it is now thought by many, will help secure such goals.

CONCLUSION

*". . . a Utilitarian Calculus of Convenience, Self—interest,
and the Chances of a Grand Scientific Payoff."*

D URING THE EARLY YEARS OF THE COLD WAR, A JOURNAL ARTICLE recounted
how several toxic substances were introduced into the systems of "mice,
guinea pigs, and humans."[1] The humans subjected to the toxic substances were
not members of the Boston Philharmonic Orchestra, the Massachusetts Cham-
ber of Commerce, or the Harvard University faculty, but mentally challenged
young males at the Wrentham State School. Injected with dangerous substances
and then routinely bled to observe the negative impact, the Wrentham subjects
were labeled "volunteers," like the mice and guinea pigs.

A few children at the Fernald State School, Wrentham, and other institutions were old enough and had sufficient cognitive ability to understand what
was happening. However, many others were either too impaired or too young to
comprehend how they were being manipulated. Like the State Boys of Fernald,
a few would learn the truth decades after their involvement as test subjects.
Most have never learned how they were once sacrificed to benefit scientific
advancement.

Researchers, many motivated by the noblest of causes, others by the prospect of fame and fortune, gravitated to orphanages, hospitals, and institutions
for the "feebleminded" when in need of test subjects to conduct a clinical
trial. The ethical constraints for such dubious acts sorely lacking or in some
cases embraced as a brilliant maneuver was spurred on by an exploitative ethos
reeked of eugenics and paternalism. That raw, utilitarian spirit, combined with
a ramped—up sense of urgency during World War II and the Cold War that
followed, contributed to an unrestrained atmosphere that fostered scientific
research and some valuable discoveries. However, those advances often came
at the expense of orphans and the physically and intellectually downtrodden.

Physicians tried to rationalize their conduct by arguing the need for isolation, control, and predictability in their research protocols. However, they never

adequately explained why their choices were always facilities like the Skillman Center for Epileptics, the Iowa Sailors Home for Orphans, and the Wrentham State School, over the many prep schools and colleges that held individuals of similar ages and were usually more convenient as a travel destination. Though most would undoubtedly deny any eugenic influence, the preponderance of evidence suggests that doctors knew which people they could risk harming and with whom they could not take such liberties.

Doctors were either ignorant of or all too willing to abandon medical codes of conduct such as the Hippocratic Oath, American Medical Association directives, and the Nuremberg Code. They routinely trafficked in children to operationalize some bit of medical research. And institutions like Letchworth Village, Vineland State Colony for the Feebleminded, the Pennhurst School, Sonoma State, and St. Vincent's Orphanage were happy to accommodate the great men of science by opening their doors to expand our knowledge of disease and improve the human condition. For Mark Dal Molin, Gordon Shattuck, and thousands of other children, that open-door policy would prove the final crushing blow to already grim, compromised lives in austere custodial institutions.

The most zealous of the medical profession were not inherently evil men and women or crass charlatans. However, they passionately pursued a particular vaccine or held a defiant stance in favor of one treatment regimen or another that placed children in great jeopardy. During the Cold War, radiation experiments or so-called tracer studies incorporated minimal amounts of radioactive substances. Constantine Maletskos of MIT underscored his attempt to use the "smallest amount possible" of radioactivity on the Fernald subjects, but as experts freely admit, not even the smallest dose of radioactivity can genuinely be called safe.[2] Thyroid uptake studies are another story, especially in infants just a few hours or days old. There is no telling how many individuals died or suffered from rare cancers due to those injudicious experiments.

Acclaimed physicians like Lauretta Bender and Walter Freeman were equally blind to the damage they were doing. Bender was too quick to see childhood schizophrenia or autism in troubled youngsters and only slightly less quick to prescribe ECT and LSD as the proper remedy. Freeman was equally determined to cure the world of myriad psychological maladies through the use of crude prefrontal lobotomies that he believed did not even require hospitalization. In the time it takes to boil an egg, he believed he could cure phobias, depression, anxiety, and a propensity for violence. Even children who argued with their stepmother could be helped with a few jabs of a simple ice pick-like instrument.

Others like Wendell Johnson and Henry Murray had their pet theories and knew whom to experiment with to support those theories.

This less well known and occasionally sordid history of medicine's wholesale commodification and abuse of children in human research reminds us of the comment of Yale law professor Jay Katz when surmising the damage inflicted on American citizens in secret Cold War experiments. He wrote that "all this is a frightening example of how thoughtlessly human beings, including physicians, can treat human beings for noble purposes."[3] It should also remind us of the significant human and societal costs that accompany a ruthless search for knowledge. Children, society's most vulnerable and defenseless group for research purposes, were often sacrificed in that quest for advancement.

We are approaching the sixtieth anniversary of the infamous Jewish Chronic Disease Hospital case in which Sloan-Kettering cancer researcher Chester Southam was allowed to inject live cancer cells into infirmed patients. Three conscientious physicians blew the whistle on the project, causing it to be abruptly terminated. We might ask why there have been so few instances of doctors taking principled stands and thwarting unethical experimentation.[4]

Why, one is forced to ponder, were there no doctors during the four-decade long Tuskegee syphilis study who were willing to expose the fact that sick and dying men were going untreated? Why was no opposition heard after the experiment had been repeatedly written about in medical journals over the years? Why did no one raise concerns about Lauretta Bender's overuse of ECT on children or her controversial use of LSD on autistic children, reports on which appeared in journal articles? Why did the medical profession allow Walter Freeman to travel around the country like a surgical Pied Piper performing lobotomies on adults and children as if he were conducting some routine and innocuous health survey? Furthermore, why did Wendell Johnson's Iowa orphans have to endure psychically damaging speech sessions without someone standing up and attempting to put a stop to it?

Was there no one at Bellevue Hospital in the early 1940s who recognized that six-year-old Ted Chabasinski was not suffering from schizophrenia and was too young for a battery of twenty electroshock treatments? Was there no one at the Fernald School who recognized that twelve-year-old Charlie Dyer had had enough of the Science Club and was willing to risk serious injury and death by climbing up to the building's rafters to avoid any more time as an experimental guinea pig?

Much is written about the "blue wall of silence" in police departments and the innercity "street codes" that silence witnesses of violent crime, but an argument can be made that the moral amnesia and ethical paralysis of those in the medical and psychological research professions are equally formidable. As Dr. Hyman Strauss has argued, "A conspiracy of silence developed in which an effort to suppress the disclosure of these practices to the membership and the proper authorities was quite apparent."

All too infrequently, individuals in the medical community come forward to declare some research mischief unacceptable. As one disenchanted observer commented in 1921 after learning that a New York pediatrician at the Hebrew Infant Asylum had experimentally induced rickets in young children, "No devotion to science, no thought of the greater good to the greater number, can for an instant justify the experimenting on helpless infants, children pathetically abandoned by fate and entrusted to the community for their safeguarding. Voluntary consent by adults should, of course, be the *sine qua non* of scientific experimentation."[5]

Of course, the research physician had his own thoughts on the matter, and they were based on a utilitarian calculus of convenience, self-interest, and the chances of a grand scientific payoff. The use of the unworthy as test "material" only lessened the odds of getting caught if something untoward should occur. "Research on institutionalized children," wrote one investigator, "offered scientific advantages because the standardized conditions in the asylum approximated those conditions which are insisted on in considering the course of infection among laboratory animals, but which can rarely be controlled in a study of infection in man."[6]

One might naturally ask what it was about those few physicians that made the abuse of patients and test subjects offensive to them and not to the many others who followed orders or went about their business as if nothing untoward were occurring. Why were there so few who had the moral capacity to discern a wrong being committed and the personal courage to speak up about it? Thousands have suffered consequently.

Integrity is just one of the principles that undergird our emerging codes of ethics over the years. In addition to ensuring that researchers do not fudge data, fabricate results, or plagiarize, integrity also mean blowing the whistle on violations of ethical principles. As this book has shown, the principles of autonomy, justice, nonmaleficence, veracity, and beneficence have been embedded into our research culture with varying degrees of success.[7] Textbooks and college ethics courses may stipulate that subjects have the right to refuse to be incorporated in research, be free from coercion, go unharmed, and be told the truth about an experiment. However, often, one or more of these principles were jettisoned in deference to the lofty experiment under consideration.

For most of the last century, codes of ethics regarding human experimentation were little known and rarely enforced. The Oath of Hippocrates and the American Medical Association's first code of ethics, formalized in 1903, were ignored or not seen as applicable to medical research. Granted, occasionally, the sobering pronouncements of the great men of science about research parameters, but the practical impact of these high-minded statements was negligible. Dr. William Osler, for example, may have articulated, "We have no right to use patients entrusted to our care for the purpose of experimentation unless direct benefit to the individual is likely to follow," but how many hospital ward physicians actually practiced it?

Even Osler, however, understood the limits of high-minded rhetoric, especially when matched against the attraction of scientific experimentation and all that it represented. "Enthusiasm for science has, in a few instances, led to regrettable transgressions of the rules," admitted Osler. "But these are mere specks which in no way blur the brightness of the picture, one of the brightest in the history of human effort which portrays the incalculable benefits to man from the introduction of experimentation into the art of medicine."

These "specks" or embarrassing episodes that Osler refers to would increase in number and severity after 1907, but not so much that the medical profession clamped down and made a concerted effort to rectify the problem. Antivivisectionists would protest and mobilize against researchers and their "specks" of indiscretion, but they were easily marginalized and routinely cast aside as uninformed, highly emotional do-gooders. No legislation proposed to protect human subjects during this period came to fruition.

Year after year and decade after decade, medical researchers went about their business with few legal or ethical restraints to harness their insatiable appetite for combatting a dreaded disease or the scientific exploration of some medical curiosity. Doctors' authority, dedication, and zeal, not to mention their conquering diseases like polio and discovering wonder drugs like penicillin, allowed them a wide berth in scientific endeavors. The confluence of the popularization of scientific heroes, gods of science, and the devaluation of specific institutionalized populations by a clamorous eugenics movement contributed to a potent brew that celebrated triumphant outcomes and dismissed those who were sacrificed in the effort as little more than throwaway people. Few, if any, would contemplate why we so clearly saw a multitude of vices occurring in Nazi Germany's medical establishment during the 1940s but ignored our sins in the use of vulnerable populations as test subjects.

Cracks in the morally fragile façade would appear in the 1960s and grow more visible with the revelations of unethical experimentation by Henry Beecher and Maurice Pappworth, the federal government's early effort to establish the concept of Institutional Review Boards, and the various political and social protest movements that were occurring at the time. And finally, the stunning 1972 revelation regarding the Tuskegee syphilis study was the shot across the bow of America's casual indifference to the harm that was being perpetrated on thousands of devalued citizens; a healthy percentage of them we can now say were the neglected and abandoned children housed in stark institutionalized settings.

The last quarter of the twentieth century would prove an overdue corrective of the laissez-faire atmosphere that had long characterized medical research in America. Experimentation would now be subjected to institutional oversight committees, increased paperwork, assurances that test subjects understood what they were participating in, and additional safeguards against coercion, bribes, and misleading information. Abuse of test subjects in medical research would still occur. However, the levels of exploitation and mistreatment were significantly reduced. Both doctors and institutions were now fully cognizant of restrictive codes and regulatory guidelines that established ethical boundaries within which they could work.

One of the most dramatic changes would be the rather sudden end to the long tradition of using asylums, orphanages, hospitals, and prisons as research mills. With access to cheap and available domestic "material" closed off, investigators and their sponsors began looking abroad for new "fertile fields" of experimental opportunity.

Those far-flung fields of experimental endeavor beyond our shores proved exceedingly fruitful. It is estimated that 70 percent of all drug approvals are based partly on research data accumulated outside the United States.[8] Institutions like Sonoma State Hospital, the Ohio Soldiers' and Sailors' Orphans Home, the Pennhurst School, and the Vineland State Colony for the Feeble-minded have been replaced by China, India, and Brazil as sites for critical Phase I drug studies.

The motivating factors pushing Big Pharma and research organizations abroad are identical to those that encouraged them to enter America's great human warehouses during the last century. First and foremost is the continuing need for human subjects. As one observer commented, "currently, pharmaceutical sponsors are engaged in a turf war over human subjects." The upshot of the offshore research boom is that it is cheaper to do research abroad, where it is easier to recruit test subjects. Many of the subjects incorrectly believe they are being treated and where there is less likelihood that negatively impacted individuals will seek legal counsel.[9]

The gains from these new fields of opportunity have not come without some setbacks, including numerous injuries and death. It should be no surprise that these deaths have had as significant an impact on the American consumer as did the medical experiments on the feebleminded in the 1940s and 1950s.

Granted, there has been much improvement in the protection of experimental test subjects in recent decades. However, any self-congratulatory celebration should be tempered with the understanding that we have not only moved the majority of our drug testing abroad but have quite possibly adopted the practices of an earlier era in which society's outcasts were routinely exploited and were only of value as experimental "material."

If we have learned anything from our sad history of using institutionalized children as research subjects, it is our propensity to marginalize those most in need and our willingness to jettison inconvenient ethical constraints to follow the path offering the greatest rewards.

As uncomfortable as it may be, history must be acknowledged and made available to forthcoming generations. Moreover, we as a society must be ever vigilant that such paternalism and utilitarian practices never return, nor be outsourced abroad so that the burden of scientific advancement is relegated to vulnerable populations in lesser developed countries. Scientific progress and the medical advances it fosters is a process we can all celebrate. However, the attainment of such triumphs on the backs of children and other powerless groups makes their realization all the less impressive and praiseworthy.

EPILOGUE

THE 21ST CENTURY RECKONING

Efforts to Remove/Contextualize Eponyms for Medical Researchers Undeserving of Glorification.

BEFORE, DURING, AND FOLLOWING THE PUBLICATION OF OUR 2013 EDITION of *Against their Will*, the authors have been aware of and involved with attempts to eradicate or contextualize the glorification of names of medical researchers who had committed ethical violations of the sort mentioned in our book. So, we have chosen to add an epilogue to the expanded version of our *Against their Will* book that speaks to the unwarranted glorification of three deceased medical researchers who committed serious ethical violations. While their research may not have been focused exclusively on children, who are the concern of our book, or their research may not have been conducted in America, we use them here as examples of the need for some further thoughts and action more than those already taking place in many spheres in recent years. As exemplified by eponym removal/ contextualization, we believe that such a reckoning should occur for many of the researchers exposed in our book.

Gregory Dober was actively involved in discovering archival records that tied Dr. Thomas Parran, the 6th Surgeon General of the United States, to the initiation of the infamous Tuskegee research study. This discovery, along with his active support, led to the removal in 2018 of the Parran name from the building that houses the Graduate School of Public Health at the University of Pittsburgh.

Just a few years after our book was initially published, Judith Newman read with horror and amazement two new publications in 2018 that used recently discovered archival records to reveal that Hans Asperger's Clinic in Vienna had become an essential part of Nazi operations.[1] Dr. Asperger himself had transferred dozens of children declared unworthy to a known "euthanasia" ward. Newman then conducted qualitative research regarding the continuing usage of the Asperger eponym and posted a petition in the hopes of removing or contextualizing the use of the term Asperger Syndrome to describe/label high functioning persons on the Autism Spectrum. There are numerous examples of eponym removals or disease renaming's involving other Holocaust—involved physicians and researchers.[2] Even the strategy of using phrases such as "the disease formerly known as . . ." has been suggested for such cases.[3]

Finally, Allen Hornblum directly witnessed the use of vulnerable populations as experimental test subjects when he began working in prisons a half—century ago. He actively pursued exposing such unethical practices starting in 1993 when he investigated dermatological researcher Dr. Albert Kligman and the University of Pennsylvania's medical experiments in the Philadelphia Prison System and institutions housing vulnerable children. That effort resulted in Hornblum's publication of *Acres of Skin* in 1998 and *Sentenced to Science in 2007*. It continues with new and broader initiatives for the University to face a reckoning for their support of Kligman and their continued glorification of his name.

Hornblum will provide details in his narrative regarding ongoing initiatives to remove the Kligman eponym; to convince the University to teach their students about the human cost of Kligman's research; to formally apologize to the victims and their families, and even to compensate the victims (or their heirs) for these past injustices.

We know that such unwarranted continuations of name glorifications may sometimes be due to a lack of knowledge about the "facts," or a focus on the researcher's more extensive opus of work, or to financial (i.e., donation) considerations, or to a teleological (goal-oriented) justification for the researcher's actions suggesting that we may have learned something important from their "unethical" research, or that their findings benefitted the larger society. But we will use just these three medical researchers, Drs. Parran Asperger, and Kligman, as examples of why we prefer a deontological (ethical principle-based) approach that would suggest there is no justification for the harms these researchers intentionally inflicted. We take a more objective view than a relativistic one as we believe there are indeed universal values like "do no harm" and that sacrificing one for the many (especially without the assent/consent of the "one") is a violation of professional, ethical principles and is unworthy of glorification.

DOBER AND THOMAS PARRAN.

The effort to put together a book like *Against Their Will* requires critical time spent on "paper chases." The coauthors and I invested vast amounts of time in university and state libraries. In addition, the "chase," as noted by our extensive bibliography, required countless hours of interviews and investigation in the archives of researchers and others connected with the topic.

One of the archives I visited was the Dr. Thomas Parran, Jr. archive at the University of Pittsburgh ("Pitt"). Dr. Parran was the 6th Surgeon General of the United States from 1936-1948. He was the founder and first dean of the School of Public Health at the University of Pittsburgh from 1948-1958. The Parran archive is extensive, utilizing 76 linear feet containing approximately 139 boxes. In addition, a nine—story building, built—in 1957 housing the School of Public Health, was named Parran Hall in 1969.

In 2010, while reviewing documents in the Parran–archives, one of the folders I reviewed was titled *Macon County Ala. Rosenwald Fund, Study by Dr. Parran et al.* Having read the sordid history of the Tuskegee Syphilis Study ("Study") over the years, primarily from James Jones's *Bad Blood* and other sources, I knew that Macon County and the Rosenwald Fund were of importance to the Study. Macon County is the home of Tuskegee Institute, where the United States Public Health Service established its headquarters for the Study and the Rosenwald Fund, an essential donor to the fight against syphilis in the South at that time.

While perusing through the various documents in the folder, I found a memo dated eight months before the commencement of the Study. It was a typed memo that traced Parran's trip to Macon County during January 1932 as a representative of the Rosenwald Fund. The memo's finer point was: "If one wished to study the natural history of syphilis in the negro race uninfluenced by treatment, this county would be an ideal location for such a study." I thought it was worthy of subsequent follow-up.

A few years later, after *Against Their Will* was initially published, I would further investigate the memo's details and Parran's specific role in the Study. The memo would lead me to more archives, such as the National Archives in College Park, MD, and Georgetown University. The investigation required the filing of numerous Freedom of Information Act (FOIA) requests and hours of discussions with other individuals knowledgeable of the history and ethics of the Study. Ironically, as I was working in the Parran archives, Wellesley College professor and noted historian Susan Reverby was reviewing documents, independently, in the John C. Cutler archives at the University of Pittsburgh. Cutler became a professor at Pitt in 1967 and was the acting Dean of its Graduate School of Public Health from 1968–69.

In 2010, Reverby had discovered documents that she shared with the Center for Disease Control from Cutler's papers. Cutler, a researcher during Parran's tenure as the Surgeon General, ran experiments from 1946-48 in Guatemala.[4] The experiments involved infecting men and women in prison with sexually transmitted diseases. In 2011, during a later government investigation by the Presidential Commission for the Studies of Bioethical Issues, Parran knew about the Study and did not halt it despite the unethical and dangerous protocol.[5] Despite the findings, Pitt retained Thomas Parran's name on the school building in 2011. At that time, Pitt noted that their charge was to investigate the findings but not recommend a name change of the building.

However, other national organizations became outraged at the revelations. In 2013, the American Sexually Transmitted Disease Association renamed its "Thomas Parran Award" for lifetime achievement in research to the "The ASTDA Distinguished Career Award."[6] The deflection away from Parran for the Guatemala experiments at Pitt appeared to have resulted from much of the blame being placed on Cutler and his cadre of researchers.

In 2017, after I completed most of the field research on Parran and Tuskegee, my coauthor, Allen Hornblum, and I decided to prepare a manuscript regarding the findings of Parran's further involvement in the Tuskegee Syphilis Study. Our manuscript concludes that Parran's influence was much more significant than previously disclosed for the impetus of the Study. In July 2017, the *Philadelphia Inquirer* published a story regarding the unpublished manuscript and findings.[7] At the time, the *Inquirer* reached out to Pitt and sent them the manuscript. Pitt's statement on Parran acknowledged his accomplishments and shortcomings but noted that the University "has no immediate plans" to change the building's name. In the Fall of 2017, at the request of the Pitt Dean of the Graduate School of Public Health, Dr. Donald Burke, I met with him to discuss the findings. Dr. Burke, being a historian of medicine, listened intently and concurred that the memo in the archives was authentic

In January 2018, Dean Burke sent a letter to the University's Office of Diversity and Inclusion (ODI) informing them of current information that may be relevant to the issue of having a building named after Dr. Parran. His final statement in the letter, "I now request that the University of Pittsburgh consider whether it is consistent with its mission to have the main Graduate School of Public Health building named for Thomas Parran."[8]

The University, now having a protocol in place through the ODI to address such situations, formed a review committee at the request of Dean Burke to consider the possible removal of Dr. Parran's name from the school building. The committee was charged to review Burke's concern and make a recommendation through a report to the Chancellor regarding the disposition of the building name.

So, what changed that did not happen after the Guatemala experiments were revealed a few years earlier? First, the University now had a policy and protocol to review institutional concerns that impact the greater University community and are not subject to other University policies and procedures. Second, after the *Inquirer* article, public health graduate students started to question the person's history whose name resided on the building where they attend classes.

In the Fall of 2017, several public health graduate students contacted me and requested that I meet with them. They wanted to understand more about the role of Thomas Parran in the Tuskegee Syphilis Study. I met with several of the students to discuss the manuscript and the findings in the archive. In the meeting, they displayed disappointment and concern that many of their African American, Latino, and Asian-American student colleagues attend class in a building linked to the history of the Tuskegee and Guatemala studies.

Dean Burke requested that a "town hall" type meeting occur at the school. On March 29, 2018, a symposium titled "Thomas Parran: His Career, His Name, and His Legacy" was sponsored by the Graduate School of Public Health. Dean Burke assembled a panel with diverse thoughts and varying opinions on the issue. The panel speakers invited were historian Susan Reverby, Tuskegee historian Bill Jenkins, Kirk Savage, a professor at Pitt specializing in public monuments, and myself. This meeting gave students, faculty, and committee members information about Parran and the Study. It also provided an opportunity to voice concerns and participate in a question-and-answer session.

After Dean Burke's January letter, the Pitt graduate students can be credited with keeping the pressure on the university to remove Parran's name from their classroom building. In February 2018, the Pitt Graduate Student Organizing Committee began collecting petition signatures to rename Parran Hall. The petition campaign eventually garnered over 1,300 signatures. The students noted on social media, "We view Parran Hall as a constant reminder of the legacy of racism in the academic, scientific, and medical, communities. . . ."[9] The students and student newspaper continued to cover the story after the March 2018 symposium. The students and student newspaper agreed, it was time to move on and remove Parran's name from their class building.

The ODI Committee charged with issuing a report for the Board of Trustees recommended removing the name of Parran from the building. In the transmittal of the report to the Trustees, Patrick Gallagher, Chancellor, and Chief Executive made the following comment:

In my view, there is a reasonable likelihood that if the Board knew of Dr. Parran's involvement in the two studies at issue here, which took place before he was Dean, one could easily conclude that the decision to permanently honor Dr. Parran would not have taken place. Both studies conducted human trials on vulnerable populations without informed consent. These actions are fundamentally at odds with the University's core values.[10]

Finally, in June 2018, after reviewing the ODI Committee's report, the Board of Trustees released a statement recommending the removal of Parran's name from the building.

The removal of Parran's name in 2018 resulted from two converging vital elements: 1) a protocol was finally in place to investigate and deliberate on these types of issues and 2) an active student body that wanted their school to be transparent and systematically deliberate the issue. The protocol that Pitt followed should be a model for future similar cases at other schools and institutions.

The removal of names from buildings or monuments often creates the argument that it's a removal of history and "cancel culture." Thomas Parran, as Surgeon General, was responsible for many significant accomplishments that benefited the country. He was an advisor in Franklin Roosevelt's cabinet and instrumental in enacting the Social Security Act of 1935 and the Hill-Burton Act of 1946. Being an appointed member of the administration of the President of the United States is an esteemed honor and privilege. However, having two of the most unethical and harmful medical trials in America linked to his resume, Tuskegee, and Guatemala, is something that should not be ignored or taken lightly. In this case, the removal of Parran's name was done fairly, with transparency and deliberation. It is not often that an institution would have the moral courage to take such a bold move. Pitt showed how it should be accomplished. But more importantly, Pitt showed it could be accomplished.

NEWMAN AND HANS ASPERGER.
This book began with a discussion of the impact of the Eugenics movement in this country in the early 1900s. The notion of good-gened worthy people and bad-gened unworthy people was certainly also prevalent in Eastern Europe. In fact, according to Silberman, author of *Neurotribes*, American eugenicists received a warm welcome in Germany to secure the future of their race after the decimation of WWI.

As the National Socialist party rose to power in the 1930s, the body of American eugenic law became the blueprint for protecting their race against dysgenic influences. And according to Sheffer, author of *Asperger's Children,* many physicians "slid passively into Nazi racial hygiene practices, forced sterilizations, human medical experiments, [internment] and murder," especially for those members of the populace who did not/could not feel the right emotions toward the collective.[11] Sheffer continues that neuropsychiatrists played the most prominent role in this negative eugenics, or cleansing, by sorting the population into categories.

And, as will be seen in this discussion of Hans Asperger, as Austria slid into Fascism and the Third Reich, and as social work and special education initiatives were therefore altered, the original intention to help so-called "defective" children often turned to catastrophic harm.

When Hans Asperger began his work in the Curative Education Clinic of the Children's Hospital at the University of Vienna, the influence of Dr. Erwin Lazar's holistic "therapeutic education" philosophy still loomed large, and the milieu therapy that was practiced with the young patients was individualized and respectful. The Clinic was viewed as a microcosm of a humane society.[12] Well-known medical researchers and practitioners such as Drs. Ani Weiss and George Frankl were there in the 1920s and were respectively the staff psychologist and the staff physician at the Clinic when Hospital Director Hamburg hired Asperger in May of 1931.

Asperger saw over 200 children with symptoms such as social awkwardness, precociousness, and a fascination with rules and schedules. While he seems to have thought he was the first to notice these children, much had already been written about such patients under terms such as *adolescent psychosis.*[13] Even Drs. Weiss and Frankl, from Asperger's own Clinic, had authored several such publications.

At first, Asperger seemed opposed to using any labels or diagnoses regarding his patients. He affectionately referred to those high functioning children and therefore considered remediable or educable as his "little professors." The distinction between those children considered valuable or worthy and those who were not becoming more and more a focal point as he moved through the 1930s and into the early 1940s.

Asperger quickly rose in the ranks at the Clinic, mainly because 3200 of the 5000 physicians in Vienna who were Jews or liberals were being forced to retire, leave the country, or be deported to the concentration camps. Dr. Anni Weiss emigrated to the United States in 1934, and Dr. George Frankl was forced to emigrate in 1937 as the University of Vienna was slowly but surely being transformed into a center for racial improvement. It is assumed that since Hans

Asperger stayed and benefitted from frequent promotions primarily due to the vacancies left by Jewish colleagues, he would have had to sign a loyalty oath to Hitler as all physicians who stayed were forced to do.[14]

It was "In this climate of rabid fanaticism on October 3, 1938, [that] Asperger gave his first public talk on autism in history, in a lecture hall at the University Hospital.[15] While he focused on the high functioning among his clients, he was at this point still arguing that not everything that steps out of line and is thus "abnormal" must necessarily be "inferior." He argued that rather than racial hygiene, we could train the person to cope with special challenges. But Sheffer argues that the bulk of the 1938 treatise was disparaging and more of a political statement than scientific research.[16] The words were a tribute to Nazi ideals, declaring that the individual was subordinate to the state. She further notes that a bit of benevolence was only tagged on at the end of the talk. Asperger may have still argued that his "little professors," compared to those on the rest of the spectrum, may make great code breakers, and this may have been to save or protect them. Still, he would very soon slide even further down the slippery slope of ethics, as you will see by saying that all autistic children were devoid of Gemüt, which determined one's worth to society. Gemüt was essential to an individual's connection to the Volk or the collective.[17]

The Nazi annexation of Austria took place in 1938, and those Viennese doctors and nurses who remained were required by government decree to register all children born with congenital abnormalities. They received a small sum for each report sent to a panel of 3 medical experts in Berlin. The panel, primarily based on a child's IQ, decided whether the child should live or die. By the end of August 1940, children were being sent to so-called *euthanasia* wards where they were painfully starved to death or were administered massive doses of barbiturates, developed pneumonia and died. The primary children's killing ward for all of Austria was Vienna's Am Spiegelgrund institution.

The new findings about Asperger reveal that he was slowly expanding his involvement with the Nazi regime. For example, in the early 1940s, Asperger signed up for 12 hours a week as a medical psychiatric expert for Vienna's Public Health Office, which was "the central Reich agency that assessed individual's value to the regime and assigned their fates."[18] His Clinic had become an essential part of government operations. In addition to the fact that at least 35 of the 44 youths transferred to Spiegelgrund by Asperger's commission did die there, he also recommended transfers as a medical consultant for the Nazi administration. And, since the records are incomplete, given that the Clinic was bombed in 1944, the total number of children referred and killed for their aberrant behavior is likely higher.

While Asperger never actually joined the Nazi Party, he joined the Father-land Front, had solid far-right-wing credentials, and was a self-proclaimed eugenicist. He not only survived but thrived.[19]

While at the start of his career he had been opposed to diagnosis, by 1944, when Asperger published his 1943 postdoctoral thesis entitled *Autistic Psychopathy in Childhood*, he had assigned this rather negative label to his former "little professors." The term *psychopathy* was chosen to signify those who threaten the social order—a term used by Asperger when Nazism fully controlled his world.[20] According to Sheffer, Asperger's diagnosis of autistic psychopathy emerged from the very values of the Third Reich. By the time of his publication in 1944, Asperger had been drafted into the Wehrmacht as an ambulance driver and then a surgeon. Still, he continued to participate remotely with his Clinic until it was bombed and destroyed in the summer of 1944.

Some have argued, at least before the recent revelations that are based on actual case records of Asperger's patients, that he may still have been trying to protect the high functioning among his clients and was only entirely dismissive of the lower functioning patients who did not possess community spirit or Gemüt that was so essential to an individual's connection to the Volk or the collective.[21] It is the case that Asperger even said that the so-called calendar people with "crackpot" interests were of no social value either. He would speak of some of their superior traits as valuable but then argue that the positive traits "do not outweigh the negative ones."[22] For us, the devaluing of any life is the relevant issue here.

Sheffer points out that "Asperger was neither a zealous supporter nor an opponent of the regime. He was an exemplar of this drift into complicity" and became gradually reconciled to Nazi rule.[23] Asperger's concept of autistic psychopathy did "not arrive fully formed . . . but emerged bit by bit, shaped by the values and interactions of psychiatry, state, and society."[24] According to Sheffer, "Asperger's definition of autistic psychopathy sharpened year by year, as he described the patients in ever more judgmental, social, and eugenicist terms, and incorporated ever more elements of Nazi child psychiatry" and Fascist rhetoric such that from 1938 to 1941 to 1944 he grew more and more critical.[25]

Asperger was, according to Silberman, living in the gray zone that morally ambiguous position of subjects of the Reich who performed their jobs under Nazi rule, making horrific compromises and trade-offs they may never have made under normal conditions.[26] But the new files reveal that Asperger *did* participate in Vienna's child-killing system on multiple levels. He was very close to fervent party members like Hamburger, his mentor, and Jekelius, the Director of Spiegelgrund. And "through his numerous positions in the Nazi state, Asperger sent dozens of children to Spiegelgrund where children in Vienna were killed."[27] His affiliation with child euthanasia leaders, states Sheffer, was an active, not a passive, choice."[28] He was a conscious participant.

One of the reasons that we may not have been more aware of Asperger's actions is when his 1944 publication was finally translated from German into English in the 1980s by Lorna Wing and in the 1990s by Uta Firth, the introduction was not included. This very introduction contained disturbing descriptions of anomalous or defective Gemüt—an introduction in which Asperger defined autism and Nazism as inverse states of being.

Recall that in 1944 the syndrome was referred to as autistic psychopathy. It was not named Asperger's Syndrome until Lorna Wing's translation in 1982. Dr. Wing, a child psychiatrist and parent of a high functioning autistic child, actually asked her physician husband to translate Asperger's 1944 paper from German into English. She then chose to honor Asperger when she published the translation by naming the autism disorder "Asperger's Syndrome." It was not her intention that this name be solely equated with high functioning persons, but it was and still is by many professionals and laypersons.

The 4th edition of the Diagnostic and Statistical Manual (DSM-4), published in 1994 and used as the basis for formal diagnosing of patients, did introduce Asperger Syndrome as a separate diagnosis indicating higher functioning autism. But since such distinctions created some confusion, Asperger Syndrome is no longer listed in the DSM-5 published in 2013. There is instead just the umbrella term of Autism Spectrum Disorder as a Pervasive Developmental Disorder. Note that this change occurred before the 2018 revelations about Asperger's ties to the Nazi regime. However, as stated in an editorial entitled "What's in a name?" in *The Lancet*, "The [Asperger] term has been removed from DSM-5 but is still commonly used in the public domain."[29] The editorial continues that "the use of the term Asperger's syndrome, in light of the recent discoveries, might now elicit more negative associations for the patients or their families than they have experienced previously."

Evidence for the common use of the *Asperger* label could be seen, for example, in early 2021, when Elan Musk hosted Saturday Night Live and referred to himself as the first host with Asperger's, or at least as the first to admit it. Some medical doctors continue to use the Asperger term with their clients as they assume that parents will be less upset with this as an informal diagnosis since it continues to imply higher functioning. When I, along with two of my undergraduate students, interviewed a mother of a child on the Autism spectrum, she spoke of a *recent* medical appointment in which the doctor advised her to "say *Asperger* when trying to get services for my child." We also called a few organizations that still contained Asperger's name in their titles to inquire if they were considering a change of name for their organizations. Those names have now been changed.[30]

While some persons with an official diagnosis of Asperger's may prefer to keep this "label" to identify themselves as a member of a community or neurotribe of "Aspies," others are disturbed by the news of Asperger's past.[31] Even during our interviews, a young adult male on the autism spectrum reflected, after some information-sharing about Hans Asperger's actions, that "The emotional connotation of this history may now be stronger than my connection to the word Asperger."

Of the 36 undergraduate students that were interviewed, only 12% knew anything about Asperger's unethical actions, 80% thought that eponym removal was justified for cases of research misconduct, 75% said they'd be willing to sign a petition for removal of the Asperger eponym, and 55% would support using the term "high functioning Autism."

We believe it is essential to continue to educate those around us about Asperger's involvement in the deaths of atypical children during the 1940's so that we all think twice before glorifying his name. We know of his collaboration during the Third Reich. He did not leave Vienna. He did not protest. He participated. He seems far less a hero than we had thought. Thus, we consider it essential to remove or contextualize this Asperger eponym whenever and wherever the term *Asperger Syndrome* continues to be used.

HORNBLUM AND ALBERT KLIGMAN.

"My father, Leodus Jones . . . was a human guinea pig who endured both mental and physical assaults at the hands of a prominent dermatologist and prestigious university while incarcerated in the Philadelphia Prison System in the 1960s. The experience," Adrienne Jones Alston goes on to write in the April 6, 2021, issue of *Merion West*, "proved catastrophic both for him and my entire family."[32]

Though a child at the time of her father's incarceration and bewildered by his periodic absence, her father's return proved even more difficult, if not "frightening." His "strangely marked skin and paranoid behavior" was terrifying, and the chilling memories of the physical and mental changes he exhibited haunted her for years. Jones Alston would also spend time behind bars and struggle with the connection between her troubled past and her father's. Now better informed about both their lives, she's fired up and taking action. She aims to force "the University of Pennsylvania and the many pharmaceutical companies and government entities that exploited imprisoned African Americans as cheap and available research material" under the direction of famed dermatologist Dr. Albert M. Kligman "to apologize and pay reparations to the families they harmed."[33]

Jones Alston's gripping narrative of being "daddy's little girl . . . enjoying a home with two loving parents," only to see it all crumble under the emotional strain and turmoil of her father's experience as a cellblock guinea pig. She is now on a mission to shake up her intransigent, affluent opponents. Kligman, a world-renowned researcher and creator of the highly profitable Retin, a cosmetics line, died in 2010. Still, the University of Pennsylvania, one of America's elite universities, continues to operate as if nothing untoward occurred. She plans to take the university to the moral woodshed for a public spanking at every opportunity.

The embarrassing thrashing by an African American woman for her father's descent into psychological turmoil—and that of the many "black prisoners who were injected with radioactive isotopes, smeared with dioxin, and given an assortment of chemical warfare agents" while locked in cellblock cages—was just the latest in a series of withering opinion pieces, op-ed articles, and student marches over the past year. The *Philadelphia Inquirer* published a similarly scathing report by Jones Alston just weeks earlier.

She would not be alone in her condemnation of Penn, however. A public reckoning seemed underway. Some commentaries were now coming from prominent corners of the education arena, such as a critical November 2019 *Chronicle of Higher Education* article, which focused on Penn's ethics and institutional priorities. "Colleges are questioning the morality of accepting research funds from Jeffrey Epstein, who was accused of sexually molesting young girls, and the Sacklers, makers of OxyContin. They are searching their souls," wrote investigative reporter Alex Kafka, "over institutional ties to slavery and Jim Crow era exploitation." Penn, however, proves itself an outlier and rewards Kligman with "a lectureship . . . and not one, but two chaired professorships."[34]

The criticism of Kligman and Penn, especially being compared to sexual predators and corporate exploiters, caused many medical professionals to wince. Some organizations cut ties with the famed researcher. For example, the Society for Investigative Dermatology, after what they called "careful deliberation," decided to discontinue the annual *Albert M. Kligman Leadership Lecture & Award.*[35] But the Board and leadership of the University of Pennsylvania proved unmoved by the growing crop of critics and seemed to double down in their resolve that Kligman and Penn had done nothing wrong.

But there were clear signs that the formidable, though conscienceless Ivy League institution was showing cracks in its armor. Dr. Jules Lipoff, an Assistant Professor of Clinical Dermatology at Penn's Medical School, co-authored an opinion piece in the *Philadelphia Inquirer,* taking the school to task for continuing to honor Kligman despite his troubling research record.[36] It was the first time, albeit decades after the prison experiments ended, and 10-years after Kligman's passing, that a member of Kligman's own academic department raised concerns about the school continuing to honor one of the most prolific exploiters of vulnerable subjects and practitioners of unethical medical research in American history.

In addition to faculty, students were now taking an increasing interest in the school's dubious fealty to a proven and long-time abuser of intellectually challenged children and prison inmates. In May 2021, three undergraduates wrote a searing indictment of Penn's "ties with systemic racism" and its inability "to adequately address the legacy of Dr. Albert Kligman." In a lengthy *Daily Pennsylvanian* article, they pointed out that "Kligman's name remains across multiple areas within Perelman School of Medicine. Professorships, research labs, and a lectureship all bear his name. Displays in the atrium of the Hospital of the University of Pennsylvania and at Perelman Center for Advanced Medicine highlight his contributions to Penn's legacy . . . by proudly displaying his name without context and neglecting to formally apologize or publicly consider reparations. The university implies that they don't see the trauma that Kligman inflicted as worthy of acknowledgment or compensation. This is unacceptable."[37]

The students urged "Penn to stop waffling around . . . confront the full picture of its legacy, admit its complicity in the Kligman experiments, and formally apologize." They excoriated university leadership "for a longstanding pattern of . . . using black bodies without consent for the advancement of science and medicine."

The well—reasoned treatise was so ethically sound; one would have thought it emanated from one of the school's many bioethicists. But that wasn't the case. Despite the growing criticism, Penn's Center for Bioethics has been silent on the issue. Though led over the years by formidable academic talents like Arthur Caplan and Ezekiel Emanuel, who regularly comment to the media on everything from the Tuskegee Syphilis Study and gene-editing advances to stem cell research and Covid vaccine efficacy, it would be only natural for one of them to utter a pithy statement on the Kligman controversy. But that was not to be. One would be hard pressed to find any of the nearly three dozen or so bioethics faculty members commenting on the school's unsavory history of using powerless, marginalized people as human guinea pigs.

The conspiracy of silence confirms Carl Elliot's observation, "Don't count on bioethicists to help set the record straight. The field of bioethics has been thoroughly captured by academic medicine" to the point that "a lot of academic health centers think they can count on their bioethicists to keep quiet if there is a scandal."[38] In her own right, Amy Gutmann, Penn's president and a bioethicist who Chaired President Obama's National Bioethics Commission, exemplifies how corporate influence trumps ethics. In some way, during her tenure as university president, she could have addressed the grievances of the many African Americans who were used as research "material." But she chose to ignore the issue. It has been long observed that Penn's so-called ethicists learn early on; never bite the hand that feeds you.

The continuing silence reflected the very same mindset and actions of Kligman's departmental colleagues over a half-century ago when he was mining the riches his captive guinea pigs represented. Years later, while researching the *Acres of Skin* saga, one doctor after another sheepishly replied when I asked, "Did you really believe it was ethical to use the incarcerated and intellectually challenged children as test subjects for so many medical experiments over so many years?" Eminent mid-20th century physician-researchers like Drs. Walter Shelley and Clarence Livingood embarrassingly admitted they were "skeptical" and had "reservations" about their younger colleague's prison operation. Though they claimed to have "kept their distance" from it, both pointed to the prison's value as a "training ground for dermatology residents" and alluded to "all the money it brought the department" as reasons for its longevity.

One young resident initially had "no qualms" about Kligman's research program and, "thought it very beneficial," only to suddenly leave for a medical residency at Harvard and become an outspoken critic of the entire money-making scheme Holmesburg Prison represented, was Dr. A. Bernard Ackerman. Though he would go on to be one of the world's pre-eminent dermatopathologists with a lengthy list of publications and medical triumphs, his one year at Penn would stand out as a disheartening, "searing experience." "What was purported to be a research institute at Holmesburg, under the direction of Albert M. Kligman and the auspices of the Department of Dermatology at the University of Pennsylvania," he would testify at a Philadelphia City Council hearing, "was little more than a commercial operation in which Dr. Kligman, the University of Pennsylvania, and possibly others, reaped huge financial dividends."

Ackerman told lawmakers, Penn had an "obligation" to "set ethical standards . . . stay alert to violations of the Nuremberg Code . . . ensure the research was serious and meaningful . . . set standards for informed consent . . . and mandate that scientific work at Holmesburg was truly scientific.[39] It did not. It had an obligation to us to make a clear distinction between commerce and medicine. It did not." Regrettably, Dr. Ackerman was one of the very few to break ranks and call out Kligman and Penn for their long-running breach of ethical medical standards.

As Greg Dober has written concerning Pitt's quite similar reckoning with past medical research indiscretions of a prominent faculty member, university leaders finally learned they could no longer bury Thomas Parran's embarrassing initiatives and decisions. Even contextualized plaques proved insufficient; his name would have to be removed from the Graduate School of Public Health Building. On the other hand, Penn had been unbending on the issue; Albert Montgomery Kligman remained an honored figure at the university.

With that troubling history in mind as I wrote my contribution to the epilogue in August 2021, I concluded with Dr. Ackerman's powerful statement of a quarter-century ago, "An end should come to the University of Pennsylvania's stonewalling, rationalizations, excuses, and denials about what went on at Holmesburg and the schools for mentally disabled children in New Jersey. Until the wrongs at Holmesburg and the schools for children are acknowledged and rectified, in some measure, by the University of Pennsylvania, there will always be a blot, worse than any dermatologic blemish, on its escutcheon. If the University of Pennsylvania is not ashamed, it should be shamed by force of moral authority and public outrage."[40]

The ink was not yet dry on that final sentence when, late on a Friday afternoon on August 20, 2021, the university sent out a press release announcing a *"Statement on Penn Medicine's Recognition of the Legacy of Albert Kligman, MD, Ph.D."* After recognizing Kligman's many "groundbreaking contributions to the field of dermatology," the release admitted, "the work done by Dr. Kligman was terribly disrespectful of individuals, many of whom were imprisoned Black men, denying them the autonomy and informed consent which the medical community now considers to be foundational underpinnings for conducting ethical research."[41] The release went on to say, "Penn Medicine apologizes for the pain Dr. Kligman's work caused to incarcerated individuals, their families, and our broader community."[42]

For a powerful institution that had turned a cold shoulder on ethical guidelines, not to mention common decency, as well as the historical record and the community in which it resides, the long-awaited apology was significant. And so were other promised changes, including the "sunsetting" of the Kligman lectureship, "renaming a Kligman professorship," and several other programmatic initiatives designed to "better reflect the University of Pennsylvania's commitment to inclusion, innovation, and impact."[43]

However, one should not lose sight that the victory would never have been attained without the collective effort of the concerned, the dedicated core of activists who saw a wrong and tried to correct it. If not for them, Kligman's name would remain in the hallowed halls of Penn Medicine. Ackerman, Anthony, Jones-Alston, Lipoff, the Penn students, and Hornblum are not household names with great influence, but their individual efforts were significant enough to impress a large university that it must change course. The return of students on campus during the Fall semester only promised more tumult. In the end, they needed to confront an ethical and moral dilemma of their own making.

Similarly, under the prodding of faculty member Judith Newman, Penn State University soon followed suit. Though Kligman had donated large sums of money to his alma mater over the years, the university decided to revoke the Kligman name from a Distinguished Alumni Award, an Alumni Fellow award, as well as from four scholarship/fellowship endowments, and a room name in the Art Museum, as the "research of the renowned dermatologist does not correspond with Penn State's values."[44] Suddenly, an iconic figure in the annals of medical research had become too controversial and too great a burden to bear despite his financial support. A historical reckoning had occurred; the two largest and most renowned academic institutions in the state of Pennsylvania decided to separate themselves from a tarnished alum and employee.

As with the Parran case at the University of Pittsburgh and Kligman at the University of Pennsylvania, student activists, faculty, and historical researchers like Dober, Hornblum and Newman have pointed the way, showing the highly educated, well-paid school decision-makers what road to take. In short, how a major institution of higher education should act. The Pitt, Penn, and Penn State cases involving the troubled histories of celebrated faculty should be a role model for others around the country who have come upon similar faculty embarrassments and institutional conundrums. Granted, the challenges of such initiatives are great, and the battle years long, but doing the right thing has its own rewards.

EPILOGUE CONCLUSION

We fully understand that controversy surrounds such eponym removal/contextualization initiatives as some see such campaigns as overly politicized and part of a "cancel culture" movement. They may argue we cannot or should not judge

20th-century researchers by present-day standards . . . as though there was ever a time when it was acceptable for medical researchers to do harm!

Opponents of eponym removal may also use "erasure" arguments suggesting that history is immutable and cannot be changed. On the other hand, we are not locked into either established or revisionist history. We believe that we should remember the past, but new historical revelations may dictate reappraisal. Recently discovered documents, such as Asperger's medical files or those revealing former Surgeon General Thomas Parran's connection to the Tuskegee Syphilis Study, requires serious historians and medical chroniclers to reexamine the experiment's true origin. Evidence, not politics, should be the key determinant if a reckoning is in order.

We are cognizant that retrospective moral judgments are difficult to traverse, filled with moral landmines, political bias, and decades of distance. However, as complex and problematic that undertaking may be, there are more than enough examples of questionable, if not egregious, medical research during the last century to learn. As we have stated, the confluence of a much-accepted eugenics movement, a celebration of heroic medicine, and the impetus of World War II fostered a research environment that demanded scientific triumph at the expense of ethics. Thousands of marginalized individuals, especially many institutionalized children, were caught in the experimental maelstrom that followed.

We believe, especially given the current zeitgeist of reckoning, it is undoubtedly time to demonstrate our communal sense of regret. Our book has exposed many perpetrators who committed these moral and ethical crimes. Our sincere hope is that *Against Their Will* illuminates the many wrongs that occurred, sparks debate, and serves some constructive role in underscoring the importance of ethics in medical research.

Such cavalier treatment of children and other vulnerable persons at the hands of medical researchers should never happen again. Charlie Dyer, Mark Dal Molin, and the thousands of other institutionalized children incorporated in scientific research against their will remain unknown, while men like Hilary Koprowski, Saul Krugman, and Albert Kligman were accorded iconic status as medical geniuses. But a society that so readily sacrifices one group for the other—no matter how grand the goal and devalued the subjects—must eventually recognize that a moral reckoning is in order. That moment—that reckoning—is now underway. We encourage its progress with all deliberate speed.

NOTES

INTRODUCTION

1. Numerous interviews were conducted with Charlie Dyer, both in person and over the phone, between 2009 and 2012, about his recollections of the Fernald Training School and his participation in the Science Club medical experiments.

2. Edwin Black, *War Against the Weak: Eugenics and America's Campaign to Create a Master Race* (New York: Four Walls Eight Windows, 2003), p. 55.

3. Elof Axel Carlson, *Times of Triumph, Times of Doubt: Science and the Battle for Public Trust* (New York: Cold Spring Harbor Press, 2006), p. 50.

4. James W. Trent Jr., *Inventing the Feeble Mind: A History of Mental Retardation in the United States* (Berkeley: University of California Press, 1994), p. 136.

5. Ibid., p. 163.

6. In addition to the wide net that had been used to capture the many troubled souls residing in asylum and hospital wards throughout the country, specific remedial solutions eugenics boards around the nation were still utilizing such sterilization. For example, in North Carolina, the state eugenics board functioned until 1977 in the hope that it would "keep welfare rolls small, stop poverty, and improve the gene pool." Kim Severson, "Thousands Sterilized, a State Weighs Restitution," *New York Times*, December 10, 2011.

7. Soviet premier Nikita Khrushchev's pointed comment, "We will bury you," was not so much a threat of war or nuclear destruction between the United States and the Soviet Union as a statement of the inevitability of Marxist thought and economics. Most Americans, however, interpreted it as a not-so-veiled threat of impending conflict between the world's two superpowers.

8. Adam B. Ulam, *The Communists: The Story of Power and Lost Illusions 1948–1991* (New York: Scribners, 1992), p. 52.

9. Dyer interviews.

10. One of the best examples of this phenomenon was Dr. Austin R. Stough, an Oklahoma physician who began a small-town medical practice during the Great Depression. By the end of his career, he had made millions of dollars conducting clinical trials for the pharmaceutical industry in three different state prison systems. Walter Rugerber, "Prison Drug and Plasma Projects Leave Fatal Trial," *New York Times*, July 29, 1969.

11. Quoted in Allen M. Hornblum, *Acres of Skin: Human Experiments at Holmesburg Prison* (New York: Routledge, 1998), p. 37.

12. James Jones, *Bad Blood: The Tuskegee Syphilis Experiment* (New York: Free Press, 1981).

CHAPTER 1: THE AGE OF HEROIC MEDICINE

1. Paul Starr, *The Social Transformation of American Medicine* (New York: Basic Books, 1982), p. 81.

2. Ibid., p. 83.

3. Ibid., p. 143.

4. Paul de Kruif, *The Sweeping Wind*, (New York: Harcourt, Brace & World, 1962), p. 13.

5. Ibid., 19.

6. Ibid.

7. Ibid., p. 58.

8. Ibid., p. 59.

9. Paul de Kruif, *The Sweeping Wind*, (New York: Harcourt, Brace & World, 1962), p. 115.

10. Ibid., p. 118.

11. Paul De Kruif, *Microbe Hunters* (New York: Harcourt Brace, 1926), 309.

12. Ibid., p. 315.

13. Ibid., p. 349.

14. Ibid., p. 303.

15. Ibid., p. 314.
16. Ibid.
17. Ibid., p. 318.
18. Ibid., p. 315.
19. Ibid., p. 349.
20. Hansen, Ibid., p. 152.
21. Though a well-paid studio hand and in his fifties with a weak heart, Faust became a war correspondent. It was while covering the conflict in Italy in 1944 that he succumbed to extensive shrapnel wounds and posthumously received a commendation for bravery from President Roosevelt.
22. Gustav Eckstein, *Noguchi* (New York: Harpers, 1931), p. 103.
23. *Time* Magazine issues of May 18, 1931, and August 6, 1931.
24. Susan Lederer's article, "Hideyo Noguchi's Luetin Experiment and the Antivivisectionists" in *ISIS* (1985, 76, 31-48) is the best source of information on the subject.
25. Ibid., p. 36.
26. It should also be pointed out that the 400-plus page, 1931 biography made no mention that he had used institutionalized children in his leutin experiment.
27. Paul De Kruif, *Life Among the Doctors* (New York: Harcourt, Brace, 1949), p. 3.
28. Ibid., p. 20.
29. Susan Lederer, *Subjected to Science* (Baltimore: Johns Hopkins University Press, 1995), p. 50.
30. Gerald L. Geison, "Pasteur's Work on Rabies: Reexamining the Ethical Issues," *Hastings Center Report* 8 (1978), pp. 26–33.
31. Henry Heiman, "A Clinical and Bacteriological Study of the Gonococcus Neisser in the Male Urethra and in the Vulvovaginal Tract of Children," *Journal of Cutaneous and Genito - Urinary Diseases* 13 (1895), pp. 384–87.
32. George M. Sternberg and Walter Reed, "Report on Immunity against Vaccination Conferred upon the Monkey by the Use of the Serum of the Vaccinated Calf and Monkey," *Transactions of the Association of American Physicians* 10 (1895), pp. 57–59.
33. Samuel McClintock Hamill, Howard C. Carpenter, and Thomas A. Cope, "A Comparison of the Pirquet, Calmette, and Moro Tuberculin Tests and Their Diagnostic Value," *Archives of Internal Medicine* 2 (1908), p. 405.
34. Godfrey R. Pisek and Leon Theodore LeWald, "The Further Study of the Anatomy and Physiology of the Infant Stomach Based on Serial Roentgenograms," *American Journal of Diseases of Children* 6 (1913), pp. 232–44.
35. Albert Leffingwell, "Illustration of Human Vivisection," 1907.

CHAPTER 2: EUGENICS AND THE DEVALUING OF INSTITUTIONALIZED CHILDREN

1. Edwin Black, *War Against the Weak* (New York: Four Walls Eight Windows, 2003), p. 41.
2. The best article on the Letchworth Village castration is Paul Lombardo's "Tracking Chromosomes, Castrating Dwarves: Uninformed Consent and Eugenic Research," *Ethics & Medicine* 25, No. 3 (Fall 2009).
3. The condition known today as Down syndrome or Trisomy 21 was commonly referred to derisively as "mongolism" through much of the nineteenth and twentieth centuries; the term was used to describe those "idiotic and imbecilic" children of European or Caucasian background with "atavistic features" of a Mongolian from Asia. First described by John Langdon Haydon Down, a British physician, in 1866, the condition and whether it was hereditary or congenital would confound and stimulate scientific debate for generations.
4. Letter from Charles B. Davenport to Dr. C. S. Little, July 12, 1929. Papers of Charles B. Davenport at the American Philosophical Society (cited hereafter as C. B. Davenport Papers).
5. Ibid.
6. The child's father was deceased, and his mother was said to be "of low mentality." Paul Lombardo describes her as "so lacking in comprehension that her consent would probably not be legally valid." "Tracking Chromosomes, Castrating Dwarves," p. 156.
7. Black, *War Against the Weak*, p. 14.
8. Francis Galton, *Hereditary Genius: An Inquiry into Its Law and Consequences* (London: Macmillan, 1869); *Natural Inheritance* (London: Macmillan,1899).

9. Black, *War Against the Weak*, p. 16.

10. Phillip Reilly, "The Surgical Solution: The Writings of Activist Physicians in the Early Days of Eugenical Sterilization" *Perspectives in Biology and Medicine*, Vol. 26, No. 4, Summer 1983, p. 646.

11. William T Belfield, "The sterilization of criminals and other defectives by vasectomy." *Journal of the New Mexico Medical Society* (1909), pp. 21–25.

12. Lewellys F. Barker, "The Importance of the Eugenic Movement and Its Relation to Social Hygiene," Journal of the American Medical Association 54 (1910): 2017–2022; and G. Frank Lydston, "Sex Mutilations in Social Therapeutics," *New York Medical Journal* 95 (1912), pp. 677–85.

13. Phillip Reilly, p. 643.

14. Martin W. Barr, "Some Notes on Asexualization; with a Report of Eighteen Cases," *Journal of Nervous & Mental Disease* 51, No. 3 (March 1920), p. 232.

15. Phillip Reilly, "The Surgical Solution: The Writings of Activist Physicians in the Early Days of Eugenical Sterilization" *Perspectives in Biology and Medicine*, Vol. 26, No. 4, Summer 1983, p. 643.

16. Daniel J. Kevles, *In the Name of Eugenics* (New York: Knopf, 1985), p. 47.

17. Leon F. Whitney, *The Case for Sterilisation* (London: John Lane, 1935), p. 76.

18. . Ibid., p. 2.

19. Alexander Johnson, "To Eliminate the Defectives," December 28, 1932, pp. 1–3.

20. Whitney, *Case for Sterilisation*, p. 99. Whitney's book is a clear and powerful statement about the era and the attitudes of eugenicists. However, unfortunately, it is littered with demeaning references to those with disabilities and those placed in institutions involuntarily. For example, in addressing the elimination of such individuals, Whitney states, "Undoubtedly society would be better off without such, though the assertion has been made that we need them for our drudgery—for the dirty work of the world," p. 100.

21. Black, *War Against the Weak*, p. 99.

22. Ibid., p. 126.

23. From the turn of the century to the Great Depression, public institutions in America continued to grow in both numbers and population. By 1923, there were over 42,000 people in institutions, a number that would grow to 50,000 just three years later. By the mid-1930s, the population was over 81,000. James W. Trent Jr., *Inventing the Feeble Mind: A History of Mental Retardation in the United States* (Berkeley: University of California Press, 1994), p. 199.

24. Daniel J. Kevles, *In the Name of Eugenics: Genetics and the Uses of Human Heredity* (New York: Knopf, 1985), pp. 47, 53.

25. Ibid., p. 58.

26. Ibid., p. 55.

27. Black, *War Against the Weak*, p. 94.

28. Lombardo, "Tracking Chromosomes, Castrating Dwarves."

29. Letchworth Village Cornerstone Program, June 14, 1933.

30. Letter from Charles B. Davenport to Henry H. Goddard, March 18, 1909. C. B. Davenport Papers

31. Eugenic Record Office Questionnaire. C. B. Davenport Papers.

32. Letter from Henry Goddard to Charles B. Davenport, April 13, 1910. C. B. Davenport Papers.

33. Letter from Charles B. Davenport to H. H. Goddard, April 18, 1910. C. B. Davenport Papers, p. 3. Davenport would further mollify his concerned colleague about the potential for "exploitation" by stating "the danger seems slight since people do not object so much to facts being known as to their relation to those facts being known. The families" being addressed in their publications "might just as well be on the planet Mars so far as any danger of their being identified by other people goes," p. 4.

34. In adapting Binet's intelligence tests to English and the American educational landscape, Goddard coined a new term for the highest class of feebleminded individuals. The three categories of I.Q. differentiation—idiot, imbecile, and moron—would remain part of institutional profiling for generations.

35. Letter from Henry Goddard to Charles B. Davenport, October 25, 1915. C. B. Davenport Papers.

36. Dozens of ERO questionnaires concerning university coursework can be found in the C. B. Davenport Papers.

37. The University of California Questionnaire. C. B. Davenport Papers.

38. Letter from Adolf Meyer to Charles B. Davenport, April 28, 1921. C. B. Davenport Papers.

39. Letter from F. Heiermann, S.J., to Harry B. Laughlin, February 16, 1920. C. B. Davenport Papers.

40. Walter Lippmann, "The Abuse of the Tests," *New Republic*, November 15, 1922, p. 297.

41. Quoted in Kevles, In the Name of Eugenics, p. 138.

42. Letter from E. B. Conklin to Charles B. Davenport, February 9, 1909. C. B. Davenport Papers.

43. Kevles, *In the Name of Eugenics*, p. 75.

44. Black, *War Against the Weak*, p. 75.

45. Whitney, *Case for Sterilisation*, p. 195.

46. Gregory Michael Dorr, *Segregation's Science*, (Charlottesville: University of Virginia Press, 2008), p. 53.

47. Ibid., p. 55.

48. Paul Lombardo and Gregory Dorr, "Eugenics, Medical Education, and the Public Health Service: Another Perspective on the Tuskegee Syphilis Experiment" *Bulletin of the History of Medicine*, Vol. 80, No. 2, Summer 2006, p. 302.

49. Dorr, p. 63.

50. Ibid., p. 116.

51. Ralph Brave and Kathryn Sylva, "Exhibiting Eugenics: Response and Resistance to a Hidden History" *The Public Historian*, Vol. 29, No. 3, p. 37.

52. Key PHS physicians such as Hugh Cumming, Taliaferro Clark, and Raymond Vonderlehr were involved in the Macon County syphilis study and all were graduates of the University of Virginia. It would appear that the PHS made a concerted effort to recruit Virginia educated students, and explains at least in part, why there were no complaints within the PHS about the unethical nature of the four-decade long experiment. Lombardo and Dorr, pp. 291–316.

53. Kevles, *In the Name of Eugenics*, p. 110.

54. Ibid., p. 111.

55. Letter from Charles B. Davenport to C. S. Little, August 8, 1924. C. B. Davenport Papers.

56. Letter from Charles B. Davenport to C. S. Little, May 27, 1927. C. B. Davenport Papers.

57. Letter from C. S. Little to Charles B. Davenport, January 16, 1935. C. B. Davenport Papers.

58. Report of the Meeting of the Letchworth Village Research Council, January 15, 1936. C. B. Davenport Papers.

59. Letter from Charles B. Davenport to Elizabeth W. Buck, July 26, 1939. C. B. Davenport Papers.

60. Lombardo, "Tracking Chromosomes, Castrating Dwarves," p. 156.

61. Dr. Henry Heiman, "A Clinical and Bacteriological Study of the Gonoccus Neisser in the Male Urethra and in the Vulvo-vaginal Tract of Children," *Journal of Cutaneous and Genitourinary Diseases* 13 (1895), p. 385.

CHAPTER 3: WORLD WAR II, PATRIOTISM, AND THE NUREMBERG CODE

1. Paul Julian Weindling, *Nazi Medicine and the Nuremberg Trials* (New York: Palgrave, 2004), p. 7.

2. Ibid., p. 270.

3. Nazi Doctors Trial, United States v. Karl Brandt, Nuremberg, Germany, June 13, 1947, pp. 9173-9174. Future citations will refer to Doctors Trial. The death of 13 inmates at Bilibid Prison in the Philippines in 1905 due to either "criminal negligence" or possibly more serious charges has never been fully explained to the satisfaction of many. Dr. Richard P. Strong inoculated 24 prisoners with an anti-cholera serum, an experiment that seemed more for his own scientific interest than any therapeutic benefit for the prisoners. When inmates subsequently became seriously ill and began dying it was quickly discovered that the serum actually contained bubonic plague. Initially brought up on charges, Strong not only escaped prosecution, but he also eventually returned to the island years later to perform additional medical experiments. He would go on to become Harvard Medical School's first professor of tropical medicine. One of the better articles on the incident is Kristine A. Campbell's "Knots in the Fabric: Richard Pearson Strong and the Bilibid Prison Vaccine Trial's, 1905-1906" *Bulletin of the History of Medicine*, Vol. 68, No. 4, Winter, 1994, p. 600.

4. Ulf Schmidt, *Justice at Nuremberg* (New York: Palgrave Macmillan, 2004), pp. 134–35.

5. Doctors Trial, p. 9215.

6. For a more detailed account of prisoners' motivation for participation in medical experiments see Allen Hornblum's *Acres of Skin* (Routledge, 1998).

7. The Green Committee, named after Dwight Green, the governor of Illinois, was a device by Ivy to try an legitimize after the fact that the Stateville malaria experiments were ethical and consistent with the law. In fact, the committee never met or issued a report when Ivy took the stand at Nuremberg. As Ulf Schmidt generously states, "Ivy was coming close to perjury" on several occasions when he was queried by defense attorneys about the committee's findings. Schmidt, pp. 234–35.

8. Doctors Trial. The trial and conviction of Leopold and Loeb for the brutal murder of young Bobby Franks dominated the news media in the mid-1920s. Servatius mistakenly said Leopold "was condemned to fifteen years…for murder" when, in fact, the sentence was considerably longer, life plus 99 years. That sentence would actually become the title of a book Leopold would write several years later that would be instrumental in his successful bid for a gubernatorial pardon in the 1950s. Leopold's book devotes several chapters on the Stateville Prison malaria experiments and graphically describes the chills, raging fevers, and recurring discomfort the test subjects endured.

9. Though German lawyers argued, "900 prisoners condemned to death" were targeted as test subjects, Kristine Campbell stated that most sentences ranged from "life imprisonment" to a "few days of arrest." She also stated that "prison guards urged those on who were reluctant" to participate.

10. Defense counsel, and the defendants themselves, brought up a host of inconsistencies and what they deemed as medical and military excesses by the victors that were the equal in ethical horror as to what they were being charged with. Defendants Karl Brandt and Gebhardt, for example, argued that the dropping of atomic bombs on Hiroshima and Nagasaki than their experiments on chemical weapons and sulphonamides – did not both have a strategic rationale?

11. Weindling, *Nazi Medicine and the Nuremberg Trials*, p. 279.

12. Schmidt, *Justice at Nuremberg*, p. 206.

13. Doctors Trial, pp. 9239-240.

14. Ibid. pp. 9241-242.

15. Schmidt, *Justice at Nuremberg*, p. 207.

16. Ibid., p. 206.

17. Doctors Trial, p. 9242.

18. Ibid.

19. Schmidt, *Justice at Nuremberg*, p. 137.

20. Ibid. p. 139.

21. Ibid. p. 140.

22. Jay Katz, "The Consent Principle of the Nuremberg Code: It's Significance Then and Now" *The Nazis Doctors and the Nuremberg Code* (New York: Oxford University Press, 1992), p. 227.

23. David J. Rothman, *Strangers at the Bedside: A History of How Law and Bioethics Transformed Medical Decision Making* (New York: Basic Books, 1991), p. 36.

24. Ibid.

25. Jay Katz, "The Consent Principle of the Nuremberg Code: It's Significance Then and Now" *The Nazis Doctors and the Nuremberg Code* (New York: Oxford University Press, 1992), p. 227.

26. Jay Katz, Final Report of the Advisory Committee on Human Radiation Experiments, (New York: Oxford University Press, 1996), p. 234.

27. Sheldon H. Harris, *Factories of Death* (New York: Routledge, 1994), p. 219.

28. A more complete list of diseases applied to humans would include "plague, typhoid, parathyroid A and B, typhus, smallpox, tularemia, infectious jaundice, gas gangrene, tetanus, cholera, dysentery, glanders, scarlet fever, undulant fever, tick encephalitis, songo or epidemic hemorrhagic fever, whooping cough, diphtheria, pneumonia, bysipelas, epidemic cerebrospinal meningitis, venereal diseases, tuberculosis, salmonellas, frostbite, and countless other diseases." Moreno, p. 106.

29. According to Harris, the State-War-Navy Coordinating Subcommittee for the Far East was "charged with achieving two objectives" regarding biological warfare weapons. It was critical the Soviets not learn "anything relating to Japanese BW research" and equally important that "Japanese BW research experts provided American scientists with all the data they had previously amassed." Ibid., p. 209.

30. According to Weindling, the U.S. "employed in all 765 German and Austrian scientists and engineers for military research under the Paperclip scheme. P. 309.

31. Presidential Commission for the Study of Bioethical Issues, *Ethically Impossible: STD Research in Guatemala from 1946 to 1948* (Washington, D.C.: September 2011).

32. Ibid., pp. 76, 77, and 106.

33. Rothman, *Strangers at the Bedside*, p. 30.

34. Letter from Robert Ward to Dr. Joseph Stokes Jr., April 12, 1943. Papers of Dr. Joseph Stokes Jr., American Philosophical Society. Cited hereafter as J. Stokes Papers.

35. Ibid., p. 2.

36. Letter from Dr. Joseph Stokes Jr. to Dr. Paul de Kruif, November 15, 1935. J. Stokes Papers.

37. Letter from Dr. Joseph Stokes Jr. to Dr. Paul de Kruif, April 25, 1936. J. Stokes Papers.

38. Jonathan Moreno, *Undue Risk* (New York: W.H. Freeman, 2000), p. 16.

39. Rothman, *Strangers at the Bedside*, p. 31.

40. Ibid., p. 33.

41. Moreno, *Undue Risk*, p. 15; Rothman, *Strangers at the Bedside*, p. 32.

42. Rothman, *Strangers at the Bedside*, p. 36.

43. Bernard E. Harcourt, "Making Willing Bodies: The University of Chicago Malaria Experiments on Prisoners at Stateville Penitentiary" May 2011, p. 2.

44. Ibid.

45. Rothman, p. 36.

46. Eventually Gov. Adlai Stevenson would commute or parole 317 of the nearly 500 prisoners who took part in the experiment. Too public and controversial a figure to initially receive a commutation of his sentence, Leopold would be granted one subsequent to the publication of his well-received book. Though many applauded his sacrifice, skeptics believe he cunningly orchestrated events to win the public's sympathy and earn a gubernatorial pardon.

47. "Prison Malaria: Convicts Expose Themselves to Disease so Doctors can Study It" *Life* Magazine, June 4, 1945, pp. 43-46.

48. Moreno, p. 36.

49. Major Sabib's Laboratory, "Proposed Budget for Neurotropic Virus Disease Commission," July 1, 1944, to June 30, 1945, in the Papers of Dr. Joseph Stokes, Jr. at the American Philosophical Society. P. 1.

50. Letter from S. Bayne-Jones to Dr. Joseph Stokes, Jr. October 5, 1944, in the Papers of Dr. Joseph Stokes, Jr. in the American Philosophical Society.

51. Yale Hepatitis Laboratory, Ibid.

52. Report on activities of the Board for the Investigation and Control of Influenza and Other Epidemic Diseases in the Army, January 31, 1944, in the Papers of Dr. Joseph Stokes, Jr. at the American Philosophical Society.

53. Ibid., p. 8.

54. Letter from Dr. Joseph Stokes, Jr. to Dr. Ellen G. Potter, April 11, 1945, in the Papers of Dr. Joseph Stokes, Jr. at the American Philosophical Society.

55. Ibid.

56. Letter from Dr. Joseph Stokes, Jr. to Dr. Ellen G. Potter, May 16, 1945, in the Papers of Dr. Joseph Stokes, Jr. at the American Philosophical Society.

57. Letter from John R. Neefe to Brig. General Stanhope Bayne-Jones, October 12, 1944, in the papers of Dr. Joseph Stokes, Jr. at the American Philosophical Society.

58. Letter from John R. Neefe to Dr. J. B. Spradley, September 28, 1944, Papers of Dr. Joseph Stokes, Jr. at the American Philosophical Society.

59. Committee on Medical Research, Office of Scientific Research and Development, Monthly Progress Report No. 19, December 8, 1944. National Archives, College Park, Md.

60. Committee on Medical Research, Office of Scientific Research and Development, Monthly Progress Report No. 18, October 3, 1944. National Archives, College Park, Md.

61. Rothman, p. 33.

62. Letter from Robert Ward to Dr. Stokes, April 7, 1943. J. Stokes Papers.

63. Annual report of the Commission on Neurotropic Virus Diseases, March 27, 1945, p. 4.

64. Ibid., p. 5.

65. Letter from S. Bayne-Jones to Captain John R. Neefe, August 4, 1944. J. Stokes Papers.

66. Elizabeth P. Maris, Geoffrey Rake, Joseph Stokes Jr., Morris P. Shaffer, and Gerald C. O'Neil, "Studies on Measles: The Results of Chance and Planned Exposure to Unmodified Measles Virus in Children Previously Inoculated with Egg-Passage Measles Virus," Journal of Pediatrics 23, No. 6 (1943), p. 29.

67. Ibid., p. 17.

68. Letter from John R. Neefe to Maj. Walter P. Havens Jr. September 1, 1944. J. Stokes Papers.

69. Joseph Stokes Jr. "Mission to MTOUSA and ETOUSA at the request of the Surgeon General, U. S. Army, to Study the Prevention and Treatment of Epidemic Hepatitis." J. Stokes Papers.

70. Letter from Joseph Stokes Jr. to Brig. Gen. S. Bayne-Jones, September 21, 1944. J. Stokes Papers. Joseph Stokes Jr. "Mission to MTOUSA and ETOUSA at the request of the Surgeon General, U. S. Army, to Study the Prevention and Treatment of Epidemic Hepatitis." J. Stokes Papers.

71. Letter from John R. Neefe to Brig. Gen. Stanhope Bayne-Jones, May 17, 1945. J. Stokes Papers

72. Letter from Brig. Gen. S. Bayne-Jones to Capt. John R. Neefe, April 11, 1945. J. Stokes Papers.

73. Rothman, *Strangers at the Bedside*, p. 48.

74. Ibid

75. Ibid., p. 50.

76. Jordan Goodman, Anthony McElligott, and Lara Marks, *Useless Bodies* (Baltimore: Johns Hopkins University Press, 2003), p. 12.

CHAPTER 4: IMPACT OF THE COLD WAR ON HUMAN EXPERIMENTATION

1. Author interviews with Karen Alves, October 26, 2001, and June 5, 2012.

2. Cerebral palsy is a neurologic disorder caused by damage to the motor control centers of the developing brain during pregnancy or childbirth resulting in limitations to movement and posture.

3. Esther M. Pond and Stuart A. Brody, *Evolution of Treatment Methods at a Hospital for the Mentally Retarded*, Department of Mental Hygiene, 1965, pp. 1–14. A copy is maintained by Bancroft Library, University of California, Berkeley.

4. Rebecca Leung, "A Dark Chapter in Medical History," *60 Minutes*, CBS, February 11, 2009.

5. Karen Alves would subsequently learn that LPNI 8732 stood for Langley Porter Neurological Center Patient Number 8732.

6. Neuropathology report on Mark Dal Molin, LPNI #8732, July 6, 1961. Supplied by his sister, Karen Alves.

7. Autopsy report for Mark Dal Molin, #19139, May 30, 1961.

8. Application for Research Grant, "An Etiological and Diagnostic Study of Cerebral Palsy," National Institutes of Health, October 20, 1952, p. 2.

9. Nathan Malamud, Hideo H. Itabashi, Jane Castor, and Harley B. Messinger, "An Etiologic and Diagnostic Study of Cerebral Palsy," *Journal of Pediatrics* 65, No. 2 (August 1964), p. 271.

10. Alves interviews. (See 1 above.)

11. Hepatitis Studies—Pennhurst: Results, Tissue Culture Experiment #2," August 15, 1947, p. 1. Joseph S. Stokes Jr. papers at the American Philosophical Society. Cited hereafter as J. Stokes Papers.

12. Ibid., p. 2.

13. Ibid., p. 3.

14. Presidential Commission for the Study of Bioethical Issues, *Ethically Impossible: STD Research in Guatemala from 1946 to September 1948*, September 2011.

15. Distribution of Volunteers for Next Hepatitis Experiment, undated. J. Stokes Papers. Plans for Jaundice Experiments. American Philosophical Society.

16. David J. Rothman, *Strangers at the Bedside: A History of How Law and Bioethics Transformed Medical Decision Making* (New York: Basic Books, 1991), p. 51.

17. Ibid., p. 52.

18. Ibid., p. 53.

19. Ibid., p. 55.

20. "The Nuremberg Trial against German Physicians," Journal of the American Medical Association 135, No. 13, November 29, 1947, p. 867.

21. Oral History Project of the Advisory Committee on Human Radiation Experiments, January 13, 1995, p. 2.

22. Ibid.

23. Authors' interview with Dr. Chester Southam, July 28, 1996.

24. Authors' interview with Dr. A. Bernard Ackerman, September 9, 1996.

25. Letter from Joseph Stokes Jr. to Col. William B. Stone, October 15, 1947. J. Stokes Papers.

26. Letter from Joseph Stokes Jr. to Dr. Colin MacLeod, February 11, 1948. J. Stokes Papers.

27. Letter from C. J. Watson to Lt. Col. Frank L. Bauer, April 12, 1948. Papers of Joseph Stokes, Jr., American Philosophical Society.

28. Letter from Dr. John R. Paul to Dr. Joseph Stokes Jr., February 18, 1948. J. Stokes Papers.

29. Letter from Dr. Joseph Stokes Jr. to Dr. Colin MacLeod, February 11, 1948. J. Stokes Papers.

30. Dr. Richard B. Capps, "Proposed Studies on Liver Disease," March 10, 1951. J. Stokes Papers.

31. Ibid.

32. The membership list of the Sub-Committee on the Allocation of Volunteers of the Armed Forces Epidemiological Board included Dr. Irving Gordon of the Division of Laboratories& Research for the Department of Health; Dr. Roderick Murray of the National Institutes of Health; Dr. Cecil Watson,

director of the Commission on Liver Disease and professor at the University of Minnesota; Dr. Colin MacLeod, president of the AFEB; and Colonel A. J. Rapalski, a key administrator of the AFEB at the Office of the Surgeon General. J. Stokes Papers.

33. Letter from Frank L. Bauer to Dr. Joseph Stokes Jr., April 26, 1950. J. Stokes Papers.

34. Letter from Dr. Joseph Stokes Jr. to Dr. Cecil J. Watson, February 8, 1951. J. Stokes Papers.

35. Armed Force, Epidemiological Board, Office of Medical History, U.S Army Medical

36. Letter from Dr. Joseph Stokes Jr. to Dr. Cecil J. Watson, February 4, 1953. J. Stokes Papers.

37. Letter from Dr. Joseph Stokes Jr. to Dr. Cecil J. Watson, February 5, 1953. J. Stokes Papers.

38. Letter from Alex M. Burgess to Dr. Joseph Stokes Jr. December 10, 1945. J. Stokes Papers.

39. Memorandum from Andy Burgess to Homer L. Morris on Volunteer Experimental Sub jects. J. Stokes Papers, p. 2.

40. Susan E. Lederer, *Subjected to Science: Human Experimentation in America before the Second World War* (Baltimore: Johns Hopkins University Press, 1997), p. 137.

41. Letter from Dr. Colin M. MacLeod to Dr. Herman E. Hillsboe, December 3, 1952. J. Stokes Papers, p. 1.

42. Ibid., p. 2.

43. Joseph Stokes Jr., "A Clarification of the Question of Ethical Responsibility in the Exposure of Human Beings to Certain Infectious Agents," February 4, 1953, p. 1. J. Stokes Papers.

44. Ibid., p. 4.

45. Ibid., p. 6.

46. Letter from Dr. Roderick Murray to Dr. Joseph Stokes Jr., November 13, 1952. J. Stokes Papers.

47. Ibid., p. 2.

48. Unsigned and undated memo on the subject of prisoner compulsion. Papers of Joseph Stokes, Jr., American Philosophical Society.

49. Both *Acres of Skin: Human Experiments at Holmesburg Prison; A True Story of Abuse and Exploitation in the Name of Medical Science* (New York: Routledge, 1998) and *Sentenced to Science: One Black Man's Story of Imprisonment in America* (University Park: Pennsylvania State University Press, 2007) by Allen M. Hornblum provide an historical accounting of prison research in America and the reasons inmates chose to participate in experimental studies.

50. Department of Defense Resolution concerning House of Delegates of the American Medical Association. J. Stokes Papers.

51. Letter from Dr. Joseph Stokes Jr. to Dr. Paul Havens, November 10, 1952. J. Stokes Papers.

52. Letter from Nate Hazeltine to Dr. Colin Macleod, February 10, 1953. J. Stokes Papers.

53. Letter from Colin M. MacLeod to Dr. Joseph Stokes, Jr., November 6, 1952, in the Papers of Joseph Stokes, Jr. at the American Philosophical Society, p. 1.

54. Letter from Joseph Stokes, Jr. to Dr. Richard B. Capps, June 17, 1954, in the Papers of Joseph Stokes, Jr. at the American Philosophical Society, p. 1.

55. Letter from Dr. Joseph Stokes Jr. to Harry Von Bulow, Jr., July 7, 1954. J. Stokes Papers.

56. Letter from H. Von Bulow to Dr. Joseph Stokes Jr., July 12, 1954. J. Stokes Papers.

57. Letter from H. Von Bulow to Dr. Joseph Stokes Jr., August 31, 1954. J. Stokes Papers.

58. Letter from Dr. Joseph Stokes Jr. to Dr. Herald Cox, August 24, 1954. J. Stokes Papers.

59. Letter from Herald R. Cox to Dr. Joseph Stokes Jr., August 26, 1954. J. Stokes Papers.

60. Letter from Dr. Joseph Stokes Jr. to Mrs. Rose Antman, September 28, 1955. J. Stokes Papers.

61. Paul Starr, *The Social Transformation of American Medicine: The Rise of a Sovereign Profession and the Making of a Vast Industry* (New York: Basic Books, 1982), p. 335.

62. Ibid., p. 336.

63. J. Edgar Hoover, *Masters of Deceit: The Story of Communism in America and How to Fight It* (New York: Henry Holt, 1958), p. 331.

64. Paul A. Offit, *The Cutter Incident: How America's First Polio Vaccine Led to the Growing Vaccine Crisis* (New Haven, CT: Yale University Press, 2005), p. 84.

65. Christopher Simpson, *Blowback: The First Full Account of America's Recruitment of Nazis and Its Disastrous Effect on the Cold War, Our Domestic and Foreign Policy* (New York: Collier Books, 1988), p. 3.

66. Allen Weinstein and Alexander Vassiliev, *The Haunted Wood: Soviet Espionage in America—The Stalin Era* (New York: Modern Library, 1999), p. 300.

67. Richard Rhodes, *Dark Sun: The Making of the Hydrogen Bomb* (New York: Simon & Schuster, 1995), p. 260.

68. James S. Ketchum, *Chemical Warfare Secrets Almost Forgotten: A Personal Story of Medical Testing of Army Volunteers* (Santa Rosa, CA: ChemBook, 2006), p. 3.

69. Advisory Committee on Human Radiation Experiments, *Final Report of the Advisory Committee on Human Radiation Experiments* (New York: Oxford University Press, 1996), p. 2.

70. Ibid.

71. John D. Marks, *The Search for the Manchurian Candidate: The CIA and Mind Control; The Secret History of the Behavioral Sciences* (New York: W. W. Norton, 1979), p. vii.

72. Authors' interview with Dr. James Ketchum, July 23, 2012.

73. Ibid., p. 247.

74. Authors' interview with Dr. Enoch Callaway, October 30, 2010.

75. Marks, *The Search for the Manchurian Candidate*, p. 25.

76. Ibid., p. 63.

77. Bufotenine is a psychedelic neurotransmitter found in certain toads, mushrooms, and plants.

78. Marks, *The Search for the Manchurian Candidate*, p. 142.

79. Ibid., p. 150.

80. Harvey Weinstein, *Father, Son and CIA* (Halifax: Goodread Biographies, 1990), p. 294

81. Marks, *The Search for the Manchurian Candidate*, p. 18.

82. Alton Chase, *Harvard, and the Unabomber: The Education of an American Terrorist* (New York: Norton, 2002).

83. Henry K. Beecher, "Ethics and Clinical Research," *New England Journal of Medicine* 274, No. 24 (June 16, 1966), pp. 1354–360.

84. David J. Rothman, "Ethics and Human Experimentation: Henry Beecher Revisited," *New England Journal of Medicine* 317, No. 19 (November 5, 1987), p. 1195.

85. Beecher, "Ethics and Clinical Research," p. 1354.

86. Rothman, "Ethics and Human Experimentation," p. 1196.

87. Maurice Pappworth, *Human Guinea Pigs* (Boston: Beacon Press, 1967).

CHAPTER 5: VACCINES

1. Interview with Pat Clapp, August 5–7, 2012.

2. Henry W. Pierce, "State Halts Use of Retarded as Guinea Pigs" *Pittsburgh Post Gazette*, April 11, 1973; Henry W. Pierce, "State Kills Testing of Meningitis Shots" *Pittsburgh Post Gazette*; Delores Frederick, "Experiments on Humans Denied Here" *Pittsburgh Press*, April 12, 1973.

3. Pierce, "State Kills Testing of Meningitis Shots" *Pittsburgh Post Gazette*, April 12, 1973.

4. Pierce, "State Halts Use of Retarded as Guinea Pigs" *Pittsburgh Post Gazette*, April 11, 1973.

5. Pierce, April 12, 1973.

6. Delores Frederick, "Courts, Not Parents, Have Word on Retarded Tests, Wecht Says" *Pittsburgh Press*.

7. "Retarded at Hamburg State Drugged" April 20, 1973, p. 13.

8. Gabriel Ireton, "Polk Chaplin Defends use of Patient Pens" *Pittsburgh Post Gazette*, June 21, 1973, p. 6.

9. "Designed Cage, Doctor Admits."

10. Letter from Helene Wohlgemuth to James H. McClelland, April 16, 1973.

11. William H. Wilder, "Report of the Committee for the Study of the Relation of Tuberculosis to Diseases of the Eye" *Journal of the American Medical Association*, Vol. LV, No. 1, June 2, 1910, p. 21.

12. Susan E. Lederer, *Subjected to Science*, (Baltimore: Johns Hopkins, 1995), p. 80.

13. Louis M. Warfield, "The Cutaneous Tuberculin Reaction" *Journal of the American Medical Association*, Vol. L, No. 9, February 29, 1908, p. 688.

14. L. Emmett Holt "A Report Upon One Thousand Tuberculin Tests in Young Children" *Archives of Pediatrics*, January 1909, p. 3.

15. Ibid., pp. 2, 7.

16. N. Paul Hudson, Edwin H. Lennette, and Francis B. Gordon, "Factors of Resistance in Experimental Poliomyelitis" *The Journal of the American Medical Association*, June 13, 1936, Vol. 106, No. 24, p. 1.

17. "The Prophylaxis of Poliomyelitis" Ibid., p. 15.

18. Ibid., p. 17.

19. Ibid., p. 33.

20. Morris Schaeffer, "William H. Park: His Laboratory and His Legacy" *American Journal of Public Health*, November 1985, Vol. 75, No. 11, p. 1301.

21. "New Infantile Paralysis Vaccine is Declared to Immunize Children" *New York Times*, August 18, 1934, p. 1; "Will Give Children Paralysis Vaccine" *New York Times*, August 21, 1934, p. 1.

22. Schaeffer, Ibid.

23. "Questions Safety of Paralysis Virus" *New York Times*, October 9, 1935.

24. "Dr. Brodie Upholds Paralysis Vaccine" *New York Times*, November 3, 1935.

25. Shaeffer, Ibid.

26. "Paralysis Vaccine Discontinued Here" *New York Times*, December 27, 1935.

27. Paul Offit, *The Cutter Incident* (New Haven: Yale University Press, 2005), p. 35.

28. David Oshinski, *Polio: An American Story* (New York: Oxford, 2005), p. 151.

29. Jonas E. Salk, Harold E. Pearson, Philip N. Brown, and Thomas Francis, Jr. "Protective Effect of Vaccination Against Induced Influenza B" *Journal of Clinical Investigation*, July 1945, Vol. 24 (4), pp. 547–53.

30. Oshinski, Ibid.

31. Letter from Gale H. Walker to Honorable William C. Brown, February 4, 1952, Salk Archives, University of California, San Diego, p. 1.

32. Letter from Hilding Bengs to Dr. Gale H. Walker, March 18, 1952, Salk Archives, University of California, San Diego.

33. Oshinski, p. 132.

34. Irena Koprowska, *A Woman Wanders through Life and Science* (Albany: State University of New York Press, 1997), p. 298.

35. Interview with Dr. Hilary Koprowski, September 14, 2009.

36. Koprowska, p. 298.

37. Ibid., p. 299.

38. Koprowski interview.

39. Saul Benison, *Tom Rivers: Reflections on a Life in Medicine and Science* (Cambridge: MIT Press, 1967), p. 465.

40. Ibid. p. 467.

41. "Poliomyelitis: A New Approach" *The Lancet*, March 15, 1952, p. 552.

42. Howard A. Howe, "Criteria for the Inactivation of Poliomelitis," Committee on Immunization, December 4, 1951, Meeting, Mandeville Special Collections Library, University of California, San Diego, p. 3.

43. Howard A. Howe, "Antibody Response of Chimpanzees and Human Beings to Formalin-Inactivated Trivalent Poliomyelitis Vaccine" *American Journal of Epidemiology* 56, (No.3) 1952, pp. 265–86.

44. "The Prophylaxis of Poliomyelitis" is a transcript of the April 30, 1936, meeting in Baltimore, Maryland, p. 4.

45. Werner Henle, Gertrude Henle, and Joseph Stokes, Jr. "Demonstration of the Efficacy of Vaccination Against Influenza Type A By Experimental Infection of Human Beings." *Journal of Immunology*, Vol. 46, 1943, p. 163.

46. Ibid. p. 166.

47. Elizabeth P. Maris, Geoffrey Rake, Joseph Stokes, Jr., Morris F. Shaffer, and Gerald C. O'Neil "Studies on Measles: The Results of Chance and Planned Exposure to Unmodified Measles Virus in Children Previously Inoculated with Egg-Passage Measles Virus" *Journal of Pediatrics*, Vol. 22, No. 1, January 1943, p. 17.

48. Letter from Richard Capps to Dr. Joseph Stokes, Jr., November 30, 1950, in the Papers of Dr. Joseph Stokes, Jr. at the American Philosophical Society.

49. Ibid. Handwritten comments at top of page.

50. Saul Krugman, "The Willowbrook Hepatitis Studies Revisited: Ethical Aspects" *Reviews of Infectious Diseases*, Vol. 8, No. 1, January-February 1986, p. 158.

51. "Was Dr. Krugman Justified" *World Medical News*, October 15, 1971, p. 29.

52. Stephen Goldby, "Experiments at the Willowbrook State School" *The Lancet*, April 10, 1971, p. 749.

53. Ibid.

54. "Was Krugman Justified," p. 29.

55. Saul Krugman, "The Willowbrook Hepatitis Studies Revisited: Ethical Aspects" *Reviews of Infectious Diseases*, Vol. 8, No. 1, January-February 1986, p. 157.

56. Robert Ward, Saul Krugman, Joan P. Giles, and Milton A. Jacobs, "Endemic Viral Hepatitis in an Institution Epidemiology and Control" (undated document ca. 1956 from the New York University Medical School Archives), p. 3.

57. The stool virus was developed in the following manner. "A 20% aqueous suspension was prepared from stools of 6 patients in the first 8 days of observed jaundice. Three centrifugations were carried out, 1 at 2000 RPM and 2 at 8500 RPM for 1 hour. The supernate was heated at 56 degrees C for ½ hour and treated with penicillin 1000units and chloramphenicol 100 ug/ml. before sterility was achieved. This sterile suspension was inoculated into 5 monkeys (1 ccintracerebrally), 47 suckling mice, Hela and monkey kidney tissue cultures No changes occurred in any of these test objects and the monkeys' spinal cords and brain stems showed no evidence of poliomyelitis lessions." Ward, p. 5.

58. Ibid., p. 6.

59. Ibid., p. 7.

60. Letter from Saul Krugman to Harold H. Berman, January 27, 1960, in the Papers of Saul Krugman at the New York School of Medicine Archive.

61. Letter from Robert Ward to Dr. Harold H Berman, March 29, 1957, in the Papers of Saul Krugman at the New York University School of Medicine Archives.

62. Ibid., pp. 2–4.

63. Letter from Saul Krugman to Harold H. Berman, April 27, 1959, in the Papers of Dr. Saul Krugman at New York University School of Medicine Archives.

64. Letter from Alfred M. Prince to Dr. Saul Krugman, November 29, 1960, in the Papers of Saul Krugman at New York University School of Medicine Archives.

65. Letter from Saul Krugman to Captain Alfred M. Prince, December 14, 1960, in the Papers of Saul Krugman at the New York School of Medicine Archives.

66. Letter from Saul Krugman to Jack Hammond, August 2, 1965, in the papers of Saul Krugman at the New York University School of Medicine Archives.

67. Letter from Saul Krugman to Jack Hammond, July 12, 1966, in the Papers of Saul Krugman, at the New York University School of Medicine Archives.

68. Letter from Jack Hammond to Saul Krugman, November 24, 1967, in the Papers of Saul Krugman at the New York University School of Medicine Archives.

69. Lawrence K. Altman, "Immunization id Reported in Serum Hepatitis Tests" New York Times, March 24, 1971, p. 1.

70. Letter from Stanley A. Plotkin to Mr. Robert Morrow, March 15, 1972, in the Papers of Saul Krugman at the New York University School of Medicine Archives.

71. Stanley A. Plotkin, David Cornfield, and Theodore H. Ingalls "Studies of Immunization with Living Rubella Virus Trials in Children with a Strain Cultured from an Aborted Fetus" *American Journal of Disability and Children*, Vol. 110, October 1965, p. 382.

72. Stanley A. Plotkin, J.D. FarQuhar, M. Katz, and C. Hertz, "Further Studies of an Attenuated Rubella Strain Grown in WI-38 Cells" *American Journal of Epidemiology*, Vol. 89, No. 2, September 6, 1968, p. 238.

73. George T. Harrell, S.F. Horne, Jerry K. Aikawa, and Nancy J. Helsabeck "Trichinella Skin Tests in an Orphanage and Prison: Comparison with Serologic Tests for Trichinosis and with the Tuberculin Reaction" *Journal of Clinical Investigation*, Vol. 26, No. 1, January 1947, p. 64.

74. Johannes Ipsen, Jr. "Bio-Assay of Four Tetanus Toxoids (Aluminum Precipitated) in Mice, Guinea Pigs, and Humans" *Journal of Immunology*, Vol. 70, No. 4, 1953, pp. 426–34.

75. Ibid., p. 433.

76. Louis W. Sauer and Winston H. Tucker, "Immune Responses to Diptheria, tetanus, and Pertusis, Aluminum Phosphate Absorbed" *Journal of Public Health*, Vol. 44, Issue 6, 1954, p. 785.

77. Ibid.

78. Stephen Millan, John Maisel, C. Henry Kempe, Stanley Plotkin, Joseph Pagano, and Joel Warren "Antibody Response of Man to Canine Distemper Virus" *Journal of Bacteriology*, Vol. 79, No. 4, 1960, p. 618.

CHAPTER 6: SKIN, DIETARY, AND DENTAL STUDIES

1. Interview with Margaret Grey Wood, February 2, 1996.

2. Interview with Paul Gross, January 22, 1996.

3. More on Dr. Gross' experiment with Paritol can be found in Albert M. Kligman, "Pathologic Dynamics of Human Hair Loss" *Archives of Dermatology*, Vol. 83, February 1961, pp. 37–59.

4. Interview with A. Bernard Ackerman, February 1, 1996, and September 9, 1996.

5. A more complete accounting of Dr. Kligman's Holmesburg research operation can be gleaned in Hornblum's *Acres of Skin* (New York: Routledge, 1998).

6. See Hornblum's *Acres of Skin* for a detailed account of Kligman's Holmesburg Prison operation.

7. Ibid.

8. Kligman's many ringworm articles caused a member of the Holmesburg Prison medical staff to inquire if he would take a look at the athlete's foot problem at the institution. Kligman visited the jail and immediately viewed it as "a fertile field" of investigatory opportunity. He quickly began performing experiments on the inmates and would remain there for the next 24 years.

9. Albert M. Kligman, "The Pathogenesis of Tinea Capitis Due to Microsporum Audouini and Microsporum Canis," *Journal of Investigative Dermatology*, Vol. 18, No. 3, March 1952, p. 231.

10. Ibid., p. 246.

11. Albert M. Kligman and W. Ward Anderson, "Evaluation of Current Methods for the Local Treatment of Tinea Capitis" *Journal of Investigative Dermatology*, No. 16, March 1951, p. 162.

12. Ibid., p. 166.

13. For additional information, one can peruse Herbert Goldschmidt and Albert M. Kligman, "Experimental Inoculation of Humans with Ectodermotropic Viruses" *Journal of Investigative Dermatology*, Vol. 31, No. 3, September 1958, p. 176; John S. Strauss and Albert M. Kligman, "Effect of X-Rays on Sebaceous Glands of the Human Face" *Journal of Investigative Dermatology*, Vol. 33, No. 6, December 1959, p. 347; Allen M. Hornblum, *Acres of Skin*, p. 36.

14. Albert M. Kligman, "Hyposensitization Against Rhus Dermatitis" *Archives of Dermatology*, Vol. 78, July 1958.

15. Life Magazine, September 5, 1955; and Hornblum, *Acres of Skin* (New York: Routledge, 1998).

16. Francis P. Coombs and Thomas Butterworth, "Atypical Keratosis Pilaris" *Archives of Dermatology*, Vol. 62, No. 2, August 1950, p. 305.

17. Hornblum, Ibid., p. 37.

18. Botho F. Felden, "Epilation with Thallium Acetate in the Treatment of Ringworm of the Scalp of Children" *Archives of Dermatology and Syphilology*, Vol. 17, No. 2, February 1928, p. 185.

19. Robert E. Swain and W.G. Bateman, "The Toxicity of Thallium Salts," *The Journal of Biological Chemistry*, December 9, 1909, p. 147.

20. Ibid.

21. G. B. Dowling, "The Treatment of Ringworm of the Scalp by Thallium Depilation," *The British Medical Journal*, August 13, 1927, p. 261.

22. Ibid., p. 192.

23. Howard Ticktin, "Hepatic Dysfunction and jaundice in Patients" *New England Journal of Medicine*, Vol. 267, No. 19 (1962), pp. 964–68.

24. Isaac A. Abt, "Spontaneous Hemorrhages in Newborn Children" *Journal of the American Medical Association*, Vol. 40, No. 5, January 1903, p. 290.

25. Ibid.

26. Ibid., p. 291.

27. Joann G. Elmore and Alvan Feinstein, "Joseph Goldberger: An Unsung Hero of American Clinical Epidemiology" *Annals of Internal Medicine* Vol. 121, No. 5, September 1994, p. 372.

28. Alan M. Kraut, *Goldberger' War* (New York: Hill and Wang, 2003), p. 105.

29. Ibid., p. 106.

30. Donald J. Barnes "Effect of Evaporated Milk on the Incidence of Rickets in Infants" *Journal of the Michigan State Medical Society*, Vol. 31, 1932, p. 397.

31. Victor A. Najjar and L. Emmett Holt, "The Biosynthesis in Man and its Implications in Human Nutrition" *Journal of the American Medical Association*, Vol. 123, No. 11, November 1943, p. 683.

32. Victor A. Najjar and George C. Johns, George C. Mediary, Gertrude Fleischmann and L. Emmett Holt, "The Biosynthesis of Riboflavins" *Journal of the American Medical Association*, Vol. 126, No. 6, October 1944, pp. 357–58.

33. Pauline B. Mack, Alice Knapper Milsom, and Paul L. Carney, "A Study of Two Levels of Bread Enrichment in Children's Diet" *Monographs of the Society for research in Child Development*, Vol. 18, No. 2, 1953, pp. 1–92.

34. Herbert I. Goldman, Samuel Karelitz, EliSelfter, Hedda Acs, and Norman B. Schell, "Acidosis in Premature Infants Due to Lack of Lactic Acid," *Pediatrics*, Vol. 27, 1961, p. 928.

35. Ibid., p. 929.

36. Norman B. Schell, Samuel Karelitz, and Bernard S. Epstein, "Radiographic Study of Gastric Emptying in Premature Infants," *The Journal of Pediatrics*, Vol. 62, No. 3, March 1963, p. 343.

37. Basil G. Bibby, "A Test of the Effect of Fluoride-containing Dentifrices," *Journal of Dental Research*, Vol. 24, No. 6, 1945, pp. 297–303.

38. Julian D. Boyd and Kenneth E. Wessels, "Epidemiologic Studies in Dental Caries: The Interpretation of Clinical Data Relating to Caries Advance," *American Journal of Public Health*, Vol. 41, August 1951, p. 978.

39. Ibid., p. 979.

40. Ibid., p. 983.

41. R.L. Glass and S. Fleisch, "Diet and Dental Caries: Dental Caries Incidence and the Consumption of Ready-to-Eat Cereals," *Journal of the American Dental Association*, Vol. 88, No. 4, April 1974, pp. 807–13; N.H. Rowe, R.H. Anderson, and L.A. Wanninger, "Effects of Ready-to-Eat Breakfast Cereals on Dental Caries Experience in Adolescent Children" *Journal of Dental Research*, Vol. 53, No. 1, January 1974, pp. 33-36; Thomas J. Hill, John Sims, and Millicent Newman, "The Effect of Penicillin Dentifrice On the Control of Dental Caries" *Journal of Dental Research*, Vol. 32, 1953, pp. 448–52.

42. A.D. Steinberg, S.O. Zimmerman, and M.L. Bramer, "The Lincoln Dental Caries Study: The Effect of acidulated Carbonated Beverages on the Increase of Dental Caries" *Journal of the American Dental Association*, Vol. 85, No. 1, 1972, pp. 81–89.

CHAPTER 7: RADIATION EXPERIMENTS ON CHILDREN

1. Authors' interviews with Gordon Shattuck. Numerous interviews were conducted with Shattuck in Waltham and Beverly, Massachusetts, as well as by phone, between July 2010 and August 2011.

2. Case Record Folder for Gordon C. Shattuck, Walter E. Fernald State School, April 23, 1947, p.1.

3. Samuel G. Howe, "A Selection from Report Made to the Legislature of Massachusetts" in Steven Noll and James W. Trent Jr. *Mental Retardation in America* (New York: New York University Press) 2004, p. 23.

4. Ibid., p. 26.

5. Walter E. Fernald died on the evening of November 27, 1924. The Massachusetts legislature declared on July 1, 1925, that the Massachusetts School for the Feeble-minded would become the Walter E. Fernald State School. Guy Pratt Davis, *What Shall the Public Schools Do for the Feeble-Minded?* (Cambridge, MA: Harvard University Press, 1927).

6. Marie E. Daly, "History of the Walter E. Fernald Development Center," p. 2.

7. Quoted in Michael D'Antonio, *The State Boys Rebellion* (New York: Simon & Shuster, 2004), p. 19.

8. Shattuck interviews.

9. Authors' interviews with Charles Dyer. Numerous interviews were conducted with Dyer in Waltham and Beverly, Massachusetts, as well as by phone, between July 2010 and August 2011.

10. Authors' interviews with Austin LaRocque. Numerous interviews were conducted with LaRocque in Waltham and Beverly, Massachusetts, as well as by phone, between Septemeber 2009 and August 2011.

11. Shattuck interviews.

12. Clinical data and Further Experimental Details – Experiment No. 1, March 28, 1950.

13. Dyer interviews.

14. LaRocque interviews.

15. Scott Allen, "Radiation Used on Retarded," *Boston Globe*, December 26, 1993.

16. Ibid.

17. Shattuck interviews.

18. Radiation abuse stories would saturate media outlets around the nation.

19. "Fernald's Atomic Café," Boston Globe, December 29, 1993.

20. Eileen Welsome, "Plutonium Experiment," *Albuquerque Tribune*, November 15–17, 1993.

21. Phillip Campbell, Department of Mental Retardation memo, April 15, 1994, pp. 29-37.

22. Task Force on Human Subject Research, "A Report on the Use of Radioactive Materials in Human Subject Research that Involved Residents of State-Operated Facilities within the Commonwealth of Massachusetts from 1943 to 1973," April 1994. (Hereafter cited as Massachusetts Task Force Report.)

23. Quoted in ibid., p. 33.

24. Ibid., pp. 36–38.

25. Ibid., p. 35.

26. Quotations from Letter from Robert S. Harris to Dr. Malcolm Farrell, December 19, 1945. Massachusetts Task Force Report, pp. 1, 2, 4–5.

27. Letter from Clifton T. Perkins to Malcolm J. Farrell, December 27, 1945. Massachusetts Task Force Report.

28. "Report of Progress in Research," Report II, July 1, 1945, to June 30, 1946, Nutritional Biochemistry Laboratories, Department of Food Technology, Massachusetts Institute of Technology, pp. 11–12.

29. Letter from Robert S. Harris to Dr. Clemens E. Benda, April 13, 1949, "Outline of Proposed Experiment to Determine the Absorption of Calcium by Children and the Effect of Phytates upon Absorption." Massachusetts Task Force Report, p. 1.

30. Ibid., p. 2.

31. Letter from Clemens E. Benda to Paul Aberhold, May 18, 1949. Massachusetts Task Force Report, p. 1.

32. From the Papers of Clemens Ernst Benda, M.D., 1898–1975, Countway Medical Library. Harvard Medical School.

33. Regrettably, much of Benda's personal correspondence and research notes are at Countway Medical Library and have been sealed and are unavailable to the public and medical historians.

34. Letter from S. Allan Lough to Dr. Robley D. Evans, September 28, 1949. Massachusetts Task Force Report, p. 1.

35. Letter from S. Allan Lough to Dr. Clemens E. Benda, November 3, 1949. Massachusetts Task Force Report, p. 1.

36. Ibid.

37. Ibid., p. 2.

38. Letter from Malcolm J. Farrell to Parents, November 2, 1949. Massachusetts Task Force Report, p. 1.

39. Letter from Robert S. Harris to Clemens E. Benda, May 1, 1953. Massachusetts Task Force Report, p. 1.

40. Ibid.

41. Ibid., p. 2.

42. Quotations from Letter from Clemens E. Benda to Dear Parent, May 28, 1953. Massachusetts Task Force Report, p. 1.

43. In a letter to a parent, Benda said he had learned of the "plan to take your son [name redacted] on vacation on July 1st." Benda informed the child's mother that her son was "cooperating in a science test" that was deemed "extremely important" and that he was needed at the institution for further tests. He then requested that the family's vacation be changed "from Wednesday, July 1st, to Friday, July 3rd." Letter from Clemens Benda to Mrs. [name redacted], June 29, 1953. Massachusetts Task Force Report.

44. For example, one child from Ward 22 was said to have been born in 1940, had a mental age of 82 an IQ of 55, and weighed 140 pounds. Science Club Boys, 6/5/53. Massachusetts Task Force Report.

45. In the early to mid-1950s, Fernald hosted a broad array of research projects. Benda admitted in a 1953 annual report that the school's research department was involved in a "larger field of investigations than in previous years" and now included work on "neuropathological and biochemical aspects of mongolism," work with Harvard's Department of Food Research" on metabolism studies, feeding and mating experiments on rats and mice, along with the MIT food metabolism research. Annual report of the Research Laboratory, Walter E. Fernald State School, July 1952 June 1953. Massachusetts Task Force Report.

46. Letter from Clemens E. Benda to Atomic Energy Commission, September 29, 1953. Massachusetts Task Force Report, p. 1.

47. Ibid.

48. Felix Bronner, Clemens E. Benda, Robert S. Harris, and Joseph Kreplick, "Calcium Metabolism in a Case of Gargoylism Studied with the Aid of Radiocalcium," *Journal of Clinical Investigation* 37 (1958), pp. 139–47.

49. Letter from Jack R. Ewalt to Superintendent, June 1, 1956. Massachusetts Task Force Report, p. 1.

50. Quoted in Allen, "Radiation Used on Retarded."

51. Authors' interviews with Constantine Maletskos by telephone on February 22, 2011, and at Spaulding Rehabilitation Hospital, Boston, April 28, 2011.

52. The calcium studies were published by F. Bronner, R. S. Harris, C. J. Maletskos, and C. E. Benda, "Studies in Calcium Metabolism. Effect of Food Phytates on Calcium Uptake in Children on Low Calcium

Breakfasts," *Journal of Nutrition* 54 (1954), pp. 523–42; F. Bronner, R. S. Harris, C. J. Maletskos, and C. E. Benda, "Studies in Calcium Metabolism. Effects of Food Phytates on Calcium 45 Uptake in Children on Moderate Calcium Breakfasts," *Journal of Nutrition* 59 (1956), pp. 393–406; and F. Bronner, R. S. Harris, C. J. Maletskos, and C. E. Benda, "Studies in Calcium Metabolism. The Fate of Intravenously Injected Radiocalcium in Human Beings," *Journal of Clinical Investigation* 35 (1956), pp. 78–88.

53. Henry K. Beecher, "Ethics and Clinical Research," *New England Journal of Medicine* 274 (June 16, 1966), p. 24.

54. G. S. Kurland, J. Fishman, M. W. Hamolsky, and A. S. Freedberg, "Radioisotope Study of Thyroid Function in 21 Mongoloid Subjects, Including Observations in 7 Parents," *Journal of Clinical Endocrinology & Metabolism* 17, No. 4 (April 1957), p. 552.

55. Massachusetts Task Force Report, p. 14.

56. Ibid.

57. Ibid., p. 18. The study was published in 1962 by K. M. Saxena, E. M. Chapman, and C. V. Pryles, "Minimal Dosage of Iodide Required to Suppress Uptake of Iodine-131 by Normal Thyroid," *Science* 138 (1962), pp. 430–31.

58. K. M. Saxena and C. V. Pryles, "Thyroid Function in Mongolism," *Journal of Pediatrics* 67 (1965), pp. 363–70.

59. C. E. Benda, C. J. Maletskos, J. C. Hutchinson, and E. B. Thomas, "Studies of Thyroid Function in Myotonia Dystrophica," *American Journal of Medical Sciences* 228 (1954), pp. 668–72.

60. Memo from Dr. Roy Shore to the Task Force, March 5, 1994, p. 1; and Memo from Joseph L. Lyon to Task Force. Massachusetts Task Force Report, p. 1.

61. Letter from Dr. Brian Macmahon to Doe West, February 24, 1994. Massachusetts Task Force Report, p. 1.

62. Authors interview with Joseph Almeida, September 7, 2009.

63. Authors' phone interview with Sandra Marlow, April 10, 2010.

64. Authors' interviews with Doe West in Boston, April 28, 2010, and April 29, 2011.

65. George H. Lowery, William H. Beierwalters, Isadore Lampe, and Henry J. Gomberg, "Radioactive Uptake Curve in Human: Studies in Children," *Pediatrics* 4 (1949), p. 628.

66. Van Middlesworth, "Radioactive Iodide Uptake of Normal Newborn Infants" *American Journal of Diseases in Children* 38 (1954), p. 439.

67. Ibid., p. 441.

68. Edgar E. Martmer, Kenneth E. Corrigang, Harold P. Chareneau, and Allen Sosin, "A Study of the Uptake of Iodine by the Thyroid of Premature Infants," *Pediatrics* 17 (1955), p. 507.

69. Richard E. Ogborn, Ronald E. Waggener, and Eugene VanHove, "Radioactive-Iodine Concentration in Thyroid Glands of Newborn Infants," *Pediatrics* 28 (1960), p. 771.

70. Krishna M. Saxena, Earle M. Chapman, and Charles V. Pryles, "Minimal Dosage of Iodide Required to Suppress Uptake of Iodide-131 by Normal Thyroid," *Science* 138 (1962), p. 430.

CHAPTER 8: PSYCHOLOGICAL TREATMENT

1. Authors' interviews with Ted Chabasinski, March 15, 2010, and October 26, 2011.

2. Unpublished manuscript by Ted Chabasinski provided to author

3. "The Papers of Lauretta Bender," Brooklyn College Library Archive.

4. Ibid.

5. In 1938, Bender wrote "A Visual Motor Gestalt Test and Its Clinical Use" a reproducing nine figures derived from the work of Gestalt psychologist Max Wertheimer. The Bender-Gestalt Test would become one of the most used tests by clinical psychologists to measure perceptual motor skills and perceptual motor development along with neurological intactness.

6. Lauretta Bender, "Theory and Treatment of Childhood Schizophrenia," *Acta Paedopsychiatrica* 34 (1968), p. 301.

7. Joel Braslow, *Mental Ills and Bodily Cures* (Berkeley: University of California Press, 1997), p. 96.

8. Ibid., p. 100.

9. Ibid., p. 101.

10. Bender, "Theory and Treatment of Childhood Schizophrenia."

11. Ibid.

12. Lauretta Bender, "One Hundred Cases of Childhood Schizophrenia Treated with Electric Shock," *Transactions of the American Neurologic Association* 762 (1947), p. 168.

13. Braslow, Mental Ills and Bodily Cures, p. 98.

14. Quoted in E. Shorter and D. Healy, *Shock Therapy* (New Brunswick, NJ: Rutgers University Press, 2007), p. 86.

15. Quoted in ibid., p. 87.

16. Ibid., p. 137.

17. Jack El-Hai, *The Lobotomist: A Maverick Medical Genius and His Tragic Quest to Ride the World of Mental Illness* (Hoboken, NJ: John Wiley, 2007), p. 107.

18. Ibid., p. 1.

19. Walter Freeman, "The Religion of Science." Papers of Walter Freeman, George Washington University Archives (cited hereafter as Freeman Papers).

20. Quoted in El-Hai, *The Lobotomist*, p. 180.

21. Quoted in ibid., p. 248.

22. Quoted in ibid., p. 91.

23. Edward Shorter, *A History of Psychiatry: From the Era of the Asylum to the Age of Prozac* (New York: John Wiley, 1997), p. 227.

24. "Lobotomy Disappointment," *Newsweek*, December 12, 1949, p. 51.

25. Quoted in El-Hai, *The Lobotomist*, p. 199.

26. Ibid., pp. 174–75.

27. Walter Freeman and James W. Watt, "Schizophrenia in Childhood," February 26, 1947. Freeman Papers.

28. Ibid.

29. Ibid., p. 4.

30. Ibid.

31. Ibid., pp. 6–7.

32. Ibid., p. 8.

33. Letter from James W. Watts to Mr. Oliver E. Denham, June 7, 1961. Freeman Papers.

34. Common expression used by inmates in the Philadelphia Prison System, where author Allen Hornblum worked in the 1970s.

35. El-Hai, *The Lobotomist*, p. 267.

36. Howard Dully, *My Lobotomy* (New York: Three Rivers Press, 2007), p. 102.

37. Ibid., p. 91.

38. Quoted in ibid., p. 98.

39. Ibid., p. 268.

40. Shorter, *History of Psychiatry*, p. 227.

41. O. J. Andy, "Thalamotomy in Hyperactive and Aggressive Behavior," *Confinia Neurologica* 32 (1970), p. 322.

42. Ibid., p. 324.

43. Peter R. Breggin, "Campaigns Against Racist Federal Programs by the Center for the Study of Psychiatry and Psychology," *Journal of African American Men* 1, No. 3 (1995), p. 6.

44. United States Congress. Senate. Committee on Labor and Public Welfare. Subcommittee on Health. Quality of Health Care—Human Experimentation, 1973, Hearings, Ninety-third Congress, first session, on S. 974.

45. Ibid.

46. Benedict Carey, "Surgery for Mental Ills Offers Both Hope and Risk," *New York Times*, November 27, 2009.

47. Braslow, *Mental Ills and Bodily Cures*, p. 143.

48. The word "enthusiast" was repeatedly used in describing the scientific mind-set of Dr. Albert M. Kligman, the famous University of Pennsylvania dermatologist who created lucrative creams for acne and wrinkled skin but also had a long history of using vulnerable populations in his research (See chapter 6). Friends and colleagues of Kligman defended his penchant for sometimes risky, if not dangerous experimentation by explaining "Al was not a venal or menacing person. He was just an enthusiast interested in a wide variety of dermatological subjects." Interviews collected by Allen Hornblum for *Acres of Skin: Human Experiments at Holmesburg Prison: A True Story of Abuse and Exploitation in the Name of Medical Science*, (New York: Routledge, 1998).

49. John Marks, *The Search for the Manchurian Candidate* (New York: Norton, 1979), p. 25.

50. Quoted in Martin A. Lee and Bruce Shlain, *Acid Dreams* (Weidenfield, NY: Grove, 1985), p. xxiv.

51. Marks, *Search for the Manchurian Candidate*, p. 28.

52. Ibid., p. 66.

53. Harold A. Abramson (1967) The Use of LSD (D-Lysergic Acid Diethylamide) In the Therapy of Children, *Journal of Asthma Research*, 5:2, pp. 139–43.

54. Stephen Kinzer, *Poisoner in Chief: Sidney Gottlieb and the CIA Search for Mind Control* (New York, NY, Henry Holt and Company, 2019), p. 99.

55. A number of doctors had questionable histories with LSD research. Harold Abramson, for example, worked for both the army and the CIA and was the last physician (albeit an allergist) to see Frank Olson before he went out the window of his Statler-Hilton hotel room. Paul Hoch was the head of the Psychiatric Institute's mescaline research program that killed Harold Blauer, and Harold Isbell ran the controversial drug research program at Lexington Federal Penitentiary.

56. Lee and Schlain, *Acid Dreams*, p. 45.

57. Lauretta Bender, "Discussion," in *Child Research in Psychopharmacology*, ed. Seymour Fisher (Springfield, IL: Charles C. Thomas, 1959), p. 41.

58. Lee and Schlain, *Acid Dreams*, p. 63.

59. Lauretta Bender, Gloria Faretra, and Leonard Cobrinik, "LSD and UML Treatment of Hospitalized Disturbed Children," *Recent Advances in Biological Psychology*, Vol. 5, 1963, p. 37.

60. Ibid., p. 85.

61. Lauretta Bender, "A Twenty-five Year View of Therapeutic Results" *Evaluation of Psychiatric Treatment* (New York: Grune and Stratton, 1964), p. 141. Hoch, Paul H., Zubin Joseph American Psychopathological Association.

62. Lauretta Bender, "Children's Reactions to Psychotomimetic Drugs," *Psychotomimetic Drugs* (1970), p. 268.

63. Ibid., p. 270.

64. Ibid.

CHAPTER 9: PSYCHOLOGICAL ABUSE

1. Much of our account of the Monster Study comes from Jim Dyer's groundbreaking articles on the study. Jim Dyer, "Ethics and Orphans: The Monster Study," *San Jose Mercury News*, July 25, 2001. According to the *San Jose Mercury News*, Jim Dyer, their reporter on assignment for the newspaper, did not notify authorities of the Iowa State Archive of this fact or of the actual purpose of his research when he approached them for access to the material in question. Although Dyer was a graduate student at the time and claimed to be doing scholarly research, the archive is not open to journalists. The newspaper's editors claimed to be unaware of this ethical breach, and although they viewed Dyer's article as "an important investigative story," they admitted, "It's unfortunate we can't endorse some of the methods used to report it."

2. Quoted in ibid.

3. Ibid.

4. Mary Tudor, "An Experimental Study of the Effect of Evaluative Labelling on Speech Fluency," Master of Arts thesis, Graduate College of the State University of Iowa, August 1939, p. 98.

5. Ibid., p. 67.

6. Quoted in Dyer, "Ethics and Orphans."

7. Tudor, "Experimental Study," pp. 116, 117.

8. Ibid., p. 148.

9. Ibid., p. 147.

10. Dyer, "Ethics and Orphans."

11. Quoted in ibid.

12. Tom Owen, "When Words Hurt: Stuttering Study Story Missed the Mark," The Gazette (Iowa City), July 12, 2003.

13. Associated Press, "Iowa Pays Victims of Abusive 1930's Stuttering Experiment Paid Almost $1 Million," Fox News, August 20, 2007.

14. Rodney G. Triplet, "Henry A. Murray: The Making of a Psychologist?" *American Psychologist* 47, No. 2 (February 1992), pp. 299–307.

15. Ibid., p. 300.

16. Alston Chase, *Harvard, and the Unabomber* (New York: W. W. Norton, 2003), p. 361.

17. Ibid., p. 362.

18. Ibid., p. 363.

19. O. I. Lovaas and James Q. Simmons, "Manipulation of Self-Destruction in Three Retarded Children," *Journal of Applied Behavior Analysis* 2, No. 3 (1969), p. 149.

20. Ibid., p. 156.

21. E. Garralda, "Psychophysiological Anomalies in Children with Emotional and Conduct Disorders," *Psychological Medicine* 21 (1991), pp. 847–57.

22. 24. Clemens Kirschbaum, Dirk H. Helhammer, Christian J. Strasburger, Elisabeth Tilling, Renate Kamp, and Harold Luddecke, "Relationships between Salivary Cortisol, Electrodermal Activity and Anxiety under Mild Experimental Stress in Children," Frontiers of Stress Research (1989), pp. 383–87.

23. Stephanie van Goozen, Walter Matthys, Peggy T. Cohen-Kettenis, Victor Wiegant, and Herman van Engeland, "Salivary Cortisol and Cardiovascular Activity During Stress in Oppositional-Defiant Disorder Boys and Normal Controls," *Biological Psychiatry* 43 (1998), p. 531.

24. Connie Lamm, I. Granic, P. D. Zelano, and Marc D. Lewis, "Magnitude and Chronometry of Neutral Mechanisms of Emotion Regulation in Subtypes of Aggressive Children," *Brain and Cognition* 77, No. 2 (November 2011), pp. 159–69.

CHAPTER 10: REPRODUCTION AND SEXUALITY EXPERIMENTS

1. Amy Goodman, "The Case Against Depo-Provera," *Multinational Monitor* 6, Nos. 2 & 3 (February 1985), http://www.multinationalmonitor.org/hyper/issues/1985/02/conference.html.

2. "The Law: Sterilized: Why," *Time Magazine*, July 23, 1973.

3. United States Congress. Senate Committee on Labor and Public Welfare. Subcommittee on Health. Quality of Health Care – Human Experimentation, 1973, Hearings, Ninety-third Congress, first session, S. 974. Washington, U.S. Gov't. Printing Office. (Hereafter cited as Human Experimentation hearing.)

4. Interviews with Jessie Bly, May 6, 2010, and November 9, 2012.

5. Human Experimentation hearing, p. 74.

6. Ibid., p. 75.

7. Bly interview.

8. Human Experimentation hearing, p. 82.

9. Ibid., p. 77.

10. Ibid., p. 10.

11. Ibid., p. 12.

12. Ibid., p. 120.

13. *Relf vs. Weinberger*, Civil Action No. 1557 – 73, filed July 31, 1973.

14. Jane Lawrence, "The Indian Health service and the Sterilization of Native American Women" *American Indian Quarterly*, Vol. 24, No. 3, Summer 2000, pp. 400-19.

15. Andrea Smith, *Conquest: Sexual Violence and American Indian Genocide* (Boston: South End Press, 2005), p. 88.

16. Ibid.

17. Elof Axel Carlson, *Times of Triumph, Times of Doubt: Science and the Battle for Public Trust* (New York: Cold Spring Harbor Press, 2006).

18. Everett Flood, "The Advantages of Castration in the Defective," *Journal of the American Medical Association* 29, No. 17 (October 1897), p. 833.

19. Ibid.

20. Philip Reilly, "The Surgical Solution: The Writings of Activist Physicians in the Early Days of Eugenical Sterilization," *Perspectives in Biology and Medicine* 26 (1983), p. 646.

21. Marie E. Kopp, "Surgical Treatment as Sex Crime Prevention Measure," *Journal of Criminal Law and Criminology* 28, No. 5 (1938), p. 693.

22. Louis A. Lurie, "The Endocrine Factor in Homosexuality," *American Journal of the Medical Sciences* 208, No. 2 (August 1944), p. 180.

23. Harriet Washington, *Medical Apartheid* (New York: Doubleday, 2006), p. 63.

24. Jeffrey S. Sartin, "J. Marion Sims, the Father of Gynecology: Hero or Villain?" *Southern Medical Journal* 97, No. 5 (May 2004), p. 500.

25. P. Knightley, H. Evans, E. Potter, and M. Wallace, *Suffer the Children: The Story of Thalidomide* (New York: Viking Press, 1979), p. 3.

26. Ibid., p. 45.

27. Ibid., p. 47.

28. Ibid., p. 113.

29. Mary V. Seeman, "Women's Issues in Clinical Trials," in *Clinical Trials in Psychopharmacology: A Better Brain*, ed. Marc Hertzman and Lawrence Adler (Hoboken, NJ: Wiley, 2010), p. 89.

30. A. Goodman, J. Schorge, and M. F. Greene, "The Long-term Effects of In Utero Exposures—The DES Story," *New England Journal of Medicine* 364, No. 22 (2011), pp. 2083–2084.

31. Robert N. Hoover et al., "Adverse Health Outcomes in Women Exposed in Utero to Diethylstilbestrol," *New England Journal of Medicine* 365 (2011), pp. 1304–314.

32. G. I. M. Swyer, "An Evaluation of the Prophylactic Antenatal Use of Stilboestrol" *American Journal of Obstetrics and Gynecology* 58, No. 5 (1949), pp. 994–1009.

33. Arthur L. Herbst, "Diethistilbestrol and Adenocarcinoma of the Vagina," *American Journal of Obstetrics and Gynecology* 181, No. 6 (1999), pp. 1576–578.

34. *New York Times* articles from April 16, 1978, and February 27, 1982.

35. Goodman, p. 2084.

36. Eileen Welsome, *The Plutonium Files* (New York: Dial Press, 1999), p. 220.

37. Ibid., p. 221.

38. Ibid., p. 225.

CHAPTER 11: RESEARCH MISCONDUCT

1. Paul A. Offit, *Autism's False Prophets: Bad Science, Risky Medicine, and the Search for a Cure* (New York: Columbia University Press, 2008), p. 37.

2. Editorial, "Wakefield's Article Linking MMR Vaccine and Autism was Fraudulent," *British Medical Association*, 342, January 5, 2011.

3. William Broad and Nicholas Wade, *Betrayers of the Truth: Fraud and Deceit in the Halls of Science* (New York: Simon and Schuster, 1982), p. 23.

4. Ibid., p. 37.

5. Mazur, Allan "Allegations of Dishonesty in Research and Their Treatment by American Universities" *Minerva* 27 (1989).

6. Ibid.

7. David J. Miller, "Personality Factors in Scientific Fraud and Misconduct," in *Research Fraud in the Behavioral and Biomedical Sciences*, ed. David J. Miller and Michael Hersen (New York: Wiley, 1992), p. 129.

8. Alexander Kohn, *False Prophets: Fraud and Error in Science and Medicine* (New York: Blackwell, 1986), p. 54.

9. Ibid., p. 55.

10. Broad and Wade, *Betrayers of the Truth*, p. 199.

11. Arthur Jensen, "Scientific Fraud or False Accusations? The Case of Cyril Burt," in Miller and Hersen, *Research Fraud in the Behavioral and Biomedical Sciences*, p. 118.

12. Tom Collins and Selwyn Raab, "Charge Hospital Shot Live Cancer Cells Into Patients" *New York World-Telegram*, January 20, 1964, p. 1.

13. Ibid.

14. William Newman M.D. and Chester Southam M.D., "Virus Treatment in Advanced Cancer," *Cancer*, Vol. 7, No. 1, January 1954, p. 107.

15. Interview with Selwyn Raab – December 9, 2011.

16. Letter from Chester M. Southam to Emanuel Mandel, July 5, 1963, in *Experimentation with Human Beings* (New York: Russell Sage Foundation, 1972), p. 11.

17. Ibid.

18. Interview with Chester Southam – October 3, 1996.

19. Ibid. Additional information can be gleaned from Hornblum's, Acres of Skin.

20. Interviews with Dr. Avir Kagan – November 3 & 5, 2011.

21. Ibid.

22. Affidavit of Dr. David Leichter, September 12, 1963, in Katz, p. 13.

23. Affidavit of Dr. Deogracias Custodio, January 3, 1964, in Katz, pp. 25–26.

24. Kagan Interviews.

25. Louis J. Lefkowitz, Petitioner's Post-Hearing Memorandum, in Katz, p. 48.

26. Elinor Langer, New York Verdict Affirms Patient's Rights, in Katz, p. 64.

27. Board of Regents Disciple Committee, in Katz, p. 62.

28. Kagan interview.

29. Ibid.

30. Charles J. Glueck, Margot J. Mellies, Mark Dine, Tammy Perry, and Peter Laskarzewski, "Safety and Efficacy of Long-Term Diet and Diet Plus Bile Acid-Binding Resin Cholesterol-Lowering Therapy in 73 Children Heterozygous for Familial Hypercholeserolemia," *Pediatrics* 78, No. 2 (August 1986), pp. 338–48.

31. Mark B. Roman, "When Good Scientists Turn Bad," *Discover* 9, No. 4 (1988), pp. 55, 57.

32. Paul Connett, James Beck, and H. S. Micklem, *The Case against Fluoride: How Hazardous Waste Ended Up in Our Drinking Water and the Bad Science and Powerful Politics That Keep It There* (White River Junction, VT: Chelsea Green, 2010).

33. Roman, "When Good Scientists Turn Bad," p. 52.

34. Ibid.

35. Miller, "Personality Factors in Scientific Fraud and Misconduct," p. 136.

36. Alan Poling, "The Consequences of Fraud," in *Research Fraud in the Behavioral and Bio-medical Sciences*, p. 146.

CONCLUSION

1. J. Ipsen, "Bioassay of Four Tetanus Toxoids in Mice, Guinea Pigs, and Humans," *Journal of Immunology* 70 (1952), pp. 426–34.

2. Interview with Constantine Maletskos, April 28, 2011, at Spaulding Rehabilitation Hospital, Boston.

3. Jay Katz, *Final Report of the Advisory Committee on Human Radiation Experiments* (New York: Oxford University Press, 1996), p. 544.

4. In the summer of 1963, Drs. Avir Kagan, Perry Ferskos, and David Leichter refused to participate in a cancer experiment at the Jewish Chronic Disease Hospital and subsequently went to the press to expose what they considered unethical medical research. Subsequent media coverage led to an investigation, several hearings, and two doctors being sanctioned by medical boards.

5. Susan Lederer and Michael Grodin, "Historical Overview: Pediatric Experimentation" in *Children as Research Subjects: Science, Ethics and Law*, ed. Michael A. Grodin and Leonard H. Glantz (New York: Oxford University Press, 1994), pp. 3–25.

6. Ibid.

7. Autonomy suggests that the research participant is a voluntary participant in the research process and has the power to agree to or withdraw from the experiment at any time. The issue of autonomy becomes increasingly complex and dissatisfying when applied to procuring informed consent from underage children and their parents. The principle of justice or fairness concerns equal access to or from research studies and protections against bribes and forms of coercion. The principle of nonmaleficence concerns the assurance that no harm of a physical or psychological nature will result. Veracity means that only the truth about a research project will be communicated, and beneficence means the promotion of good for the participant or for society at large.

8. U.S. Food and Drug Administration, "Global Participation in Clinical Trials Report," 2015-2016, FDA, (Silver Spring, Md: FDA, 2017), p. 6.

9. Adriana Petryna, *When Experiments Travel: Clinical Trials and the Global Search for Human Subjects* (Princeton, NJ: Princeton University Press, 2009), p. 19.

EPILOGUE

1. Czech, H. "Hans Asperger, National Socialism, and "race hygiene" in Nazi-era Vienna." Molecular Autism, (2018) 9, 29. Sheffer, E. *Asperger's children: the origins of autism in Nazi Vienna*. (W. W. Norton & Co., New York 2018).

2. Kondziella, D. "Thirty neurological eponyms associated with the Nazi era." *European Neurology*, (2009) 62(1), 56–64. Strous, R. D. & Edelman, M. C. "Eponyms and the Nazi Era: Time to Remember and Time for Change." *Israeli Medical Association Journal*, (2007) 9, 207–14. Vajda, F., Davis, S., Byrne, E. "Names of infamy: Tainted eponyms." *Journal of Clinical Neuroscience*, (2015) 22(4), 642–44.

3. Kondziella, D. "Thirty neurological eponyms associated with the Nazi era." *European Neurology*, 62(1), (2009), 56–64.

4. Reverby, Susan M. ""Normal exposure" and inoculation syphilis: A PHS "Tuskegee" doctor in Guatemala, 1946–1948." *Journal of Policy History* 23, no. 1 (2011), pp. 6–28.

5. Presidential Commission for the *Study of Bioethical Issues "Ethically Impossible" STD Research in Guatemala from 1946 to 1948*, Washington D.C, September 2011, Table 2, p. 114.

6. Vergano, Dan "Sexual diseases research award renamed after vote", USA Today, April 11, 2013, Available online at https://www.usatoday.com/story/tech/sciencefair/2013/04/11/parran-award-renamed/2074771/.

7. Bender, William, "Did a U.S. surgeon general come up with the idea of the notorious Tuskegee syphilis experiment?", *Philadelphia Inquirer*, July 20, 2017.

8. Graduate School of Public Health Dean, Dr. Donald Burke letter to Pamela Connelly, Office of Diversity, and Inclusion at the University of Pittsburgh. January 8, 2018. Available via https://www.publichealth.pitt.edu/Portals/0/Main/News/2017%20News%20images/Ltr_to._P_Connelly_from_D_Burke_re_Parran_2018-01-08.pdf.

9. Dyer, Ervin "Public Health Symposium Panelists Discuss Legacy of Parran Hall Namesake" *University Times*, Vol 50, Issue 16, April 12, 2018.

10. Chancellor Patrick Gallagher memorandum to the University of Pittsburgh Board of Trustees, 2018. Available via https://www.diversity.pitt.edu/sites/default/files/Memorandum%20Parran%20Hall%20Name-FINAL.PDF.

11. #3, 114.

12. Silberman, S. *NeuroTribes: The Legacy of Autism and the Future of Neurodiversity*. (Penguin Random House: New York 2015).

13. Ibid.

14. Ibid., p. 137.

15. Ibid., p. 128.

16. Sheffer, E. *Asperger's children: the origins of autism in Nazi Vienna*. (W. W. Norton & Co., New York 2018).

17. Ibid., p. 19.

18. Ibid., p. 92.

19. Ibid., pp. 46–47.

20. Ibid., p. 85.

21. Ibid., p. 19.

22. Ibid., p. 178.

23. Ibid., p. 21.

24. Ibid., pp. 22–23

25. Ibid., p. 214.

26. Silberman, S. *NeuroTribes: The Legacy of Autism and the Future of Neurodiversity*. Penguin (Random House: New York, 2015), p. 1.

27. Ibid., p. 16.

28. Sheffer, E. *Asperger's children: the origins of autism in Nazi Vienna*. (W. W. Norton & Co., New York, 2018), p. 138.

29. What's in a name? [Editorial]. (2018). The Lancet, 5(6), 451. Available via https://doi.org/10.1016/S2215-0366(18)30188-3.

30. Newman, J., Zere, A., & Kane, C. "Let us not honor researchers who have caused harm: removing or contextualizing eponyms for Dr. Hans Asperger and Dr. Albert Kligman. "Poster presented at the *32nd APS Annual Convention*, May 21-24, 2020, in Chicago, IL, USA. [Due to the Pandemic this became a virtual conference with access from June 1st-Sept. 1st, 2020].

31. Hendry, R. I am autistic and after the news about Hans Asperger, I think it's time the condition was renamed. *The Independent Voices*, (2018) 15:23.

32. Jones-Alston, Adrianne, "Penn's Imprisoned Black 'Guinea Pigs' Deserve an Apology and Reparations." *MerionWest*, April 6, 2021. Available via https://merionwest.com/2021/04/06/penns-imprisoned-black-guinea-pigs-deserve-an-apology-and-reparations/.

33. Ibid.

34. Kafka, Alexander C. "This researcher exploited prisoners, children and the elderly. Why does Penn still honor him?" *The Chronical of Higher Education*, Vol. 66 , No. 12 (2019).

35. Ibid.

36. Adamson, Adewole and Lipoff, Jules, "Penn must cut ties with Dr. Albert Kligman, who conducted unethical human research experiments on Black men / Opinion." *Philadelphia Inquirer*, January 4, 2021.

37. Hamid, Hiba and Lachhwani, Karishma and Romero Mark, "Penn needs to face dermatologist Albert Kligman's legacy," *Daily Pennsylvanian*, Guest Column, June 19, 1921.

38. Kafka, Alexander C. "This researcher exploited prisoners, children and the elderly. Why does Penn still honor him?" *The Chronical of Higher Education*, Vol. 66, No. 12 (2019).

39. Ackerman, A. Bernard, Hearings in Philadelphia City Council on "The Failure of Responsibility by the City of Philadelphia and the University to Prisoners at Holmesburg Prison between the early 1950's and the 1970's" February 22, 1999.

40. Ibid.

41. J. Larry Jameson MD, PhD, "Statement on Penn Medicine's Recognition of the Legacy of Albert Kligman, MD, PhD." Available via: https://www.med.upenn.edu/evpdeancommunications/2021-08-20-283.html

42. Ibid.

43. Ibid.

44. Administration, "University revokes name, rescinds awards in light of questionable practices." Penn State News, Sept, 30, 2021. Available at https://www.psu.edu/news/administration/story/university-revokes-name-rescinds-awards-light-questionable-practices/.

BIBLIOGRAPHY

BOOKS

Annas, George J., and Michael A. Grodin. *The Nazi Doctors and the Nuremberg Code: Human Rights in Human Experimentation.* New York: Oxford University Press, 1992.

Beauchamp, Tom L. *Standing on Principles.* New York: Oxford University Press, 2010.

Benison, Saul. *Tom Rivers: Reflections on a Life in Medicine and Science.* Cambridge, MA: MIT Press, 1967.

Bennett, Abram Elting. *Fifty Years in Neurology and Psychiatry.* New York: Intercontinental Medical Book Corp., 1972.

Birstein, Vadim J. *The Perversion of Knowledge.* New York: Westview Press, 2001.

Black, Edwin. *War against the Weak: Eugenics and America's Campaign to Create a Master Race.* New York: Four Walls Eight Windows, 2003.

Blatt, Burton. *Christmas in Purgatory: A Photographic Essay on Mental Retardation.* Boston: Allyn & Bacon, 1966.

Braslow, Joel. *Mental Ills and Bodily Cures: Psychiatric Treatment in the First Half of the Twentieth Century.* Berkeley: University of California Press, 1997.

Breggin, Peter, and Ginger Breggin. *The War against Children of Color: Psychiatry Targets Inner City Youth.* Monroe, ME: Common Courage Press, 1998.

Bruinius, Harry. *Better for All the World: The Secret History of Forced Sterilization and America's Quest for Racial Purity.* New York: Knopf, 2006.

Buchanan, David, Celia Fisher; and Lance Gable, eds. *Research with High-Risk Populations: Balancing Science, Ethics, and Law.* Washington, DC: American Psychological Association, 2009.

Carlson, Elof Axel. *Times of Triumph, Times of Doubt: Science and the Battle for Public Trust.* Cold Spring Harbor, NY: Cold Spring Harbor Laboratory Press, 2006.

Chase, Alston. *Harvard and the Unabomber.* New York: W. W. Norton, 2003. Cole, Leonard A. *The Eleventh Plague.* New York: W. H. Freeman, 1997.

Collins, Anne. *In the Sleep Room: The Story of the CIA Brainwashing Experiments in Canada.* Toronto: Lester & Orpen Dennys, 1988.

D'Antonio, Michael. *The State Boys Rebellion: The Inspiring True Story of American Eugenics and the Men Who Overcame It.* New York: Simon & Schuster, 2004.

Davis, Guy Pratt. *What Shall the Public Schools Do for the Feeble-Minded? A Plan for Special-School Training under Public School Auspices.* Cambridge, MA: Harvard University Press, 1927.

De Kruif, Paul. *Life Among the Doctors.* New York: Harcourt, Brace, 1949. De Kruif, Paul. *Microbe Hunters.* New York: Harcourt, Brace, 1926.

De Kruif, Paul. *The Sweeping Wind.* New York: Harcourt, Brace, & World, 1962.

Dorr, Gregory Michael. *Segregation's Science: Eugenics and Society in Virginia.* Charlottesville: University of Virginia Press, 2008.

Dowdall, George W. *The Eclipse of the State Mental Hospital: Policy, Stigma, and Organization.* Albany: State University of New York Press, 1996.

DuBois, James M., Jill E. Ciesla, and Kevin E. Voss. "Research Ethics in US Medical Education: An Analysis of Ethics Course Syllabi." *In Research of Research Integrity,* ed. by N. H.

Steneck and M. D. Sheetz. Bethesda, MD: Department of Health and Human Services, 2001.

Dully, Howard, and Charles Fleming. *My Lobotomy*. New York: Three Rivers Press, 2007.

El-Hai, Jack. *The Lobotomist: A Maverick Medical Genius and His Tragic Quest to Rid the World of Mental Illness*. Hoboken, NJ: John Wiley & Sons, 2005.

Epstein, Steven. *Inclusion: The Politics of Difference in Medical Research*. Chicago: University of Chicago Press, 2007.

Flexner, Abraham. *Abraham Flexner: An Autobiography*. New York: Simon & Schuster, 1960.

Goodman, Jordan, Anthony McElligott, and Lara Marks. *Useful Bodies: Humans in the Service of Medical Science in the Twentieth Century*. Baltimore: Johns Hopkins University Press, 2003.

Goliszek, Andrew. *In the Name of Science*. New York: St. Martin's Press, 2003.

Guerrini, Anita. *Experimenting with Humans and Animals: From Galen to Animal Rights*. Baltimore: Johns Hopkins University Press, 2003.

Harris, Sheldon H. *Factories of Death: Japanese Biological Warfare, 1932–45 and the American Cover-up*. New York: Routledge, 1994.

Harvey, A. McGehee. *Science at the Bedside: Clinical Research in American Medicine, 1905–1945*. Baltimore: Johns Hopkins University Press, 1981.

Heberer, Patricia, and Jurgen Matthaus, eds. *Atrocities on Trial: Historical Perspectives on the Politics of Prosecuting War Crimes*. Lincoln: University of Nebraska Press, 2008.

Hooper, Edward. *The River: A Journey to the Source of HIV and AIDS*. New York: Little, Brown, 1999.

Hoover, J. Edgar. *Masters of Deceit: The Story of Communism in America and How to Fight It*. New York: Henry Holt, 1958.

Hornblum, Allen M. *Acres of Skin: Human Experiments at Holmesburg Prison; A True Story of Abuse and Exploitation in the Name of Medical Science*. New York: Routledge, 1998.

Institute of Medicine. *Ethical Conduct of Clinical Research Involving Children*. Washington, DC: National Academy of Sciences, 2004.

Katz, Jay "The Consent Principle of the Nuremberg Code: It's Significance Then and Now" *The Nazis Doctors and the Nuremberg Code*, (New York: Oxford University Press, 1992)

Ketchum, James S. *Chemical Warfare: Secrets Almost Forgotten*. Self-published, 2006.

Kevles, Daniel J. *In the Name of Eugenics: Genetics and the Uses of Human Heredity*. New York: Knopf, 1985.

Kraut, Alan M. *Goldberger's War: The Life and Work of a Public Health Official*. New York: Hill and Wang, 2003.

Lederer, Susan E. *Subjected To Science: Human Experimentation in America before the Second World War*. Baltimore: Johns Hopkins University Press, 1995.

Lewis, Sinclair. *Arrowsmith*. New York: Signet Classic, 1998.

Moreno, Jonathan. *Undue Risk: Secret State Experiments on Humans*. New York: W. H. Freeman, 2000.

Noll, Steven. *Feeble-Minded in Our Midst: Institutions for the Mentally Retarded in the South, 1900–1940*. Chapel Hill: University of North Carolina Press, 1995.

Noll, Steven, and James W. Trent Jr. *Mental Retardation in America*. New York: New York University Press, 2004.

Oldstone, Michael B. A. *Viruses, Plagues, & History*. New York: Oxford University Press, 2010.

Oshinsky, David M. *Polio: An American Story*. New York: Oxford University Press, 2005.

Pappworth, M. H. *Human Guinea Pigs: Experimentation on Man*. Boston: Beacon Press, 1967.

Parascandola, John. *The Development of American Pharmacology*. Baltimore: Johns Hopkins University Press, 1992.

Parsons, Robert P. *Trail to Light: A Biography of Joseph Goldberger*. New York: Bobbs-Merrill, 1943.

Petryna, Adriana. *When Experiments Travel: Clinical Trials and the Global Search for Human Subjects*. Princeton, NJ: Princeton University Press, 2009.

Poling, Alan. "The Consequences of Fraud." In *Research Fraud in the Behavioral and Biomedical Sciences*, ed. by David Miller and Michael Hersen. New York: John Wiley & Sons, 1992.

Rhodes, Richard. *Dark Sun: the Making of the Hydrogen Bomb*. New York: Simon & Schuster, 1995.

Rosenberg, Charles E. *The Care of Strangers: The Rise of America's Hospital System*. New York: Basic Books, 1987.

Rosenberg, Charles E. *No Other Gods: On Social Thought*. Baltimore: Johns Hopkins University Press, 1997.

Ross, Colin. *Bluebird: Deliberate Creation of Multiple Personality by Psychiatrists*. Richardson, TX: Manitou Communications, 2000.

Ross, Lainie Friedman. *Children in Medical Research: Access versus Protection*. New York: Oxford University Press, 2006.

Rothman, David J. *Strangers at the Bedside*. New York: Basic Books, 1991.

Schmidt, Ulf. *Justice at Nuremberg: Leo Alexander and the Nazis Doctors' Trial*. New York: Palgrave, 2006.

Scull, Andrew. *Madhouse: A Tragic Tale of Megalomania and Modern Medicine*. New Haven, CT: Yale University Press, 2005.

Shorter, Edward, and David Healy. *Shock Therapy: A History of Electroconvulsive Treatment in Mental Illness*. New Brunswick, NJ: Rutgers University Press, 2007.

Simpson, Christopher. *Blowback: The First Full Account of America's Recruitment of Nazis, and Its Disastrous Effect on Our Domestic and Foreign Policy*. New York: Weidenfeld & Nicolson, 1988.

Skloot, Rebecca. *The Immortal Life of Henrietta Lacks*. New York: Crown, 2010.

Slaughter, Frank G. *Daybreak: The Story of a Young Doctor Faced with a Momentous Challenge*. New York: Doubleday, 1958.

Slaughter, Frank G. *East Side General: A Violent Drama of Death and Love in a Big City*. New York: Permabook, 1952.

Slaughter, Frank G. *Spencer Brade, M.D.* New York: Doubleday, 1942.

Spitz, Vivien. *Doctors from Hell: The Horrific Account of Nazi Experiments on Humans*. Boulder, CO: Sentient, 2005.

Starr, Paul. *The Social Transformation of American Medicine*. New York: Basic Books, 1982.

Stern, Alexandra Minna. *Eugenic Nation: Faults and Frontiers of Better Breeding in Modern America*. Berkeley: University of California Press, 2005.

Tierney, Patrick. *Darkness in El Dorado: How Scientists and Journalists Devastated the Amazon*. New York: W. W. Norton, 2000.

Trent, James W. Jr. *Inventing the Feeble Mind: A History of Mental Retardation in America*. Berkley: University of California Press, 1994.

Tyor, Peter L., and Leland V. Bell. *Caring for the Retarded in America: A History*. Westport, CT: Greenwood Press, 1984.

Vaughan, Roger. *Listen to the Music: The Life of Hilary Kroprowski*. New York: Springer, 2000.

Weindling, Paul J. *Nazi Medicine and the Nuremberg Trials*. New York: Palgrave, 2004.

Weinstein, Allen, and Alexander Vassiliev. *The Haunted Wood: Soviet Espionage in America*. NewYork: Random House, 1999.

Weinstein, Harvey. *Father, Son and the CIA*. Halifax, Nova Scotia: Goodread Biographies, 1990.

Welsome, Eileen. *The Plutonium Files: America's Secret Medical Experiments in the Cold War*. New York: Dial Press, 1999.

Whitaker, Robert. *Mad in America: Bad Science, Bad Medicine, and the Enduring Mistreatment of the Mentally Ill.* New York: Perseus, 2002.

Whitney, Leon F. *The Case for Sterilisation.* London: John Lane, 1935.

Zenderland, Leila. *Measuring Minds: Henry Herbert Goddard and the Origins of American Intelligence Testing.* New York: Cambridge University Press, 1998.

Zimbardo, Philip. *The Lucifer Effect: Understanding How Good People Turn Evil.* New York: Random House, 2007.

ARTICLES

Abt, Isaac A. "Spontaneous Hemorrhages in Newborn Children." *Journal of the American Medical Association* 40, No. 5 (January 1903): 200.

Allen, Scott. "MIT Official Tells More of Radiation Experiments at Fernald," *Boston Globe,* December 30, 1993.

Allen, Scott. "MIT Records Show Wider Radioactive Testing at Fernald," *Boston Globe,* December 31, 1993.

Allen, Scott. "Radiation Used on Retarded," *Boston Globe,* December 26, 1993.

Altman, Lawrence. "Immunization Is Reported in Serum Hepatitis Tests," *New York Times,* March 24, 1971.

Andy, O. J. "Neurosurgical Treatment of Abnormal Behavior." *American Journal of the Medical Sciences* 252, No. 2 (1966): 232–238.

Andy, O. J. "Thalamotomy in Hyperactive and Aggressive Behavior." *Confinia Neurologica* 32 (1970): 332.

Armstrong, David. "Experiment Records Search Ordered at State Facilities," *Boston Globe,* December 31, 1993.

Armstrong, David. "State Expects Further 1940s–50s Revelations," *Boston Globe,* December 29, 1993.

Associated Press. "Iowa Pays Victims of Abusive 1930's Stuttering Experiment Paid Almost $1 Million," *Fox News,* August 20, 2007.

Barker, Lewellys. "The Importance of the Eugenic Movement and Its Relation to Social Hygiene." *Journal of the American Medical Association* 54 (1910): 2017–2022.

Barnes, Donald. "Effect of Evaporated Milk on the Incidence of Rickets in Infants." *Journal of the Michigan State Medical Society* 31 (1932): 397.

Barr, Martin W. "Some Notes on Asexualization with a Report on 18 Cases." *Journal of Nervous & Mental Disease* 51, No. 3 (March 1920): 232.

Bartlett, Donald L., and James B. Steele. "Deadly Medicine," *Vanity Fair,* January 2010.

Beecher, Henry K. "Ethics and Clinical Research." *New England Journal of Medicine* 274, No. 24 (June 16, 1966): 1354–1358.

Benda, C. E., C. J. Maletskos, J. C. Hutchinson, and E. B. Thomas. "Studies of Thyroid Function in Myotonia Dysttrophien." *American Journal of Medical Sciences* 228 (1954): 668–672.

Bender, Lauretta. "Children's Reactions to Psychotomimetic Drugs." *Psychotomimetic Drugs* (1970): 268.

Bender, Lauretta. "D-Lysergic Acid in the Treatment of the Biological Features of Childhood Schizophrenia." *Diseases of the Nervous System* 27 (1966): 43–46.

Bender, Lauretta. "One Hundred Cases of Childhood Schizophrenia Treated with Electric Shock." *Transactions of the American Neurologic Association* 762 (1947): 168.

Bender, Lauretta. "Theory and Treatment of Childhood Schizophrenia." *Acta Paedopsychiatrica* 34 (1968): 301.

Bender, Lauretta, Gloria Faretra, and Leonard Gobrinik. "LSD and UML Treatment of Hospitalized Disturbed Children." *Recent Advances in Biological Psychology* 5 (1963): 37.

Bennett, A. E. "Preventing Traumatic Complications in Convulsive Shock Therapy by Curare." *Journal of the American Medical Association* 114, No. 4 (1940): 322–324.

Bibby, Basil G. "A Test of the Effect of Fluoride-Containing Dentifrices." *Journal of Dental Research* 24, No. 6 (1945): 297–303.

Black, W. C. "The Etiology of Acute Infectious Gingivostomatitis." *Journal of Pediatrics* 30 (1942): 145–160.

Boyd, Julian D., and Kenneth E. Wessels. "Epidemiologic Studies in Dental Caries." *American Journal of Public Health* 41 (August 1951): 978.

Bradley, Charles. "The Behavior of Children Receiving Benzedrine." *American Journal of Psychiatry* 94 (1937): 577–585.

Brave, Ralph, and Kathryn Sylva. "Exhibiting Eugenics Response and Resistance to a Hidden History." *Public Historian* 29, No. 3 (Summer 2007): 37.

Breggin, Peter R. "Campaigns Against Racist Federal Programs by the Center for the Study of Psychiatry and Psychology." *Journal of African American Men* 1, No. 3 (1995): 6.

Brodbeck, Arthur J., and Orvis C. Irwin. "The Speech Behavior of Infants Without Families." *Child Development* 17, No. 3 (September 1946): 145–156.

Brunner, Felix, Robert S. Harris, Constantine J. Maletskos, and Clemens E. Benda. "Studies in Calcium Metabolism. Effects of Food Phytates on Calcium Uptake in Children on Low-Calcium Breakfasts." *Journal of Nutrition* 54, No. 4 (December 1954): 523–542.

Buckman, John. "Lysergic Acid Diethylamide." *British Medical Journal*, July 30, 1966, p. 302.

Buckman, John. "Theoretical Aspects of L.S.D. Therapy." *International Journal of Social Psychiatry* 13, No. 2 (1967), pp. 126–38.

Burman, Michael S. "Therapeutic Use of Curare and Erythroidine Hydrochloride for Spastic and Dystonic States." *Archives of Neurology and Psychiatry* 41 (1939): 307–327.

Campbell, Eric G. "Financial Relationships Between Institutional Review Board Members and Industry." *New England Journal of Medicine* 355, No. 22 (November 2006): 2321–2329.

Campbell, Kristine "Knots in the Fabric: Richard Pearson Strong and the Bilibid Prison Vaccine Trial's, 1905-1906" *Bulletin of the History of Medicine*, Vol. 68, No. 4, Winter, 1994, p. 600.

Carey, Benedict. "Surgery for Mental Ills Offers Both Hope and Risk," *New York Times*, November 27, 2009.

Collins, Tom, and Selwyn Raab. "Charge Hospital Shot Live Cancer Cells into Patients," *New York World-Telegram*, January 20, 1964.

Colquhoun, John. "Why I Changed My Mind about Water Fluoridation." *Perspectives in Biology and Medicine* 41, No. 1 (): 29–44.

Coombs, Francis, P., and Thomas Butterworth. "Atypical Keratosis Pilaris." *Archives of Dermatology* 62, No. 2 (August 1950): 305.

Curran, William J., and Henry K. Beecher. "Experimentation in Children." *Journal of the American Medical Association* 10, No. 1 (October 6, 1969): 77–83.

Daniel, F. E., and S. E. Hudson. "Emasculation of Masturbation—Is It Justifiable?" *Texas Medical Journal* 10, No. 4 (): 239.

Darby, William, Paul Hahn, Margaret Kaser, Ruth Steinkamp, Paul Deneen, and Mary Cook. "The Absorption of Radioactive Iron by Children 7–10 Years of Age." *Journal of Nutrition* 33, No. 1 (1947): 107–119.

Dowling, G. B. "The Treatment of Ringworm of the Scalp by Thallium Depilation." *British Medical Journal* 2, No. 3475 (August 1927): 261–263.

"Dr. Brodie Upholds Paralysis Vaccine," *New York Times*, November 3, 1935.

Dyer, Jim. "Ethics and Orphans: The Monster Study," *San Jose Mercury News*, July 25, 2001.

Eckstein, Gustov Noguchi (New York: Harpers, 1931) p. 103.

Editorial. "Effects of L.S.D." *British Medical Journal*, No. 5502, June 18, 1966, p. 1495.

Editorial. "Fernald's Atomic Café," Boston Globe, December 29, 1993. Editorial. "Lobotomy Disappointment," *Newsweek*, December 12, 1949, p. 51.

Editorial. "The Nuremberg Trial against German Physicians." *Journal of the American Medical Association* 135, No. 13 (November 1947): 135.

Editorial. "Poliomyelitis: A New Approach." *Lancet* (March 1952): 552.

Editorial. "Therapeutic Orphans." *Journal of Pediatrics* 72, No. 1 (January 1968): 119–120.

Editorial. "The Treatment of Diphtheria Carriers." *Journal of the American Medical Association* 67, No. 19 (November 4, 1916): 1372.

Editorial. "Wakefield's Article Linking MMR Vaccine and Autism Was Fraudulent." *British Medical Journal* 342 (January 2011).

Elliot, Carl. "Guinea-Pigging," *The New Yorker*, January 7, 2008, pp. 36–41.

Elmore, Joann G., and Alvan Feinstein. "Joseph Goldberger: An Unsung Hero of American Clinical Epidemiology." *Annals of Internal Medicine* 121, No. 5 (September 1994): 372.

Engler, M. "Prefrontal Leucotomy in Mental Defectives." *Journal of Mental Science* 94 (October 1948): 844–850.

Falusi, Adeyinka, O. I. Olopade, and C. O. Olopade. "Establishment of a Standing Ethics/Institutional Board in a Nigerian University." *Journal of Empirical Research on Human Research Ethics* 2, No. 1 (March 2007): 21–30.

Felden, Botha. "Epilation with Thallium Acetate in the Treatment of Ringworm of the Scalp of Children." *Archives of Dermatology and Syphilology* 17, No. 2 (February 1928): 185.

Finn, S. B., and H. C. Jamison. "The Effect of a Dicalcium Phosphate Chewing Gum on Caries Incidence in Children." *Journal of the American Medical Association* 74, No. 5 (April 1967): 987–995.

Flood, Everett. "Notes on the Castration of Idiot Children." *American Journal of Psychology* 10, No. 2 (January 1899): 300.

Flood, Everett. "The Advantages of Castration in the Defective." *Journal of the American Medical Association* 29, No. 17 (October 1897): 833.

Frederick, Delores. "Experiments on Humans Denied Here." Pittsburgh Press, April 12, 1973.

Frederick, Delores. "Courts, Not Parents, Have Word on Retarded Tests, Wecht Says," *Pittsburgh Press*.

Freeman, Walter. "Psychosurgery: Present Indications and Future Prospects." *Journal of the California Medical Association* 88, No. 6 (June 1958): 429–434.

Galvin, Kevin. "Kennedy Plans Hearings on Radiation Tests," *Boston Globe*, December 30, 1993.

Geison, Gerald L. "Pasteur's Work on Rabies: Reexamining the Ethical Issues." *Hastings Center Report* 8 (1978): 26–33.

Glantz, Leonard H. "Protecting Children and Society." *Journal of and Medical Ethics* 7, No. 2 (June 1979): 4–5.

Glass, R. L. "Effects on Denial Caries Incidence of Frequent Ingestion of Small Amounts of Sugars and Stannous EDTA from Chewing Gum." *British Dental Journal* 145 (1981): 95–100.

Glueck, Charles J., Margot J. Mellies, Mark Dine, Tammy Perry, and Peter Laskarzewski. "Safety and Efficacy of Long Term Diet and Diet Plus Bile Acid-Binding Resin Cholesterol-lowering Therapy in 73 Children Heterozygous for Familial Hypercholestarolemia." *Pediatrics* 78, No. 2 (August 1986): 338–348.

Goldberger, Joseph. "The Etiology of Pellagra." *Public Health Reports* 29, No. 26 (June 26, 1914): 373–375.

Goldberger, Joseph. "Experimental Pellagra in the Human Subject Brought About by a Restricted Diet." *Public Health Reports* 30, No. 46 (November 12, 1915): 3336–3339.

Goldman, Herbert, Samuel, Karelitz, and Norman Schell. "Acidosis in Premature Infants Due to Lactic Acid." *Pediatrics* 27 (1961): 928.

Goldschmidt, Herbert, and Albert Kligman. "Experimental Inoculation of Humans with Ectodermotropic Viruses." *Journal of Investigative Dermatology* 31 No. 3 (September 1958): 176.

Gorski, David. "On the Ethics of Clinical trials of Homeopathy in Third World Countries." *Science Based Medicine* (March 2008).

Hamill, Samuel M., Howard C. Carpenter, and Thomas A. Cope. "A Comparison of the Pirquet, Calmette, and Moro Tuberculin Tests and Their Diagnostic Value." *Archives of Internal Medicine* 2 (1908): 405.

Hansen, Bert. "Medical History for the Masses: How American Comic Books Celebrated Heroes of Medicine in the 1940s." *Bulletin of the History of Medicine* 78, No. 1 (Spring 2004): 148–191.

Harcourt, Bernard E. "Making Willing Bodies: Manufacturing Consent Among Prisoners and Soldiers, Creating Human Subjects, Patriots, and Everyday Citizens—The University of Chicago Malaria Experiments on Prisoners at Stateville Penitentiary." February 6, 2011. University of Chicago Law & Economics, Olin Working Paper No. 544; University of Chicago, Public Law Working Paper No. 341. Available at SSRN: http://ssrn.com/abstract=1758829 or http://dx.doi.org/10.2139/ssrn.1758829.

Henle, Werner, Gertrude Henle, and Joseph Stokes, Jr. "Demonstration of the Efficacy of Vaccination Against Influenza Type A by Experimental Infection of Human Beings." *Journal of Immunology* 46 (1943): 163–175.

Holt, L. Emmett. "A Report Upon One Thousand Tuberculin Tests in Young Children." *Archives of Pediatrics* (January 1909): 1–10.

Hoover, Robert N. "Adverse Health Outcomes in Women Exposed In Utero to Diethylstilbestrol." *New England Journal of Medicine* 365 (2011): 1304–1314.

Howe, Howard A. "Antibody Response of Chimpanzee and Human Beings to Formalin Inactivated Trivalent Poliomyelitis Vaccine." *Journal of Experimental Medicine* 80, No. 5 (November 1944): 383–390.

Howe, Howard A. "Criteria for the Inactivation of Poliomyelitis." *Committee on Immunization*, December 4, 1951 Meeting, Mandeville Special Collections Library, University of California, San Diego, 3.

Hudson, N., Edwin Lennette, and Francis H. Gordon. "Factors of Resistance in Experimental Poliomyelitis." *Journal of the American Medical Association* 106, No. 24 (June 1936): 1.

Ipsen, J. "Bio-assay of Four Tetanus Toxoids in Mice, Guinea Pigs, and Humans." *Journal of Immunology* 70 (1952): 426–434.

Ireton, Gabriel. "Polk Chaplin Defends Use of Patient Pens," Pittsburgh Post-Gazette, June 21, 1973.

Jervis, George A., Ferdinand F. McAllister, and Bruce M. Hogg. "Revascularization of the Brain in Mental Defectives." *Neurology* 3 (1953): 871–878.

Kaempffert, Waldemar. "Turning the Mind Inside Out," *Saturday Evening Post*, May 24, 1941.

Kligman, Albert M. "Hyposensitization Against Rhus Dermatitis." *Archives of Dermatology* 78 (July 1958): 47–72.

Kligman, Albert M. "The Pathogenesis of Tinea Capitis Due to Microsporum Audouini and Microsporum Canis." *Journal of Investigative Dermatology* 18, No. 3 (March 1952): 231.

Kligman, Albert M., and W. Ward Anderson. "Evaluation of Current Methods for the Local Treatment of Tinea Capitis." *Journal of Investigative Dermatology*, No. 16 (March 1954): 162.

Knowles, Frank Crozer. "Molluscum Contagiosum: Report of an Institutional Epidemic of Fifty-Nine Cases." *Journal of the American Medical Association* 53, No. 9 (August 28, 1909): 671.

Knox, Richard. "Studies Fail by Today's Standards," *Boston Globe*, December 31, 1993.

Kong, Delores. "Ex-Resident Recalls Fernald Club," *Boston Globe*, December 29, 1993.

Koprowski, Hilary, Thomas W. Norton, Klaus Hummeler, Joseph Stokes Jr., Andrew D. Hunt, Agnes Flack, and George A. Jervis. "Immunization of Infants with Living Attenuated Poliomyelitis Virus." *Journal of the American Medical Association* 162, No. 14 (December 1, 1956): 1281–1288.

Krugman, Saul. "The Willowbrook Hepatitis Studies Revisited: Ethical Aspects." *Reviews of Infectious Diseases* 8 No. 1 (January 1986): 158.

Krugman, Saul, Robert Ward, Joan Giles, Oscar Bodansky, and A. Milton Jacobs. "Infectious Hepatitis: Detection of Virus during the Incubation Period and in Clinically Inapparent Infection." *New England Journal of Medicine* 261, No. 15 (October 8, 1959): 729–734.

Kurland, J. G., S. Fishman, M. W. Hamolsky, and A. S. Freedberg. "Radioisotope Study of Thyroid Function in 21 Mongoloid Subjects including Observations in 7 Parents." *Journal of Clinical Endochronology and Metabolism* 17 (1957): 552–560.

Ladimer, Irving. "Ethical and Legal Aspects of Medical Research on Human Beings." *Journal of Public Law* 3 (1954): 467–511.

Lamm, Connie, L. Granie, P. D. Zelano, and Marc D. Lewis. "Magnitude and Chronometry of Neutral Mechanisms of Emotion Regulation in Subtypes of Aggressive Children." *Brain and Cognition* 77, No. 2 (November 2011): 159–169.

Lawrence, Jane. "The Indian Health Service and the Sterilization of Native American Women." *American Indian Quarterly* 24, No. 3 (Summer 2000): 400–419.

Lederer, Susan. "Hideyo Noguchi's Lutein Experiment and the Antivivisectionists." *Isis* 76 (1985): 31–48.

Lederer, Susan. "Political Animals: The Shaping of Biomedical Research Literature in Twentieth-Century America." *Isis* 83 (1992): 61–79.

Lee, Gary. "U.S. Should Pay Victims, O'Leary Says," *Washington Post*, December 29, 1993.

Lippmann, Walter. "The Abuse of the Tests," *New Republic*, November 15, 1922, p. 297.

Lombardo, Paul A. "Tracking Chromosomes, Castrating Dwarves: Uninformed Consent and Eugenic Research," *Ethics & Medicine* 25, No. 3 (Fall 2009): 149–164.

Lombardo, Paul, A., and Gregory Dorr. "Eugenics, Medical Education and the Public Health Service: Another Perspective on the Tuskegee Syphilis Experiment." *Bulletin of the History of Medicine* 80, No. 2 (Summer 2006): 302.

Lovaas, O. I., and James Q. Simmons. "Manipulation of Self-Destruction in Three Retarded Children." *Journal of Applied Behavior Analysis* 2, No. 3 (1969): 149.

Lowery, George H., Walter H. Beierwalters, Isadore Lampe, and Henry Gomberg. "Radioiodine Uptake Curve in Humans." *Pediatrics* 4 (1949): 627–633.

Lurie, Louis A. "The Endocrine Factor in Homosexuality." *American Journal of the Medical Sciences* 208, No. 2 (August 1944): 180.

Lydston, G. Frank. "Sex Mutilations in Social Therapeutics." *New York Medical Journal* 95 (1912): 677–685.

Mack, Pauline B., Alice Knapper Milsom, and Paul L. Carney. "A Study of Two Levels of Bread Enrichment in Children's Diet." *Monographs of the Society for Research in Child Development* 18, No. 2 (1953): 1–92.

Maris, Elizabeth P., Geoffrey Rake, Joseph Stokes, Jr., Morris F. Shaffer, and Gerald C. O'Neil. "Studies on Measles: The Results of Chance and Planned Exposure to Unmodified Measles Virus in Children Previously Inoculated with Egg Passage Measles Virus." *Journal of Pediatrics* 22, No. 1 (January 1943): 17.

Martmer, Edgar E., Kenneth E. Corrigang, Harold Chareneau, and Allen Sosin. "A Study of the Uptake of Iodine by the Thyroid of Premature Infants." *Pediatrics* 17 (1955): 507.

Mashek, John. "Official Asks Damages for Test Victims," *Boston Globe*, December 29, 1993.

Matsuyama, Steven S., and Lissy F. Jarvik. "Cytogenetic Effects of Psychoactive Drugs." *Genetics and Pharmacology* 10 (1975): 99–132.

Mazur, Allan. "Allegations of Dishonesty in Research and Their Treatment by American Universities." *Minerva*, 27 (1989): 177.

McChamill, Samuel, Howard Childs Carpenter, and Thomas Cope. "A Comparison of the Von Pirquet, Calmette, and Moro Tuberculin Tests and Their Diagnostic Value," *Archives of Internal Medicine* 2, No. 5 (1908): 405–447.

Middlesworth, Van. "Radioactive Iodide Uptake of Normal Newborn Infants." *American Journal of Diseases in Children* 38 (1954): 439.

Millan, Stephan, John Maisel, Henry Kempe, Stanley Plotkin, Joseph Pagano, and Joel Warren. "Antibody Response of Man to Canine Distemper Virus." *Journal of Bacteriology* 79, No. 4 (1960): 618.

Mitchell, Ross G. "The Child and Experimental Medicine." *British Medical Journal*, March 21, 1964, p. 721.

Najjar, Victor, and L. Emmett Holt, "The Biosynthesis of Thiamine in Human Nutrition." *Journal of the American Medical Association* 123, No. 11 (November 1943): 683–684.

Najjar, Victor, George Johns, George Mediary, Gertrude Fleischmann, and L. Emmett Holt. "The Biosynthesis of Riboflavins." *Journal of the American Medical Association* 126, No. 6 (October 1944): 357–358.

Noguchi, Hideyo. "Experimental Research in Syphilis." *Journal of the American Medical Association* 58, No. 16 (April 20, 1912): 1163–1171.

"New Infantile Paralysis Vaccine Is Declared to Immunize Children," *New York Times*, August 18, 1934.

Ogborn, Richard E., Ronald E. Waggener, and Eugene VanHove. "Radioactive Iodine Concentration in Thyroid Glands of Newborn Infants." *Pediatrics* 28 (1960): 771.

Owen, Tom. "When Words Hurt: Stuttering Study Story Missed the Mark," *Gazette* (Cedar Rapids, Iowa), July 12, 2003.

"Paralysis Vaccine Discontinued Here," *New York Times*, December 27, 1935.

Pierce, Henry W. "State Halts Use of Retarded as Guinea Pigs," *Pittsburgh Post-Gazette*, April 11, 1973.

Pierce, Henry W. "State Kills Testing of Meningitis Shots," *Pittsburgh Post-Gazette*, April 12, 1973.

Pisek, Godfrey R., and Leon Theodore LeWald. "The Further Study of Immunization with Living Rubella Virus Trials in Children with a Strain Cultured from an Aborted Fetus." *American Journal of Disability and Children* 110 (October 1965): 382.

Plotkin, Stanley, David Cornfield, and Theodore H. Ingalls. "Studies of Immunization with Living Rubella Virus Trials in Children with a Strain Cultured from an Aborted Fetus." *American Journal of Disability and Children* 110 (October 1965): 382.

Plotkin, Stanley, J. D. Farquhar, M. Katz, and C. Hertz. "Further Studies of an Attenuated Rubella Strain Grown in WI-38 Cells." *American Journal of Epidemiology* 89, No. 2 (September 6, 1968): 238.

Porcaro, Edward T. "Experimentation with Children" *Journal of Law and Medical Ethics* 7, No. 2 (June 1979): 7–9.

"Prison Malaria: Convicts Expose Themselves to Disease So Doctors Can Study It," *Life*, June 4, 1945, 43-46.

"Psychosurgery," *Time*, November 30, 1942.

Puga, Anna. "Energy Chief Fighting a Culture of Secrecy," *Boston Globe*, December 31, 1993.

"Questions Safety of Paralysis Virus," New York Times, October 9, 1935.

Reilly, Philip. "The Surgical Solution: The Writings of Activist Physicians in the Early Days of Eugenical Sterilization." *Perspectives in Biology and Medicine* 26 (1983): 646.

Rezendes, Michael. "For Markey, Belated Vindication," *Boston Globe*, December 30, 1993.
Rezendes, Michael. "Rep. Markey Vindicated by U.S. Disclosure of Radiation Experiments," *Washington Post*, December 31, 1993.
Ritts, R. E. "A Physician's View of Informed Consent in Human Experimentation." *Fordham Law Review* 36 (1967–68): 631–638.
Roman, Mark B. "When Good Scientists Turn Bad," *Discover*, 9, No. 4 (1988): 55.
Rothman, David J. "Ethics and Human Experimentation." *New England Journal of Medicine* 317, No. 19 (November 5, 1987): 1195–1199.
Rothman, David J. "Were Tuskegee and Willowbrook 'Studies in Nature'?" *Hastings Center Report* 12, No. 2 (April 1982): 5–7.
Rowe, N. H., R. H. Anderson, and L. A. Wanninger. "Effects of Ready to Eat Breakfast Cereals on Dental Caries Experience in Adolescent Children." *Journal of Dental Research* 53, No. 1 (January 1974): 33–36.
Salk, Jonas E., Harold E. Pearson, Philip N. Brown, and Thomas Francis, Jr. "Protective Effect of Vaccination Against Influenza B." *Journal of Clinical Investigation* 24 (July 1945): 547–553.
Saltus, Richard. "Some Fernald Research Defended," *Boston Globe*, December 28, 1993.
Sartain, Jeffrey S. "J. Marion Sims, the Father of Gynecology: Hero or Villain?" *Southern Medical Journal* 97, No. 5 (May 2004): 500.
Sauer, Louis W., and Winston H. Tucker. "Immune Responses to Diphtheria, Tetanus, and Pertussis, Aluminum Phosphate Adsorbed." *Journal of Public Health* 44, No. 6 (1954): 785.
Saxena, Krishna M., Earle M. Chapman, and Charles V. Pryles. "Minimal Dosage of Iodide Required to Suppress Uptake of Iodide-131 by Normal Thyroid." *Science* 138 (1962): 430.
Saxena, Krishna M., and C. V. Pryles. "Thyroid Function in Mongolism." *Journal of Pediatrics* 67 (1965): 363–370.
Schaeffer, Morris. "William H. Park: His Laboratory and His Legacy." *American Journal of Public Health* 75, No. 11 (November 1985): 1301.
Schneider, Keith. "1950 Memo Shows Radiation Test Doubts," *New York Times*, December 28, 1993.
Schneider, Keith. "Energy Official Seeks to Assist Victims of Tests," *New York Times*, December 29, 1993.
Schneider, Keith. "U.S. Expands Inquiry into Its Human Radiation Tests," *New York Times*, December 31, 1993.
Seidelman, William E. "Mengele Medicus: Medicine's Nazi Heritage." *Milbank Quarterly* 66, No.
2 (1988): 221–235.
Sharpe, Leon M., Wendell C. Peacock, Richard Cooke, and Robert S. Harris, "The Effect of Phytate and Other Food Factors on Iron Absorption." *Journal of Nutrition*, 1949, 433-445.
Shribman, David. "Clinton Orders Conference on Radiation Tests," *Boston Globe*, December 31, 1993.
Shribman, David. "Stepping Back from Progress," *Boston Globe*, December 31, 1993;
Steinberg, A. D., S. O. Zimmerman, and M. L. Bramer. "The Lincoln Dental Caries Study: The Effect of Acidulated Carbonated Beverages on the Increase of Dental Caries." *Journal of the American Dental Association* 85, No. 1 (1972): 81–89.
Sternberg, George M., and Walter Reed. "Report on Immunity against Vaccination Conferred upon the Monkey by the Use of the Serum of the Vaccinated Calf and Monkey." *Transactions of the Association of American Physicians* 10 (1895): 57–59.
Stokes, Joseph, Jr., John A. Farquahar, Miles E. Drake, Richard B. Capps, Charles S. Ward, and Albert W. Kitts. "Infectious Hepatitis: Length of Protection by Immune Serum Globulin." *Journal of the American Medical Association* 147, No. 8 (October 20, 1951): 714–719.

Stokes, Joseph, Jr., Robert E. Weibel, Eugene B. Buynak, and Maurice R. Hilleman. "Live Attenuated Mumps Virus Vaccine." *Pediatrics* 39, No. 6 (December 1959): 363.

Strauss, John S., and Albert M. Kligman. "Effect of X-Rays on Sebaceous Glands of the Human Face." *Journal of Investigative Dermatology* 33, No. 6 (December 1959): 347.

Swain, Robert E., and W. G. Bateman. "The Toxicity of Thallium Salts." *Journal of Biological Chemistry*, December 9, 1909, p. 147.

Swyer, G. I. M. "An Evaluation of the Prophylactic Antenatal Use of Stilboestrol." *American Journal of Obstetrics* 58, No. 5 (1949): 994–1009.

Tate, Nick. "Clinton Calls High-level Conference on Radiation Testing," *Boston Herald*, December 31, 1993.

Tate, Nick. "Radiation Study was Widespread at Fernald," *Boston Herald*," December 30, 1993.

Tate, Nick. "State Probes Report Patients Fed Radioactive Food," *Boston Herald*, December 28, 1993.

"The Law: Sterilized: Why?" *Time* Magazine, July 23, 1973.

Ticktin, Howard. "Hepatic Dysfunction and Jaundice in Patients." *New England Journal of Medicine* 267, No. 19 (1962): 964–968.

Triplet, Rodney G. "Henry Murray: The Making of a Psychologist?" *American Psychologist* 47, No. 2 (February 1992): 299–307.

Van Goozen, Stephanie, Walter Matthys, Peggy T. Cohen-Kettenis, Victor Wiegant, and Herman van Engeland. "Salivary Cortisol and Cardiovascular Activity During Stress in Oppositional-Defiant Disorder Boys and Normal Controls." *Biological Psychiatry* 43 (1998): 531.

Warfield, Louis M. "The Cutaneous Tuberculin Reaction." *Journal of the American Medical Association* 50, No. 9 (February 1908): 688.

Wells, Kathleen, and Lynn Sametz. "Involvement of Institutionalized Children in Social Science Research." *Journal of Clinical Child Psychology* 14, No. 3 (Fall 1985): 245–251.

Wilder, William H. "Report on the Committee for the Study of the Relation of Tuberculosis to Diseases of the Eye." *Journal of the American Medical Association* 55, No. 1 (July 2, 1910): 21

"Will Give Children Paralysis Vaccine," *New York Times*, August 21, 1934.

Williams, Jonathan H., and Walter Freeman. "Evaluation of Lobotomy with Special Reference to Children," *Association for Research in Nervous and Mental Disease* 31 (1953): 311–318.

Wilson, C. J. "Ready-to-Eat Cereals and Dental Caries in Children: A Three-Year Study." *Journal of Dental Research* 58, No. 9 (September 1979): 1853–1858.

Wong, Doris Sue. "DMR's Plan for Self-Probe Is Assailed," *Boston Globe*, December 30, 1993.

Woody, Kathleen. "Legal and Ethical Concepts Involved in Informed Consent to Human Research." *California Western Law Review* 18 (1981): 50–79.

ARCHIVE COLLECTIONS

College of Physicians of Philadelphia, Philadelphia, Pennsylvania.

Documents on the history of Sonoma State Hospital at Bancroft Library, University of California, Berkeley, California.

Medical Archive, University of Pennsylvania Medical School. National Archives, College Park, Maryland.

New York Academy of Medicine, New York, New York.

Peace Collection, Swarthmore College, Swarthmore, Pennsylvania. Pennsylvania State Archive, Harrisburg, Pennsylvania.

Pennsylvania State Library, Harrisburg, Pennsylvania. University of Pittsburgh Archives, Pittsburgh, Pennsylvania.

Papers of Henry Beecher, Countway Library, Harvard Medical School, Boston, Massachusetts.
    Papers of Walter Freeman, George Washington University Archive, Washington, DC
Papers of Saul Krugman, New York University Medical Archive, New York, New York. Papers
    of Joseph Rauh, Library of Congress, Washington, DC
Papers of Jonas Salk, Mandeville Special Collections Library, University of California, San Di-
    ego. Papers of Joseph Stokes Jr., American Philosophical Society, Philadelphia, Pennsylvania.

REPORTS
Advisory Committee on Human Radiation Experiments. The Human Radiation Experiments.
    Final Report of the Presidents' Advisory Committee. New York: Oxford University Press,
    1996.
Presidential Commission for the Study of Bioethical Issues. "Ethically Impossible" STD
    Research in Guatemala from 1946 to 1948. Washington, DC, September 2011.
Report of Progress in Research. Report II, July 1, 1945 to June 30, 1946, Nutritional Biochem-
    istry Laboratories, Department of Food Technology, Massachusetts Institute of Technology.
Task Force on Human Subject Research. A Report on the Use of Radioactive Materials in
    Human Subject Research that Involved Residents of State-Operated Facilities within
    the Commonwealth of Massachusetts from 1943 through 1973. Department of Mental
    Retardation, April 1994.
United States Congress, Senate Committee on Labor and Public Welfare. Subcommittee on
    Health. Quality of Health Care—Human Experimentation, Hearings, Ninety-third Con-
    gress, First Session, on S. 974. Washington, DC: U.S. Government Printing Office, 1973.

ADDITIONAL SOURCES
Daly, Marie E. "History of the Walter E. Fernald Development Center," n.d.
Freeman, W., and James W. Watts. "Schizophrenia in Childhood: Its Modification by Prefrontal
    Lobotomy." Paper read at the Institute of Living, February 26, 1947, pp. 1–9.
Leung, Rebecca. "A Dark Chapter in Medical History," *60 Minutes*, CBS, February 11, 2009.
    Nazi Doctors Trial. United States v. Karl Brandt, Nuremberg, Germany, June 13, 1947, pp.
9173–9174.
Tudor, Mary. "An Experimental Study of the Effect of Evaluative Labeling on Speech Fluency."
    Master of arts thesis, Graduate College of the State University of Iowa, August 1939.

INTERVIEWS
Former Test Subjects

Anthony, Edward—November 8, 2012
Almeida, Joseph—September 7, 2009.
Chabasinski, Ted—March 15, 2010, October 26, 2011 and November 2, 2011.
Dyer, Charles—February 21, 2011 and November 2, 2011.
Frank, Leonard—October 4, 2011.
Larocque, Austin—September 11, 2009, October 9, 2009.
Shattuck, Gordon—July 18, 2010, February 21, 2011, March 9 & 25, 2011.

Physicians & Scientists

Ackerman, A. Bernard–February 1, 1996, September 9, 1996.
Callaway, Enoch—October 25, 2011.
Gross, Paul—January 22, 1996.

Kagan, Avir—November 3 & 5, 2011.
Kelsey, Frances—January 12, 1995.
Ketchum, James—February 15, 1995, February 6, 1996, October 25, 2011.
Kligman, Albert—January 10, 1995. Koprowsky, Hilary–
Livingood, Clarence—September 4, 1996.
Lisook, Alan—January 13, 1995, March 23,1995 and January 19, 1996.
Maletskos, Constantine—February 22, 2011and April 28, 2011.
Southam, Chester—July 28, 1996 and October 3, 1996.
Wecht, Cyril—August 5, 2009.
Wood, Margaret Grey—February 2, 1996.
Urbach, Frederick—February 7, 1996.

Additional Interviews

Alves, Karen—November 2, 2011.
Arbiblit, Don—July 1, 2009.
Bly, Jessie—May 6, 2010 and November 9, 2012.
Borseth, Eric—July 29, 2009.
Clapp, Pat—October 12, 2011 and August 5, 2012.
Hagerty, Dennis—October 30, 2011.
Cowen, June—August 28, 2009.
Hahn, Christine—August 7, 2011.
Kaye, Jeffrey—October 26, 2011.
Levin, Joseph—August 31, 2009 and May 3, 2010.
Lombardo, Paul—August 13, 2010.
Lurz, Paul—April 21 & 26, 2010.
Marlow, Sandra—April 10, 2010.
Milstein, Alan—July 1, 2009.
Misilo, Fred—August 28, 2009 and April 26, 2010.
Oaks, David—March 15, 2010.
Parascandola, John—June 6, 2010.
Power, Jack—November 27, 2012.
Scheberlein, Robert—May 3, 2010.
Scull, Andrew—August 15, 2011.
Sharav, Vera—September 21, 2011.
West, Doe—April 20, 2010 and April 28, 2011.

INDEX

Aberhold, Paul, 165
Abramson, Harold, 96, 196
Abt, Isaac, 138–39
acidosis, 140–41
Ackerman, Bernard, 83, 131–33, 262–64
Acres of Skin (Hornblum), 250, 262
Almeida, Joseph, 171
Alves, Karen, 75, 78, 272n5
Alving, Alf Sven, Dr., 65–66
American Medical Association (AMA), 56, 82, 90
Andy, O. J., 191–93
Armed Forces Epidemiological Board (AFED), 68, 71, 84–85, 87–88, 90–91, 272n32,
Armstrong, Donald, 108
Army-McCarthy hearings, 1
Arrowsmith (Lewis), 14–15, 17, 19–20, 200
Asperger Syndrome, 250, 258–59
Asperger, Hans, Dr., 249–50, 254–59, 265
autism, 196–97, 228–30, 243, 250, 256, 258–59
Autism Spectrum Disorder, 258
Bad Blood (Jones), 9, 251
Barker, Lewellys F., 32
Barton, Clara, 22
Bateman ,W. G., 137
Beecher, Henry K, 98, 120–22, 169, 239, 246
Bell, Alexander Graham, 33
Bellevue Hospital, 176–77, 180, 244
Belfield, William T., 32, 46
Benda, Clemens, 151, 163–69, 171, 279n43 & n45
Bender-Gestalt Test, 180
Bender, Lauretta, 177–83, 193–94, 197–99, 243, 280n5
Bentley, Elizabeth, 94
Berman, Harold, 124
Betrayers of the Truth (Broad and Wade), 230
Bini, Lucio, 181
Blackwell, Elizabeth, 22
Blauer, Harold, 195, 282n55
Bly, Jessie, 214–17
Bodian, David, 114
Boston Globe, 159–60
Boston Herald, 160
Boston University School of Medicine, 170
Bowman Gray School of Medicine, 127
brainwashing, 194, 196, 200, 207
Braslow, Joel, 181–82, 193
Breggin, Peter R., 192–93

Breuning, Stephen E., 240–41
Broad, William, 230, 232–33
Brodie, Maurice, 108–10, 112
Brown, James, 218
Bryan, William Jennings, 39
Buck v. Bell, 44
Burbank, Luther, 33
Burgess, Anna, 214
Burke, Donald, 252–53
Burt, Cyril, 232–33
California Home for the Care and Training of Feeble-minded Children, 76
Callaghan, Miss (social worker), 176, 178
Callaway, Enoch, 95
Calmette test, 105–106
Cameron, Ewen, 96–97, 196
Camp Akiba hepatitis outbreak, 71
Campbell, Phillip, 160
Capps, Richard, 119
Carrington, Charles, 32
Carver, George Washington, 26
castration, 26–27, 30–33, 41, 45–46, 220–21, 267n2
Central Intelligence Agency (CIA), 95, 194, 209
Cerletti, Ugo, 181
Chabasinski, Teddy, 176, 179–80, 182–84, 194, 244
Chambers, Whittaker, 94
Charles H Miner State Hospital, 101
Chemie Grunenthal, 224
Children's Hospital of Philadelphia, 63, 80, 117–18
Children's Hospital at the University of Vienna, 255
Clapp, Pat, 100–103, 105
Clinton, Bill, 77
Columbia University, 58, 195
Committee of Medical Research (CMR), 64
Communism, 1, 5, 9, 93, 194–95, 210
Compton, Karl, 169
Conklin, E. G., 40
Cornell University, 36, 40, 95
Creedmore State Hospital, 194, 197–98
Cronin, A. J., 18
curare, 8
Cushing, Harvey, 17
Custodio, Deogracia, Dr., 237
Cutler, John C., 251–52
D. T. Watson Home, 110, 116, 236

ABOUT THE AUTHORS

ALLEN M. HORNBLUM is a Philadelphia based author and historian who investigates controversial and long neglected subjects. He has written books on a cross section of topics running the gamut from organized crime and Soviet espionage to sports and medical ethics. He has a varied and extensive work history that includes many years in various facets of the criminal justice system as well as college instruction. He taught at Temple University for over two decades, and has lectured widely at colleges such as Columbia, Princeton, and Brown as well as numerous law and medical schools including; Drexel Law School, Temple Law School, Jefferson Medical School, and Washington Medical School in St. Louis. As a journalist he has written for a cross-section of journals, magazines and newspapers including; *The British Medical Journal*, the *Philadelphia Inquirer*, the *New York Post*, the *Baltimore Sun*, the *Daily Beast*, and *Tablet*.

JUDITH L. NEWMAN has been a faculty member of Penn State Abington College's Department of Human Development and Family Studies for over four decades. She teaches a wide range of course on Life-span development, and much of her research has focused on children's concepts of family, death, and disease. She has published articles in the Behavioral Mind

GREGORY J. DOBER is an adjunct professor at Lake Erie College of Osteopathic Medicine, and has written on a wide array of issues impacting the incarcerated for *Prison Legal News* and the *American Journal of Bioethics*.

Made in the USA
Monee, IL
19 February 2025

12197690R00184